SECOND EDITION

eBay HACKS™

David A. Karp

O'REILLY®

Beijing • Cambridge • Farnham • Köln • Paris • Sebastopol • Taipei • Tokyo

eBay Hacks,™ Second Edition
by David A. Karp

Printed in the United States of America.

Published by O'Reilly Media, Inc., 1005 Gravenstein Highway North, Sebastopol, CA 95472.

O'Reilly Media, Inc. books may be purchased for educational, business, or sales promotional use. Online editions are also available for most titles (*safari.oreilly.com*). For more information, contact our corporate/institutional sales department: (800) 998-9938 or *corporate@oreilly.com*.

Editor:	Brian Sawyer	**Production Editor:**	Jamie Peppard
Series Editor:	Rael Dornfest	**Cover Designer:**	Emma Colby
Executive Editor:	Dale Dougherty	**Interior Designer:**	David Futato

Printing History:

August 2003: First Edition.

June 2005: Second Edition.

This book uses RepKover™, a durable and flexible lay-flat binding.

ISBN: 0-596-10068-X
[M]

Contents

Credits

About the Author

David A. Karp is that dangerous combination of compulsive writer and eBay fanatic.

He discovered eBay in the late 1990s while looking for a deal on an electric cat-litter box. As an avid collector of toys of all kinds, he immediately saw eBay's potential to quench his thirst for second-hand consumer electronics, handmade brass trains, and obscure parts for discontinued products of all kinds. Soon thereafter he began selling on eBay, and now trades religiously, taking breaks occasionally to write books. He still has the litter box.

Educated in mechanical engineering at U.C. Berkeley, David consults on Internet technology, user-interface design, and software engineering. He has written ten power-user books (available in nine languages), including the bestselling Windows Annoyances series. David also writes occasionally for *PC Magazine* and is a contributing editor for *ZTrack Magazine*. Noted recognition has come from *PC Computing* and *Windows* magazines, the *San Francisco Examiner*, and *The New York Times*.

David spends some of his spare time outside with his camera, but often finds it difficult to tear himself away from a good movie. He likes hiking and skiing—almost as much as he enjoys talking about them. David scored 30.96647% on the Geek Test (*www.innergeek.us/geek.html*), earning a rating of "Total Geek." Animals and children trust him. He can make 15-minute brownies in less than 10 minutes, and he never gets tired of the Simpsons.

Contributors

The following people contributed code and inspiration for some of the hacks in this book:

- Todd Larason is a C and Perl programmer currently residing in Portland, Oregon; he's always interested in new technologies, challenges and obsessions. You can read more about his various obsessions at *www.molehill.org*.
- Adam Trachtenberg is the author of *Upgrading to PHP 5* and coauthor of *PHP Cookbook*, both published by O'Reilly Media. He began using PHP in 1997 and is a frequent speaker at conferences on XML, web services, and PHP 5. Trachtenberg cofounded and served as vice president for development at two companies, *Student.Com* and *TVGrid.Com*. At both firms, he led the front- and middle-end web site design and development. He lives in San Francisco, California and at *www.trachtenberg.com*. He has a B.A. and an M.B.A. from Columbia University.
- Samuel L. Clemens (1835–1910) worked as a typesetter between the ages of 11 and 21, during which time he also wrote humorous travel letters for regional newspapers. He assumed the pen name "Mark Twain" (the term used on steamboats as a warning that a river's depth is only two fathoms deep) in 1861 while writing for the Virginia City *Territorial Enterprise*, and was first made famous in 1864 by the story "The Celebrated Jumping Frog of Calaveras County," which he wrote as a reporter in San Francisco. He is best known for having written *The Innocents Abroad*, *The Adventures of Tom Sawyer*, *The Adventures of Huckleberry Finn*, and literally thousands of memorable quotes, several of which adorn the pages of this book. Despite having died 93 years before this book was written, Clemens provided immeasurable inspiration to this and many other authors.

Best eBay Pop-Culture References

This is Spinal Tap. In the DVD commentary track of the 1984 Rob Reiner film, the members of the heavy-metal band Spinal Tap (David St. Hubbins, Nigel Tufnel, and Derek Smalls) wax nostalgic about the guitars seen in the movie, stating that many of them can now be found on eBay.

The Simpsons (episode BABF22). Homer loses his life savings in the stock market, except for a few dollars which he spends on a cowbell. He rings the cowbell gently, only to have it break apart in his hands, and yells, "Damn you, eBay!"

Spider-Man 2. After having been discarded in a trash can, Peter Parker's Spider-Man costume is rescued by a garbage man who delivers it to the

Daily Bugle. When the man is offered fifty bucks for the suit by the newspaper's editor-in-chief, J. Jonah Jameson, the man scoffs, "I can get more than that on eBay."

Acknowledgments

I'd like to start by thanking Dale Dougherty and Rael Dornfest for coming up with this terrific series of books, and Tim O'Reilly for talking me into writing this particular volume.

Thanks to Dale Dougherty and Rael Dornfest (again) for their guidance and steadfast ideas of exactly what a "hack" should be. Additional thanks to Ruth Kampmann, Nancy Kotary, and Jim Sumser for their roles in the bizarre series of events that led to the inception of this book. Thanks to Brian Sawyer and Jamie Peppard for their help on this second edition.

Thanks to Adam Trachtenberg, Jeffrey P. McManus, and Jeff Huber of eBay for their help with the eBay API and some other aspects of the marvelous, sometimes mysterious, and always-changing computer system behind the curtains at eBay. I'd also like to thank Todd Larason, who provided code that served as the basis for many of the scripts in Chapter 8.

Thanks to Shannon Sofield, Dave Nielsen, and Dave Burchell (authors of *PayPal Hacks*), who provided insight, workarounds, and code, some pieces of which have wriggled their way onto the pages of this book.

Thanks to my sister, Deborah Karp, for her help with some of the backdrop advice in Chapter 5 and inspiration for "Sell a Broken VCR on eBay" **[Hack #51]**.

An extra-special hello to Addie, whose photo can be found somewhere in this book. And thanks to my brother, Jeffrey A. Karp, who not only is responsible for the aforementioned photo, but made a contribution to my last book, *Windows XP Annoyances for Geeks,* Second Edition, for which he was not properly attributed. He was also bitten by the dog featured in Figure 5-11.

Finally, my everlasting love to my partner, Torey Bookstein. *Taffeta darling!*

Preface

eBay is more than just a web site. It's a community of millions of people in all parts of the world, all of whom are buying and selling with varying degrees of experience, ingenuity, and, of course, intelligence. eBay refers to the universe it has created as the "eBay Marketplace," which is indeed an apt description.

What makes eBay great is *access*. As a buyer, you have access to things you can't get anywhere else: antique toys, used computer equipment, rare movie posters, handmade clothing, cheap cell-phone accessories, furniture, music, and everything in between. And as a seller, you have access to *buyers* all over the world, willing to shell out money for just about anything you can take a picture of.

eBay has become a vital tool for collectors of all sorts. In my first few weeks of exploring eBay, I found a rare toy train that hasn't been made since I was a kid drooling over pictures in a catalog. In fact, thanks to eBay, I rediscovered a hobby I had loved in my childhood, and met others who have done the same.

Origins

eBay is big. Very big. At any given time, there are over 18 million items for sale, with an average of $680 worth of transactions taking place every *second*. And these numbers will undoubtedly be even higher by the time you get around to reading this.

But like most big things, eBay started out small. As the story goes, eBay was born of a dinner conversation between Pierre Omidyar and his wife, Pam, about PEZ™ dispensers. As it turns out, this, like many origin stories, is a myth (this one was cooked up by eBay PR whiz Mary Lou Song); but the fact remains that eBay still has that PEZ-dispenser feel, and that's what keeps customers coming.

What This Book Is...and Isn't

"Hacks" are generally considered to be "quick-and-dirty" solutions to programming problems or interesting techniques for getting a task done. As any experienced eBayer will tell you, there are plenty of tasks involved in buying and selling on eBay, and anything that can be done to make those tasks easier, faster, or more effective will improve your eBay experience significantly.

This book is not a "hand holding" guide. It will not walk you through the process of bidding on your first auction or creating your first auction listing. The fact is that just about anybody can figure those things out for themselves in a few minutes. (If that weren't true, eBay wouldn't have tens of millions of active buyers and sellers.)

But despite the title, this book is also not about "hacking into a system" or anything so nefarious. Quite the contrary: in fact, you'll find in this book a very real emphasis on trading responsibly and ethically, as well as extensive tools and tips for protecting yourself as both a buyer and a seller.

The hacks in this book address the technological and diplomatic challenges faced by all eBay members, written from the perspective of an experienced eBayer who loves challenges as much as solutions.

Essentially, you'll find in this book the tools to help you trade smarter and safer, make more money, and have fun doing it.

Hacking a Dynamic System

Change is the handmaiden Nature requires to do her miracles with.
—Mark Twain

eBay is constantly evolving and changing to meet the needs of its ever-growing community (as well as its business partners). Every two weeks, in fact, eBay introduces new features and changes to its site. Some changes are subtle, like moving the location of a button or link, or updating an obscure policy. Other changes are much more dramatic.

While the first edition of this book was being written, for instance, eBay added the Calculated Shipping feature [Hack #59], substantially changed the licensing and pricing for its Developers Program (see Chapter 8), and introduced an entirely new auction page design. And all of these changes occurred within a period of about 30 days.

There is no such thing as eBay 2.0 or eBay 2.1, a fact that can create quite a challenge for tinkerers. But, by their very nature, hacks are experimental, and not necessarily impervious to breakage or obsolescence.

Much changed on eBay since the first edition of eBay Hacks was written. eBay consolidated its non-paying bidder process and fraud reporting tools into the handy Dispute Console [Hack #40] and [Hack #89] and changed the design of the feedback profile page [Hack #1]. eBay introduced the *Subtitle* listing upgrade [Hack #46] and eliminated the essentially useless *Featured on Home Page* upgrade. And a few new restrictionswere put in place concerning JavaScript in listing descriptions and revisions to running listings.

In most cases, the results of these changes were cosmetic and didn't cause any real problems. But it's important to be aware that even though policies will frequently be updated, prices will almost always go up, and new features will be added (and older ones deprecated) faster than you can keep track of them, the methodologies and strategies in this book should remain pretty much the same.

This does mean, however, that some of the hacks in this edition may need minor modifications to work within the confines of the system. If you encounter a problem, just visit *www.ebayhacks.com* to see if there's a solution (or to suggest one of your own).

Fortunately, whenever eBay closes a door, they try to open a window (or at least a vent), which means that hacking will always be a part of using eBay, and the hacker will always have a home.

Practical Matters

eBay requires only a web browser, an email account, and a sense of adventure. But to use the hacks in this book, you'll want to make sure you have all of the following:

Recent web browser. Your web browser is your portal to the entire eBay universe, so make sure you're not using browser software released before the fall of the Berlin wall.

The vast majority of malware (malicious software, such as spyware and adware) has been designed to target the most common browser, namely Internet Explorer running on a Windows PC. If you're using Internet Explorer, you should seriously consider abandoning it in favor of a more secure browser, such as Mozilla Firefox (available for free from www.mozilla.org). In addition to the added safety, Firefox sports a streamlined interface, an effective popup-blocker, tabbed browsing, configurable skins, and hundreds of cool extensions.

The hacks in this book were designed for and tested on Mozilla Firefox 1.0 or later, Mozilla Suite 1.7 or later, and Internet Explorer 6.0 or later. These are all free downloads from their respective makers (e.g., *mozilla.org* and *microsoft.com*), so no excuses! Earlier web browsers will cause all sorts of problems, such as pages not displaying correctly and forms not working properly. And newer browsers can also prefill forms and remember passwords, which can be very handy on eBay.

Email account. A reliable email account and an email address that is not likely to change in the short term are vital requirements for using eBay.

Email application. Email is how buyers and sellers communicate with one another, but many eBay members underestimate the need for a reliable program to read and send email. A good email program will do the following:

- Store all sent and received messages indefinitely.
- Allow you to search and sort stored messages quickly.
- Include the original message when you send a reply.
- Automatically separate eBay-related email from all other correspondence using filters.
- View the HTML source of an email message to see whether it is genuine or merely a spoofed eBay or PayPal message.
- Send and receive attachments.

> Note that free web-based services such as Hotmail and Yahoo! Mail, while convenient, are not really suitable for use on eBay. They don't store old email permanently, they don't give you sufficient control over spam filters (see below), and they lack other features. Plus, the supposed anonymity offered by these services means that they're often abused by spammers and scam artists. As a result, you may have a harder time gaining trust [Hack #8] among other eBay members if you have a *hotmail.com* or *yahoo.com* email address.

Some of the more suitable email software packages include Eudora (*eudora.com*), Mozilla Thunderbird (*mozilla.org*), and Outlook/Outlook Express (*microsoft.com*). And if you find that you need web-based email access (i.e., for traveling or work), contact your ISP to see if a private web-based interface to your email account is available.

Control over your spam filter. If your ISP filters out your spam, it may be deleting legitimate email messages intended for you, such as questions from customers and payment instructions from sellers. Worst of all, you'll never know that it's happening. See "What to Do When Your Email Doesn't Get Through" [Hack #9] for solutions, including an example of a suitable spam filter.

The ability to tilt your head to the left. If you are able to correctly interpret smileys ;) and other "emoticons," you can properly discern when someone is kidding in an email message or auction description. This ability can mean the difference between being happy with a transaction and rushing to file a dispute with eBay's fraud department.

A digital camera. If you're going to sell on eBay, you'll need a digital camera, or barring that, a film camera and some sort of scanner. See Chapter 5 for hacks dealing with taking photos, getting them into your computer, and putting them in your eBay listings.

A credit card. Credit cards are the best means of protection when buying on eBay; see "Send Payment Quickly and Safely" **[Hack #33]** for details. But even if you don't use it to pay for purchases, a credit card will help you get past some barriers, allowing you sell (see Chapter 4) and verify your identity **[Hack #8]**.

Fun. You must have fun on eBay. Otherwise, what's the point?

Getting Started with the Code in This Book

One of the ways *eBay Hacks* is different from other eBay books you might've read is that the solutions contained herein are not limited to the features available on the eBay web site. Rather, the hacks in this book make use of other websites, third-party software tools, and programming code you can type in, customize, and run yourself.

You don't have to type any of the code in this book by hand! Just go to *ebayhacks.com*, click The Hacks, and select the hack or section in which the code appears.

Some of this code is simple, requiring no prior experience and only a little patience. Depending on the task at hand, though, some other code examples may require some programming experience and a larger amount of the aforementioned patience. (Each hack is adorned with a little thermometer to indicate its complexity, as described in "Conventions Used in This Book," later in this preface.) What follows is a little background on the languages and concepts used in the hacks that employ code.

eBay's home is the Web, a heterogeneous place governed by well-defined standards. In most cases, the concepts presented in this book work with any programming language or platform you might be using with your web site. However the example code is primarily kept to three language and platform combinations, each inhabiting its own niche of the Internet ecology: HTML for creating web content, JavaScript for adding interactivity to web pages, and Perl for server-side (CGI) scripting. Programming for the eBay API is a somewhat different animal and is discussed in the introduction to Chapter 8.

HTML

HTML (Hypertext Markup Language) isn't so much a programming language as a schema used to add formatting to plain text. As a seller on eBay, you use HTML tags to dress up your auction descriptions and to create web content.

You don't need to be proficient in HTML to start using it; see "Format the Description with HTML" **[Hack #52]** for an introduction and crash course. The more HTML you know, the more of it you can employ to enhance your listings.

JavaScript

JavaScript is a scripting language (not to be confused with the Java programming language) used to add interactivity to otherwise-static web pages. For instance, when you click thumbnail photos in some eBay auctions to view their larger versions right on the same page, you're running JavaScript code embedded in the auction page. JavaScript comes in handy if you want to construct an interactive photo album **[Hack #79]** with photos hosted on your own server **[Hack #76]**, for example.

JavaScript code is placed within `<script></script>` tags on an HTML-formatted web page, such as the description in an eBay listing. When someone views your auction, the JavaScript code is executed by the browser client (e.g., Internet Explorer, Mozilla Firefox), which is why it's categorized as *client-side* scripting.

If you want to use the same JavaScript code in all your eBay listings, you can place the code in a file on your web server (say, *scripts.js*), and then merely reference it by placing the following line in your listing descriptions:

```
<script src="http://www.your.server/scripts.js"></script>
```

where *http://www.your.server/your-scripts.js* is the full URL of your *scripts.js* file. Any JavaScript code in this book that appears inside a `<script></script>` structure can be used in this way; just remove the opening `<script><!--` and closing `--></script>` tags, and you're good to go!

eBay imposes some restrictions on the use of JavaScript in listing descriptions, presumably in an effort to reduce the risk of abuse. Among the more-useful JavaScript elements specifically prohibited in descriptions are the window.open statement and eval() function. If you try to submit a listing containing one of these prohibited statements, you'll get this confusing and largely inaccurate error message:

> Your listing cannot contain javascript (".cookie", "cookie(", "replace(", IFRAME, META, or includes), cookies or base href.

Although none of the code in this book uses these forbidden statements, it is entirely possible that eBay may have introduced additional restrictions by the time you read this. As with all the code in eBay Hacks, be sure to visit ebayhacks.com for any applicable corrections, updates, or workarounds.

If you're using Firefox or Mozilla, you can use the JavaScript Console to see error messages and warnings generated by your JavaScript code as you test it. To open the JavaScript Console window, type `javascript:` (including the colon) in the address bar and press Enter. If you're using Internet Explorer, you can get something similar by downloading the Microsoft Script Debugger (available for free from *www.microsoft.com/downloads/*).

Note that there are other ways to add interactivity to web pages, such as VBScript, Java, and (now deprecated) ActiveX controls, but none are as widely supported and seamless as JavaScript.

Perl

In order to show up-to-date information on a web page, such as the current price and the amount of time left on an eBay auction page, its content must be dynamically generated. In most cases, this is done by a program on the web server before the page is sent to the browser. Although just about any programming language is capable of generating web content, most of the hacks in this book use Perl for this purpose. See the "Using CGI Scripts" sidebar for details.

Perl (Practical Extract and Report Language) is a great choice for "server-side" scripting because it's simple, easy to learn, requires no expensive or complicated development environment, and works on any computing platform. If you're using Unix, Linux, or Mac OS X, Perl is almost certainly already installed on your system. If you're using Windows, you can get ActiveState's ActivePerl for free at *www.activestate.com/Products/ActivePerl/*.

Using CGI Scripts

Every web server has a dedicated folder (directory) in which scripts or programs are placed. Instead of displaying the *contents* of the scripts, as would happen with ordinary HTML files, the web server software runs the scripts and displays their *output* instead. This special script directory is typically called *cgi-bin*, wherein CGI stands for "common gateway interface." Refer to your web server software's documentation for details on setting up a *cgi-bin* directory, or contact your administrator (ISP) if you're renting space on someone else's web server.

Now, copying the Perl scripts discussed throughout this book into your *cgi-bin* directory is easy enough; the hard part can be making them work.

Provided that the scripts are in the correct location, all you need to do on Unix systems is to make them executable, like this:

```
chmod +x gallery.pl
```

where `gallery.pl` is the filename of the script.

On Windows systems, each Perl script must have a filename that ends with *.pl*. Then, you'll need to associate the *.pl* filename extension with your Perl interpreter. In most cases, this will be done for you when you install Perl.

The last step is to reference the script with the proper URL, like this:

```
http://www.ebayhacks.com/cgi-bin/gallery.pl
```

where `www.ebayhacks.com` is the address of your server, `cgi-bin` is the public name of your *cgi-bin* directory (not always the same as the private name), and `gallery.pl` is the filename of your script. If all goes well, you should see the output of the script in your web browser. (It's important to note that not all Perl scripts in this book are CGI scripts.)

If you get an error when you try to run the script from your browser, try running it from the command line instead to see more-detailed error messages.

Some hacks in this book require the use of Perl modules, extensions to the Perl language that add functionality you'd otherwise have to program from scratch. See the "Installing Perl Modules" sidebar for details.

Perl scripts are simply text files; you can edit them with any plain-text editor, such as Notepad in Windows or emacs in Unix. (Note that word processors, such as Word and Wordperfect are not suitable for this task, as they'll jumble up the text file with proprietary formatting data.)

Installing Perl Modules

(Adapted from Google Hacks *by Tara Calishain and Rael Dornfest)*

A few hacks in this book make use of add-on Perl modules, useful for turning dozens of lines of messy code into a couple of concise commands. If your Perl script resides on a server maintained by someone else (typically an ISP administrator), you'll have to request that they install the module before you can reference it in your scripts. But if you're the administrator, you'll have to install it yourself:

Installing on Unix, Linux, and Mac OS X. Assuming you have the CPAN module, have root access, and are connected to the Internet, installation should be no more complicated than:

```
% su
% perl -MCPAN -e shell
cpan> install WWW::Search::Ebay
```

Note that capitalization counts; copy-and-paste the module name for an exact match. If the install fails, you can try forcing an installation by typing:

```
cpan> force install WWW::Search::Ebay
```

Go grab yourself a cup of coffee, meander the garden, read the paper, and check back once in a while. Your terminal's sure to be riddled with incomprehensible gobbledegook that you can, for the most part, summarily ignore. You may be asked a question or three; in most cases, simply hitting Return to accept the default answer will do the trick.

Installing on Windows. If you're running Perl under Windows, you'll need the Programmer's Package Manager, which is incedentally included with ActiveState's ActivePerl distribution. (If you don't have it, you can get it at *aspn.activestate.com/ASPN/Downloads/ActivePerl/PPM/*.) PPM grabs nicely-packaged module bundles from the ActiveState archive and drops them into place on your Windows system with little need of help from you. Simply launch PPM from inside a Command Prompt window (Start → Run → `cmd.exe`) and tell it to install the module:

```
C:\>ppm
PPM> install WWW-Search-eBay
```

At this point, installation proceeds just like Unix, discussed above.

Once a Perl module has been successfully installed, you can reference it from your Perl programs.

To run a Perl script in Windows, as long as filename has the *.pl* file extension,* you can double-click the file icon to start Perl and execute the script. If the script provides text output, you'll want to run it from a Command Prompt window (Start → Run → `cmd.exe`) instead; just go to the folder containing the script (type `cd` *`foldername`*), type the name of the script file, and press Enter.

To run a Perl script in Unix, Linux, or Mac OS X, open a terminal window, go to the folder containing the script (`cd` *`foldername`*), type *`./scriptfilename`* (where *`scriptfilename`* is the filename of the script), and press Enter.

If you want to learn more about Perl, the book to get is *Programming Perl*, Third Edition (also known as the "Camel Book") by Larry Wall, Tom Christiansen, and Jon Orwant.

Using Code Examples

This book is here to help you get your job done. In general, you may use the code in this book in your programs and documentation. You do not need to contact us for permission unless you're reproducing a significant portion of the code. For example, writing a program that uses several chunks of code from this book does not require permission. Selling or distributing a CD-ROM of examples from O'Reilly books *does* require permission. Answering a question by citing this book and quoting example code does not require permission. Incorporating a significant amount of example code from this book into your product's documentation *does* require permission.

We appreciate, but do not require, attribution. An attribution usually includes the title, author, publisher, and ISBN. For example: "*eBay Hacks*, Second Edition by David A. Karp. Copyright 2005 O'Reilly Media, Inc., 0-596-10068-X."

If you feel your use of code examples falls outside fair use or the permission given above, feel free to contact us at *permissions@oreilly.com*.

How This Book Is Organized

This book goes beyond the instruction page to the idea of "hacks"—tips, tricks, and techniques you can use to make your experience with eBay more profitable, more fun, less exasperating, and (if you enjoy such things) more challenging.

On a daily basis, eBay users assume many different roles: consumer, seller, technical support specialist, diplomat, teacher, nuisance, application developer, nuclear safety inspector, web designer, and, of course, hacker. With

* To show file extensions in Windows, open Windows Explorer, and go to Tools → Folder Options → View tab, and turn off the "Hide extensions for known file types" option.

that in mind, the hacks (and chapters) in this book are divided into four main sections.

Hacks for All

Chapter 1, *Diplomacy and Feedback*
: Feedback in the eBay world is like credit in the real world: you use it to buy and sell things, you build it up over a long time, and you protect it like a first-born child. This chapter introduces eBay's feedback system and describes the many different ways to maintain a good feedback profile and use it to inspire trust in others.

Hacks for Buyers

Chapter 2, *Searching*
: The only way to find anything on eBay is by searching, either by typing keywords into search boxes or by browsing through category listings. The hacks in this chapter describe how to find auctions that other bidders will likely miss, focus your searches with a variety of tools, and even create an automated search robot.

Chapter 3, *Bidding*
: This chapter explains both how bidding is *supposed* to work, and how it actually works in the real world. It also shows different ways—such as sniping—to use eBay's proxy bidding system your win rate while spending less money.

Hacks for Sellers

Chapter 4, *Selling*
: The beauty of eBay is that anything you buy can be sold, sometimes for more than you paid for it. This chapter shows strategies involved with selling, such as which listing upgrades work best, how to promote your items without spending extra money, how to format your listings with HTML and JavaScript, and how to protect yourself from deadbeat bidders.

Chapter 5, *Working with Photos*
: Photos can make or break an auction. This chapter shows you not only how to take good pictures and put them in your auctions, but also includes specific code you can use for cool presentations.

Chapter 6, *Completing Transactions*
: The hacks in this chapter will give you the selling tools to help receive payments, ship your packages, and protect yourself while doing it.

Chapter 7, *Running a Business on eBay*

If selling on eBay is your full-time job (or if you just wish it were), the tools in this chapter will help you sell more in less time and with less effort. Streamline listing creation, communications, and checkout, and make more money while you're at it.

Hacks for Developers

Chapter 8, *The eBay API*

To the delight of anyone interested in hacking, eBay's API lets developers write applications to communicate directly with the eBay servers. But it's not just for developers—anyone with a computer or web server and a little time to learn Perl can write (and use) quick-and-dirty scripts to search, retrieve auction information, leave feedback, and much more.

How to Use This Book

You can read this book from cover to cover if you like, but for the most part each hack stands on its own. So feel free to browse, flipping around to whatever sections interest you most.

If you're a Perl "newbie," you might want to try some of the easier hacks (earlier in the book) and then tackle the more extensive ones as you get more confident. If you want more information on Perl, such as the background and documentation not found in this book, see *perl.oreilly.com*. Likewise, go to *scripting.oreilly.com* for more information on JavaScript, and check out *web.oreilly.com* for help with HTML.

Conventions Used in This Book

The following is a list of the typographical conventions used in this book:

Italic

Used to indicate new terms, URLs, filenames, file extensions, directories, program names, and, of course, for emphasis. For example, a path in the filesystem will appear as */Developer/Applications*.

`Constant width`

Used to show code examples, anything that might be typed from the keyboard, the contents of files, and the output from commands.

`Constant width italic`

Used in examples and tables to show text that should be replaced with your own user-supplied values.

Color
: The second color is used to indicate a cross-reference within the text, and occasionally to help keep the author awake during late-night writing binges.

You should pay special attention to notes set apart from the text with the following icons:

This is a tip, suggestion, or general note. It contains useful supplementary information about the topic at hand.

This is a warning or note of caution. When you see one of these, your safety, privacy, or money might be in jeopardy.

The thermometer icons found next to each hack indicate the relative complexity of the hack:

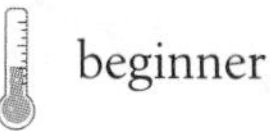

beginner moderate expert

How to Contact Us

We have tested and verified the information in this book to the best of our ability, but you may find that features have changed (or even that we have made mistakes!). As a reader of this book, you can help us to improve future editions by sending us your feedback. Please let us know about any errors, inaccuracies, bugs, misleading or confusing statements, and typos that you find anywhere in this book.

Please also let us know what we can do to make this book more useful to you. We take your comments seriously and will try to incorporate reasonable suggestions into future editions. You can write to us at:

O'Reilly Media, Inc.
1005 Gravenstein Hwy N.
Sebastopol, CA 95472
(800) 998-9938 (in the U.S. or Canada)
(707) 829-0515 (international/local)
(707) 829-0104 (fax)

To ask technical questions or to comment on the book, send email to:

bookquestions@oreilly.com

For more information about this book and others, see the O'Reilly web site:

http://www.oreilly.com

For details about *eBay Hacks,* Second Edition, including examples, errata, reviews, and plans for future editions, go to:

http://www.oreilly.com/catalog/ebayhks2/

Code examples, additions and corrections, and other related miscellany can be found at:

http://www.ebayhacks.com/

Safari Enabled

When you see a Safari® Enabled icon on the cover of your favorite technology book, that means the book is available online through the O'Reilly Network Safari Bookshelf.

Safari offers a solution that's better than e-books. It's a virtual library that lets you easily search thousands of top tech books, cut and paste code samples, download chapters, and find quick answers when you need the most accurate, current information. Try it for free at *http://safari.oreilly.com*.

Got a Hack?

To explore Hacks books online or to contribute a hack for future titles, visit:

http://hacks.oreilly.com

Diplomacy and Feedback

Hacks 1–9

eBay is a community of buyers and sellers, not just a mere web site or piece of software. It's a complex social system of which you are an active member. Success on eBay depends not only on your ability to master the technical tasks of bidding and selling, but on your ability to communicate with other eBay members and your willingness to contribute to the community in a positive way.

Feedback is the basis of trust on eBay. Each eBay member has his or her own *member profile*, a public collection of comments left by other eBay members. Each individual feedback comment is tied to a transaction in which the particular member took part. Feedback comments are marked either positive, negative, or neutral, and are added accordingly in the summary that appears at the top of the page.

A member's *feedback score* is the number representing the sum of all positive comments, minus the sum of all negative comments. (Note, however, that multiple comments left by a single user will never count more than one point.) This number, shown in parentheses after a member's user ID, is a useful tool in determining the trustworthiness and experience level of any given eBay member.

It's important to note that the feedback score alone does not give you a sufficient picture of any member's personal history. Before you do business with any other member, make sure to click the member's feedback score and appraise the profile **[Hack #1]** as a whole.

Feedback is taken very seriously on eBay, and with good reason. A seller who deals honestly and fairly with his customers will earn lots of positive feedback over the years. In turn, that good reputation will earn the seller more money from subsequent listings. Likewise, a buyer with a good reputation is more likely to get the benefit of the doubt from a seller (should anything go wrong with a transaction) than a buyer with a bad reputation.

And as you'd expect, dishonest or unreliable sellers and deadbeat bidders are likely to earn a higher percentage of negative feedback, and thus have a harder time doing business on eBay. All of this contributes to a system that allows you to buy from and sell to other eBay members who are otherwise complete strangers.

Leaving Feedback

You can leave feedback for another member only if you are both involved in a transaction, namely a completed auction. The actual task of leaving feedback is quite simple; simply go to the completed auction page and click Leave Feedback. Choose a rating (positive, neutral, or negative) and type a "review" in the space provided. You have only 80 characters in which to explain what the other eBay member did right (or wrong), so make every word count.

Here are some guidelines for writing appropriate feedback:

Positive. As long as a transaction goes reasonably well, you should always leave positive feedback for the other party.

If you're a bidder, you'll want to reward the seller for shipping quickly, responding to questions promptly, and describing the item accurately; for example:

- "Quick shipping, great deal, overall friendly service. A credit to eBay."
- "Item better than described; trustworthy seller. Highly recommended!"

As a seller, you'll likewise want to leave positive feedback for bidders who pay right away.

- "Lightning-fast payment. Reliable buyer. Thanks for your business!"
- "Quick to pay, friendly emails. This eBayer makes selling a pleasure!"

Negative. Negative feedback is unfortunately overused on eBay, and is, in most cases, unnecessary.

If at all possible, always try to resolve the problem with the other party instead of leaving negative feedback. If you're a buyer, for example, and you're not happy with the transaction, contact the seller to see if he will make it right before you give up and post negative feedback. Not only will you avoid possible feedback retaliation, but you might stand to get some money out of it as well.

One of the most common causes of negative feedback is a breakdown in communication, often for purely technical reasons. For instance, a single misconfigured spam filter may inadvertently delete a seller's payment instructions or a buyer's question. It's your responsibility to make sure your email gets through to the other party **[Hack #9]**.

As a bidder, you should leave negative feedback only if you paid and never received the item, if the seller significantly misrepresented the item and did not offer a refund, or if the seller defrauded you in some way. (Note that unless the seller is also the *manufacturer* of the item, it's not fair to leave negative feedback simply because you don't like the item you purchased. And remember, you can always resell the item if you're not happy.) For example:

- "Seller sent damaged item; completely uncooperative about refund."
- "Warning: seller took money and never shipped. Had to dispute charge."

If you're a seller, you should leave negative feedback only for deadbeat bidders who don't pay. (It's not acceptable to penalize a bidder for returning an item as a result of your mistake.) For example:

- "Bid high and then disappeared! No response to numerous emails."
- "Beware! Bidder paid with a bad check!"

Neutral. While neutral comments don't affect the feedback score or positive feedback percentage, they carry the stigma of a complaint. For this reason, leave neutral feedback only when you have a legitimate complaint but can't bring yourself to penalize the member with negative feedback. For example, neutral feedback might be appropriate for a bidder who repeatedly does not follow payment instructions, or a seller who packs an item so poorly that it arrives damaged. A few examples:

- "Poor packing job, shipping took a long time. Seller slow to respond."
- "Seller listing products he doesn't have. Waited a month for a refund."
- "Condition wasn't great; seller too busy to care. Not recommended."
- "Bidder took a month to send payment, but eventually paid in full."

Overall, you should remember the purpose of the feedback system when writing feedback for another member. The point of negative and neutral comments is to serve as warnings to other eBay members and to help show a pattern of misconduct. Unless the other person caused you a real problem or cost you money unnecessarily, your feedback comment should be positive and should reward the person for what they did right. Don't use negative or neutral feedback frivolously; for example, don't dock a seller for putting a mailing label on crooked.

Finally, never use feedback as a means of coercion, and don't let other eBay members blackmail you by threatening to leave negative feedback. Any buyer or seller who lets another member get away with murder—simply because they don't want that person to retaliate with negative feedback—does the entire eBay community a disservice.

HACK #1 Appraise an eBayer's Reputation

Quickly decipher a pattern of behavior from the comments in a Member Profile profile to determine someone's trustworthiness.

Trust is the foundation of the eBay marketplace. Whether you're a buyer about to make a purchase from an eBay seller, or you're a seller trying to figure out if a customer is a deadbeat bidder, you can use the feedback system to gauge the trustworthiness of any eBay member in just a few seconds. Unfortunately, the information that's most useful isn't necessarily right on the surface.

Click the *feedback score*, the number in parentheses shown next to any eBay user's member ID, to view his Member Profile page. At the top of the profile page, eBay shows a summary and distribution of past feedback comments, as shown in Figure 1-1.

Here you'll see the total number of positive, negative, and neutral comments, as well as how many of each were received by the user in the past month, the past six months, and the past year. These statistics add a little perspective to older entries, especially negative ones.

Each member's numeric feedback score is also supplemented with a "positive feedback" percentage, which is calculated by dividing the number of positive comments by the total number of positive and negative comments. The problem is that this figure can be somewhat misleading. For instance, a member with 19 positive comments and 1 negative comment would have a positive feedback percentage of 95%. Compare this with someone who, having received 288 positives and 12 negatives, is awarded a 96% feedback percentage. The second member in this example has a better percentage, but most eBayers would agree that 12 complaints is excessive for someone with a feedback score under 300. And the first member's sole complaint may be little cause for concern, especially if she is an eBay newbie.

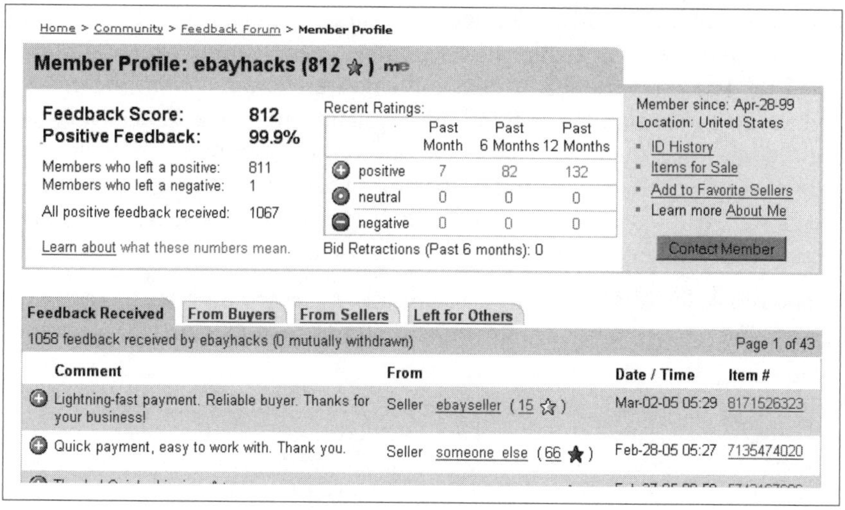

Figure 1-1. The Recent Ratings box gives a brief picture of an eBay member's feedback history

Another problem with the percentage calculation is that neutral comments are not part of the equation. For instance, a seller with 34 positive comments and 8 neutral comments will have a seemingly perfect positive feedback percentage of 100%. On the surface, such a seller would have a better rating than someone with 792 positives and only one negative comment.

Clearly, numbers alone are not always sufficient to gauge the reputation of an eBay member. Although these brief statistics provide enough information to confirm that a particular member is not overly burdened with complaints, there are times when you'll want to investigate further.

Digging Deeper

As you become more proficient with eBay, you'll start to notice certain red flags [Hack #25] in listings, such as suspicious photos, overly restrictive payment terms, and dubious auction descriptions. But, as is often the case on eBay, you might be willing to overlook some of these warnings in the pursuit of a good deal. Or, you might be interested in a particularly rare item and, as such, be somewhat more likely to accept the risks of an uncertain transaction. In these cases, it can help to dig into the seller's feedback profile to find out exactly who you're dealing with.

Click the From Buyers tab to show only feedback the member earned as a seller, and then click the listing numbers next to some of the recent feedback comments to see what items have been earning praise for the seller.

Likewise, look for negative and neutral comments (as described in the next section), and see what other customers have been complaining about. See when the less favorable feedback comments were left and what the posters had to say. For example, a handful of complaints may have all been left during a week when the seller was in the hospital or even when the seller was new to eBay. On the other hand, if the lion's share of a seller's negative comments were entered within the last week, it might show a pattern of dissatisfaction with an item the user recently started selling.

Finally, look for replies and follow-ups [Hack #5] to see how much the seller cares about his reputation (or how riled-up prior customers may've gotten).

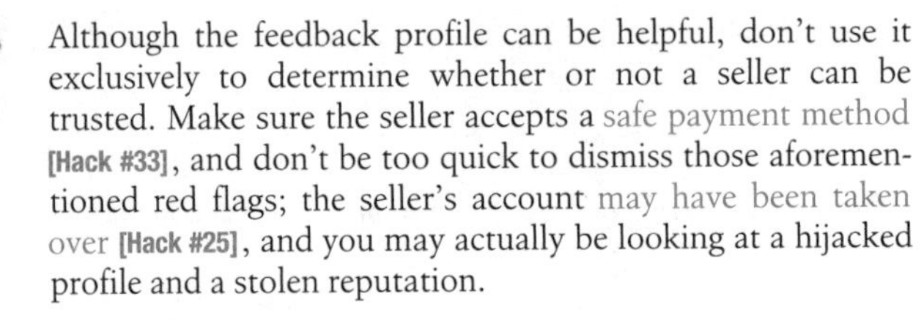

Although the feedback profile can be helpful, don't use it exclusively to determine whether or not a seller can be trusted. Make sure the seller accepts a safe payment method [Hack #33], and don't be too quick to dismiss those aforementioned red flags; the seller's account may have been taken over [Hack #25], and you may actually be looking at a hijacked profile and a stolen reputation.

By the same token, perhaps you're a seller waiting for payment for a completed auction. Do you give the customer the benefit of the doubt and wait a few more days, or do you take the next step and file a nonpaying bidder alert [Hack #68]? To find out, go to the buyer's Member Profile page, click the From Sellers tab, and look for past instances of delinquency. For instance, if the buyer's record is stellar, perhaps the problem is that your payment instruction emails (or the customer's own emails to you) aren't getting through [Hack #9].

Search for Specific Comments

As a given member accumulates feedback, a pattern of behavior emerges. However, sometimes it's necessary to look beneath the pattern and investigate a few individual transactions. After all, the way someone handles a single complaint is often more telling than 10 pages of positive comments.

Feedback is shown in chronological order, with the most recent feedback comments at the top. eBay provides no sorting or searching features, so your options are pretty limited. This is purely intentional; eBay has made a point of encouraging members to "look at the person's reputation as a whole, not just a single component of his or her reputation." While this stance is admirable, the lack of sorting tools ends up making the day-to-day use of the feedback system just a little more frustrating.

Now, in the old days, you could use your web browser's Find feature to locate all occurrences of the word "Complaint," which accompanied every negative feedback comment in a person's member profile. Shortly after the first edition of *eBay Hacks* came out, eBay changed the design of the page and replaced the words "Praise," "Complaint," and "Neutral" with green, red, and gray icons, respectively. Since icons aren't searchable as text, the change broke this handy little searching shortcut. But all is not lost! There are still a few other ways to accomplish this task.

Start by scrolling to the bottom of the user's feedback profile page. At the end of the list, you'll see page numbers that allow you to see older comments. Beneath that, shown in Figure 1-2, is an "Items per page" option. Choose 200, the maximum, and the page will automatically refresh and show the new, longer listing.

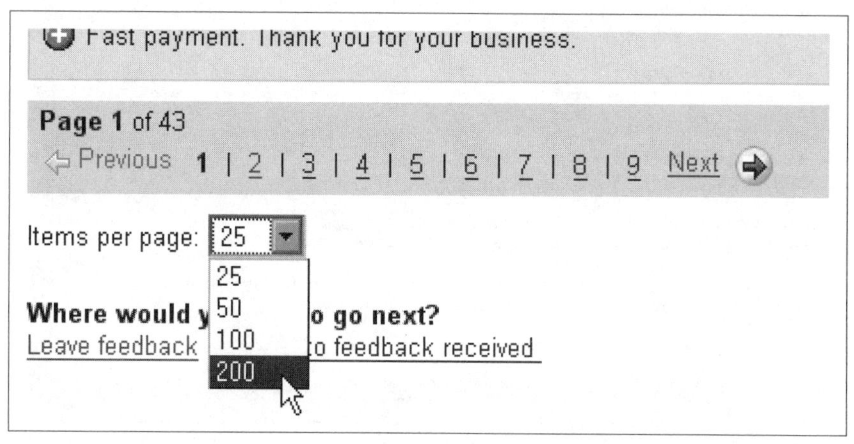

Figure 1-2. Make it easier to search through feedback comments by showing more comments on each page

Next, start at the top and, while scrolling down the page, look for red dots. The Recent Ratings box at the top of the page should give you a clue as to where recent complaints will be located, and how many you'll find.

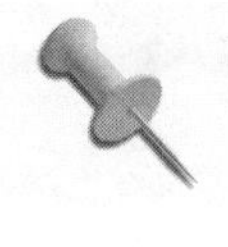

Click the From Buyers or From Sellers tabs to restrict your searches to comments the member received as a seller or a buyer, respectively. You can also get a pretty good idea of the member's demeanor by searching for feedback he or she has left for other members by clicking the Left for Others tab.

Although the bright red "negative" icons are easy to spot, gray "neutral" comments are all but invisible. And if you're a little color blind or just impatient, you'll probably want something a little more automated and foolproof.

Another way to locate individual comments is to search the page's HTML code [Hack #52] for the icon filename. To do this, go to View → Source (if you're using Internet Explorer) or View → Page Source (if you're using Mozilla/Firefox). Then, press Ctrl-F to open the Find dialog and type `iconneg` to search for negative comments (or `iconneu` for neutral comments).

The first instance of each icon you'll find will be for those in the Recent Ratings box (Figure 1-1); just press F3 (in Notepad/Internet Explorer) or Ctrl-G (in Mozilla/Firefox) to find the next one. The corresponding comment appears immediately below the code, as shown in Figure 1-3.

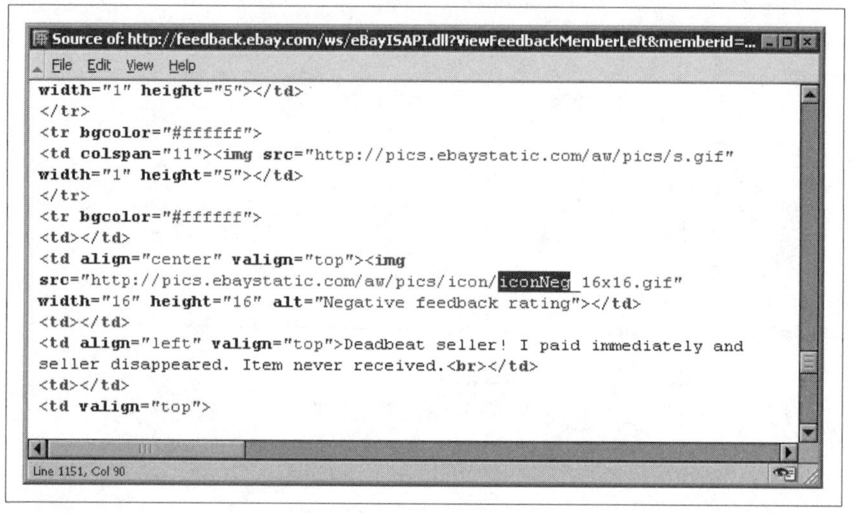

Figure 1-3. Locate negative and neutral feedback comments by searching the HTML of the feedback page

You may also wish to search a person's feedback profile for your own user ID to see if you've left feedback for that person; for this you can use the browser's built-in Find feature (Ctrl-F). Better yet, look for the Feedback Left and Feedback Received icons in the Sold and Won sections of My eBay [Hack #29].

Distill Negative and Neutral Comments

Suffice it to say, eBay doesn't make it easy to locate negative or neutral comments in a member's feedback profile. Fortunately, the Toolhaus Negative/Neutral Feedback tool does!

To list all the negative and neutral comments received by an eBay member, go to *toolhaus.org*, type (or paste) the member ID in the box, and click Received By. Or, to show the complaints the member left for others, click Left By.

For quicker access to the Negative/Neutral Feedback tool, users of Mozilla or Firefox can install the eBay Negs! extension by going to *extensionroom.mozdev.org/more-info/ebaynegs*. To use it, highlight an eBay member ID on a page, right-click the text, and select Open eBay Negs. If you're using Internet Explorer on Windows, see *toolhaus.org/negs-menu-IE.html* for a rather sketchy Windows Registry hack.

Another cool tool, Mutual Feedback (*toolhaus.org/cgi-bin/mutual*) allows you to show the feedback comments two users have left for one-another. Both Toolhaus tools are free, but you're encouraged to support the author with a donation on the site.

See Also

- See Chapter 8 for details on the eBay API and ways to retrieve and search through feedback using only a few lines of code. If you're feeling particularly adventurous, you can make your own Feedback Search Tool [Hack #123].

HACK #2 Use Prefabricated Feedback

Save time by storing prewritten feedback for future use.

It won't take you long to get tired of writing feedback comments for the various buyers and sellers with whom you trade. You always end up saying the same thing, so why bother typing it every time?

The solution is simple. Write two generic, all-purpose positive feedback comments, one for buyers and one for sellers, and place them in a plain-text file saved on your hard disk. Remember that each comment can be no longer than 80 characters, including any spaces and punctuation. (Your text editor may have a *column* indicator to tell you how many characters you've typed.)

When it comes time to leave feedback for someone, open the text file, highlight the appropriate comment, and press Ctrl-C to copy. Then, click the Feedback Review field and press Ctrl-V to paste.

Naturally, you can store as many prefabricated feedback comments as you like (variety is the spice of life, after all). Just be careful not to place any negative comments in this file, lest you select the wrong line in haste.

Feedback for Multiple Auctions

Go to My eBay → Feedback → Leave Feedback, and you'll see a list of all closed auctions for which you have not yet left feedback, as shown in Figure 1-4. Simply go down the list, pasting your prefabricated comment for any deserving transactions.

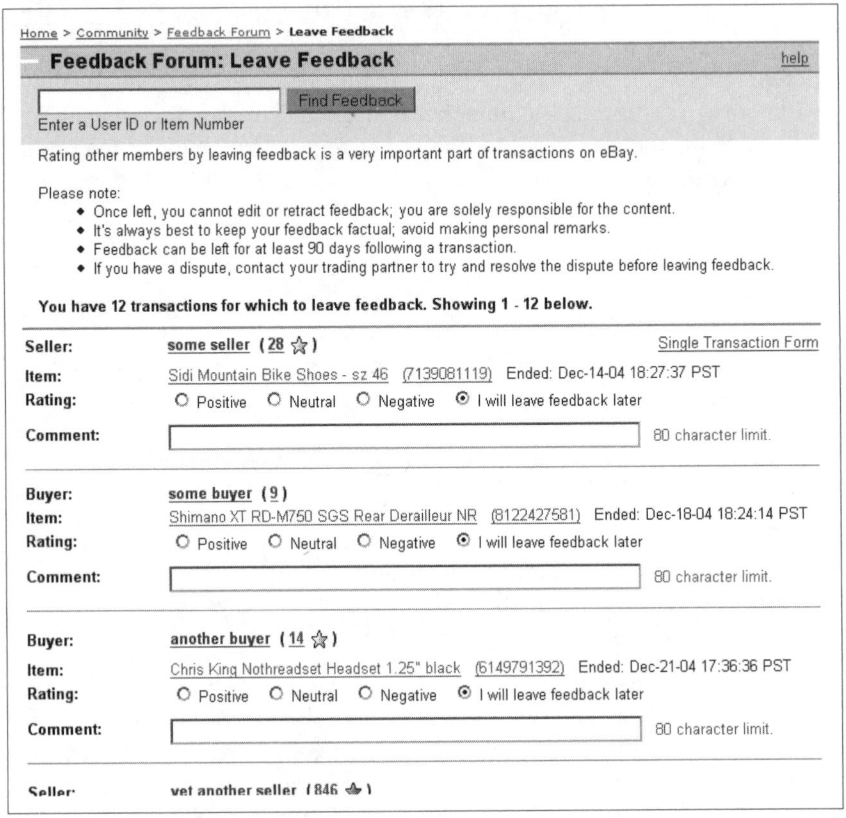

Home > Community > Feedback Forum > **Leave Feedback**

Feedback Forum: Leave Feedback help

[ ] Find Feedback
Enter a User ID or Item Number

Rating other members by leaving feedback is a very important part of transactions on eBay.

Please note:

- Once left, you cannot edit or retract feedback; you are solely responsible for the content.
- It's always best to keep your feedback factual; avoid making personal remarks.
- Feedback can be left for at least 90 days following a transaction.
- If you have a dispute, contact your trading partner to try and resolve the dispute before leaving feedback.

You have 12 transactions for which to leave feedback. Showing 1 - 12 below.

Seller: some seller (28 ☆) Single Transaction Form
Item: Sidi Mountain Bike Shoes - sz 46 (7139081119) Ended: Dec-14-04 18:27:37 PST
Rating: ○ Positive ○ Neutral ○ Negative ⊙ I will leave feedback later
Comment: [ ] 80 character limit.

Buyer: some buyer (9)
Item: Shimano XT RD-M750 SGS Rear Derailleur NR (8122427581) Ended: Dec-18-04 18:24:14 PST
Rating: ○ Positive ○ Neutral ○ Negative ⊙ I will leave feedback later
Comment: [ ] 80 character limit.

Buyer: another buyer (14 ☆)
Item: Chris King Nothreadset Headset 1.25" black (6149791392) Ended: Dec-21-04 17:36:36 PST
Rating: ○ Positive ○ Neutral ○ Negative ⊙ I will leave feedback later
Comment: [ ] 80 character limit.

Seller: yet another seller (846 ☆)

Figure 1-4. Leave feedback for dozens of auctions at a time without typing a single word

Make sure to choose the corresponding rating (positive, negative, or neutral) for each transaction, and then click Leave Feedback when you're done.

Right-Click-o-Rama

Users of Windows XP, Me, and 2000 can use their context menus for even quicker access to prefabricated feedback. Start by installing Creative Element Power Tools (*www.creativelement.com/powertools*) and enabling the "Copy file contents to the Clipboard" option.

Next, create at least two plain-text files (one for buyers and one for sellers), each with only a single feedback comment on the first line, and save them to your hard disk. (Make sure to use a plain-text editor, such as Notepad, instead of a word processor.) Give each file a name that describes its contents, such as *Standard Seller Feedback.txt* or *Positive Buyer Feedback.txt*.

When you're ready to leave feedback, just right-click one of the files and select Copy File Contents. Then, click the Feedback Review field and press Ctrl-V to paste in the feedback text.

Feedback for International Users

Saving feedback is also handy when you want to have several different prefabricated comments at your fingertips. For instance, when leaving feedback for an eBay member in another country, you'll probably want to write in the user's native language. And every time you go to the trouble of constructing a comment in a foreign language, you should save it for future use. Eventually, you'll have a folder filled with filenames like *Positive feedback for Swedish buyers.txt* and *French feedback comments.txt*.

If you're not familiar with the member's native language, use a free online translator to help you out **[Hack #37]**.

See Also

- Some of the auction management tools discussed in Chapter 7 also have features to leave feedback automatically for buyers who have paid.
- See "Leave Feedback with the API" **[Hack #119]** for details on using the eBay API to leave feedback for other members.

HACK #3 Avoid Negative Feedback

Protect your feedback profile—and your reputation—from the proverbial slings and arrows of disgruntled eBayers.

In most cases, negative feedback is unnecessary. And I'm sure that if you just received negative feedback, you'll agree in a heartbeat. But the reason that negative feedback is unnecessary is that it's usually avoidable. Complaints are usually lodged for one of the following reasons:

A buyer's expectations weren't met. A buyer will leave negative feedback for a seller if the item doesn't arrive quickly, if the item isn't in as good condition as promised, or if the seller isn't responsive to emails.

All of these are avoidable: see "Master Expectation Management" [Hack #50] and "Damage Control Before and After You Ship" [Hack #88] for tips to effectively prevent customers from being disappointed, both before and after the sale.

But it's important to note that sometimes there's only so much a seller can do to please a customer. For this reason, sellers must also do everything possible to convince their customers—especially inexperienced ones—to communicate any problems or concerns to the seller *before* they go ahead and leave feedback.

If you're the seller, probably the easiest way to do this is to include a note inside all your packages with your email address (and phone number, if you wish) and the assurance that, if the customer has a problem, you'll do everything you can to make the situation right. Sometimes the note alone is enough to make the customer happy.

Deadbeat bidder. A seller will leave negative feedback for a bidder who doesn't pay. If you're a bidder, you can avoid this by quite simply not bidding when you don't intend to follow through and purchase the item. Sellers can usually prevent deadbeat bidders from bidding on their auctions—or rather, prevent bidders from *becoming* deadbeats—by following the tips in "Keep Out Deadbeat Bidders" [Hack #68].

Communication breakdown. One of the most common causes of failed transactions—and the resulting negative feedback—is one party's inability to receive email sent by the other. See "What to Do When Your Email Doesn't Get Through" [Hack #9] for a variety of solutions.

Retaliation. A single negative feedback comment will often result in a reciprocal retaliatory feedback. Unfortunately, this is human nature, and there's not much you can do about it. What's worse, though, is that many eBay members don't leave negative feedback where appropriate out of fear of retaliation. See "Withhold Feedback" [Hack #6] for an approach that may work to your advantage in these situations.

Any buyer or seller who lets another member get away with murder, simply for fear of retaliation, does the entire eBay community a disservice. Anyone who tries to blackmail you by threatening to leave negative feedback can be suspended for doing so; see the "SafeHarbor" sidebar for details.

It might ease your mind to know that in all the years I have been using eBay, not a single deadbeat bidder who received negative feedback from me has ever retaliated. Not one.

SafeHarbor

SafeHarbor is essentially eBay's policy police. While that sounds like the last thing in the world that would interest a hacker, it's actually a quite valuable tool.

Most of eBay's policies have been put in place to protect buyers and sellers, as well as to maintain the integrity of the marketplace and the level of trust within the community. If you feel that another user is dealing unfairly or abusing the system in some way, you can notify eBay SafeHarbor by going to this address:

http://pages.ebay.com/help/contact_inline/

Some of the situations covered by eBay's policies include:

- Listings for items not in the seller's possession (pre-sale)
- Spam, phishing, and illegal account takeovers **[Hack #25]**
- Copyright violation (e.g., stolen auction photos **[Hack #75]**, selling copyrighted material)
- Abuse of the system (e.g., keyword spamming **[Hack #47]**)
- Feedback extortion

If you'd like eBay to investigate a listing or another member, navigate through the choices on this page, click Continue, and then click Email.

Etiquette and Netiquette

It goes without saying that there are some very simple things you can do on an everyday basis to avoid negative feedback, and most of them involve simple etiquette. For example:

- Be friendly, even if you're not in a friendly mood.
- Write in complete sentences.
- Respond quickly when someone emails you, even if you don't yet have an answer.
- Be patient, and don't panic if you don't get immediate responses to your emails.
- Be forgiving and understanding, especially with new eBay members. Take a little time to educate newbies rather than penalizing them for their inexperience.
- Sellers: treat your customers like gold. Understand that when you have a bidder's money, they can get anxious, suspicious, and downright demanding if you don't reply to their emails quickly.

- Buyers: sellers aren't employed by you, so be nice. Courtesy, gratitude, and patience will go far. For instance, instead of complaining to the seller about a package that hasn't yet arrived, ask the seller for the tracking number [Hack #29] and take matters into your own hands.
- Be diplomatic, even if it means sometimes swallowing your pride.

See Also

- If someone has left negative feedback for you, see "Reply and Follow Up to Feedback" [Hack #5] for tips to help with damage control, or "Remove Unwanted Feedback" [Hack #7] for a way to have it removed.

HACK #4 Receive Feedback Notifications

Have eBay email you or send a text message to your cell phone whenever someone leaves feedback for you.

You can leave feedback for someone as long as you've taken part in a listing that completed successfully within the past 90 days. Among other things, this means that someone else can do the same for you.

Most of the time—and provided you've been good—the other person will leave a positive feedback comment for you, at which point you can leave reciprocal feedback [Hack #6] or even post a reply [Hack #5] whenever you happen to get around to it. But if someone leaves a complaint, you'll want to know right away (especially if it has been 89½ days since the listing closed).

By slightly misusing an eBay notification feature intended for cell phones, you can receive an email whenever someone leaves feedback for you. Here's how to set it up:

1. Start by going to My eBay → eBay Preferences.
2. Find the "Notification preferences" entry at the top of the page, and click the View/Change link to the right.
3. Click the "Add or change notification services" link.
4. Click the Subscribe link for the "eBay Wireless Email" service.
5. Choose the "Send wireless email alerts to the address below" and then enter your email address in the box.

This feature is intended for use by cell phones and pagers, most of which have email addresses associated with them (e.g., *123456789@somewirelessprovider.com*). If you'd like to receive notifications on your cell phone, contact your wireless provider to determine your cell phone's email address.

Click Save Changes when you're done.

6. At this point, you should be returned to the "Change Your Notification Preferences" page. Scroll down to the "Feedback notification" section, and turn on the "Receive Wireless Email" option underneath it.

If the "Receive Wireless Email" checkbox doesn't appear under "Feedback notification," you've stumbled upon an eBay bug. In some cases, eBay doesn't properly rebuild this page when you've changed your wireless notification settings; if this happens to you, try coming back in a few hours. If the problem isn't resolved, contact eBay for assistance.

Click Save Changes when you're done.

From now on, you'll receive a brief email every time someone leaves you feedback, and your reputation will never be marred without your knowledge.

HACK #5 Reply and Follow Up to Feedback

A little damage control will help save a bruised reputation.

The game isn't over when another eBay member leaves feedback for you; you have the opportunity to respond to any feedback comment in your profile. Although this feature is handy for thanking users for leaving you positive feedback, its real value is for damage control when someone leaves neutral or negative feedback for you.

Often, one's instinct is to use this tool as a means of retaliation—to "get back" at the other user for leaving a nasty comment. But given the importance of feedback in the eBay community, your main goal should be to use it to lessen the impact of such comments on your own reputation.

For example, consider the following complaint lodged against you, a seller, by an unhappy bidder:

> Item arrived damaged; very expensive to repair. Lousy seller.

Obviously, this is the wrong response:

> Stupid buyer! What a jerk for complaining! Now you get nothing.

Think of the message this sends to *other* people, prospective future customers, who might scrutinize your feedback profile [Hack #1]. It doesn't address the problem, and since your response shows up only in your *own* feedback profile, it only serves to hurt you. Instead, consider this reply:

> Please contact me with all problems, and I'll do my best to make it right.

This sends a subtle message to the buyer, should he ever choose to return and view your feedback, but more importantly, it makes it appear to other bidders that *you* are the reasonable one, and this particular customer was nothing more than a crackpot. It also reassures potential customers that you will address problems and won't just leave your bidders twisting in the wind.

If you feel the bidder will be understanding and cooperative once you follow up with an email, you may wish to request to have the feedback retracted [Hack #7]. Naturally, getting no bad feedback is the most desirable outcome.

The same approach applies if you're a bidder, and a seller leaves the following feedback for you:

> Deadbeat! Buyer bid high and never paid. Avoid this guy!

The common response among inexperienced bidders is often to do nothing, either for fear that something bad will happen to them, or simply because of a lack of familiarity with the system. A response that explains why the aforementioned nonpayment might have been reasonable is usually the best choice:

> "Seller never responded to emails; I gave up and purchased another one."
> "Seller changed the terms of the sale, and I couldn't comply."
> "I was in the hospital getting a finger transplant, so I couldn't click Pay Now."

But again, when a seller leaves negative feedback for you, the first course of action should be to contact the seller and try to resolve the problem. If everything is worked out, the seller might be willing to cooperate in having the feedback removed [Hack #7].

See "Retract Your Bid Without Retracting Your Bid" [Hack #32] for some reasonable approaches a bidder can use to get out of a deal, often unscathed by negative feedback.

First Reply to Feedback

To reply to feedback left about you, go to My eBay → Feedback → Go to Feedback Forum → Reply to feedback received, and a special version of your feedback profile will appear.

Click Reply next to the appropriate comment. (Be careful that you choose the right one, because replies to feedback cannot be retracted.) The Reply to Feedback Received page will appear, as shown in Figure 1-5.

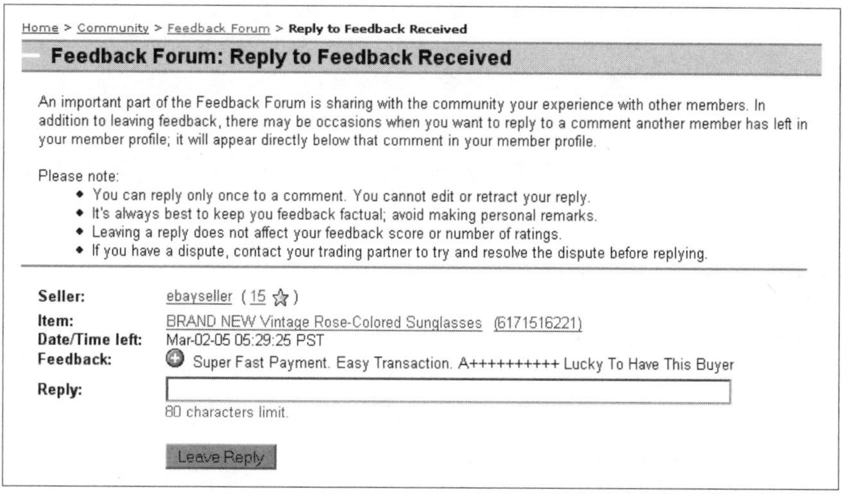

Home > Community > Feedback Forum > **Reply to Feedback Received**

Feedback Forum: Reply to Feedback Received

An important part of the Feedback Forum is sharing with the community your experience with other members. In addition to leaving feedback, there may be occasions when you want to reply to a comment another member has left in your member profile; it will appear directly below that comment in your member profile.

Please note:

- You can reply only once to a comment. You cannot edit or retract your reply.
- It's always best to keep you feedback factual; avoid making personal remarks.
- Leaving a reply does not affect your feedback score or number of ratings.
- If you have a dispute, contact your trading partner to try and resolve the dispute before replying.

Seller: ebayseller (15)
Item: BRAND NEW Vintage Rose-Colored Sunglasses (6171516221)
Date/Time left: Mar-02-05 05:29:25 PST
Feedback: Super Fast Payment. Easy Transaction. A++++++++++ Lucky To Have This Buyer
Reply:
80 characters limit.

Leave Reply

Figure 1-5. Respond to any comments left for you in your feedback profile

Inspect the original comment, and then type your response and click Leave Reply when you're done. Note that you can post only one reply to any single feedback comment, so make it count!

Follow Up to Feedback

Once you leave feedback for another eBay user, you can leave a single follow-up comment that appears beneath your original comment. There are several reasons you might want to do this:

Damage control. As a responsible eBay user, you may wish to do damage control on another user's feedback profile. For example, if you've left negative feedback for someone and they've since rectified the problem, you can return and post a follow-up, reassuring other people that the issue was eventually addressed.

Correct a mistake. On the other hand, if you leave a positive comment for someone who immediately thereafter causes you trouble (thinking, of course, that it's safe to do so), you can amend your comment with a negative follow-up.

Continue the conversation. If you've left feedback for someone, and they've responded to it, as described earlier in this hack, you may wish to post a follow-up response. Note that it isn't required that someone reply to a comment before you can post a follow-up.

Although your follow-up won't have any effect on the recipient's feedback rating, anyone inspecting the profile [Hack #1] will see what you've written. But more importantly, your follow-ups appear in the Left for Others section of your own Member Profile, and will contribute to how you appear to your prospective future customers, should they take the time to look.

To post a follow-up comment, go to My eBay → Feedback → Go to Feedback Forum → Follow up to feedback left.

HACK #6 Withhold Feedback

Know when to hold 'em, and know when to leave 'em.

The trouble with the global village is all the global village idiots.
—Paul Ginsparg

The biggest flaw (and in some ways, the biggest strength) of eBay's feedback system is the risk of retaliation. You leave negative or neutral feedback for someone, and they will—without considering the circumstances or who's at fault—do the same for you. That is the fear, and that is the reason why many people simply let problems slide.

But the risk of retaliation also reminds people that they are responsible for their own words; if there were no consequences, people would leave negative feedback with abandon, and we'd have even more problems on our hands.

I won't deny that the risks sometimes outweigh the gains. Sometimes a bidder has a seemingly legitimate reason for not paying. Perhaps a seller is inexperienced, and while a particular transaction might not have gone very smoothly, it wasn't due to any malice by the seller. Do these people necessarily deserve blemishes on their records? Perhaps not, but they don't necessarily deserve praise, either. In other words, sometimes the best move is no move at all.

Who Goes First

Often the fear of retaliation can work to your advantage. Say you're a seller, and someone has just purchased an item from you. The bidder pays in full, and you go ahead and reward the bidder with positive feedback. But when the bidder receives the item, he's not happy. Since you've already played your hand, the bidder then feels free to file negative feedback, or simply threatens to do so.

On the other hand, if you withhold feedback, the bidder will be much more likely to pursue a diplomatic solution to any problems that come up. Instead of leaving negative feedback, the bidder might politely request a refund, or, better yet, might even go away and not bother you at all.

For this reason, a wise seller will usually wait until the customer has left positive feedback, or at least wait for confirmation that the item has been received and the buyer is happy.

But what about the buyer? If an otherwise happy bidder leaves positive feedback for the seller, isn't there still risk of negative feedback from the seller?

In a word, no. Once a seller has shipped, the seller has everything he or she might've wanted. Unless the bidder does something grievously wrong, the seller has no reason to leave anything but positive feedback.

If There's Doubt

Not everybody retaliates. Some people never even leave feedback, negative or otherwise. If you're worried about retaliation, there's a pretty easy way to predict what any given user will do. Just go to the user's feedback profile page and click the Left for Others tab to view all feedback written about others by that member.

Here, you'll be able to easily tell how diligent someone is about leaving feedback, how prone she is to leaving negative feedback, and how likely she is to retaliate if a complaint is lodged against her. See "Appraise an eBayer's Reputation" [Hack #1] for ways to more easily locate individual negative comments on the member profile page.

Just in Case

One of the best ways to lessen the effect of a single negative or neutral comment in your profile is to bury it with more-recent positive comments. And, as luck would have it, there's a way to help determine the order of feedback comments you receive.

Suppose you're anticipating negative feedback from someone; once it arrives, it'll stick out like a sore thumb. But it just so happens you've completed one or two other recent transactions, for which you're expecting *positive* comments.

The key is to withhold feedback for the positive transactions until the threat of the negative comment has passed. If you get a negative comment, go ahead and leave positive feedback for any applicable transactions right away; with any luck, those members will reciprocate and leave positive comments for you soon thereafter. The more-recent comments will appear above the older negative one, effectively burying it.

Naturally, there are no guarantees; this tip works only under the assumption that the other eBay members are withholding their feedback until they get comments from you, as described earlier in this hack. But sometimes, all it takes is a little careful timing to make the best out of a bad situation.

Remove Unwanted Feedback

Strike a deal with the other party and mutually agree to withdraw feedback comments.

eBay doesn't kid around when it comes to feedback, and neither do most users. Although eBay is quite clear about stating that every member who leaves feedback is responsible for his or her own words and that, once posted, feedback cannot be retracted, there is indeed a way out.

In fact, there are several circumstances under which eBay will remove a feedback comment:

- The feedback comment contains offensive language, personal identifying information, links to pictures or web sites, or false claims with regard to eBay policies or law-enforcement organizations.
- The feedback was used as a means of coercion or blackmail.
- eBay receives a court order finding that the feedback is slanderous, libelous, defamatory, or otherwise illegal, or as a result of a settlement agreement.
- Both you and the other member complete the Mutual Feedback Withdrawal process described in this hack.
- eBay is notified by SquareTrade to remove the feedback, as explained later in this hack. (Useful if you can't get ahold of the other member.)

Go to *pages.ebay.com/help/policies/feedback-removal.html* for the complete scoop.

Mutual Feedback Withdrawal

eBay introduced the Mutual Feedback Withdrawal process to give two parties involved in a dispute an incentive to reconcile, even after they've left feedback for one another. The concept is simple; after each of you have cooled down and realized that you'd both be willing to retract what you've written in exchange for a clean slate, you both visit the Mutual Feedback Withdrawal page, shown in Figure 1-6, and follow the instructions.

The hard part, though, comes when you have to swallow your pride, reach out to the other person, and try to convince him or her to complete the

Home > Community > Feedback Forum > **Mutual Feedback Withdrawal**

Feedback Forum: Mutual Feedback Withdrawal Need Help?

You are about to initiate mutual feedback withdrawal for item 5643167676. For the feedback to be withdrawn, ebay_buyer must also agree and complete the process within 90 days from the end of the listing or 30 days from the date the feedback was left.

Please review the information below before sending your request.

Buyer:	ebay_buyer (591)
Item:	Sony RM-X7 RMX7 Car Stereo Audio Remote Control (5643167676)
Date/Time:	Jan-18-05 12:48:56 PST
Feedback you left:	Very fast payment, good communication, no problems. A pleasure to deal with. A+
Feedback you received:	Thanks! Quick shipping. A+
Message to buyer: (optional)	Up to 200 characters.

Continue > Cancel request

Figure 1-6. Provided the other party agrees, you can use the Mutual Feedback Withdrawal process to neutralize unwanted feedback comments

Mutual Feedback Withdrawal process along with you. The best approach is to send a conciliatory, carefully worded email to the other member, like this:

> I'm truly sorry for the misunderstanding. I'd like to make things right, so to that end, I'm willing to retract the feedback I've left for you. If you'll agree to do the same, please go to *feedback.ebay.com/ws/eBayISAPI.dll?MFWRequest* and follow the instructions. Please let me know if you have any questions.

This approach is simple, direct, and friendly. Most importantly, it includes the address of the Mutual Feedback Withdrawal start page (also available at *pages.ebay.com/help/policies/feedback-removal.html*), so that the other person doesn't have to hunt for it.

To be even more helpful, include the listing number **[Hack #13]** as well, since you'll both need it. The easier you make it for the other party to cooperate, the less likely he will give up.

There are a few restrictions to the Mutual Feedback Withdrawal process. First of all, it doesn't actually result in a totally clean slate. Rather, "withdrawn" feedback comments remain permanently in each person's member profile; only the negative (or neutral) aspect of the comments is removed, along with the corresponding effect on the feedback score.

Second, there's a time limit. You can initiate the Mutual Feedback Withdrawal process only within 30 days of the last feedback left, or within 90 days of the end of the listing, whichever is *later*. Once the deadline has passed, your only option is to use SquareTrade dispute resolution services.

SquareTrade

SquareTrade offers dispute resolution services (similar to eBay's own Dispute Console [Hack #68]), with an optional live mediator (at additional cost). It's a good option when the deadline to use eBay's Mutual Feedback Withdrawal has passed, or when you can't get ahold of the other party. Here's how it works:

1. You go to *www.squaretrade.com* and click File a Case. There is no time limit.
2. SquareTrade sends email messages to both parties.
3. If both parties independently agree to have their feedback removed, SquareTrade sends a removal request to eBay.

   If, on the other hand, the other party doesn't respond to any of the SquareTrade emails within 14 days, you'll be allowed to request that the offending feedback comment be removed. The restriction is that the case must be filed within 90 days of the date of the feedback, thus preventing eBay members from attempting to remove old feedback from those who have long since left eBay or changed email addresses.
4. eBay removes the feedback, or rather removes the "negative" (or neutral) aspect of the comment, along with the corresponding affect on the feedback score.

If, for whatever reason, you're unable to remove negative or neutral feedback from your own profile, at least do some damage control [Hack #5].

Improve Your Trustworthiness Quickly

Don't let an apparent lack of experience hurt your success on eBay.

Bad credit? No credit? No problem!
—Ernie's Used Cars

A low feedback rating can hurt a buyer or seller nearly as much as a feedback profile with an excessive amount of negative comments. Luckily, there are a few things newbies can do to gain trust within the eBay community.

Newbie Buyers

Many sellers, primarily those who have had a bad experience with a non-paying bidder, are understandably apprehensive about bidders with low or zero feedback. So, if you see an auction in which the seller has written a warning about such bidders, drop him a quick note by clicking "Ask seller a question," just to let him know you're serious.

If you're a seller, see "Keep Out Deadbeat Bidders" [Hack #68] for effective ways of dealing with newbie buyers as well as bidders who don't pay.

Newbie Sellers

It's harder to be a new seller on eBay than a new buyer; a seller with low or zero feedback will have a hard time selling anything. Trust, after all, takes on a bigger role when someone else's money is at stake.

The best thing to do (and, coincidentally, the most fun) is to buy a few things before you start selling. Not only is this an easy way to build up feedback, but it will give you some experience in what it's like to be a buyer, which will ultimately make you a better seller.

Note that eBay will also lift some restrictions when you've beefed up your feedback. For instance, once you reach a feedback rating of 10 (even if all the comments are left for you as a buyer), you'll be able to use the Buy It Now feature in your own auctions. For those who can't wait, eBay provides the ID Verify service, described in the next section.

When you finally do start selling, make sure to set your payment terms such that your customers will be able to pay safely. If you accept a safe and convenient payment method such as PayPal [Hack #85], you'll undoubtedly get more bids from buyers who otherwise wouldn't give you the time of day.

ID Verify

If you're a United States resident and have five dollars burning a hole in your pocket, go to Site Map → ID Verify to begin eBay's ID Verification. The process, which takes only a few minutes, simply involves entering some information that is cross-checked by eBay and VeriSign.

Ultimately, what you get out of it is a little ID Verify checkmark icon next to your user ID on eBay. Not everyone will know what it means, but those who click the icon will see the page shown in Figure 1-7.

Help : Buy : ID Verify - Mozilla

ID Verify

An extra mark of security

Some sellers choose to get ID Verified through eBay as an extra sign of security for buyers. When a member gets ID Verified, a third-party company working with eBay confirms the member's identity by cross checking their contact information across consumer and business databases.

You'll see (the ID Verify icon) in verified members' feedback profiles.

Related Help topic

- Trusting the Seller Overview

If you have not found the information you are looking for, please ask a question

eBay Home | Using eBay Help |

Figure 1-7. This reassuring page is shown to anyone who clicks the ID Verify icon next to your user ID

Trust, as much as any sales pitch, is what will earn bids on your auctions. The ID Verify logo is a bidder's assurance that you are who you say you are. Although it's not a substitute for substantive feedback, the ID Verify icon will help new sellers appear more trustworthy to many bidders.

Negative Feedback

New users are more prone to getting negative feedback, typically as a result of inexperience. If you receive negative feedback, don't hesitate to do a little damage control [Hack #5]. And if the other party is willing, you might even be able to get it withdrawn [Hack #7].

eBay allows you to hide your feedback profile by making it "private," which might appeal to someone who has just received negative feedback. But don't do it; it's a trap! The implication that you have something to hide will be more damaging than any single negative comment.

HACK #9 What to Do When Your Email Doesn't Get Through

Use other means to contact buyers and sellers, and avoid the most common cause of negative feedback.

Email is the life's blood of the eBay community. Sellers use it to send payment instructions to buyers, buyers use it to send questions to sellers, and eBay uses it for just about everything.

Unfortunately, there are times when your email never makes it to the other party, either bouncing back or disappearing into the ether. There are two common reasons why your email may never make it to its intended recipient:

- The other member's registered email address is out of date. In this case, any emails sent to that address should be bounced back to you. (Note that any user can update their registered email address by going to My eBay → Personal Information.)
- The other member has an overly aggressive spam filter, which might simply delete all email from unknown addresses (including yours). The spam filter may be running on the recipient's computer or may even be employed by the recipient's Internet Service Provider (ISP) without his or her knowledge. This means you'll never know if your email made it to its destination.

> Any spam filter that deletes email without your approval is ultimately going to lead to a lot of trouble, and possibly some expense and negative feedback. Instead, use a *passive* spam filter like SpamPal (*www.spampal.org*) that simply marks suspicious email as spam, so that your email software (discussed in the Preface) can filter it accordingly. That way, you can inspect it—or even search for lost messages—before deleting it permanently. Refer to the documentation that comes with your spam filter and email program for further details. Also, contact your ISP and make sure they aren't deleting any of your email.

Fortunately, there are a bunch of different tools you can use to get a message through to another eBay member, useful for those times when standard email fails:

Contact an eBay Member form. Click any eBay member's user ID and then click Contact Member to send an email via eBay's mail server. This is useful if you suspect that another member's spam filter is deleting your mail, since it's likely to approve all email originating from *eBay.com*. However, since successful delivery relies on the registered email address in the recipient's eBay account, this won't help if the recipient's address is wrong.

If the recipient is a seller, and you make contact through a currently running auction, eBay will save your message and allow the seller to respond right on the eBay web site [Hack #67]. Even if the seller never receives the email, she'll see your question the next time she views the listing page or visits the Selling section of her My eBay page. This feature isn't available for listings that have ended, but if you're trying to contact a seller for a completed listing (which is common), you can always do so through another one of the seller's listings.

Use a different ISP. If you have an email account with another ISP, try sending your email from there. This will also help get around spam filters. If you don't have another account, you can try getting a free backup address at *mail.yahoo.com* or *www.gmail.com*.

Look in the auction description. If you're a bidder trying to contact a seller, look in the auction description and payment instructions section to see if the seller has specified an alternate email address or phone number. Even if you're not bidding on one of this user's auctions, she may have one or more auctions currently running or recently completed [Hack #18] that might contain this information.

See where the member's photos are hosted. If you're trying to contact a seller who is hosting his own photos [Hack #76], right-click a photo in one of the seller's auctions, and select Properties (if you're using Internet Explorer) or View Image (if you're using Mozilla/Firefox) to see the address of the photo. If the address indicates the photo is residing on a server other than *ebay.com*, there's a chance you can use it to extract the seller's email address. For instance, if the address is *http://www.someprovider.net/~bob/skateboard.jpg*, then you can try contacting the seller at *bob@someprovider.net*. Of course, it's possible that the seller is just using someone else's photo, but it's worth a shot.

About Me. If the member's user ID is accompanied by a little red and blue "me" icon, click the icon to view her About Me page [Hack #62], which might also have alternate contact information.

Modify your own photos. If you're having trouble contacting one of your winning bidders and you're hosting your own auction pictures [Hack #76], you can use your photos as another means of communication. Simply add large, extremely clear text to one of your photos instructing the bidder to email you immediately. For best results, increase the canvas size and place dark red text in the whitespace *above* the image (which will be more obvious than text placed in the photo).

Piggyback on PayPal. Try sending a token invoice or payment through PayPal [Hack #33] of, say, a few cents, and include your message in the Optional Instructions field. Even if the user doesn't receive PayPal's notification email, your note will appear the next time she logs into PayPal.

Alternate PayPal email address. If you've completed a PayPal transaction with the person in question-either as a buyer or seller-log into *PayPal.com*, find the transaction in your payment history, and see if the person's PayPal account is connected with a different email address than the one eBay has on file. If so, try sending your messages to that address as well.

File a dispute. Although it's a rather drastic step, you can almost always get someone's attention by reporting an Unpaid Item [Hack #89] (if you're a seller) or by reporting an Item Not Received [Hack #41] (if you're a buyer). But the best part is that the dispute process includes a two-way message system, in which both parties can write messages and see the entire discussion right on the eBay web site. It's the only way to contact another member for a completed auction that doesn't rely on email. You can view all open disputes by going to My eBay → Dispute Console.

Additional contact information. Provided that you and the other member are both involved in a transaction, go to Advanced Search → Find Contact Information, and enter the person's member ID and relevant item number in the spaces provided. eBay will then email both parties with each other's street address and phone number, which you can use as a last resort.

In nearly all cases, one of these methods will get your message across when email fails. Make sure that you inform the other person that you have had trouble sending email, and don't be afraid to request that they take steps to rectify the problem. Strangely enough, people are often indifferent to the situation, but suggesting that yours is probably not the only email that isn't getting through is usually enough to convince the recipient to snap into action.

See Also

- If you're a seller, and your high bidder isn't replying to your emails, you may have a deadbeat bidder on your hands. See "Keep Out Deadbeat Bidders" [Hack #68] and "Deal with Stragglers, Deadbeats, and Returns" [Hack #89] for ways to deal with this problem.

CHAPTER TWO

Searching

Hacks 10–24

Without the ability to search, eBay would be close to worthless. Think about it: at any given time, there are close to 20 million items for sale on eBay, and that number keeps growing. If you were only able to flip through them like pages in a magazine (a magazine a quarter of a mile thick, mind you), you'd never find anything.

Searching on eBay is an art, often requiring you to think a little creatively. Sometimes you have to get into the minds of potential sellers to predict how they might describe the item you're looking for; other times you just have to be a little devious.

Now, basic searching on eBay is a piece of cake. Just type a word into eBay's search box and press Enter, or type more than one word to narrow your search. By default, all searches simply cover auction titles, but you can include auction descriptions as well by clicking the "Search title and description" checkbox (available everywhere except in the little search box in the eBay page header).

The hacks in this chapter take it several steps further, covering the advanced search syntax, showing you how to carefully control the scope of your searches, and including several ways to find things that would otherwise elude you. After all, the best deals (and the best finds) are usually the items that most people don't see.

HACK #10 Focus Your Searches with eBay's Advanced Search Syntax

Simplify your searches by making them a little more complicated.

Why should exhaustive searches be so...exhausting? Whether you're performing a quick one-time search or repeating the same search every other day, you can dramatically improve the efficiency of your searches and the relevance of your search results with some simple modifications to your queries.

You could fine-tune your searches by using the Advanced Search form, but this can be cumbersome and is mostly unnecessary due to the advanced search syntax.

Excluding Unwanted Results

Simply precede a search term with a minus sign (–) to eliminate any search results containing that term. For example, the query:

```
sunglasses -men's
```

will show all auctions containing "sunglasses" but not "men's", which should, at least in theory, show you a list of women's sunglasses. (Note that there's no space between the minus sign and the term "men's".) This approach is typically more effective than something like "women's sunglasses" because it will also include any auctions for gender-neutral sunglasses.

Naturally, you can exclude multiple terms, like this:

```
sunglasses -men's -children's -ugly
```

The scope of the excluded terms is the same as the scope of the search; that is, if you're searching only titles, the exclusions will apply only to titles. For example, the previous example may bring up some auctions with "ugly" in the description, provided the word doesn't appear in the title.

Exclusions open up a little paradox in eBay's search tool. In most cases, expanding a title-only search to include titles and descriptions will increase the number of search results. But when you exclude a word, a title-and-description search may return *fewer* results than the same search performed only on titles. Although this is caused by nothing more than the increased likelihood of finding one of the excluded terms when you search descriptions, it can still sometimes be surprising.

Be careful when excluding terms, especially when searching descriptions, because some sellers are sloppy with the words they include in their auctions. For instance, you might type:

```
digital camera -refurbished
```

to eliminate any refurbished (a.k.a. "factory reconditioned" or "factory renewed") cameras from your searches. But any listing that contains the phrase "Brand new; not refurbished" will also be excluded from your search. See the "Evolution of a Search" sidebar for additional examples.

Evolution of a Search

Adding exclusions to a search is typically an evolutionary process. Say you're searching for a plasma TV; you'd begin your search by typing:

```
plasma tv
```

which, not surprisingly, brings up some 2657 listings. About half of those are merely for plasma TV wall mounts, so you refine your search:

```
plasma tv -mount
```

But 1300 listings is still too many (how many TVs do you need, anyway?), so you further restrict your search by looking only for Panasonic TVs:

```
plasma tv -mount panasonic
```

But then it occurs to you that some inexperienced sellers may specify the brand only in the description, so you turn on the "Search title and description" option. Of course, this means that the `-mount` exclusion will also now catch phrases you might see like "wall mount available" so you take it out. It also occurs to you that some sellers may not include the term `tv` so you take that out, too. So you're left with:

```
plasma panasonic
```

which still results in more than 1300 listings. So, you turn off the "Search title and description" option and try again. Now, you're down to a little over 500 listings. It's at this point that you decide to visit the Panasonic website and figure out exactly which model TV you want. Then, you return to eBay and do a title-and-description search for only the model number (or rather, for several variations of the model number), which results in a very-manageable selection of only 11 listings. Watch that last one; it ends in 8 minutes!

Save Time and Typing with Wildcards

Place an asterisk (*) character in or after a search term to match all words that begin with that term. For example, the query:

```
phillips screwdriver*
```

will bring up auctions for "screwdriver" and "screwdrivers." An even better choice is:

```
phil* screwdriver*
```

which will catch the common misspelling "philips" as well.

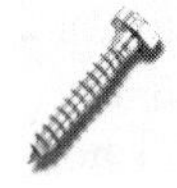

As you might expect, if your wildcard searches are too general, you'll get a bunch of irrelevant results. A recent search for "phil* screwdriver*" brought up an auction for a Beatles recording because the auction description mentioned producer Phil Spector and a reference to John Lennon having made a joke about a screwdriver.

Since wildcards can also appear in the middle of keywords, you can further focus your search with the following:

```
phil*ips screwdriver*
```

You can also use wildcards with exclusions. For example, if you're looking for women's sunglasses, you might type:

```
sunglasses -men -men's -mens
```

to exclude results you don't want. But you could also use this much simpler version:

```
sunglasses -men*
```

to exclude all the variants of auctions for men's sunglasses.

Performing OR Searches

By default, every eBay search is an AND search, meaning that each auction must match each and every search term; the more terms you specify, the narrower your search becomes. But if you're looking for multiple items, or for an item that can be described in several different ways, you can combine your terms into a single OR search.

Terms in an OR search are encased in parentheses and separated with commas. Let's say you're looking for anything by the Beatles or the Bee Gees; you'd type:

```
(beatles,bee-gees,beegees)
```

Note the absence of spaces around the commas and parentheses. You can also combine OR and AND searches; if you're looking for any videos by the Beatles, you might type:

```
beatles (video,videos,dvd,dvds,vhs)
```

Or better yet:

```
beatles (video*,dvd*,vhs)
```

Note the inclusion of singular and plural variations of some of the terms, which may or may not be necessary; see "Control Fuzzy Searches" [Hack #11] for details.

Use an OR search to consolidate several searches into a single phrase. Say you're restoring an old Porsche 356b sports car; instead of conducting individual searches for each of the parts you're still missing, try something like:

```
(356,356b) (wiper,shift knob,hub cap)
```

and look for all the parts you need on a single page of search results. Plus, you can save your search [Hack #20] or even get email updates [Hack #21] when new matching listings appear on eBay.

Looking for Phrases

Enclose phrases in quotation marks, like this:

```
"abbey road"
```

or, to look only for the CD:

```
"abbey road" cd
```

Note that the term "cd" isn't in the quotes, since it could be anywhere in the title or description. Naturally, phrase searches can be combined with exclusions, wildcards, and OR searches. Type:

```
"abbey road" -cd
```

to look for all listings *except* the CDs. Or, try:

```
("abbey road","white album") -cd
```

to include only these specific Beatles albums in your searches.

Want to see how valuable the quotation marks are in your searches? Try this:

```
abbey road -"abbey road"
```

This will show you all auctions with these two words, *except* when they appear together in the phrase "abbey road". When I tried this, the first auction that came up was a signed LP by Barry Manilow. Enough said.

Control Fuzzy Searches

Choose when and how plurals and variations of your search terms are used in searches.

For the most part, eBay searches return only listings that match your search terms exactly. That is, if you search for `possum`, you won't necessarily retrieve the same results that you would in a search for `opossum`.

Historically, to perform a *fuzzy* search, you'd have to include all the variations of a word in the search box manually, like this:

```
(opossum,possum,apossoun)
```

To accommodate singular and plural variants of a word, you'd have to type something like this:

```
(antenna,antennas,antennae)
```

The OR search commanded by the use of parentheses [Hack #10] takes care of this nicely. But it's not always necessary.

All eBay searches automatically include common plurals and a few alternate spellings of words. For instance, a search for `antenna` will also yield results matching `antennas` rendering the use of an OR search or wildcards redundant in this case. The same is true for `lens` and `lenses`, as well as `watch` and `watches`. (The equivalency of plurals doesn't necessarily carry over to phrase searches. See "Use Keywords Effectively" [Hack #47] for an example.)

Plurals aren't the only variations included in fuzzy searches; search for `spiderman` and you'll also get listings that match `spider-man`. Likewise, `t-shirt` and `tshirt` are considered equivalent, as are `Mr. T` and `Mr T`.

Unfortunately, eBay's support for fuzzy searches is a little unreliable and difficult to predict; sometimes the results include plurals and sometimes they don't. While a search for `tire` yields the same results as a search for `tires`, the same is not true for `tyre` or `tyres`. Bad spellers will be sad to learn that `paisly` is not the same as `paisley`. And while eBay equates `phone` with `phones`, a `telephone` is still an entirely different animal.

> Rather than relying on the whims of eBay's search engine, there's an easy way to test any particular variant. Just perform two searches: one for the singular version, and another for the plural (e.g., `harmonica` and `harmonicas`). Then, compare the number of items found; if they're the same, then eBay considers the two terms to be equivalent. (Since listings start and end all the time, the totals may change slightly; just repeat the search to confirm.) This tip is particularly useful if you're a seller trying to decide whether or not you need to include multiple variations of a term in your listing title [Hack #47].

The reason that eBay's fuzzy searches may seem inconsistent is that matches are based on a hand-selected dictionary of common variations and plurals, and eBay appears to be constantly revising these definitions. As the feature evolves, new matches may be added to the list while others proven to be troublesome may be removed. In an effort to keep fuzzy searches as unobtrusive as possible, though, extreme variants, such as "potato" and "tater" are unlikely to ever make the cut.

Search, Literally

Of course, the inclusion of fuzzy variations isn't always desirable. For instance, if you're looking for rooftop antennas for a Pennsylvania Railroad PA-1 locomotive (or a model of one), you wouldn't so much be interested in a book discussing the antennae of Pennsylvania cockroaches. To force eBay to search only for exact matches of words, enclose such terms in quotation marks, like this:

```
pennsylvania "antennas"
```

which is practically equivalent to:

```
pennsylvania antennas -antennae
```

Whether the quotes will be necessary, or whether you'll need to manually include variations (using parentheses), will depend on the particular search you're trying to perform.

Punctuation

To simplify searches that would otherwise require very cumbersome search phrases, nearly all forms of punctuation are considered equivalent to spaces in eBay searches. For instance, say you're looking for a 1:43-scale model car; you might expect to have to type the following:

```
car (1/43,1\43,1:43)
```

Instead, all you would need to type is:

```
car 1/43
```

where the `1/43` term will match `"1 43"`, `1:43`, `1;43`, `1\43`, `1-43`, `1.43`, `1!43`, `1@43`, `1#43`, `1$43`, `1%43`, `1^43`, `1&43`, `1_43`, `1=43`, `1+43`, and `1~43`.

Now, say the aforementioned car is a 1968 Ford GT 40; the appropriate search phrase might then be:

```
(gt40,gt-40) 1/43
```

Here, the 1/43 catches all appropriate variants, but an OR search **[Hack #10]** is still required for both versions of the car name; although `gt-40` is equivalent to `"gt 40"`, it won't match `gt40` (without any space or punctuation). This tactic is often necessary when searching for product model numbers, since most sellers aren't terribly diligent about dashes and other punctuation. For instance, if you're searching for the Sony XDP-4000X digital signal processor, you'll want to use something like this:

```
(xdp4000x,xdp-4000x)
```

Or, better yet:

```
(xdp4000x,xdp-4000x,xdp4000,xdp-4000)
```

since sellers frequently drop single letters that follow strings of numbers (like the trailing x here) for reasons that are not entirely clear. As you can imagine, eBay won't find these variants for you. Of course, you could also simplify the search with wildcards:

```
(xdp4000*,xdp-4000*)
```

Now, punctuation doesn't fall under the same rules as variations and plurals, meaning that you wouldn't be able to use quotation marks to restrict your search to include only desired variations, as discussed earlier in this hack. For instance, a search for:

```
"gt-40"
```

won't exclude variants `gt/40` or `gt:40`. This means that the two terms in this search:

```
gt-40 -gt/40
```

will cancel each other out, and you'll always get "0 items found" as a result. Of course, if you're trying to curb your spending on model cars, this type of "search sabotage" might be just the thing you need to save yourself a few bucks.

Jump In and Out of Categories While Searching

Narrow your searches by confining them to certain categories, and filter categories while you browse.

eBay uses an extensive hierarchy of categories to group similar items together. This not only enables sellers to improve the exposure of their auctions, but it helps bidders find what they're looking for and even discover new items.

When you perform a standard search, no thought is given to the categories in which the items are sorted; toaster ovens are listed right alongside antique doll clothes and rechargeable batteries. By the same token, when you browse a category, you're simply looking at a list of every item placed in that category by sellers, whether it's relevant or not.

Category listings and search results are essentially the same thing: subsets of the massive auction database that is eBay. This means that when you perform a search or browse a category, you're really just changing your filtering criteria. Fortunately, you can combine the two quite easily. Think of it as either narrowing a search by confining it to a single category, or filtering a category listing with search keywords.

Search Within a Category

Click Buy at the top of any eBay page to view a directory of the top-level categories. Choose a category here, and then a subcategory from the assortment displayed on the next page. At three levels deep and beyond, you'll see standard category views, including auction listings and a basic search field, as shown in Figure 2-1. (Note that you can also jump to a category listing from any auction by clicking the category link at the top of the page.)

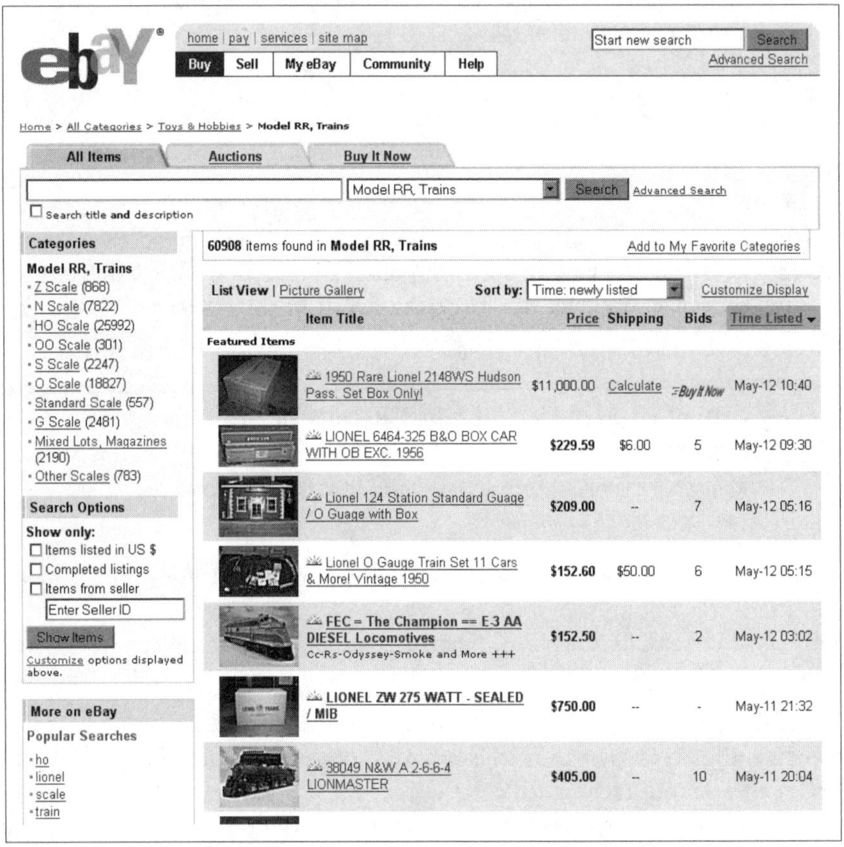

Figure 2-1. Search results and category listings use the same interface, so it's easy to switch between them

Just type your query in the search box, leave the drop-down box set to the currently selected category, and click Search. Any matching auctions found in the current category (or subcategories, if applicable) will then be shown.

To cancel the search and return to the unfiltered category view, click the right-most category link at the top of the page (just before "Search Results for...").

If you're looking for a particular item, as opposed to merely browsing, you'll probably find it easier to start with a search and then choose a category thereafter, as described next.

Categorize Your Search

Whether you started your search from a category listing or from the search box on another page, a selection of categories with matching auctions will be shown in the Matching Categories box on the left, and the current category (if applicable) will appear at the top of the page.

You can navigate through the categories without disrupting the search filter:

Up. To go up a level and broaden your search, choose the category name from the drop-down listbox next to the search text box, and click Search.

Down. To drill down to more specific categories and narrow your search, click the desired subcategory in the Matching Categories box on the left. (The numbers shown in parentheses next to the subcategory names represent the number of matching auctions those categories.)

Anywhere. To remove the category filter from your search, choose the All Categories entry from the drop-down listbox and click Search.

Bookmark a Category

Once you've gone to the trouble of composing a search and navigating through categories to narrow it, the last thing you want is to have to do it again.

To save your search, including the currently selected category, click the Add to Favorites link in the upper-right corner, and the search will show up in the Favorites section of your My eBay page [Hack #20]. Or, if you're viewing an unfiltered category listing (no search), click Add to My Favorite Categories.

The problem is that favorite categories and saved searches are shown in two different places in My eBay, as shown in Figure 2-7. To bookmark a category so that it appears alongside your favorite searches, start with an ordinary search, as described in the previous section, and then navigate to the category you'd like to bookmark. Now, erase the text in the search box and click Search.

At this point, you'll see what looks like a basic category view, except that an Add to Favorites link appears in the upper right (as opposed to the aforementioned Add to My Favorite Categories). Click Add to Favorites, and you'll be given the opportunity to save an All Items search for the selected category.

See Also

- For other ways to narrow your searches, see "Focus Your Searches with eBay's Advanced Search Syntax" [Hack #10].
- See "Tweak Search URLs" [Hack #13] for a more in-depth look at categories and how they relate to searches and auctions.

HACK #13 Tweak Search URLs

Tap into eBay's massive database right from your own address bar.

eBay is essentially a massive database. Every time you view an auction page, you're just looking at a single database record. Every time you search, you're performing a query. But even if you're not familiar with DB lingo, you can play with eBay's URLs to tweak what you see. Among other things, this makes it easier to share links with others, as well as quickly jump to certain pages on the eBay site.

Auction/Listing Pages

Most pages on eBay are generated dynamically so that you can see up-to-date listing information and customized content. In order for this to work, certain details need to be sent to eBay, and this is typically done with parameters included in web page addresses (URLs). For instance, the address of an auction page usually looks like this:

```
http://cgi.ebay.com/ws/eBayISAPI.
dll?ViewItem&category=19117&item=5958951586&rd=1
```

Here, `cgi.ebay.com` is the name of the server, `eBayISAPI.dll` is the filename of the program, `ViewItem` is the command to execute, and `item=5958951586` is a parameter. Any additional parameters are separated by ampersands (&).

As you can see, this URL is too long to fit on one line. If you've ever tried to email a long URL to a customer or friend, you know that the word-wrap feature found in most email programs will break long lines, thus disabling the URL. The solution is to shorten the URL by removing unnecessary elements. In this case, both the category and `rd` parameters are superfluous and can be removed:

```
http://cgi.ebay.com/ws/eBayISAPI.dll?ViewItem&item=5958951586
```

The remaining parameter, item, is the only one that's required; this shortened URL is only 61 characters long, thus fitting easily within the 76-character limit imposed by most email software.

The easiest way to shorten listing page URLs is to let eBay do the work. Double-click the item number in the URL (5958951586 in the above example), and press Ctrl-C to copy it to the clipboard. Then, click in the search box at the top of the eBay page, and press Ctrl-V to paste. Finally, click Search, and the page will simply reload with the shorter URL.

See the "Shorten Any URL" sidebar for another way to make long URLs easier to email.

Feedback/Member Profile pages

To view someone's Member Profile page [Hack #1], click the number in parenthesis next to the member's ID on any eBay page. The URL looks like this:

```
http://feedback.ebay.com/ws/eBayISAPI.dll?ViewFeedback&userid=ebayhacks
```

Other parameters may be present, all of which can be safely ignored or omitted. If you want to look at the feedback for a particular member without having to scour eBay for a page with the correct link, and without having to fuss with search pages, simply replace the text after the userid parameter (ebayhacks in this case) with the user ID of the member you want to look up.

The same goes for About Me [Hack #62] pages:

```
http://cgi.ebay.com/ws/eBayISAPI.dll?ViewUserPage&userid=ebayhacks
```

and eBay Stores [Hack #91] pages:

```
http://stores.ebay.com/ebayhacks
```

Most pages on eBay are like these, where it should be fairly obvious how you can change a parameter in a URL to quickly jump to another page.

Search Results and Category Listings

As described in "Jump In and Out of Categories While Searching" [Hack #12], search results and category listings are pretty much the same thing. The URL of a search for "avocado green" in the Linens, Fabric & Textiles category, for instance, looks like this:

```
http://search.ebay.com/avocado-green_Linens-Fabric-Textiles_
W0QQcatrefZC12QQfromZR40QQfsooZ2QQfsopZ2QQsacatZ940QQsojsZ1
```

And the URL of the unfiltered listing of the items in the Linens, Fabric & Textiles category looks like this:

```
http://listings.ebay.com/Linens-Fabric-Textiles_
W0QQcatrefZC4QQfclZ3QQfromZR10QQfrppZ200QQfsooZ2QQfsopZ2QQ
sacatZ940QQsocmdZListingItemListQQsofindtypeZ0
```

Shorten Any URL

Whether you're a seller trying to direct a customer to a PayPal help page, or a buyer trying to direct a seller to the Revise Your Item page [Hack #65], you'll have a much easier time of it if you just include the address (URL) of the page.

As explained in "Tweak Search URLs" [Hack #13], the biggest problem with emailing URLs is that the word-wrap feature in most email programs breaks any URLs longer than about 76 characters. Of course, the recipient can cope with this by reassembling the long URL by copying and pasting, but you should never expect him to know how to do this, or even know that he's supposed to.

Rather, use a service like TinyURL or SnipURL (both free) to create an email-friendly short version of the address. Just highlight the long URL, press Ctrl-C to copy it to the clipboard, go to the site (*tinyurl.com* or *snipurl.com*), and press Ctrl-V to paste the URL in the box. Click the button (Make TinyURL or Snip URL), and the site will generate an address that looks something like this:

```
http://tinyurl.com/4vnfa
```

The site will also report the length of the original URL and the shortened URL it has provided for you. To use the new address, highlight it, press Ctrl-C to copy, and then paste it into an outgoing email message. Test the address at any time by pasting it into the address bar of your browser and pressing Enter. The short URL will never expire.

If you find that you use these services frequently, there are a few ways to streamline the URL-shortening process:

Toolbar buttons. You can create a link on your browser's Links toolbar (much like the one in "Find Similar Items" [Hack #14]) to create a short URL in one step; instructions can be found on each of the aforementioned sites.

Browser Extension. If you use Mozilla or Mozilla Firefox, try TinyURL Creator *https://update.mozilla.org/extensions/moreinfo.php?id=126&vid=1227*, or better yet, *http://tinyurl.com/574q9*). To use the tool, right-click an empty area of the current page and select Create Tiny URL for this Page. The new address will be copied to the clipboard for you to use right away. A similar tool, MyIE2, works with Internet Explorer and SnipURL, and is available at *www.myie2.com*.

As you can see, these URLs are not quite as user-friendly as the ones illustrated earlier in this hack. But if you look closely, they're actually very similar. You can see the individual parameters, but instead of `&` symbols separating them, eBay uses `QQ`. And instead of an equals sign between the parameter name and its value, eBay uses Z. Thus, the "avocado green" search URL is equivalent to:

```
http://search.ebay.com/avocado-green_Linens-Fabric-Textiles_
W0&catref=C12&from=R40&fsoo=2&fsop=2&sacat=940&sojs=1
```

Unfortunately, after all this work, there's essentially nothing interesting you can do with this URL. You can customize the search options by clicking the Customize Display link, and you can changing your filtering options [Hack #12] with the category links to your left.

About the only thing you can do here is glean the category number (940, in this case) from the sacat parameter, which can be used to more easily specify a category when creating a listing [Hack #43]. And if you want a short URL pointing to a category listing, eBay still supports their old-style category listing URL format:

```
http://listings.ebay.com/aw/listings/list/category940
```

Just replace 940 with the number corresponding to the category you wish to view. (You can also get the category number for any of eBay's 15,000+ categories at *listings.ebay.com/aw/plistings/list/categories.html*.)

Categories are typically restricted to a single nationality. For example, a given category number at *ebay.com* won't be recognized at *ebay.de*, even though *ebay.de* may have an equivalent category that goes by a different number. See "Search Internationally" [Hack #19] for details.

View a Seller's Other Items

If you click "View seller's other items" on any auction page, you'll get an ordinary, fully-functional eBay search page, filtered [Hack #12] to show only current listings offered by the seller. It wasn't always this way, though; the "View seller's other items" page used to be a specialized listing page with very few options. This is useful because the URL of the old page still works:

```
http://cgi.ebay.com/ws/eBayISAPI.dll?ViewSellersOtherItems&userid=ebayhacks
```

which is a little friendlier than the new version:

```
http://search.ebay.com/_W0QQfgtpZ1QQfrppZ25QQsassZebayhacks
```

Both addresses do work, however, and either is appropriate for emailing or including in your listing descriptions [Hack #60].

See Also

- See "Smooth Out International Transactions" [Hack #37] for a way to change the nationality of most eBay pages by modifying the URL.
- See "Find Similar Items" [Hack #14] for another way to use search URLs.

Find Similar Items

Quickly list auctions similar to the one you're looking at with a simple JavaScript tool.

I'm always excited to discover something new while searching on eBay, but I've been around long enough to know that there's virtually no such thing as "one of a kind."

When you've found an item you're interested in, it's often helpful to seek out other auctions for similar items, either to compare prices or perhaps to find something better. Typically, this involves opening a search box and typing the name of the item for which to search. Here's a quick hack that will eliminate these steps and list similar items with a single click.

Create a new button on your browser's Links bar (see the "Customizing the Links Bar" sidebar for details) and type the following JavaScript code, all on one line, into the new link:

```
javascript:void(win=window.open('http://search.ebay.com/' +
      document.title.substring(document.title.indexOf(' - ') + 3)))
```

Make sure to note the capitalization of the JavaScript code, such as the uppercase "O" in the `indexOf` keyword. Note also the spaces around the hyphen (`' - '`). You can name the new link anything you like, such as "Find Similar."

Then, open any auction page and click the new link, as shown in Figure 2-2. (Naturally, the hack won't work on a nonauction page.) A new window will appear with search results matching the title of the auction you were just looking at, which, in theory, should contain at least one auction. At this point, you can modify and repeat the search as needed.

Figure 2-2. View a list of similar auctions by clicking this custom button on your Links bar

How It Works

The first part of the code, `win=window.open`, instructs your browser to open a new window and navigate to the URL that follows. The reason you need

Customizing the Links Bar

Modern web browsers such as Firefox, Mozilla, and Internet Explorer all have a customizable toolbar called the Links bar. The Links bar, shown in Figure 2-2, is nothing more than a small collection of easily accessible bookmarks (a.k.a. favorites, shortcuts, links) that you can click to open the corresponding pages. These are sometimes called *bookmarklets*.

The easiest way to add a custom button to the Links bar is to simply drag-and-drop the URL shortcut icon (to the immediate left of the URL) onto the bar to add the current page. Or drag any link from any open web page, bookmark, favorite, or Internet shortcut onto the Links bar.

Some of the hacks in this book use JavaScript code embedded in links placed on the Links bar. Although there's no way to create a blank button on the Links bar into which you can type the code, there are other easy ways to create such a link:

- Start by dragging-and-dropping any arbitrary link onto the Links bar. Then, right-click the new link, select Properties, and replace the URL with the appropriate JavaScript code.
- In Windows, right-click on an empty area of your desktop and go to New → Shortcut. Type the JavaScript code into the location field, choose a name, and click Finish when you're done. Then, drag and drop the new shortcut onto the Links bar.
- Create a new web page (a *.html* file) and place the JavaScript code into an <a> hyperlink tag **[Hack #52]**. Then, open the page and drag and drop the hyperlink onto the Links bar. This is typically more trouble than the other two methods, but it can be an easy way to send the link to others, especially since you can include instructions right on the same page.

JavaScript is that the search URL needs to include information from the auction shown in the current window, something a static link wouldn't be able to do.

Next comes the URL to open. The first part of the URL is taken from a standard eBay search URL, as seen in "Tweak Search URLs" **[Hack #13]**:

```
http://search.ebay.com/keywords
```

The *keywords* parameter is then completed by including the title of the currently displayed auction:

```
document.title.substring(document.title.indexOf(' - '),document.title.length)
```

wherein the auction title is extracted from the page title by taking only the text that appears *after* the hyphen (with spaces on either side) that separates the end date from the auction title.

Hacking the Hack

By default, this hack searches only auction titles. To search both titles and descriptions, you'll need to add `_W0QQftsZ2` to the end of the search URL, like this:

```
javascript:void(win=window.open('http://search.ebay.com/' +
    document.title.substring(document.title.indexOf(' - ')+3)+'_W0QQftsZ2'))
```

A variation of this hack might be used to search completed auctions instead of current auctions, which may be useful for finding how similar items have previously sold [Hack #42] or possibly seeing if the specific item on which you're bidding is being resold [Hack #25]. Just change the URL (`http://search.ebay.com/`) to that used for completed item searches:

```
http://search-completed.ebay.com/
```

Note that eBay will complain if you try to show complete auctions and search titles and descriptions at the same time, since completed items can be searched only by their titles.

HACK #15 Search for Selected Text

Highlight text in any web page and search for it on eBay with the click of a button.

So you've found an item you like while surfing the web, and it occurs to you that you can probably get it cheaply on eBay. At this point, you've learned that you can highlight the name (or model number) of the product on the page, press Ctrl-C to copy it to the clipboard, then go to eBay, paste it into a search box (Ctrl-V), and press Search to look for matching items. If this scenario sounds familiar, you'll definitely appreciate this shortcut.

Start by creating a new button on your browser's Links bar [Hack #14], and naming it "Search eBay" or something similar.

Next, if you're using Mozilla, Firefox, or Netscape, place this JavaScript code (all on one line) into the button's location field:

```
javascript:s=document.getSelection();
        for(i=0;i<frames.length;i++){s=frames[i].document.getSelection();}
        location.href='http://search.ebay.com/'+escape(s);
```

If you're using Internet Explorer, you'll need this code:

```
javascript:s=(document.frames.length?'':
        document.selection.createRange( ).text);
        for(i=0;i<document.frames.length;i++)
        {s=document.frames[i].document.selection.createRange( ).text;}
        location.href='http://search.ebay.com/'+escape(s);
```

Next, open any web page, highlight some text, and click your new search button. The next thing you'll see is a search results page with items matching your selected text.

How It Works

First, the code fills the variable `s` with any currently selected text on the page. Next, to accommodate frames (exemplified in [Hack #16]), the code searches through all frames present in the current window (if any) and, again, fills `s` with any selected text found. Then, the code executes an eBay search by combining the base search URL [Hack #13], *http://search.ebay.com/*, with the contents of `s`.

If you've spent any time programming JavaScript (introduced in the Preface), you've undoubtedly discovered differences in the support of the language between Internet Explorer and the browsers based on Mozilla (e.g., Firefox and Netscape). (Hint: this is Microsoft's fault.) Thus, regrettably, two versions of the code are needed to support the different browser's methods for retrieving selected text and negotiating frames. Ah, the fun of cross-platform scripting.

Hacking the Hack

By default, this hack searches titles only; to search titles and descriptions, change the URL in the code from `search.ebay.com` to `search-desc.ebay.com`.

HACK #16 Open Search Results in a New Window

View eBay search results and eBay listings side-by-side in two windows.

The next time you do a search on eBay that gives you 53,112 matching items, you might not be so tempted to give up if you had a quick way to go through them all. Fortunately, it's easy to plow through a large number of listings if you use multiple browser windows.

Setting up two browser windows is easy enough: with your search results open in one window, press Ctrl-N (or go to File → New → Window) to open a second window, and then resize and reposition them so they appear side-by-side on your screen. Finally, drag each link from the search results into the new window to view the corresponding listing in that window. Do this repeatedly until you've gone through them all.

To show more listings on each page of search results, click Customize Display (at the top-right of the search page), and choose a number from the Items per page list (200 is the maximum). If you're signed in, your preference will be saved for all future searches.

Although using two windows to open a bunch of links is easier than remaining confined to one, the dragging and dropping can get a little cumbersome after a short while. The good news is that it's not your only choice.

The Hack

The following solution is a hack in every sense of the word; rather than accept eBay's limitations, there's a way to frame a search results window so that links open in a new window when you click them.

Start by typing the following text into a plain-text editor (such as Notepad):

```
<frameset rows="*,1" frameborder=no>
    <frame src="http://search.ebay.com/" name="search">
    <frame src="hack.html" name="hack">
</frameset>
```

Save the file as *search.html*. Next, create a new text file, *hack.html*, containing this HTML code:

```
<html><head>
<script language="JavaScript"><!--
function fixSearch( ) {
❶ netscape.security.PrivilegeManager.enablePrivilege('UniversalBrowserRead');
❷ netscape.security.PrivilegeManager.enablePrivilege('UniversalBrowserWrite');

if (parent.search.length != 0) {
❸   for (var i=0; i < parent.search.document.links.length; i++) {
❹     if (parent.search.document.links[i].href.indexOf("ViewItem") > 0) {
        if (parent.search.document.links[i].target != '') { break; }
❺       parent.search.document.links[i].target = 'listing';

      }
    }
❻   parent.document.title = parent.search.document.title;
}
❼ setTimeout('fixSearch( )', 500)
}

//--></script>
</head><body onLoad="fixSearch( )">
</body></html>
```

Place *search.html* and *hack.html* in the same folder, and then double-click *search.html* to open it in the default browser.

Now, type something in the search box and click Search. When the new page appears, start clicking listings in the search results. As long as the current page is loaded, each listing will open in a separate window (the same separate window).

How It Works

First, the `frameset` structure in *search.html* creates a page with two frames: the `search` frame, which points to eBay's search page, and the one-pixel-high `hack` frame, which contains the script (*hack.html*).

The script itself works by exploiting what is known as the "cross-domain scripting bug," wherein a script on one server (your computer, in this case) tries to control a page on another server (eBay, in this case). Now, all modern browsers have safety features specifically designed to prevent this from happening, so lines ❶ and ❷ are required to elevate the security level of the script. Thus, the first time you use this hack, your browser displays the warning message shown in Figure 2-3. Just check the "Remember this decision" box, and click Allow to permit your script to do its job; this won't affect the security settings for any other scripts or sites.

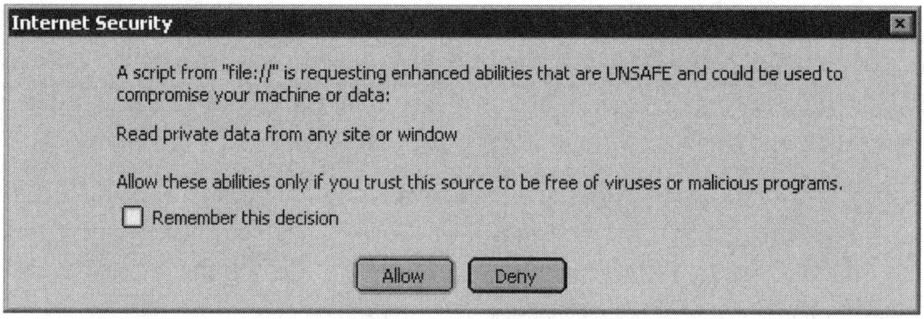

Internet Security

A script from "file://" is requesting enhanced abilities that are UNSAFE and could be used to compromise your machine or data:

Read private data from any site or window

Allow these abilities only if you trust this source to be free of viruses or malicious programs.

☐ Remember this decision

Allow Deny

Figure 2-3. Your browser warns you when you try to exploit a security flaw; just click

Next, a `for` loop ❸ iterates through all the links on the page, and checks for any containing the text `ViewItem` ❹ to ensure that only links to listings are affected. When a match is found, line ❺ is responsible for changing the *link target* of the link to a window called `listing`. (Targets are typically used with frames, wherein a link in one frame opens a page in another.) If your browser can't find the target, it opens a new window and names it `listing`. Thus, each listing link you click is opened in the same new window.

To pretty things up, line ❻ changes the title of the page to reflect the title of the eBay page in the search frame. And the `setTimeout` statement ❼ instructs your browser to run the routine once every half-second (500 milliseconds), so subsequent search pages are automatically modified, too.

Hacking the Hack

You may wish to have the script mark links as they're modified, so you can tell if the script is doing its job. To change the color of the links, add the following code immediately after line ❺:

```
parent.search.document.links[i].style.color = 'green';
```

or, to italicize the links (and preserve their color), use this instead:

```
parent.search.document.links[i].style.fontStyle = 'italic';
```

The `frameset` in *search.html* opens eBay's Advanced Search page, but if you'd rather, use your favorite searches **[Hack #20]**. Just edit *search.html* and replace the search page URL with the address of your Favorites page in My eBay, or *http://my.ebay.com/ws/ebayISAPI.dll?MyeBay&CurrentPage=MyeBayFavorites*.

The Greasemonkey Approach

I know what you're thinking: there's got to be an easier way to run a script on another site than building this elaborate frameset thing. I bet you probably didn't expect to be right!

Greasemonkey is a free Mozilla Firefox extension that lets you add your own JavaScript code to any page on any web site. The code runs as though it were part of the page itself, a fact that turns out to be remarkably convenient.

To use Greasemonkey, you'll need to have a recent version of Mozilla Firefox, which you can get for free at *www.mozilla.org* (Greasemonkey won't work with Mozilla Suite or Internet Explorer). Then, install the Greasemonkey extension by going to *www.greasemonkey.mozdev.org*, and restart Firefox.

Next, type the following code into a plain text editor (e.g., Notepad):

```
==UserScript==
// @name          eBay Hacks - Search in new window
// @namespace     http://www.ebayhacks.com
// @description   Opens search links in a separate window
// @include       http://search.ebay*
// @include       http://search-completed.ebay*
// ==/UserScript==

(function() {
  for (var i=0; i < document.links.length; i++) {
    if (document.links[i].href.indexOf("ViewItem") > 0) {
```

```
            if (document.links[i].target != '') { break; }
            document.links[i].target = 'listing';
        }
    }
})();
```

Save the file as *newwindow.user.js* (the *.user.js* suffix is essential). Note that the underlying code here is nearly identical to the JavaScript code found earlier in this hack, except that the `parent.search.` object references—used to compensate for the frameset—have been removed.

Drag the *newwindow.user.js* file onto Firefox, and then go to Tools → Install User Script. (Alternatively, you can download the script from *ebayhacks.com/userscripts/newwindow.user.js.*) When you see the Install User Script box, click OK. Then click OK again when you see the alert.

The next time you view an eBay search page, each search results link will open the listing in a separate window. You can temporarily disable or uninstall the user script by going to Tools → Manage User Scripts, or get scripts for other sites at *dunck.us/collab/GreaseMonkeyUserScripts*.

See Also

- See "Create a Split-Pane Search Tool" [Hack #105] in Chapter 8 for a way to build a customizable search page with any streamlining features you find useful.

HACK #17 Decipher Title Acronyms

Figure out what a seller means by HTF, OOAK, and AMOOFL.

To save space in listing titles, sellers often include acronyms to describe certain aspects of the item being sold in an effort to make more space for ever-important keywords [Hack #47]. The problem is that these acronyms can sometimes be a little difficult to understand, and sellers rarely take the time to spell them out in the description.

So, in an effort to foster communication and goodwill between buyers and sellers, Table 2-1 lists acronyms you might find in listing titles.

Table 2-1. Generic acronyms commonly found in auction titles

Acronym	Meaning
BIN	Buy It Now
C&R	Curio and Relic
CIB	Complete In Box
EX	Excellent condition (see Table 2-2)

Table 2-1. Generic acronyms commonly found in auction titles (continued)

Acronym	Meaning
FS	Free Shipping
FSB	Factory Sealed Box
G1 / 1G	First Generation (or 2G / G2 for Second Generation, and so on)
HTF / HTG	Hard To Find / Hard To Get
IB	In Box
LE	Limited Edition
LH	Left Handed
LN	Like New (see Table 2-2)
LNIB	Like New In Box
MIB	Mint In Box
MNH	Mint Never Hinged (stamps)
NB / NBX	No Box
NIB / NIP	New In Box / New In Package
NOS	New Old Stock
NR	No Reserve
NWT	New With Tag (clothing and beanie babies)
OB / OBX	Original Box
OOAK	One Of A Kind
OOP	Out of Print / Out of Production
PC	Piece (e.g., "2pc" means the auction comes with two total units)
PR	Pair (e.g., "2pr" means the auction comes with two pair, or four total units)
RH	Right-Hand
RTR / RTF	Ready To Run / Ready To Fly (toys, radio-controlled models)
S&H	Shipping and Handling
S/T	Self-Titled (musical albums, cds, etc.)
VG	Very Good condition (see Table 2-2)
W/	With
W/O	Without
WBX	Wrong Box
XS / XL	Extra Small / Extra Large

Naturally, these abbreviations will be different in other languages, but the methodology is the same. For example, on German eBay, you'll frequently see OVP, which stands for "ohne Verpackung." This translates to "without packaging," or in more common vernacular, "NB."

Interpreting Condition

Also used in auction titles and descriptions is a variety of different rating systems to describe the condition of the item being sold. One such system is shown in Table 2-2. Note that typically only the cosmetic appearance of an item is indicated by these terms; if you want to know whether or not the item works or the original accessories and packaging are included, check the listing description or contact the seller.

Table 2-2. Acronyms often used to describe the cosmetic condition of the item being sold

Rating	Meaning
New	Literally new; never used, includes all original packaging
Like new	Virtually perfect, nearly indistinguishable from New
Mint	Almost perfect, extremely light wear, packaging may have shelf wear; an "A" grade
Mint-	Between Mint and EX+
Ex+	Very light wear, slight marks, 85–90% of original condition
Ex	Light wear, slight marks or scratches; a "B" grade
Ex-	Between EX and VG+
Vg+	Normal wear for its age, noticeable marks or scratches, still fully functional
Vg	Slightly more than normal wear, noticeable marks, scratches, still functional; a "C" grade
Ok	Cosmetically acceptable, shows moderate to heavy wear, noticeable marks, scratching, dings, or dents

You may want to avoid using the abbreviations shown in Table 2-2 in your own auctions, mostly because they can be ambiguous and confusing, and typically aren't adequate for proper expectation management **[Hack #50]**.

Look It Up

If you stumble upon an abbreviation mysteriously absent from Tables 2-1 and 2-2, including industry-specific acronyms like AGP or DVI (in this case, for the computer industry), there are a couple of places you can go to look them up:

Acronym Finder
: Visit *www.acronymfinder.com* and type the acronym in the search box for the likely definition.

Dictionary.com
: Quick access to definitions and a pretty good thesaurus to boot.

Google
: Type `define:`*`word`* to look up any word or abbreviation.

NetLingo
: Take a look at *www.netlingo.com/emailsh.cfm* for some of the most common abbreviations found in email messages.

Wikipedia
: Just because it wouldn't be right to exclude *Wikipedia.org*.

HACK #18 Search by Seller

There are some easy ways to find items sold by a particular seller.

If for no other reason than to save money on shipping costs, you may find yourself wanting to purchase multiple items from a single seller. Although you can't specify a particular seller when typing into a basic search box, there are three other ways to search among a seller's current (or completed) auctions.

View Seller's Other Items

Probably the first thing that occurred to you is to just use the "View seller's other items" link on the auction page. If so, give yourself a gold star. This is typically the easiest way to search by seller because you can see an up-to-date listing of all the seller's current auctions.

What you'll see here is a standard search results page, filtered to show only current listings offered by the seller. At this point, you can specify some search terms [Hack #10] or choose a category [Hack #12] to narrow the search, which is particularly useful if the seller is offering several thousand items at the same time.

In the Search Options box to your left, there's a checkbox labeled "Items from Seller" right next to a textbox with the seller's member ID. As you might expect, you can broaden your search and show listings from all sellers by turning off the checkbox, or show the items offered by a different seller by typing the seller's ID in the box.

You've probably noticed that the Items from Seller checkbox and accompanying textbox aren't normally available when you do a standard search, say, by typing text into the search box at the top of any page. To add these options to all search pages, click Customize at the bottom of the Search Options box. Then, on the Customize Your Search page shown in Figure 2-4, select the "Items from specific seller" entry in the lefthand "Available search options" box. Then click the >> arrow button to move it to the right-hand "Options you want to display" box. Click Save when you're done.

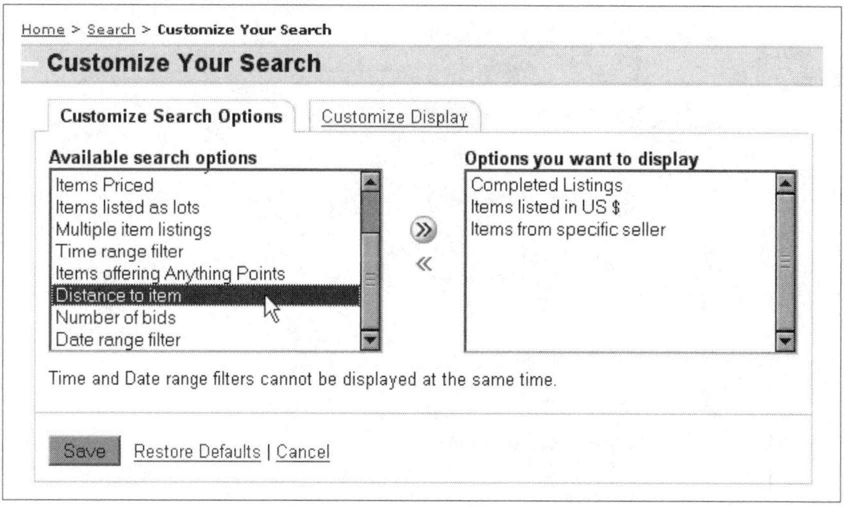

Figure 2-4. You can add new features to search pages by customizing the controls that appear in the Search Options box

Expand Your Search

The problem with the "View seller's other items" link is that its results are limited in the way any search is limited by default, namely that only items available to your country are listed. Thus you may not be seeing all the items a seller has currently listed on eBay.

To conduct a more extensive seller search, you'll have to start from scratch. First, find the ID of the seller from a listing page or from the "Items from Seller" textbox described in the last section, highlight it, and press Ctrl-C.

Then, click the Advanced Search link just underneath the little search box that appears at the top of any eBay page. If this page is short, click the "Advanced search" link at the *bottom* of the page to show the expanded version illustrated in Figure 2-5.

Paste the seller's ID into the "From specific sellers" textbox by pressing Ctrl-V, and then define the scope of your search **[Hack #19]** to include locales other than your own. At this point, you can specify additional sellers (up to 10), as long as you separate their IDs with commas.

You can exclude one or more sellers from your search by changing the Include option to Exclude (as shown in Figure 2-5), which is useful if one obnoxious seller appears to be dominating your search results, or if you simply want to avoid sellers with whom you've had previous unpleasant experiences.

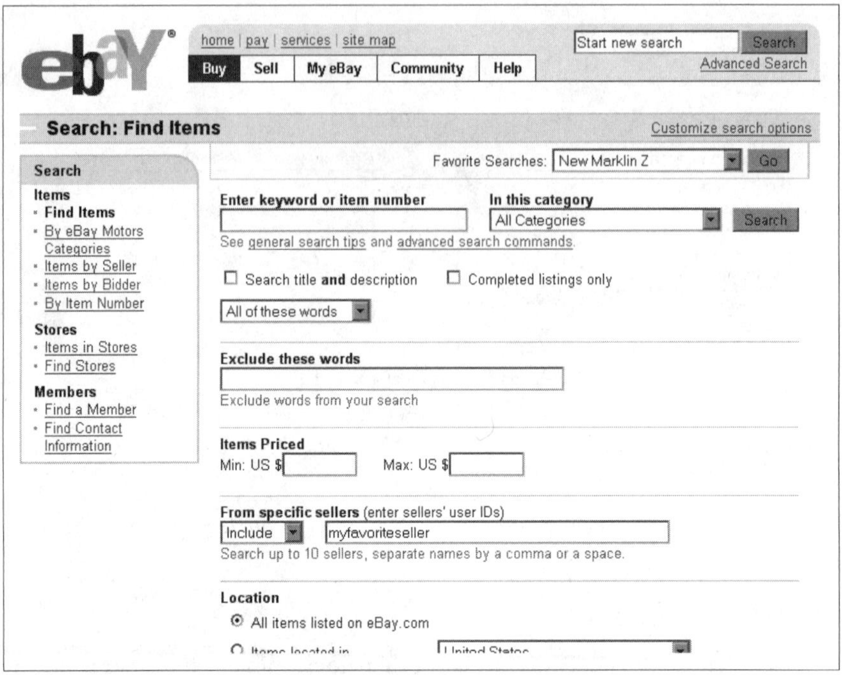

Figure 2-5. The Multiple Sellers search, hidden at the bottom of the Search → By Seller page, allows you to specify the seller in a standard keyword search

When you're ready, click Search to show all matching search results. Your search options will remain in effect until you close the window or start over with a new search.

eBay Stores

If the seller has an eBay Store [Hack #91], there may be even more listings that don't show up in standard searches. Click the little red "Store" icon that appears next to the seller's ID to view the store's inventory, which includes all standard auctions, standard Buy It Now listings, and store-only fixed-price listings.

Here, you can use the search box at the top of the page to search within this seller's store, or you can browse the seller's own custom categories (not the same as eBay's categories) to look for items that may interest you.

The Obvious

Don't forget the most direct approach of all: if you're looking for something, try contacting the seller and asking. More often than not, a seller will have more than what is currently showing up in eBay listings, and will likely be all too happy to sell you something extra.

Case in point: a few years ago, I sold a model locomotive and a few train cars to go with it. The buyer, not yet owning any compatible accessories in the scale, asked me if I had any track to sell. I happily put together an oval of track and included a power pack (transformer), and sold the accessories for a few extra dollars. I sold something I probably wouldn't have bothered to list on eBay, and my customer got a complete train set!

See Also

- See "Let's Make a Deal" [Hack #66] for some tips when contacting sellers directly.

HACK #19 Search Internationally

Use different eBay localizations to look for things outside your home town.

When you search, you're not searching all of eBay; you're searching a subset of auctions made available to your localized version of eBay. Depending on where in the world you live, you may be using any one of the following sites:

Country	eBay address
Australia	*www.ebay.com.au*
Austria	*www.ebay.at*
Belgium	*www.ebay.be*
Canada	*www.ebay.ca*
China	*www.ebay.com.cn*
France	*www.ebay.fr*
Germany	*www.ebay.de*
Hong Kong	*www.ebay.com.hk*
India	*www.baazee.com*
Ireland	*pages.ebay.com/ie/*
Italy	*www.ebay.it*
Malaysia	*www.ebay.com.my*
Netherlands	*www.ebay.nl*
New Zealand	*www.ebay.com/nz/*
Philippines	*www.ebay.ph*
Poland	*www.ebay.pl*
Singapore	*www.ebay.com.sg*
Spain	*www.ebay.es*
Sweden	*www.ebaysweden.com*

Country	eBay address
Switzerland	*www.ebay.ch*
Taiwan	*www.tw.ebay.com*
United Kingdom	*www.ebay.co.uk*
United States	*www.ebay.com*

Although all these sites share the same global auction database,* each one uses the native language and currency of the region it represents. Your eBay user account works on all eBay sites, so you can bid, search, and sell in any country eBay serves. What is dramatically different, however, is the selection of categories, and thus the search indexes.

This means that a search for decorative dog collars at *www.ebay.ch* may yield different results than the same search at *www.ebay.co.uk*.

Expanding Your Search

This limitation on international searches is nothing more than a matter of scope, and the scope of any search can be customized. There are effectively three different levels of scope in eBay searches:

Within your own localization. The default scope when you search is to look only in the categories that are native to your localization. Some categories are linked to categories on other eBay localized sites, so when searching for dog collars on the U.S. eBay site (*www.ebay.com*), for example, you will most likely see a few auctions priced in euros or pounds sterling, as shown in Figure 2-6.

All items available to your country. Click the Advanced Search link just underneath the little search box that appears at the top of any eBay page. If this page is short, click the "Advanced search" link at the *bottom* of the page to show the expanded version. Choose your country from the "Items available to..." listbox, and click Search. Here, you'll see more international items, but only those where the seller has intentionally stated that he or she will ship to your country (or, more likely, that the seller has elected to ship "worldwide").

All items, everywhere. On the expanded Advanced Search page, choose "Any country" from the "Items available to..." listbox. This will show the greatest number of search results, but it's important to realize that

* There are a few other sites, those only "associated" with eBay, that don't share the same database. Among these is *www.mercadolibre.com*, which covers Argentina, Brazil, and Mexico, and *www.auction.co.kr*, which covers Korea.

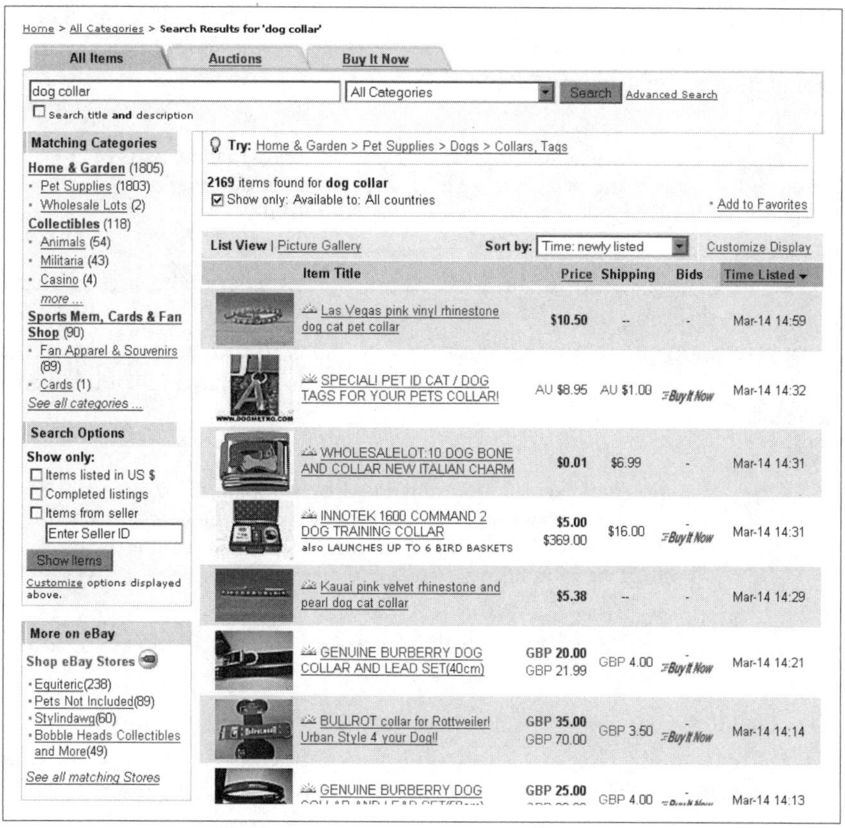

Figure 2-6. International searches show a greater percentage of foreign auctions

your searches may include auctions by sellers who are not willing to ship to your country.

There are several ways to tell if a particular auction is from a different localized eBay than your own, such as the language and currency used throughout the auction page. But there are two auction details to which you should pay particular attention. One is the Shipping section, which lists the parts of the world to which the seller is willing to ship (or "worldwide" if the seller has chosen no such restrictions), and the other is the category in which the item has been placed.

Making Sure the Seller Will Ship to You

When performing international searches, you'll inevitably run into sellers who are willing to ship only to bidders in their own country or continent. Since international shipping can often be a royal pain in the neck, this is understandable. The problem is that many sellers simply don't bother to change the Shipping option from its default (domestic shipping only) even though they may be happy to ship anywhere.

Note to sellers: those who are willing to ship to more parts of the world will get more bids, and thus more money. See "Sell and Ship Internationally" [Hack #87] for details.

So the first thing to do is check the description. Sellers who are adamant about not shipping internationally usually say so in big letters, with stern warnings to anyone in another country who dares to bid on their items. But if there's no mention of it, and you really want the item, then all you have to do is ask.

Since some sellers are intimidated by shipping internationally or may have had bad experiences with bidders from other countries, you should take special care to assure the seller that your business won't end up being a burden.

Just use the Ask Seller a Question link in the auction page and write something like:

- "Hello! I'm interested in this item; would you be willing to ship to the United States?" Keep it short and sweet, but also make it clear that you're a serious bidder and have every intention of paying quickly.
- "Pourriez-vous possiblement envoyer cet achat chez moi, aux États-Unis? Merci!" If you're writing to a seller who speaks a different language, don't be afraid to write so that they will actually understand you.

With any luck, and assuming you've left plenty of time before the auction closes, the seller should send you a favorable reply. Et voilà!

Viewing Foreign Categories

Each global eBay site has its own selection of categories. Although you can include foreign items in your searches, you can't browse foreign categories from your local eBay site. Naturally, you could switch to any of the foreign sites listed at the beginning of this hack and browse from there, but this can be exceedingly difficult if you don't understand the language.

When viewing any auction native to your local eBay site, you can jump into the auction's category by clicking the category link at the top of the page. But you won't be able to do this for most foreign auctions: the category will still be there, but the link will not. In order to browse a foreign auction's category, you need to view the auction from its native eBay site.

The URL of an auction page looks something like this:

```
http://cgi.ebay.com/ws/eBayISAPI.dll?ViewItem&item=3128013702
```

Simply change the domain name to match the native site of the auction. If you're not sure which site to use, simply look at the country specified in the auction details. For instance, to view this from within the French eBay, just change the domain to *ebay.fr*, like this:

```
http://cgi.ebay.fr/ws/eBayISAPI.dll?ViewItem&item=3128013702
```

The currency and language of the site (everything but the title and description) are automatically changed to reflect the localization you choose. More importantly, the category line will become a link, which you can then click to view other items in the same category.

Excluding Foreign Items

In some cases, eBay searches include listings from other countries, even when you don't change any special settings. For instance, if you're searching *eBay.com* (the USA site), you may see listings from *eBay.ca* (Canada) and *eBay.co.uk* (United Kingdom). This happens if the foreign items are in the same language (English, in this case) and the respective sellers have indicated that they'll ship to your country.

Since foreign transactions [Hack #37] can be more expensive (due to exchange rates, transaction fees, and shipping costs), you may wish to exclude all listings that aren't in your own country. Although you can return to the Advanced Search page and specify that only items in your country should be shown (as described earlier in this hack), there is a quicker way.

In the Search Options box on any search results page, just turn on the "Items listed in US $" option (replace "US $" with your native currency), and click Search. (If you don't see this option, click the Customize link at the bottom of the Search Options box.)

Now, this won't have exactly the same effect as the first method: rather than removing *all* foreign listings, only listings specified in a *foreign currency* will be excluded. It's still possible for an item being sold out of Hong Kong, for instance, to appear in your search results (provided that it's being sold in your native currency). But the convenience of this feature may be enough to put up with the occasional long-distance listing.

Save Your Searches

There are different ways to save your complex searches for repeated use.

Dimitri's Law states that anything you search for on eBay, you will likely search for again. Okay, there is no Dimitri, and I just made up the part about the law, but it's still a valid point.

Favorite Searches

The Favorites tab of My eBay is designed to save lists of your favorite searches, favorite categories, and favorite sellers. These lists are stored on-site and so can be accessed even if you're not at home, which can be quite convenient.

To add a new category, go to My eBay → All Favorites → Categories, and then click the "Add new category" link on the right side of the box. On the next page, you can choose and save up to four categories. Categories can be removed from the list by marking the corresponding checkboxes and clicking Delete.

Provided you haven't reached your four-category limit, you can also add a category to your list of Favorites by clicking the "Add to My Favorite Categories" link in the upper-right of any ordinary category listing **[Hack #12]**. Once you've specified four favorite categories, the link no longer appears.

The My Favorite Sellers page works similarly to the My Favorite Categories page, except that you type or paste the seller names instead of clicking. Also, there is a delay in adding new sellers to this list, so be prepared to wait about a minute before reloading the page to see a newly added seller. You can save up to 30 seller names or eBay Stores **[Hack #91]** on this list. (If you click the Sellers link on the left, you'll also see the elusive My Recent Sellers list, which shows all the sellers from whom you've made recent purchases.)

Probably the most useful of the lists is My Favorite Searches, shown in Figure 2-7, not only because you can save extremely specific and targeted search queries, but because you can save your search directly from the search page. Simply perform a search—any search, including advanced searches or searches on international eBay sites—and click the Add to Favorites link in the top right of the search page.

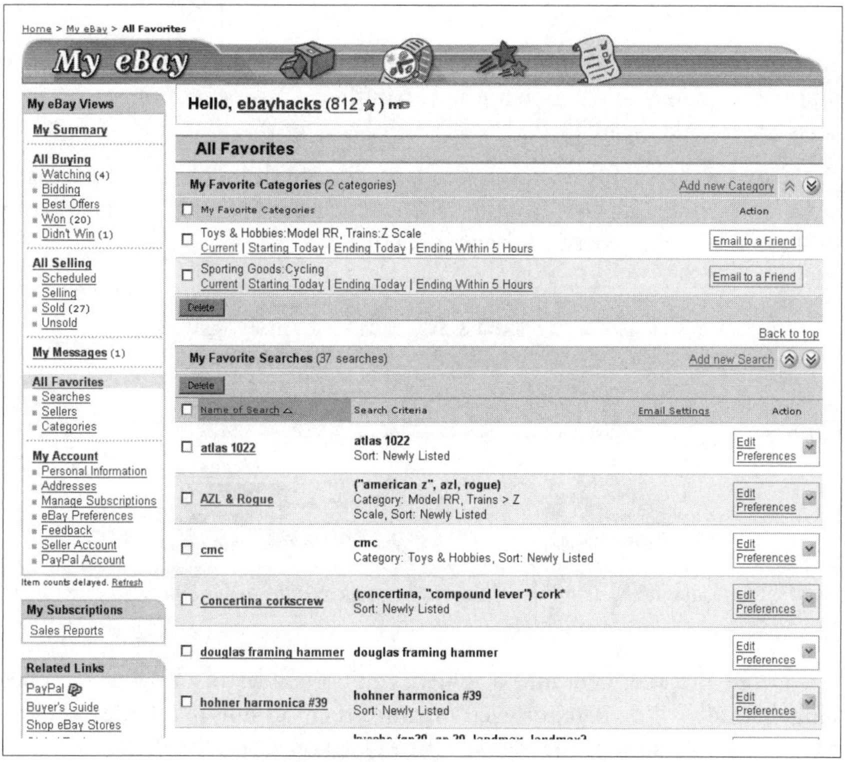

Figure 2-7. The My Favorite Searches list allows you to save up to 100 searches

Only your search query is saved, not your search results. Each time you click a favorite search, you'll see the most up-to-date search results. To save specific listings, see "Keep Track of Auctions Outside of eBay" [Hack #29].

Click the search caption to perform the search. Up to 100 different searches can be saved here, 30 of which can be configured to email you daily when new matches are found. Click Preferences to "subscribe" to a daily email notification, as well as rename a search without changing its search criteria. (See "Create a Search Robot" [Hack #21] for a more flexible tool to notify you of new listings.)

Although you can click Refine to change the parameters of an existing favorite search, it's actually easier to simply perform the search normally and make your revisions right on the search page. When you're done, click "Add to My Favorite Searches" again, click "Replace one of these with my new search," and then select the old search caption in the list to replace the old version with your newly revised search.

Quick and Dirty

Another way to save your searches involves no special features at all. Since all the parameters of a search are stored in the URL [Hack #13], all you need to do is bookmark a search to save it.

Probably the most convenient method is to create shortcuts to your favorite searches by dragging and dropping the Address Bar shortcut icon onto your desktop (or into a folder), as shown in Figure 2-8.

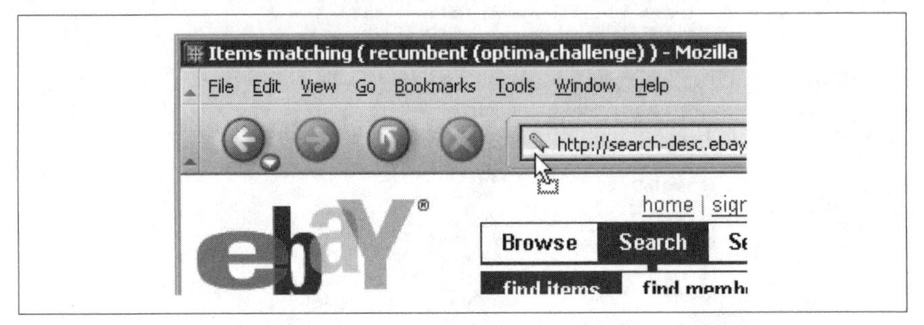

Figure 2-8. Drag the shortcut icon from your browser's Address Bar onto your desktop or into an open folder to create an Internet Shortcut

If you put the shortcuts into a folder, you'll be able to sort your searches alphabetically or by date, or even organize them in multiple folders (something you can't do with the items in the My Favorite Searches list).

A Little Spit and Polish

Instead of saving your searches as shortcut files, you can just as easily create a custom My Favorite Searches page. Start by opening a blank document in your favorite WYSIWYG web page editor (such as Mozilla Composer, which comes free with the Mozilla Suite web browser, from *www.mozilla.org*) and placing it side by side next to an eBay search window. Then, drag the Address Bar shortcut icon onto your blank web page to create a link to the search; repeat for as many searches as you like.

Your custom search links can then be renamed and organized to your heart's content. When you're done, save the page, and then open it in a browser. Or, upload it to a web server so that you (and others) can access it from anywhere.

See Also

- See "Create a Search Robot" [Hack #21] for a way to not only save your search, but to be automatically notified when new matches are found.
- "Keep Tabs on eBay with the eBay Toolbar" [Hack #23] allows you to save recent searches right in your browser's toolbar.

HACK #21 Create a Search Robot

Use a Perl script to perform searches automatically and email you the results.

A collector in search of a particular item or type of item may repeat the same search, often several times a week. A serious collector, knowing that items sometimes sell within hours of being listed [Hack #31], may repeat a search several times a *day* for an item. But who has the time?

The Favorites tab of the My eBay page, which allows you to keep track of up to 100 favorite searches [Hack #20], also has a feature to email you when new items matching your search criteria appear on the site. Just check the Preferences link next to the search caption, and then turn on the "Email me daily whenever there are new items" option.

Unfortunately, eBay's new-item notification feature will send you notifications no more than once a day, and in that time, any number of juicy auctions could've started and ended. And eBay's emails are limited to only 20 listings per message. So I created this hack to do my searches for me, and to do them as often as I see fit.

Constructing the Robot

A robot is a program that does automatically what you'd otherwise have to do manually. In this case, the goal is a robot that automatically performs an eBay search at a regular interval, and then emails you any new listings.

This hack uses a technique called *scraping*, wherein an ordinary search on the eBay site is performed and the results are extracted by parsing the page for links pointing to listings. This script uses a handful of Perl modules to accomplish this task: `LWP`, `URI`, `HTML::LinkExtor`, `HTML::HeadParser`, `Net::SMTP`, and `MIME::Lite`. See the "Installing Perl Modules" sidebar in the Preface for details.

The version of this script that appeared in the first edition of *eBay Hacks* relied on the `WWW::Search::eBay` module, which no longer works—a danger whenever you use an unofficial method for accessing another site and a reason that the eBay API, discussed in Chapter 8, is so valuable. The following script, which uses only standard modules, is based on code submitted to *ebayhacks.com* by Keith Howlette. See "Search eBay Listings" [Hack #104] for an API version of this hack.

The Code

Here's the script that does it all:

```
#!/usr/bin/perl
use strict;
use LWP 5.64;
use URI;
use HTML::LinkExtor;
use HTML::HeadParser;
use Net::SMTP;
use MIME::Lite;
❶ my $searchstring = "steam";
my $category = "19116";
my $country = ".com";
my $email = "dave\@ebayhacks.com";
my $mailserver = "my.smtpserver.com";
my $localfile = "searchresults.txt";

my ($results, %searchresults, %olditems, $title, $itemnumber);
my $pageurl =
      "http://cgi.ebay" . $country . "/ws/eBayISAPI.dll?ViewItem&item=";
❷ my $searchurl = "http://search.ebay" . $country . "/ws/search/SaleSearch";

❸ my $url = URI -> new($searchurl);
$url->query_form(
  'satitle'=> $searchstring,
  'sacat'=> $category
);

%searchresults = ();
my $browser = LWP::UserAgent -> new;
❹ my $response = $browser -> get($url);

my $link_extor = HTML::LinkExtor -> new(\&handle_links);
❺ $link_extor -> parse($response -> content);

if (-s $localfile) {
  open (INFILE, "$localfile");
    my %olditems = map { split(/=/, $_) } <INFILE>;
  close (INFILE);
  chomp %olditems;

  foreach $itemnumber (keys %olditems) {
❻   if (exists($searchresults{$itemnumber})) {
      delete $searchresults{$itemnumber};
    }
  }
}

open (OUTFILE, ">>$localfile");
  foreach $itemnumber (keys %searchresults) {
```

```
❼     print OUTFILE $itemnumber . "=1\n";
    }
  close (OUTFILE);

  my $mailbody = "The following new items have been listed on eBay:\n";
  foreach $itemnumber (keys %searchresults) {
❽   $mailbody = $mailbody . &get_title($searchresults{$itemnumber}) . "\n";
    $mailbody = $mailbody . $pageurl . $itemnumber . "\n\n";
  }

❾ if ($mailbody ne "") { &sendemail($email, $email,
                          "New $searchstring items found", $mailbody); }
  exit;

  sub handle_links {
    my ($tag, %links)=@_;
    my $key;
    if ($tag eq 'a') {
      foreach $key (keys %links) {
        if ($key eq 'href') {
          if ( $links{$key} =~ m/ViewItem/) {
            $links{$key} =~ m/item=(\d+)/;
            $searchresults{$1} = $links{$key};
          }
        }
      }
    }
  }

  sub get_title($) {
    my $itempage = LWP::UserAgent -> new;
    my $item_contents = $itempage -> get($_[0]);
    my $p = HTML::HeadParser -> new;
    $p -> parse($item_contents -> content);
    $title = $p -> header('Title');
    $title = substr($title, index($title, " - ") + 3);
    return $title;
  }

❿ sub sendemail {
    my ($to, $from, $subject, $body) = @_;
    my $msg = MIME::Lite->new (
      To      => $email,
      From    => $email,
      Subject => $subject,
      Data    => qq{ $body }
    );

    MIME::Lite->send('smtp', $mailserver, Timeout => 10);
    $msg->send;
  }
```

How It Works

Before you can use this script, you'll have to modify some of the variables near the beginning of the script, starting with line ❶. First, set `$searchstring` to the text to search (`steam` in this case) and set `$category` to the number of the category [Hack #13] you wish to search (specify `$category = ""` to search all categories). If you want to search one of the non-USA eBay sites, change `$country` to one of the domain extensions listed in "Search Internationally" [Hack #19] (e.g., `."fr"` for eBay France.

To customize the script for your system, set `$email` to your email address, and `$mailserver` to the address of your ISP's SMTP server. (The `$mailserver` parameter may not be necessary if you're using Unix or Mac OS X; see the "Hacking the Hack" section for details.) And if you want, set the `$localfile` to the full path and filename of a text file in which to save previous search results.

Once the variables are initialized, the script forms the search URL ❸ and then uses the `LWP::UserAgent` module to perform the search ❹. Next, the `HTML::LinkExtor` module scans all the links from the page ❺, and with the help of the `&handle_links` subroutine (defined at the end of the script), records links containing the text `ViewItem`.

The script then opens the text file defined as `$localfile` and checks the new search results against previously found items ❻. After duplicate items are deleted, the remaining list is saved to the text file ❼ so they won't be reported next time. The last step is to retrieve the listing titles ❽ (with the help of the `&get_title` subroutine defined at the end of the script), put them together with shortened URLs [Hack #13] provided by `$pageurl`, and email these latest findings ❾ to the address specified at the beginning of the script.

Running the Hack

The search criteria you choose are entirely up to you, but narrow searches make more sense than broad searches for this hack. For instance, the example script looks only in category `19116` (a model railroad category) for listings with the word "steam" in the title. At any given time, there may be only a handful of these items for sale on eBay, which means that you may receive a single notification per week, if that. Conversely, a search yielding hundreds of results would quickly fill up your mailbox with dozens of emails with erroneous results. Of course, you can further narrow your searches [Hack #10] to make the results in your notification emails more relevant.

The best way to run this script is automatically at regular intervals, unless you enjoy waking up at 3 a.m. and typing commands into a terminal. How frequently you run the script is up to you, but it wouldn't make sense to run it more often than you check your email. In most cases, it's sufficient to perform the search robot 3–4 times a day, but given that new auctions can show up on eBay less than a minute after being listed, you can run it once an hour if you like.

Use this script responsibly. If eBay finds that their servers are overburdened due to abuse by scrapers (which, strictly speaking, violate eBay's terms of service), they might take steps to disable them. See "Search eBay Listings" [Hack #104] for a version of this hack that uses the eBay API to perform searches.

If you're using Unix or Mac OS X, type `crontab -u` *`username`* `-e` to set up a *cron* job, where *`username`* is, not surprisingly, your username. In the editor that appears, add the following four lines:

```
0 0 * * * /home/mydirectory/scripts/search.pl
0 6 * * * /home/mydirectory/scripts/search.pl
0 12 * * * /home/mydirectory/scripts/search.pl
0 18 * * * /home/mydirectory/scripts/search.pl
```

where */home/mydirectory/scripts/search.pl* is the full path and filename of the script. Save the file when you're done. This will instruct the server to run the script every six hours: at midnight, 6:00 a.m., noon, and 6:00 p.m. For more information on *crontab*—the program used to configure cronjobs—type `man crontab` at the prompt.

If you're using Windows, open the Scheduled Tasks tool, right-click on an empty area of the window and select New. (This bypasses the cumbersome wizard and goes directly to the so-called "advanced" properties sheet.) Type the full path and filename of the script in the Run field, and then choose the Schedule tab. Turn on the "Show multiple schedules" option, and click New three times. Set up each of the four schedules to run as follows: Daily at 12:00 a.m.., Daily at 6:00 a.m.., Daily at 12:00 p.m.., and Daily at 6:00 p.m.. Click OK when you're done.

Assuming all goes well, you should eventually get an email that looks something like this:

```
To: dave@ebayhacks.com
From: dave@ebayhacks.com
Subject: New railex items found

The following new items have been listed on eBay:
Z Scale NJC Steam Set 4-6-2/Tender/Gon/Cab EX
http://cgi.ebay..com/ws/eBayISAPI.dll?ViewItem&item=5951984275

Z Scale CB&Q Steam Set 2-8-2/Tender/Gon/Cab
```

```
http://cgi.ebay..com/ws/eBayISAPI.dll?ViewItem&item=5951983974

Z Scale SOPAC RR Steam (2-8-2)/2 Gon Set NEW
http://cgi.ebay..com/ws/eBayISAPI.dll?ViewItem&item=5945397947
```

You should continue getting emails as new auctions matching your criteria are listed on eBay; just click the links in the emails to view the auctions.

Hacking the Hack

Here are some things you can do to spice up or otherwise customize the search robot:

Search titles and descriptions. By default, this script searches only titles. To search descriptions as well, change the URL prefix on line ❷ from `http://search.ebay` to `http://search-desc.ebay`.

Add more information. The email generated by the search robot includes the titles and URLs of matching listings, but you can add more information if you like. For instance, if you parse the listing title for the end date **[Hack #29]**, you can include the amount of time remaining for each listing.

Add gallery thumbnails. You can have each listing's gallery photo appear right in your email by formatting the message with HTML **[Hack #52]**. Just replace line ❽ with the following three lines:

```
$mailbody = $mailbody . "<p><a href=\"" . $pageurl . $itemnumber . "\">";
$mailbody = $mailbody . "<img src=\"http://thumbs.ebaystatic.com/pict/" .
        $itemnumber . "8080_0.jpg\"><br>"
$mailbody = $mailbody . &get_title($searchresults{$itemnumber}) . "</a>\n";
```

This modification works as long as the URL of gallery images is `http://thumbs.ebaystatic.com/pict/`*`itemnumber`*`8080_0.jpg`; if this hack ever stops working, you can find out what URL eBay is currently using for gallery images by performing any search, right-clicking any gallery image, and selecting View Image (in Mozilla/Firefox) or Properties (in Internet Explorer).

Next, if you're using Windows, you'll need to modify the mail routine to support your new HTML-formatted content; replace the entire `&sendemail` subroutine ❿ with the following:

```
sub sendemail {
  my ($to, $from, $subject, $body) = @_;
  my $msg = MIME::Lite->new (
    To      => $email,
    From    => $email,
    Subject => $subject,
    Type    => 'multipart/related'
  );
```

```
    $msg->attach(
      Type => 'text/html',
      Data => qq{ $mailbody }
    );

    MIME::Lite->send('smtp', $mailserver, Timeout => 10);
    $msg->send;
  }
```

If you're using a Mac or Unix machine, you'll need to use a different subroutine, shown next.

Send mail on Linux, Unix, Mac OS X. The &sendemail subroutine on line ⑩ works on Windows-based systems with a MIME-compatible email program installed. If you're using Unix, Linux, or Mac OS X, you probably have sendmail installed and configured on your system. In this case, you'll need to replace the &sendemail subroutine with the following:

```
sub sendemail {
  my ($to, $from, $subject, $body) = @_;
  open(MAIL,"|/usr/sbin/sendmail -t");
    print MAIL "To: $to\n";
    print MAIL "From: $from\n";
    print MAIL "Subject: $subject\n\n";
    print MAIL "$body\n";
  close(MAIL);
}
```

(You may have to change /usr/sbin/sendmail to match the location of sendmail on your system; type `which sendmail` at a terminal prompt if you're not sure.)

Consolidate multiple searches. One of the drawbacks to eBay's built-in email notification is that each search generates its own email; have 20 favorite searches, and you'll get up to 20 separate emails every day. In this hack, you can accommodate multiple searches by modifying line ❶ so that the script retrieves a list of individual keywords from a separate file and then compiles a single array from the results of all the searches. That way, you'll only get a single email, regardless of the number of different searches the robot performs.

Automatically watch new listings. Once you've been notified of newly listed auctions, you'll most likely want to keep track of their progress [Hack #29]. If you're feeling a little adventurous, you can modify the search robot script to automatically write new entries to the *track.txt* file used by the *track.pl* script in "Keep Track of Auctions Outside of eBay" [Hack #29]. That way, new auctions will automatically show up in your watching list!

Find Items by Shadowing

Become an auction stalker and leech off someone else's searching skills.

Often the best deals on eBay are the auctions that most bidders don't find, usually as a result of sellers not knowing what they're selling or not taking the time to promote them properly. The better you become at searching, the more likely you are to find the auctions that are off most bidders' radars. Sometimes, it takes nothing more than dumb luck to stumble upon a great find; occasionally, it helps to rely on other users' dumb luck (or skill) as well.

As much as eBay is a single community of millions of users, it can also sometimes feel like a bunch of microcommunities, each centered around certain genres and auction categories. As you use eBay and become more familiar with the categories in which you're interested, you'll start to recognize individual buyers who, like you, frequently return to eBay in search of more antique pottery, model trains, Ford Model A restoration parts, first-edition Hemingways, or whatever else you might collect.

As soon as someone bids on an item, that bid becomes public record,* even though the bid *amount* is kept private until the auction ends. When you see that someone has bid on something in which you're interested, all you have to do is search for other auctions on which he has bid. Not only will you discover auctions for similar items, you'll discover new items that you may not have even known to look for.

To do this, just highlight the bidder's user ID, copy it to the clipboard (Ctrl-C), go to Advanced Search → Items by Bidder, and paste (Ctrl-V) into the Enter Bidder's User ID field. Do not include completed listings, select "Even if not the high bidder," and click Search. You'll then be shown a list of all public auctions on which that member is currently bidding.

Prevent Bidders from Shadowing You

It's typically in your best interest as a bidder to have as few people as possible see an auction on which you're bidding. Fewer interested bidders means fewer bids, which, in turn, means a lower price and a higher likelihood that you'll win the auction.

Bid shadowing is not common on eBay, but is practiced by some of the more determined users from time to time. The best way to prevent others from shadowing your bids is to bid later in the auction, thereby shrinking the win-

* The exceptions are private auctions and auctions held in localizations with strict privacy laws, such as eBay Germany (*www.ebay.de*).

dow of time during which other bidders can see where you've bid. See "Snipe It Manually" [Hack #26] for a way to take this to the extreme and effectively eliminate shadowing altogether.

Keep Tabs on eBay with the eBay Toolbar

Expand your browser with eBay's custom toolbar application.

The eBay Toolbar, shown in Figure 2-9, is a free add-on program that provides a handy search box, several desktop "alert" features, and quick access to many My eBay features.

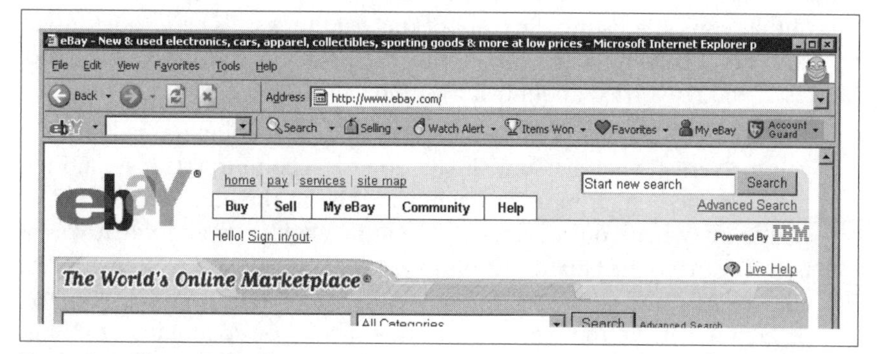

Figure 2-9. The eBay Toolbar provides several handy tools, primarily useful for bidders, such as two "alert" features not otherwise available to non-toolbar-equipped browsers

Provided you're running recent versions of Windows and Internet Explorer, you can download the eBay Toolbar at *pages.ebay.com/ebay_toolbar*. (Users of Mozilla, Firefox, Netscape, Opera, or any browser on Unix, Linux, or a Mac are unfortunately out of luck.)

In addition to providing handy links to My eBay, various eBay Search pages, the PayPal home page, and a few other hot spots, the eBay Toolbar also has some features you won't find elsewhere:

Search. The Search textbox keeps a history of the last few searches you've typed (up to 25), which can be a quick and easy way to save past searches [Hack #20]. But you have to use it exclusively, as it doesn't link up with your My Favorite Searches list, nor will it list any searches typed into the eBay site itself.

Bid Alerts. Bid Alerts notify you 10, 15, 30, 60, or 75 minutes before the end of an auction on which you've bid, which is useful if you wish to return to the auction to bid again and ensure a win. Included in the Bid Alerts menu is a handy list of all the open auctions on which you've placed at least one bid; click Refresh Bid List if it appears to be out of date.

Click the little arrow next to the eBay logo on the left side of the eBay toolbar and click eBay Toolbar Preferences to enable and customize eBay alerts.

Watch Alerts. Watch Alerts work just like Bid Alerts, but apply to items in the Items I'm Watching list [Hack #29], as opposed to items on which you've already bid. Use this feature to remind you to place a bid on items that interest you, or to set up a snipe bid [Hack #26] before it's too late.

Outbid Alerts. Let the eBay Toolbar alert you whenever someone else has outbid you on a listing. Be wary of this feature, as it's easy to let it bait you into a bidding war with another member. Instead, try sniping [Hack #26] if you're worried about being outbid.

Account Guard. Do you ever get those suspicious-looking emails asking you to "verify" your account? If you don't feel comfortable just ignoring these spoofed email messages, you can rely on the eBay Toolbar to let you know when you're viewing a genuine eBay page and when you're not. The Account Guard button turns green when you're seeing a real eBay or PayPal page, red if you're seeing a potential spoof site [Hack #25], or gray when the toolbar doesn't know what you're looking at. Naturally, you shouldn't type your eBay ID and password into your browser unless the proverbial light is green. Better yet, don't ever click any links you find in email messages; rather, type the address of the site (e.g., *ebay.com*) into your browser's address bar or use a toolbar button you trust.

Maybe you just like toolbars. Finally, there's a certain cachet to using a customized, feature-rich toolbar right on your browser that simply isn't available anywhere else.

If you're a Windows 95, Mac, or Unix user, or if you use Mozilla, Firefox, or Opera on any platform, there's a very simple alternative to the eBay Toolbar. Both Internet Explorer and Mozilla/Firefox have a fully customizable Links toolbar, which can hold not only links to web pages, but sport neat drop-down menus into which those links can be organized. See "Find Similar Items" [Hack #14] for a snazzy little example.

HACK #24 Post a Want Ad

Create a free listing on eBay's Want It Now site, and let the world know what you're looking for.

In an effort to answer the pleas of hungry collectors everywhere, eBay has created a special place where members can advertise items they're looking for, as opposed to items they're selling. To create a new want ad, go to *pages.ebay.com/wantitnow/* and click Post to Want It Now.

The rather spare Post To Want It Now form has only three self-explanatory options: Title, Description, and Category. Type a keyword-rich title [Hack #47], take time to write an effusively-friendly description, and then select the top-level category under which you'd normally expect to find your item on the main eBay site. Click Post To Want It Now when you're done.

Make sure to indicate in the description that you're willing to pay via PayPal [Hack #33], if that is indeed the case, as it will help affirm your trustworthiness among the more timid sellers that may stumble upon your ad.

Your ad will appear on the site immediately, and will remain for 60 days or until you delete it. Click View Your Post on the confirmation page to see your listing, which should look something like the one in Figure 2-10.

home | pay | services | site map
Start new search | Search
Buy | Sell | My eBay | Community | Help
Advanced Search

Placed in category: Toys & Hobbies

Ultraman Life-size Vinyl Figure for my living room Post number: 5963511836

Responses: 0 total responses
Respond >

Time left: **41 days 12 hours**
Date placed: Mar-14-05 17:05:03 PST
Location: Seattle , WA United States

Buyer information
Feedback Score: 812
Positive Feedback: **99.9%**
Member since Apr-28-99 in United States

Description

If you have a life-size Ultraman figure, I may have the perfect home for him!

I'm willing to pay one-way coach airfare to Seattle, but business-class is out of the question. Contact me right away if you have one to sell, and please send photos!

Ready to respond?

Simply click the **Respond** button below to send your listing to this buyer. Learn more about Want It Now.

Respond >

Delete this post | Top of Page

Figure 2-10. A Want It Now listing allows you to advertise what you're looking for, in the hopes that a seller will see it and contact you

Now, don't expect a flood of emails from eager sellers right away. In fact, you'll be lucky if you get any bites, mostly because it won't occur to most sellers to look on the Want It Now site for items they're thinking of selling. Instead, you'll have to be a little proactive if you want a decent response to your request. Here are some tips for getting your want ad noticed:

Sell something. Odds are that if you're an avid collector, you're also selling related items from time to time. If so, don't be afraid to include a link [Hack #60] to your Want It Now listing in your listing descriptions. That way, the people who are more-likely to have the item you're looking for will see your ad.

Use your About Me page. If you haven't done so already, create an About Me page [Hack #62] and manually add links to each of your individual want ads there. Although it may be a bit of a pain to keep this list up-to-date (something you'll have to do manually), it may be worth the trouble if you're desperate.

To see all your Want It Now posts in one place, go to *http://wantitnow-search-desc.ebay.com/ws/eBayISAPI.dll?MyPosts*. Unfortunately, there's no way to make this list available to others, so if you want to advertise your want ads, you'll have to list them manually on a separate site.

Advertise off-eBay. Since Want It Now posts remain on the site for 60 days, you'll have time to advertise them in newsgroups, online discussion forums, and other web sites. If you're feeling bold, you can even attempt to have your posts indexed on Google, Yahoo!, or any other search engine. See "Tweak Search URLs" [Hack #13] for a way to create short URLs that are easy to include in emails. Although Want It Now listings show your current feedback rating, they don't contain links to your feedback profile [Hack #1] nor do they indicate your name or eBay member ID, so you don't have to worry about your privacy when it comes to promoting your want ads.

If any prospective sellers find your want ad, and they feel as though they have something you might like, all they have to do is click the Respond button on your post, and you both will be given the option of completing the transaction through eBay. But don't hold your breath.

## CHAPTER THREE

Bidding

Hacks 25–41

The term *auction* evokes a vivid image in most people's minds: a fast-talking auctioneer at a podium, dozens of seated participants, and an assistant parading numbered collectibles across the stage, one by one, as the participants place their bids. The auctioneer quotes an opening price, and participants signal their interest by raising their hands, at which point the bid price is raised by some arbitrary amount. Bidding for each item continues until the current bid price exceeds the amount that all but one of the participants is willing to pay.

eBay's bidding system works a little differently. For one, auctions are timed, and close at a predetermined date and time, regardless of the bid price or whether or not everyone has finished bidding.

Secondly, eBay uses something called *proxy bidding*, a system that somewhat compensates for the fact that the auctions are timed. Instead of placing individual bids on an item, you simply specify a single maximum bid, and eBay does the rest. Imagine sending someone else to an auction on your behalf, giving him a certain amount of money to bid on a single item. That person, the *proxy*, would place traditional bids until he wins the auction or runs out of money.

Finally, eBay offers *fixed-price listings* that allow buyers and sellers to skip the bidding process and complete the deal with a single purchase, as though eBay were just another online store. Furthermore, the Buy It Now feature [Hack #31] allows sellers to turn their auctions into a hybrid of sorts, permitting either ordinary bidding or an instant purchase. Factoid: roughly one in four eBay listings ends with a Buy It Now or fixed-price purchase.

Proxy Bidding

The best way to understand proxy bidding is to see it in action. A seller starts an auction for an antique pocket watch, and sets an opening bid of $25.00. The duration of the auction is five days; since the auction started at

3:52 p.m. on a Thursday, it is scheduled to end at 3:52 p.m. the following Tuesday. Here's how bidding might proceed:

Time	Bid placed	Price becomes	What happened?
Friday 10:00 a.m.	Bidder 1 bids $45	$25.00	First bid; price is set at opening bid price, regardless of bidder's maximum.
Friday 5:30 p.m.	Bidder 2 bids $30	$31.00	Bidder 1's maximum bid is higher than Bidder 2's, so price rises to $1 above Bidder 2's bid.
Sunday 11:15 a.m.	Bidder 3 bids $35	$36.00	Bidder 3 is instantly outbid, just like Bidder 2.
Monday 3:41 a.m.	Bidder 4 bids $60	$46.00	Bidder 1 is finally unseated as the high bidder, and the price is raised to Bidder 1's maximum of $45, plus $1.
Tuesday 1:38 p.m.	Bidder 5 bids $50	$51.00	Another bidder comes along, but her maximum isn't as high as the current high bidder.
Tuesday 3:52 p.m.	Auction ends	$51.00	Bidder 4, who entered the highest maximum bid, wins the auction!

Here, a total of five bidders placed a total of five bids, and the final price ended up at $1.00 more than the second-highest bid. See "Take Advantage of Bid Increments" [Hack #30] for details on the $1.00 increment shown here.

In any auction with more than one bidder, the final value is always in the neighborhood of what at least two bidders are willing to pay for the item.

The problem with proxy bidding is that bidders are human, and as such, the excitement of winning can cloud their judgment. Furthermore, many bidders still think—and bid—in conventional terms. The next example paints a somewhat more realistic picture of how bidding works, using the same auction as the previous example:

Time	Bid placed	Price becomes	What happened?
Friday 10:00 a.m.	Bidder 1 bids $35	$25.00	First bid; price is set at opening bid price.
Friday 5:30 p.m.	Bidder 2 bids $28	$29.00	Bidder 1's original bid is higher than Bidder 2's, so price rises to $1 above Bidder 2's bid.
Friday 5:32 p.m.	Bidder 2 bids $32	$33.00	Bidder 2 isn't happy to have been outbid, so he bids again, and is again outbid.
Friday 5:33 p.m.	Bidder 2 bids $38	$36.00	Bidder 2 bids once again, this time finally emerging as the high bidder.
Saturday 1:40 p.m.	Bidder 1 bids $45	$39.00	Bidder 1 returns to auction, discovers that she has been outbid, and raises the stakes.

Time	Bid placed	Price becomes	What happened?
Monday 9:15 a.m.	Bidder 2 bids $45	$45.00	Bidder 2 is back. Since both bidders have specified the same maximum bid, the earlier bid takes precedence, and the price is set at $45. Bidder 2 gives up.
Tuesday 3:49 p.m.	Bidder 3 bids $50	$46.00	Bidder 3 bids at the last minute and becomes the high bidder.
Tuesday 3:52 p.m.	Auction ends	$46.00	Bidder 3 wins the auction!

Two important things happened in this second example. First, a bidding war took place between Bidder 1 and Bidder 2. Between them, they placed seven bids, but neither won the auction. It would've been much less trouble if each had simply decided how much he or she was willing to spend and then had stuck to it.

> The beauty of proxy bidding is that it also accommodates conventional bidding, allowing bidders to enter a single bid or a maximum bid with equal ease. But true proxy bidding is the better choice, because it enforces the concept of picking a maximum and sticking to it.

Second, Bidder 3 saw this war and decided to stay out of it. Instead, she waited until about three minutes before the end of the auction, and then placed her maximum bid. Since there wasn't enough time for Bidder 1 to be notified that she had been outbid, she never bid higher, and ended up losing the auction. Not only did waiting ensure a win for Bidder 3, it avoided further bidding wars, which ultimately resulted in a lower final price. This is called sniping [Hack #26].

It's important to point out that sniping doesn't guarantee a win. Quite the contrary, in fact: had either Bidder 1 or Bidder 2 entered a bid higher than $50, either would've won the auction, regardless of Bidder 3's last-minute bid. And I'm sure that at least one of the early bidders returned after the auction ended and thought "I would've been willing to pay more than that!"

HACK #25 Sniff Out Dishonest Sellers

A little research can save you a big headache.

Just because you're paranoid doesn't mean they're not really after you. And just because you take steps to protect yourself doesn't mean that there aren't sellers ready to sell you a lot of hot air. Fortunately, eBay provides a lot of tools to help you discern the good sellers from the bad.

Naturally, feedback (see Chapter 1) should be your first recourse, not only when you suspect a seller of being dishonest, but any time you bid on an item sold by someone you don't know. But there are limitations to the feedback system. For one, it relies on the intelligence of past buyers, something you can never count on. It also takes a few weeks for feedback (negative or otherwise) to make its way back to a seller, so a new seller—or an experienced member new to selling—may be able to sell under the guise of a trustworthy seller for up to a month before his reputation catches up to him.

If It Sounds Too Good to Be True...

You've heard it before, and it undoubtedly runs through your head when you're looking at certain auctions: if something sounds too good to be true, it probably is. Now, there are certainly more exceptions to this rule on eBay than at most other places, mostly due to sellers who don't know what they're selling or don't do a good job of constructing the auction. (In fact, I've gotten some great deals—even to the point of effectively getting stuff for free—simply by being more knowledgeable than the seller.) Nonetheless, don't let your desire for a deal cloud your better judgment.

The photo can be a dead giveaway, both to a dishonest seller and to an inexperienced seller who simply doesn't know any better. If the photo appears to be intentionally blurry, doctored, or simply doesn't match the item described in the auction (or other photos of the same item), it should be your first clue that something's fishy. Check out some of the seller's other auctions (both past and present) and look for inconsistencies; for example, do all the photos have the same background? If they don't, the seller may have snatched them [Hack #75] from other auctions or web sites. This can either mean that they're selling something they don't have, or merely that they're lazy (both qualities to avoid).

So how do you tell the difference between someone who is trying to rip you off and someone who simply hasn't taken the time to construct a proper listing? Assuming there's still some time left before the listing closes, ask the seller a question. Specific questions, such as those that inquire about an item's dimensions or whether or not it comes with a particular accessory, are good ways to determine whether or not the item described is actually the item you'll receive.

The Inflated Shipping Scam

One of the most common scams is to sell something for pennies, and then make up the difference in grossly inflated shipping fees. Sellers do this for three reasons. First, cheaper items show up higher in search results sorted by price and attract less-experienced buyers. Second, eBay's final-value fees are based on the final price only (not including shipping charges), so sellers avoid eBay fees by overcharging for shipping. Third, sellers typically do not refund shipping charges, so if you paid $1.00 for an item and $12.00 to ship it, you'll be unlikely to return it just to get your buck back.

> By default, eBay doesn't show shipping costs in searches. But if you click the Customize Display link in the upper-right corner of search results pages, move the "Shipping cost" entry to the right-hand Columns to Display box, and click Save, you can see how much it will cost to have each item shipped. Note that this only applies to listings in which the seller has specified a fixed shipping cost [Hack #59]; shipping costs based on your location and extra fees specified only in the description won't ever show up in search results.

So how do you tell whether high shipping charges are legitimate? The give-away is the "Additional shipping per item" amount, specified in the Payment Details at the bottom of the auction page. If the price seems artificially low with respect to the shipping charges, and it costs nearly as much to ship a second item as the first (e.g., $19.00 for the first item and $18.50 for each additional unit), then you've likely found a shipping-cost scam.

Naturally, it's up to you to determine if shipping charges are indeed excessive, given your knowledge of the weight and size of the item: $45.00 is a perfectly reasonable shipping charge for a bicycle, but not for a deck of Bicycle playing cards. See "Save Money on Shipping" [Hack #38] for more tips.

Quick to Unload?

In no time, you'll begin to appreciate the public nature of every eBay member's bidding and selling histories.* For example, you can paste a seller's User ID into the "Search by Bidder" box (see Chapter 2) to see if he's reselling something he purchased recently on eBay.

Bidder and seller histories can be invaluable, especially if you suspect a seller isn't telling you everything. You may find that the seller indeed bought the item a few weeks ago for only a few dollars, but when reselling, neglected to mention the gaping hole in the side. To find out more, contact the *original* seller to get the whole story. Similarly, if a seller has relisted an item after the original high bidder backed out, try contacting the bidder to see why he or she did not complete the transaction.

* Due to German privacy laws, the bidding and selling histories of eBay members registered in Germany (*www.ebay.de*) are kept confidential.

There's Less Than Meets the Eye

Here's another example of the "if it's too good to be true" scam: someone appears to be selling name-brand consumer electronics for far below their market value, when, in fact, they're selling only *information* on how to acquire the item advertised. If you see a $2,000 camera with a Buy It Now price of $8, then it's unlikely you'll be receiving any photographic equipment. Despite the claims made by the seller, all you'll get is an email or CD-ROM with information that is already freely available on the Web. And in most cases, the information will be nothing more than a link to a pyramid scheme, lottery, or some other type of scam. See Chapter 2, especially "Focus Your Searches with eBay's Advanced Search Syntax" [Hack #10], for ways to eliminate these types of auctions from search results.

Some sellers start their auctions with a negligibly small opening bid, such as a single cent, merely to encourage healthy bidding. This is not the same as the scam discussed here, and does not necessarily indicate any wrongdoing. Likewise, low prices in currently running auctions may be due to nothing more than the fact that time still remains for more bids. The red flag is a Buy It Now price [Hack #31] far below what it should be.

Although it's common to see items selling on eBay for less than they would in retail stores, you should also be wary of sellers who appear to be selling expensive items far below market value on eBay [Hack #42], yet much higher than the typical cost of the aforementioned "information." Such listings may be the result of account takeovers, described next.

Hostile Takeover

eBay's feedback system is useful, but not infallible. For instance, it's possible for an unscrupulous seller to "take over" someone else's account, using that person's good reputation to fool honest bidders. Here's how it works:

1. The seller obtains a list of eBay members' email addresses, typically from a company that sells such lists to spammers (not exactly the pillars of society themselves).
2. The seller sends an email to all the members on the list, carefully designed to look like it came from eBay. See the "Investigating Suspicious Emails" sidebar for ways to determine the validity of any such email you receive.

Investigating Suspicious Emails

eBay never sends emails to their members asking for user IDs or passwords. However, you've probably seen at least one email appearing to be from eBay or PayPal, warning you that your account will be suspended if you don't log in and "verify your information."

In nearly all cases, such email messages (and the sites they link to) are fraudulent, and are sent to you for the sole purpose of fooling you into divulging your eBay password, credit card number, or other sensitive information. The process is commonly known as *phishing* (not to be confused with the excellent musical group, *Phish*).

You can always tell whether a suspicious email actually came from eBay using your email program's View Source feature. Such emails (and corresponding web sites) use clever HTML and JavaScript to spoof the actual URLs of the links. With a little knowledge of HTML [Hack #52], you can quickly see whether the `<a>` tag points to a real eBay address or an obvious fake like `http://63.111.25.9`. (Be particularly aware of sneaky spoofed URLs like *http://pages.ebay.com.fakserver.com* or *ftp://pages.ebay.com@fakserver.com*.)

The other—and not very smart!— way to find out where a link takes you is to click the link to open it. If the URL shown in the browser that appears does not start with something like *pages.ebay.com* or *cgi.ebay.com* followed by a slash (/), then you have a fake on your hands. But there are ways to fake these indicators, too, so your best bet is to abstain from clicking links in emails in the first place.

Instead, type *ebay.com* into your browser's address bar manually, or use a trusted shortcut. If you're not comfortable with your own ability to spot these fakes, check out the Account Guard feature of the eBay Toolbar [Hack #23]. If you encounter a fake site or a spoofed eBay email, report it immediately by going to *pages.ebay.com/help/contact_inline/*.

These scam artists will stop at nothing to fool you into handing over your sensitive information, but in the end, it's up to you to use your head.

3. An unwitting recipient clicks a link in the email and is brought to a page that *looks* like an eBay or PayPal page, into which he types his user ID and password. The server then records the information.
4. The crook then uses the user ID and password to log into a valid eBay account. He immediately changes the password and registered email address, and then begins to sell high-priced items under the guise of the unsuspecting user, hoping to use the seller's good reputation to mask his own motivations.

Fortunately, it's usually pretty easy to tell these scams apart from legitimate auctions. First, it's always a deal that seems way too good to be true. Second, the seller mysteriously accepts payment only by money order or other postal mail-based payment service with no means of protection [Hack #33]. Finally, if you search the seller's past auctions [Hack #18], you'll most likely see a pattern that doesn't match the items currently being sold.

For example, if someone who has been selling doll clothes for years is suddenly selling dozens of top-of-the-line digital cameras for rock-bottom prices, you've probably found yourself a scam.

While shopping for digital cameras a few years ago, I came across a particularly transparent scam being perpetrated by someone with a seemingly-good feedback record. After reporting it to eBay, I contacted the seller and started asking questions. I tried to draw the seller out and exploit his one clear vulnerability: that he was a crook. For instance, when the seller demanded payment by Western Union (an obvious red flag), I tried to talk him into accepting a payment method I knew I could rescind.

The seller then replied—under the guise of eBay's SafeHarbor department—to inform me of the "legitimacy of his account and transactions." The email went on to say "We advise you to close this specific transaction, the new Western Union and eBay security system allows you to close transactions safely." It would be laughable if it weren't so dangerous. Within 24 hours, the listing was pulled from eBay, and the seller's account was suspended.

Here are a few other red flags that may indicate an account takeover:

Private Auction. If it says "User ID kept private" for the High bidder, it means the seller has elected to make the listing a "private auction." This means, among other things, that you can't see who's bidding on this or, more to the point, any of the seller's completed listings to see if they've had good experiences.

Restrictive payment methods. If the seller won't accept credit cards, PayPal, or another safe payment method [Hack #33], it could mean that he or she doesn't want to be traced once you've sent payment. Keep in mind that you get virtually no protection if you pay by check, money order, cash, or Western Union.

Unspecified or mismatched item location. If the country in which the seller is registered (viewable on the Member Profile page) doesn't match the country in which the item is specified, or neither matches the country indicated by the seller's email address, then you should be wary of sending this person any money.

Eager to sell. If there's language in the title or description urging you to use Buy It Now, or more specifically, send the seller money outside of eBay, there's a pretty good chance that something's fishy.

Don't hesitate to report suspicious listings by going to *pages.ebay.com/help/contact_inline/*. If you're the high bidder in a completed auction and you suspect fraud, you can file a fraud dispute [Hack #41] with eBay.

Taking Matters into Your Own Hands

At this point, it may have occurred to you that you could possibly do more than merely report fraudulent listings as you find them. If you're particularly scrupulous, you might take it upon yourself to bid high on an obvious scam listing so that nobody else can.

eBay's official stance is that they don't condone vigilante justice; they'd rather diligent members simply report suspicious listings or sellers, and then move on. The problem is that it can take eBay up to a day or two to respond to your report and take appropriate action. And in that time, dozens of other unsuspecting members may be taken in by a single scam artist.

As a result, many people do take matters into their own hands, with varying success. There are stories of particularly resourceful people helping law-enforcement officers track down criminals, although the vast majority of cases are those fellow eBayers silently trying to make the community just a little bit safer.

Whether you decide to pursue a scammer is up to you, but be warned: there are risks, not the least of which is that once you bid and win an auction, the seller has your email address (and possibly mailing address and phone number). If you're lucky, all you'll get is negative feedback and a flood of spam and phishing emails (see the "Investigating Suspicious Emails" sidebar).

If nothing else, be a critical thinker and listen to that little voice in your head.

HACK #26 Snipe It Manually

Bid at the last minute to simultaneously ensure that you win the auction and pay the lowest possible amount.

It shouldn't take long to figure out that it's usually better to bid later in an auction—the later the better. Many eBayers wait until the last few minutes of the auction to bid, leaving no time for lower bidders to be notified and respond with higher bids. This is called sniping, and all it takes is a little nerve and the ability to tell time.

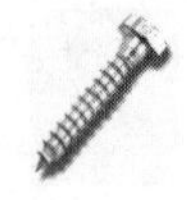

Sniping leaves no time to read the auction description carefully or to ask the seller any questions you may have. Make sure you take care of these things long before the end of the auction.

When you've found an auction you want to snipe, the first step is to track the auction [Hack #29] and make note of its closing date and time. Then, all you need to do is return to eBay a few minutes before the auction ends and place your bid.

The problem is that many eBay users make a habit of doing this, so you'll likely have competition. With multiple snipers, the prize often goes to the bidder who can enter a bid closest to the end of the auction.

With Seconds to Spare...

The most effective snipes occur within 10 to 15 seconds of the end of the auction, leaving no time for other bidders to even see your bid—not to mention outbid you—before it's too late.

Give yourself about two minutes to set up. Start by opening two browser windows (press Ctrl-N to open a second window), and open the same listing in both windows. Move and resize the two browser windows so they're side by side on your screen.

Type your maximum bid in one of the windows and click Place Bid (but do not confirm your bid on the next page). If necessary, scroll the page so that the Confirm Bid button is visible.

Then, switch to the other window and reload (refresh) the page by pressing Ctrl-R. Reload it again a few seconds later to see any changes to the current price and the time left. Repeat this until there are only 15 seconds left in the auction.

If you have a slow connection to the Internet, it will be difficult to reload the page quickly enough to see the status of the auction. Try temporarily turning off images in your browser settings to speed things up. If your connection is exceedingly slow, you'll probably have to increase your sniping margin to 20–30 seconds and hope for the best.

When the time is right, switch back to the other window, and press the Confirm Bid button to place your bid. Then, quickly reload the auction page to make sure your bid was accepted. Assuming you entered a sufficiently large bid, you should be the high bidder for the seven seconds that remain. If you cut it close enough, nobody else will even know you've bid until the auction is over.

Ethical Concerns

Some eBay members consider the ethics of sniping to be somewhat dubious in that it may appear unfair to those unfamiliar with the process. This concern is somewhat understandable. It's true that new members will lose auctions to seasoned eBayers at first, either in bidding wars or by sniping, but as they become more experienced, they'll start winning more auctions.

The choice of whether or not to snipe is yours, but it's very unlikely that any seller will complain about getting your business. (Most sellers realize that sniping prevents prices from peaking early, which might otherwise scare away potential bidders). And fellow bidders are more likely to be energized by the challenge than personally offended at being outbid. Plus, inexperienced bidders will eventually learn the system and find a method that works for them (sniping or otherwise).

Contingency Plans

Of course, things don't always work out the way we plan. The very nature of sniping leaves little time to correct errors or deal with obstacles, so it's best to prepare for them ahead of time.

For instance, say you want to snipe an item for $25; this bid amount poses no problem 2 minutes before the end of the auction, as the current price is only $17. But if, 20 seconds before the end, the bidding reaches $25, your $25 bid will be refused. Sure, you could anticipate this by bidding $26 instead, but then the same thing could happen. (What can really drive you nuts is when you bid $25 and the current price is $24.72; even though your bid is higher, eBay refuses it because it is below the minimum bid required by the bid increment [Hack #30].)

The best way to combat this—especially if you really want an item—is to open up at least one extra bidding window when sniping. The procedure is the same as ordinary sniping, except on one side you'll have the auction page, and on the other you'll have two (or more) "Confirm your Bid" windows, cascaded so that each is big enough to be functional but small enough that each Confirm Bid button is visible. In the first bidding window, you might type a bid of $25, but have the second window ready to type in a slightly higher bid if necessary.

When it comes down to the wire, click the Confirm Bid on the $25 window as you normally would. If you see the large blue letters confirming that the bid has been accepted, then there's nothing left to do. But if, instead, you see the light brown letters informing you that your bid is too low or that you've been outbid, you'll be poised and ready to enter a second, slightly higher bid in the extra window.

I know what you're thinking: why not simply enter an inordinately large bid when sniping to completely eliminate the chance of being outbid?

One of the most important, but least evident, advantages of sniping is that it bypasses the bidding wars that are so common on eBay. Bidding wars typically accomplish nothing more than unnecessarily raising the price of an auction, at which point everyone is bidding more than the item is worth. By bidding at the last minute, you not only eliminate any time for others to outbid you, but you cripple your own ability to bid more than you would normally be willing to pay for the item.

See Also

- When used in conjunction with "Take Advantage of Bid Increments" [Hack #30], sniping allows you to cut the price of an item by a few pennies to a few dollars.
- See "Keep Track of Auctions Outside of eBay" [Hack #29] for ways to mark auctions for later sniping.
- See "Snipe It Automatically" [Hack #27] if you're not going to be around when the auction ends, and you don't want to bid early.

Snipe It Automatically

Use eSnipe to snipe without actually having to be in front of a computer when the auction ends.

Sniping [Hack #26] is an effective way to increase your odds of winning an auction while simultaneously lowering the final price you pay. But there are significant drawbacks to sniping that limit its practical usefulness:

- You have to be in front of your computer, ready to bid, at the exact time the auction ends.
- It's nearly impossible to snipe two or more auctions ending at the same time.
- If your computer crashes or your Internet connection goes down moments before you snipe, you lose.
- You can easily forget to bid, or even become distracted moments before bidding time. (I can't tell you how many times I've been distracted by a doorbell ring or a good song on the radio, only to turn around and find that I've missed my two-minute sniping window.)

The solution, of course, is to simply bid early, and then return to the auction after it's over to find that you've been outbid by four cents. Fortunately, there is a better way.

A number of *sniping services* are available that will automatically place a bid for you at a specified time, typically a few minutes or seconds before the end of an auction. Some sniping services are simply standalone software programs that run on your computer, but these suffer some of the same limitations as sniping manually—namely, that your home computer be turned on and connected to the Internet at the right time. The better services are web-based, like eBay itself, and operate whether or not your computer is powered up.

When you use a sniping service, you must share your eBay ID and password so the software can log in and bid for you. While some sniping services are legitimate, there will undoubtedly be some services that use this information unscrupulously. So use caution and do your homework before trusting an unknown service with your eBay login.

One of the most well-established sniping services is eSnipe (*www.esnipe.com*). It's easy to use, very reliable, and best of all, it works. Just log into eSnipe with your eBay user ID and password, and you're ready to go. To set up a snipe, specify the listing number, the amount to bid, and the buffer time (number of seconds before the end of the auction), as shown in Figure 3-1.

eSnipe will bid for you at the specified time and then send you an email to let you know whether or not the snipe was successful. Naturally, if you are outbid or if your bid isn't high enough, eSnipe will fail.

Among other things, automatic sniping offers the distinct advantage of being able to cancel your snipe bid at any time. Compare this with bids on eBay, which can only be retracted [Hack #32] under very specific circumstances.

The Catch

There are two drawbacks to using eSnipe. First, it's not free. New users are granted a free trial period, but thereafter eSnipe charges 1% of the final price of the auction, with a minimum fee of 25 cents and a maximum fee of $10.00.* The fees are pretty small, though, and probably pay for themselves

* The fees are per auction; sniping three $2 auctions will cost you 75 cents. The exception is that all foreign auctions have a flat fee of $1, presumably because eSnipe isn't able to do an accurate currency conversion on the fly. Naturally, all quoted prices are subject to change.

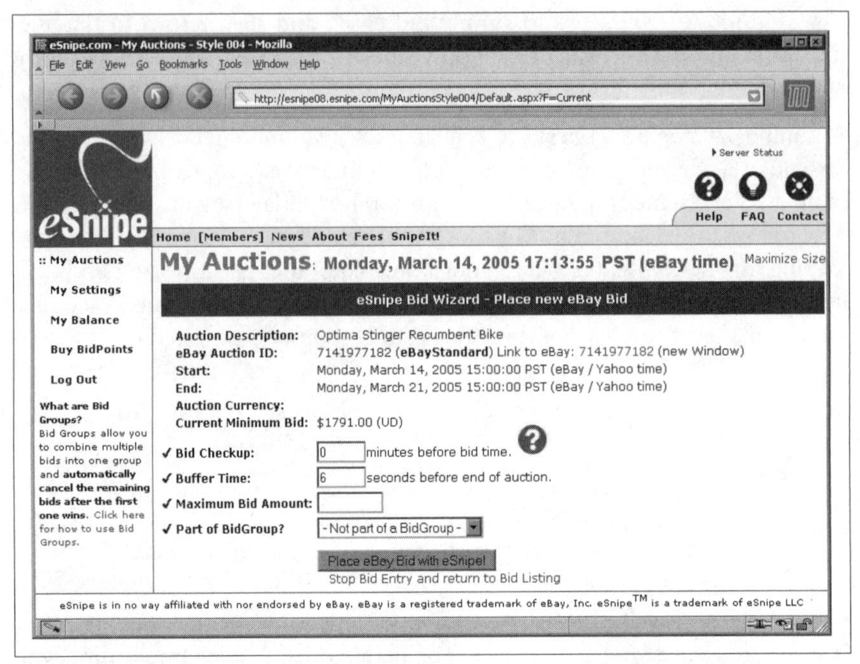

Figure 3-1. Automatic sniping tools such as eSnipe bid for you at the last minute

with the money saved by sniping. eSnipe fees are paid by purchasing "Bid-Points," which are available at a discount if purchased in bulk.

The second catch is that eSnipe is not smart. It can't read your mind or the minds of the other bidders, nor can it make decisions for you. For instance, if you enter a snipe bid of $54.03 and the price at the time of sniping is $53.99, then eBay will refuse your bid even though it's higher than the highest bid **[Hack #30]**. If you sniped the auction manually **[Hack #26]**, then you'd be able to make the call on the spot and raise your bid by the required 96 cents. See the "Where Sniping Can Go Terribly Wrong" sidebar for another case.

eSnipe offers a Bid Checkup feature, an automated email sent at a specified time before the end of the auction to notify you of any potential problems with your pending snipe, but the real-world usefulness of the feature is limited, since you probably won't be around when it arrives. And you may find the Bid Checkup email to be somewhat of a nuisance, because it only means you get two email messages notifying you of a failed snipe instead of just one. Fortunately, you can specify `0` (zero) in the Bid Checkup field to disable the feature.

Where Sniping Can Go Terribly Wrong

Although sniping usually has good results, there are circumstances under which automatic sniping can actually make things worse. Here's a case in point.

I saw a set of Go stones (used in Go, an ancient board game somewhat like chess, but with black and white stones on a 19×19 grid) for auction with an opening bid of $45. I set up an automated sniping service to bid about $50 for me, seven seconds before the end of the auction. I then promptly forgot about it; that is, until I received an email from the service shortly after the end of the auction.

It appeared that the seller had extended the auction another three days and lowered the price to $40. This happened sometime after I placed my snipe bid, so I was none the wiser until it was too late. Not wanting a bid retraction [Hack #32] to show up in my feedback profile, I let the bid stand. And since the price had been lowered and I was the only bidder, I felt like I was in a good position.

Then, another bidder came along and bid repeatedly until my $50 bid had been trounced, something that wouldn't have happened if my bid had not yet been placed (or if I had retracted the errant snipe). Since my bid was placed early, the other bidder felt compelled to outbid me, thus raising the price of the set over what I was willing to pay.

I ended up losing the auction, and the other bidder ended up paying too much, all because of what can go wrong with sniping. Had I sniped manually, I would've known to postpone my bid. Or, had I simply bid at the time I entered my snipe bid, the seller wouldn't have been able to extend the auction in the first place.

Put eSnipe on Your Toolbar

If you find yourself using eSnipe frequently, you may want to streamline the bid-entry process. Instead of opening up eSnipe, logging in, and then typing or pasting the auction number into the form, you can use eSnipe's SnipeIt feature.

Start by clicking SnipeIt! on eSnipe's toolbar and following the prompts on screen. Eventually, you'll be given a link that you can drag onto your browser's Links toolbar. (The link is the same for all supported platforms and browsers; only the screenshots in the instructions are different.)

To snipe an auction, navigate to the auction page on eBay and click the SnipeIt link on your Links toolbar. A small window will appear with all information filled in for you; just specify a bid amount and press "Place eBay Bid with eSnipe."

Alternatives to eSnipe

There are a bunch of other available sniping services, such as:

Bidnapper.com. Another sniping web site, Bidnapper offers a few unique features not offered by eSnipe, such as Contingency Bidding [Hack #28], a Seller Profile tool (which helps find negative feedback comments [Hack #1]), and even shadowing [Hack #22].

JustSnipe.com. One of the only services to offer free sniping (up to five snipes per week), JustSnipe also offers unlimited sniping for a fixed monthly fee. The membership service also offers an auction-watching tool [Hack #29].

StealthBid.com. Although similar to the other services mentioned here, StealthBid is the least expensive service for low-cost auctions. The minimum price is only 5 cents for wins of $5.00 or less, versus a minimum per-snipe code of 25 cents for the others.

See Also

- See "Snipe It Manually" [Hack #26] for the old-school approach to sniping.
- See "Snipe It Conditionally" [Hack #28] if you want to bid on several auctions but win only one.

HACK #28 Snipe It Conditionally

Automatically discard future snipes once you win an auction.

One of the best features of eSnipe [Hack #27] is its ability to cancel one or more future snipes once you win an auction.

Say you want to buy a PDA. Since PDAs are a common commodity on eBay, you'd likely be happy winning any one of a dozen different auctions for the same model. But if you were to snipe them all with eSnipe, you run the risk of winning more than one auction. The solution is to use eSnipe's Bid Groups feature.

Start by clicking the Bid Groups tab on the eSnipe site, and then clicking Create New Bid Group, as shown in Figure 3-2. Type a name for the new group under Brief Name and click Create New Folder (the Long Name and Description fields are optional).

Next, pick one of the auctions on which you want to bid and begin placing an eSnipe bid as you normally would. The only difference is that you must choose the name of the Bid Group you just created from the "Part of Bid Group?" field. Repeat the process for the other auctions in the group.

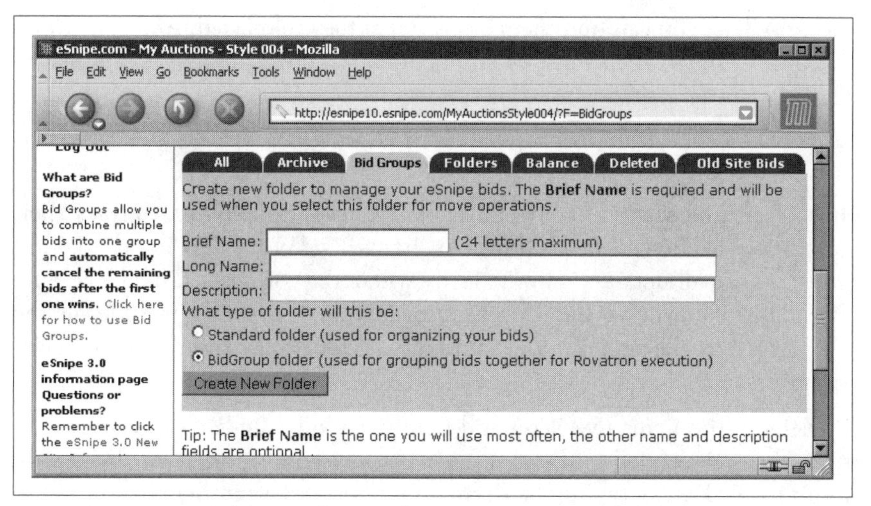

Figure 3-2. eSnipe's Bid Groups feature allows you to snipe multiple auctions until you win one

eSnipe will bid on each of the auctions in the Bid Group, one after another, until it wins one. As soon as an auction has been won, the pending bids from all remaining auctions will be canceled.

Contingency Sniping

Another service, *bidnapper.com*, offers a similar feature called *Contingency Bidding*. Instead of cancelling remaining bids once you successfully win an auction, the service *continues to bid* on successive listings if you win the first listing. Thus, you can buy three items from the same seller, say, to save on shipping fees, but you won't be stuck winning an accessory for a separate product someone else won in an earlier listing.

Keep Track of Auctions Outside of eBay

Use eBay's auction-tracking tools or create a flexible auction-watching tool better than anything eBay has to offer.

If I bought everything on eBay I wanted, I would've gone broke long ago. But I'm also a collector, and as such, I routinely track many auctions in my various fields of interest, whether or not I actually intend to bid on them.

Keeping track of auctions is among your most important tasks as a bidder—especially for items you've won—if for no other reason than to ensure that you eventually receive everything you've paid for. Tracking auctions is also an essential part of sniping **[Hack #26]** as well as selling **[Hack #43]**. If you're really after something specific, you may want to track completed auctions that didn't sell, so you can find them easily when they're relisted. And sometimes you may want to keep track of an auction's progress purely for the sake of curiosity.

Using eBay's Tracking Tools

The All Buying section of My eBay is where most people turn to track their auctions. The Items I'm Bidding On, Items I've Won, and Items I Didn't Win lists are all updated automatically whenever you place a bid or an auction on which you've bid closes, respectively. These lists include all the vitals, such as the auction titles, amounts of your bids, end dates, and closing prices.

By default, the Items I've Won and Items I Didn't Win lists show only auctions that have ended in the past few days, but you can increase their range to up to 60 days by typing the desired number of days in the box at the top of each list. And like search results, all the lists on this page can be sorted by clicking the hyperlinked column headers.

You can clean out these lists by ticking the checkboxes next to one or more auction titles and clicking Remove. However, when you delete an auction, its entry disappears into the ether with no obvious means of retrieval. (The only way to retrieve a deleted listing for items you've won is to retrieve them *all*; go to My eBay → eBay Preferences, turn on the "Retrieve removed items" checkbox in the "My eBay Preferences," and click Apply.) A better way to shorten these lists is to simply decrease the number of days back they go.

The Items I'm Watching list is a very handy tool, but it works somewhat differently than the others. It will remain empty until you choose to "watch" an auction: simply go to any auction (or fixed-price listing) page and click "Watch this item." A message then appears, confirming that item is now being tracked in My eBay; click the link to view the updated list. The Watching list is easy to use and adequate if you never track more than a few items at a time.

To have eBay send you an automatic Item Watch Reminder email for any item in your Watch list that will end within 36 hours, go to My eBay → Preferences → Notification preferences, and turn on the "Send me daily lists of all items in my watch list that will end within 36 hours" option.

The eBay toolbar [Hack #23] sports a few additional features that work in conjunction with the Items I'm Watching list, such as watch alerts and bid alerts that remind you when auctions you're watching or have bid on are about to end.

If You Want It Done Right...

As useful as eBay's tools are, you may find that none of them completely meet your needs. For example:

Limited number. You can watch a maximum of 100 listings at a time. When you reach the limit, you have to manually delete watched items before you can add more.

No long-term history. Completed listings remain in the lists for no longer than 60 days, even though they often remain in the eBay system for about 5 months.

Can't watch closed items. You can't add listings to your Watching list after they've ended, which would be useful if you're a bidder waiting for the seller to relist, or you're selling something similar yourself.

No prioritization. There's no way to prioritize items in your Watching list, which would be useful for differentiating items on which you're planning to bid and those about which you're simply curious.

No customization. The Bidding/Watching page can be cumbersome to use. For example, the way entries are divided into auctions won, auctions lost, etc., has a certain logic to it, but doesn't necessarily end up being as convenient as a single, unified list of auctions.

These limitations have prompted me to come up with something better: a fully customizable, web-based, off-site list of auctions with none of the limitations of eBay's tools. The following hack is based on a tool I created for my own use and have used every day since. There are two parts to this hack: the Perl script, used to store and display your personal list of auctions; and the link, used to activate the script and add the currently displayed auction.

The Link

The first task is to create an easy way to add any given auction to your custom list, an alternative to the Watch This Item link on auction pages. This is accomplished by placing the following snippet of JavaScript in a button on your browser's Links bar [Hack #14]:

```
javascript:void(win=window.open('http://www.ebayhacks.com/exec/track.pl?
      do=add&auction='+location.href+'&title='+document.title,'Hack'))
```

(Make sure the text appears all on one line.) You can name the new link anything you like, such as Watch Auction or simply Track.

The first few bits of the code are used to instruct your browser to open a new browser window and execute the code inside the parentheses, but it's the stuff that follows that's the most interesting. First comes the complete URL of your tracking tool, so you'll need to change `www.ebayhacks.com` to the name of your own web server, `/exec` to the name of your executable folder (usually `/cgi-bin`), and `track.pl` to the filename of your script (discussed in the following section). The second half of the URL—the text after the question mark (?)—is composed of three arguments that are passed to your script, separated by ampersands (&):

```
do=add&auction='+location.href+'&title='+document.title
```

The JavaScript code automatically inserts the auction URL (`location.href`) and page title (`document.title`) as arguments to pass to the script. One of the neat little tricks of this code is how it works with eBay's auction URL, which also includes arguments separated by ampersands:

```
http://cgi.ebay.com/ws/eBayISAPI.dll?ViewItem&item=3125058177
```

When this URL is passed to your script with the other arguments, it is automatically split into these two arguments:

```
auction=http://cgi.ebay.com/ws/eBayISAPI.dll?ViewItem

item=3125058177
```

and thus the auction number is conveniently separated for you!

The Code

The second half of this hack is a Perl script that interprets the information it receives from the JavaScript link (see the previous section), stores all your auctions in a file, and then displays a properly sorted list.

```
#!/usr/bin/perl

# *** includes ***
use Time::ParseDate;
use POSIX qw(strftime);
use LWP 5.64;
use HTML::HeadParser;
require("cgi-lib.pl");
&ReadParse;

# *** variables ***
❶ $selfurl = "http://www.ebayhacks.com/exec/track.pl";
$localfile = "/usr/local/home/ebaylist.txt";
$timeoffset = 0;
```

```
    $url = "http://cgi.ebay.com/ws/eBayISAPI.dll?ViewItem&item=";
❷   @formatting=("color=#EE0000 STYLE=font-weight:bold",
                   "color=#000000 STYLE=font-weight:bold", "color=#000000");
    $i = 0;
    $exists = 0;
❸   $numlevels = 2;

    # *** read stored list ***
    open (INFILE,"$localfile");
      while ( $line = <INFILE> ) {
        $line =~ s/\s+$//;
        $i++;
        ($enddate[$i],$priority[$i],$item[$i],$title[$i]) =
                                                     split(",", $line, 4);

        # *** see if passed auction number is in list already ***
        if (($item[$i] ne "") && ($item[$i] eq $in{'item'})) { $exists = $i; }
      }
    close (INFILE);

    # *** add latest auction to list, if valid ***
    if (($in{'auction'} =~ "ebay.com") && ($in{'item'} != "") && ($exists==0)) {
      $x = index($in{'title'}, "(");
      $y = index($in{'title'}, ")", $x);
      $z = index($in{'title'}, "-", $y);

❹     $title = &get_title($in{'item'});
      $enddate = parsedate(substr($in{'title'}, $x + 6, $y - $x - 7));

      $i++;
      ($enddate[$i], $priority[$i], $item[$i], $title[$i]) =
                                          ($enddate, 2, $in{'item'}, $title);
    }
    elsif (($in{'do'} eq "promote")) {
      $priority[$exists]--;
      if ($priority[$exists] < 0) { $priority[$exists] = 0; }
    }
    elsif (($in{'do'} eq "demote")) {
      $priority[$exists]++;
      if ($priority[$exists] > 2) { $priority[$exists] = 2; }
    }
    elsif (($in{'do'} eq "delete")) {
      splice @enddate, $exists, 1;
      splice @priority, $exists, 1;
      splice @item, $exists, 1;
      splice @title, $exists, 1;
      $i--;
    }

    # *** update list ***
    if (($in{'do'} ne "")) {
      open (OUTFILE,">$localfile");
```

```
    for ($j = 1; $j <= $i; $j++) {
      print OUTFILE "$enddate[$j],$priority[$j],$item[$j],$title[$j]\n";
    }
  close (OUTFILE);

  print "Location: $selfurl\n\n";
  exit( 0);
}

# *** sort list ***
@idx = sort criteria 0 .. $i;

# *** display list ***
print "Content-type: text/html\n\n";
print "<table border cellspacing=0 cellpadding=6>\n";

for ($j = 1; $j <= $i; $j++) {
  $formatteddate =
         strftime("%a, %b %d - %l:%M:%S %p", localtime($enddate[$idx[$j]]));

❺  $formattedtitle = "<a href=\"$url$item[$idx[$j]]\" target=\"_blank\"><font
              $formatting[$priority[$idx[$j]]]>$title[$idx[$j]]</font></a>";

  if (strftime("%v", localtime($enddate[$idx[$j]])) eq
                                              strftime("%v", localtime(time))) {
❻    $formattedtitle = "<li>" . $formattedtitle;
  }
  if ($enddate[$idx[$j]] < time) {
❼    $formattedtitle = "<strike>" . $formattedtitle . "</strike>";
  }
  else {
    $timeleft = ($enddate[$idx[$j]] - time) / 60 + ($timeoffset * 60);
    if ($timeleft < 24 * 60) {
      $hoursleft = int($timeleft / 60);
      $minleft = int($timeleft - ($hoursleft * 60));
      if ($minleft < 10) { $minleft = "0" . $minleft; }
❽        $formattedtitle = $formattedtitle .
                        " <font size=-1>($hoursleft:$minleft left)</font>";
    }
  }

  print "<tr><td>$formattedtitle</td>";
  print "<td><font size=-1>$formatteddate</font></td>";
❾  print "<td><a href=\"$selfurl?item=$item[$idx[$j]]&do=promote\">+</a>";
  print " | <a href=\"$selfurl?item=$item[$idx[$j]]&do=demote\">-</a>";
  print " | <a href=\"$selfurl?item=$item[$idx[$j]]&do=delete\">x</a></td>";
  print "</tr>\n";
}

print "</table>\n";

sub criteria {
```

```
  # *** sorting criteria subroutine ***
  return ($priority[$a] <=> $priority[$b] or $enddate[$a] <=> $enddate[$b]);
}

sub get_title($) {
  my $itempage = LWP::UserAgent -> new;
  my $item_contents = $itempage -> get($_[0]);
  my $p = HTML::HeadParser -> new;
  $p -> parse($item_contents -> content);
  $title = $p -> header('Title');
  $title = substr($title, index($title, " - ") + 3);
  return $title;
}
```

This script requires the `Time::ParseDate` Perl module, part of David Muir Sharnoff's *Time-modules-2003.0211* distribution (*search.cpan.org/perldoc?Time::ParseDate*), which is necessary to convert eBay's date notation into something Perl understands. (See the "Installing Perl Modules" sidebar in the Preface for installation instructions.) Also required is Steven E. Brenner's *cgi-lib.pl* Perl library (*cgi-lib.berkeley.edu*), which is used to parse the arguments passed from the JavaScript link, and the `LWP` and `HTML::HeadParser` Perl modules, which are used to retrieve the auction title from the listing page.

Save this script as *track.pl* and place it in your web server's *cgi-bin* directory, as described in the Preface. Note that the `$selfurl` and `$localfile` variables ❶ must be modified to match the URL of your script and the location of the local file in which the auction titles are to be stored, respectively. Also, you may need to adjust the `$timeoffset` variable to compensate for the time zone difference between eBay time (Pacific time) and your computer's clock; e.g., enter `3` if you're in eastern time (GMT–5:00).

Running the Hack

With the script in place and the JavaScript link at the ready on your browser toolbar, all that's left is to try it out. Open any auction page on eBay and click the Track link on your Links bar. A new window will open, and the auction you were just looking at will appear at the top of the list, as shown in Figure 3-3. Repeat this for as many auctions as you like; there's virtually no limit. You can even track completed auctions and auctions that you haven't won.

Click the title of any auction to open the eBay listing page in a new window. Click the **x** link to delete the entry.

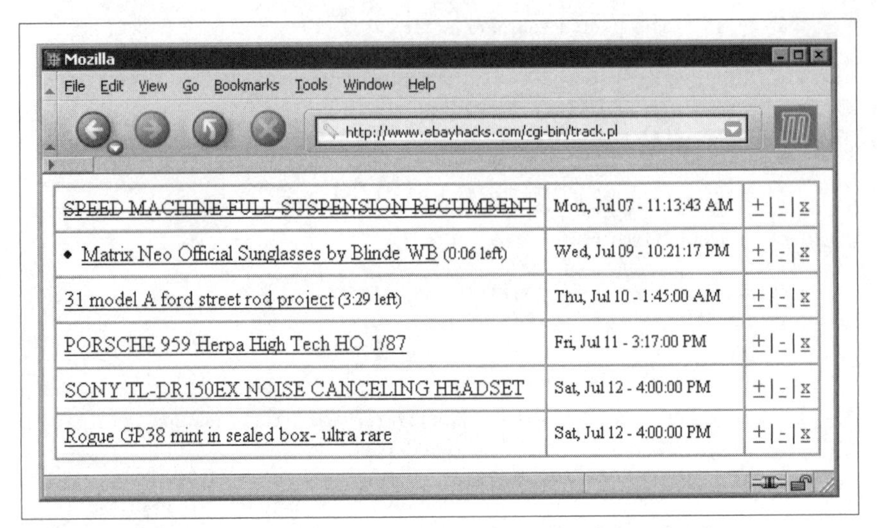

Figure 3-3. Track and prioritize auctions with this flexible web-based tool

Auctions can be prioritized; all new entries start out at the lowest priority and are shown in normal font. Click the + link to promote an auction and make its title bold. Click + again to promote the auction to the highest level and make its title red and bold. Likewise, click - to demote any entry. Higher-priority items appear higher in the list, and all auctions within a certain priority level are sorted by their closing date. I use the lowest priority for auctions on which I don't intend to bid, the medium priority for items I want, and the highest priority for items I've already bid on and won.

> Sellers often lower **[Hack #65]** the Buy It Now prices **[Hack #31]** of running auctions that haven't received bids, sometimes repeatedly. If you really want an item, it's a good idea to check back a few times before the end of the auction to see if you can snag it before someone else does.

As with all the hacks in this book, you can download the code for this hack at *ebayhacks.com*.

Hacking the Hack

Naturally, you'll want to customize this hack to suit your needs, which is really this tool's greatest advantage over eBay's Bidding/Watching page. Among the more interesting ways to hack this script are the following:

Add some spice. If you're familiar with HTML, you can add pictures and text to your heart's content. Add shading and even column headers (for sorting) to the table. Replace the +, -, and x links ❾ with more interesting icons, and add a splash of color to the page.

Add more levels. You can have as many different levels of prioritization as you like. Three levels suit my needs just fine, but you can add more by increasing the `$numlevels` variable ❸. (Keep in mind that lower numbers mean a higher priority.) The only other thing you'll need to maintain is the `@formatting` array ❷, which contains snippets of HTML code [Hack #52] (one for each priority level) that visually differentiate one priority level from another.

Add more links. Using the `$item[$idx[$j]]` variable ❺, you can also add links to bid, leave feedback, and view the bid history.

Add more users. To support multiple users, include another argument in the JavaScript link (Part 1), such as `&user=cletus`. Then, simply append the username to the filename to create a different auction list file ❶ for each user, like this:

```
$localfile = "/usr/local/home/ebaylist_\L$in{'user'}.txt";
```

Thus, the script will load the file appropriate to the specified username (in this case, *cletus.txt*).

Add more information. The script contains code that adds a little "richness" to the tool. For example, completed auctions have crossed-out titles ❼, auctions ending today are marked with round bullets ❻, and any auction ending within 24 hours shows the time left to bid ❽. I've found these additions to be quite helpful for my purposes, but you may have different needs. For example, if you're in front of your computer only during the day, you can configure the script to highlight auctions ending after 5:00 p.m. so you know you'll have to bid early or set up an automatic snipe [Hack #27].

Speed things up. The script retrieves the auction title ❹ by using the `&get_title` subroutine defined at the end of the script. This routine loads the page and then grabs the listing title, which can be time-consuming. To speed up the script, you can extract the auction title from the URL passed by the JavaScript link by replacing line ❹ with this code:

```
$title = substr($in{'title'}, $z + 2);
```

The caveat to this approach is that if the title contains an ampersand (&) or pound sign (#), the title will be broken apart, and all you'll get is the first portion. Also, the script determines the closing time and date by further parsing the title, and may not work with titles from non-U.S. sites that use a different date notation.

A more bulletproof (and only slightly more complex) solution to both of these problems would be to use the eBay API to retrieve the auction title and end date [Hack #111]. This would also enable you to reliably read the seller's name, the current price, and other auction details, all without having to resort to parsing.

Customize the pop up. The pop-up window can be customized by modifying the JavaScript code. For example, add the following to the JavaScript line:

```
,'width=400,height=300,menubar=no,status=no,resizable=yes,scrollbars=yes'
```

to assign a fixed size to the pop-up window. Make sure to place the code after `'Hack'` but before the two closing parentheses, and to include the comma and enclose the parameters as a whole in single quotes as shown. More information on these parameters can be found in any JavaScript documentation, under the `window.open` statement.

HACK #30 Take Advantage of Bid Increments

A slight adjustment to your bidding strategy will help you save money and win more auctions.

Every auction has a minimum bid, a dollar amount shown just above the Place Bid button on the auction page, as shown in Figure 3-4. If the auction hasn't received any bids, the minimum bid is the same as the starting bid. Otherwise, the minimum bid is equal to the current price plus a bid increment.

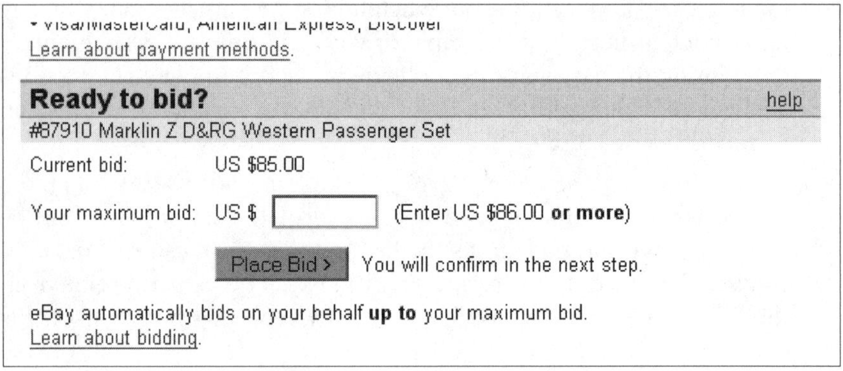

Figure 3-4. The Bidding Section shows the current bid increment and minimum bid

Bid increments, at least in theory, prevent bidders from outbidding one another by a single cent, and are calculated as follows:

Current price	Bid increment
$0.01–$0.99	$0.05
$1.00–$4.99	$0.25
$5.00–$24.99	$0.50
$25.00–$99.99	$1.00

Current price	Bid increment
$100.00–$249.99	$2.50
$250.00–$499.99	$5.00
$500.00–$999.99	$10.00
$1,000.00–$2,499.99	$25.00
$2,500.00–$4,999.99	$50.00
$5,000.00 and up	$100.00

For example, an auction currently at $68.45 will have a minimum bid of $69.45 (one dollar more), so you wouldn't be able to bid $69.00 even though it's higher than the current price.

Bid increments also come into play when calculating the current price. If there's more than one bidder, the current price is equal to the second-highest bidder's bid plus the bid increment. So if someone bids $114 and someone else bids $157, the current price will be $116.50 ($114 + $2.50), and the minimum bid for subsequent bidders will be $119 ($116.50 + $2.50).

As more bids are placed, the current price continues to rise, always equal to the second-highest bid plus the bid increment. But it gets more interesting when someone places a bid very close to the high bidder's maximum bid. The bid increment rule is compromised by another rule: eBay will never raise the current price above the highest bidder's maximum bid. Here's how this works:

- If someone bids $156.80 on this auction, it will raise the current bid to $157, even though it's only 20 cents above the second-highest bidder's maximum.
- If a subsequent bidder enters a bid of $157, the current price will be exactly $157. The original bidder will still be the high bidder, because earlier bids take precedence over later bids of the same amount.
- If the later bidder bids $157.01, the current price will be raised to $157.01 (one cent above the previous high bid), and the newcomer will become the high bidder.

This loophole effectively allows you to outbid another bidder by as little as a single cent. But why is this important, and how is this useful?

Outbidding the High Bidder

Bid amounts are always kept hidden until an auction closes. As described above, however, you can easily determine the second-highest bidder's maximum bid by subtracting the bid increment from the current price. Only the high bidder's maximum remains elusive.

Most bidders type whole, round numbers when bidding, primarily out of habit and sometimes out of laziness. You can take advantage of this by guessing a high bidder's maximum and adding a penny.

For example, if an auction with a starting bid of $7.99 has only one bidder, the current price is $7.99. If that bidder is relatively new to eBay (having a feedback rating of, say, less than 30), that bidder most likely typed either $8 or $10 as a maximum bid. Although you couldn't bid $8.01, as the minimum bid would be $8.49, you could bid $10.01 and have a pretty good chance of outbidding the other bidder by a single cent. Contrast this to a bid of $15.00, which would result in a final price of $10.50 ($10 plus the 50-cent increment). You've just saved 49 cents.

More experienced bidders won't type whole numbers, but they will likely be just as predictable. If you want to outbid someone by a single cent, try searching for past auctions they've bid on (see Chapter 2); look at the bidding history of closed auctions they didn't win, and you'll see their exact bids. Look at two or three old auctions, and you'll likely find a pattern.

Understanding bid increments is also extremely useful if you bid on an item, yet don't end up as the high bidder (wherein eBay immediately says you were outbid by someone else). If, after you bid, the current price ends up *lower* than your bid plus the bid increment (you bid $40 and the price rises to $40.17), then the high bidder's maximum bid is equal to the current price (in this case, $40.17). This means that all you need to do is place one more bid of at least $41.17 to put yourself in the lead. Combine this with sniping [Hack #27], and you've won the auction!

Taking It One Step Further

You can take steps to prevent other bidders from outbidding you by one cent (and they will) while allowing you to more readily outbid others. Instead of bidding whole, round numbers, make a habit of bidding odd numbers, such as $10.07 or $11.39. That way, if someone bids $10.01 or $11.01, respectively, you'll still be the high bidder. Likewise, you'll also be more likely to outbid others who type bid amounts like $10.01.

HACK #31 Manipulate Buy It Now Auctions

Save money with the loopholes of the Buy It Now feature.

The Buy It Now feature that appears in some auctions allows a bidder to bypass the bidding process and end an auction early at some predetermined price. Whether or not this is a good deal for the buyer, however, depends on the Buy It Now price the seller has chosen.

The Buy It Now option remains visible on the auction page until the first bid is placed, after which it disappears. (The exception is reserve-price auctions, where Buy It Now will be available as long as the reserve hasn't been met, regardless of the number of bids.) There are several ways to use this to your advantage.

Start with the Obvious

Some of the best deals on eBay are Buy It Now items, where the seller specifies too low a Buy It Now price, allowing you to snatch it before anyone else gets a chance. If you see a good price, why wait? Just click Buy It Now and end the auction without bidding.

There may be a reason that an auction has a low Buy It Now price; make sure you read the auction description carefully before you commit. And watch out for seller scams [Hack #25]. Buyers have the same obligation to complete Buy It Now transactions as those that end normally.

Click the Buy It Now tab in search results, and then sort by Newly Listed, and the newest Buy It Now auctions will appear first. This gives you a good chance to catch early deals, as they're unlikely to last more than a few hours.

Undercut the Buy It Now Feature

Auctions with too high a Buy It Now price are just as common as those with too low a Buy It Now price. But there will always be some yahoo who doesn't know any better, and will come along and buy these items anyway. If, however, you place a bid right away—say, the minimum amount—the Buy It Now option will disappear, and bidding will proceed normally. This will not only give you a chance to win the item for less than the Buy It Now amount, but will also give you more time to decide whether you really want the item. (This is an example of when it pays to bid *early*, a strategy contrary to that of sniping [Hack #26].)

This works best on auctions with artificially low starting bids, because bidding is likely to exceed your first bid and you'll be under no obligation to buy. For example, consider an auction with a Buy It Now price of $12 and a $1 minimum bid. Suppose you were to undercut the Buy It Now price by bidding $1; the item might then end up selling for less than $5, yet could easily have sold for $12 if someone who really wanted it got there before you.

Let this be a lesson to sellers to choose their starting bids and Buy It Now prices carefully. Had the seller in this example set the starting bid at $6 and the Buy It Now at $9, you might have bought it right away for $9. You would've been happy to get a deal, and the seller would've gotten twice as much for the item. See "What's It Worth?" [Hack #42] for similar strategies.

Naturally, you run the risk of the bidding exceeding the original Buy It Now price, something that happens often on eBay. But if the Buy It Now price is more than you're willing to pay, you're going to lose the auction either way.

There's also a chance that the auction won't get any other bids, and you'll end up winning the item with your starting bid. Assuming the bid was low enough, you should be happy to get a good deal. However, if you suspect that you may be stuck with something you don't want, you probably shouldn't bid, lest you be forced to try to retract your bid [Hack #32].

Let's Make a Deal

Buy It Now is an optional feature, chosen by sellers on a per-auction basis. A seller may not wish to include a Buy It Now price if she is unsure of the value of the item, or if she doesn't want to scare away early bidders with too high an opening price. The Buy It Now option is also available only to sellers with a feedback rating of 10 or higher, so sellers new to eBay won't be able to include it even if they want it. And as stated at the beginning of this hack, the Buy It Now feature disappears once bids have been placed on the auction.

For whatever reason, there will be an auction without a Buy It Now price, but that doesn't mean you can't "buy it now." Just contact the seller; in some cases, you'll be able to convince the seller to accept your offer and end the auction early.

Using eBay's resources to conduct business behind eBay's back is a blatant violation of eBay's policies. The purpose of this section is not to aide off-eBay transactions, but rather to enable communication between buyers and sellers to help close deals more quickly.

There are good and bad ways to broach the subject, and, as with many aspects of using eBay, diplomacy is very important here. The idea is to get what you want, but also to make it worth the seller's while.

Here are some *good* ways to request a Buy It Now:

"Do you have a Buy It Now price for this item?" This is polite and nonconfrontational, and the seller will typically respond with a price or ask you what you'd be willing to pay.

"Would you consider adding a Buy It Now price to this auction?" This is similar to the previous example, except that it doesn't send the message to the seller that you're trying to circumvent eBay's rules. Use this only if the auction hasn't yet received any bids. (See "Make Changes to Running Auctions" [Hack #65] for details on how sellers can accommodate this request. Remember, sellers with a feedback rating of less than 10 will not have this option.)

"Would you be willing to end the auction early for $250?" Pique the seller's interest by including a specific offer in your first email. Even if it's too low, you can always raise it later.

About half the sellers I've contacted with offers like these end up agreeing, and the other half have preferred to wait. In nearly all cases where a seller has declined to sell early to me, though, I ended up buying the item for less than my original offer. Let this be a lesson to both buyers and sellers!

Here are some examples of what *not* to do:

"Would you sell me the item for the current bid price?" Why would any seller sell at the current price when they can wait and most likely get more money? Remember, make it worth the seller's while, or they won't give you the time of day.

"I'll give you 50 bucks for it." The tone here is condescending and aggressive, and most sellers will respond poorly (if at all). Furthermore, if the bidding has been healthy and your offer is not much higher than the current price, the seller will probably take it as an insult that you'd expect her to sell so cheaply. You're asking the seller a favor, so be nice!

"What would it take to end the auction early?" Again, the tone is too aggressive, and the message offers the seller nothing for her trouble. Furthermore, it pressures the seller to quote a price right away, which is never good. Sellers put in this position will quote you a higher price for fear of quoting too low. It's much harder to haggle a seller down than to increase a low opening offer.

If a seller seems disagreeable to the whole idea, you're unlikely to convince her otherwise (unless you offer so much money that it's no longer worth *your* while).

You can often determine a seller's disposition before you write by simply reading the auction description and even the feedback comments she's left for others. If the seller's tone is relaxed and positive, then she'll be more likely to make a deal. If the prose is stiff and curt, the seller will likely want to proceed "by the book" and let the auction play out.

Assuming the seller agrees, you'll have three choices:

By the book. One, you can wait for the seller to add a Buy It Now price to the auction, and then purchase the item normally. Just make sure to check the auction page frequently and purchase it as soon as the option becomes available, lest someone beat you to it.

Become the high bidder. If the seller can't use Buy It Now for whatever reason, you can always bid and become the high bidder, with the understanding that the seller will then end the auction early and sell to you at the agreed price (regardless of the closing price of the auction). This allows both you and the seller to leave feedback for one another and use eBay's other services. Keep in mind, however, that this can be seen as a form of fee avoidance,* which is strictly prohibited on eBay.

Under the table. The other option is for the seller to cancel all bids, end the auction early, and then sell to you outside of eBay. The seller may prefer this, as it will save the eBay fees normally charged to successfully completed auctions (though possibly get her in trouble with eBay), but there will be little advantage for the buyer, because any transactions not completed through eBay aren't eligible for feedback, fraud protection, or any other services. Of course, this is also a clear violation of eBay policy, but you already knew that.

See Also

- See "Let's Make a Deal" [Hack #66] for strategies for sellers, as well as a few other options.

* Strictly speaking, it's against eBay policy for any user to intentionally circumvent the fee system, which should not be too surprising. But eBay also can't prevent members from completing transactions any way they choose, even if the end result is a coincidental lowering of the fees eBay ultimately receives.

HACK #32 Retract Your Bid Without Retracting Your Bid

Back out of an auction before it's too late.

There are many reasons you might want to back out of an auction after bidding. Obviously, if you make a mistake and bid the wrong amount or bid on the wrong auction, you'll want to retract that bid before the auction ends and you're obligated to pay.

But there are other reasonable circumstances under which you may change your mind about an auction. Sellers can make changes [Hack #65] to the description or photos, even after the item has received bids, and such changes may affect your desire for an item or your ability to pay for it. Or, if you lose your job and find your daughter needs braces, your desperate need for that 50-inch plasma TV may become slightly less desperate.

eBay takes bidding very seriously, to the point of imposing restrictions as to when and under what circumstances you can retract a bid. This is understandable, considering the scams a small minority of eBay users have propagated; look up "buying offenses" in eBay's Help for an exhaustive list (and lots of ideas, too).

By the Book

The easiest way to retract a bid is to use the "Retract my bid" form. Simply enter the auction number, choose one of the prewritten excuses from the list, and click Retract Bid. (It doesn't really matter which reason you choose; the end result will be the same.) All your bids on the auction will be canceled, and the auction's current price will be adjusted accordingly.

Not surprisingly, you can't retract a bid *after* an auction ends under any circumstances. Keep this in mind any time you bid, and especially when you snipe [Hack #26].

The problem is that bid retractions are shown on your feedback page for six months, and while it doesn't actually affect your feedback rating, excessive bid retractions may make you appear less trustworthy and certainly less serious to other members. Furthermore, a pattern of bid retractions may arouse the suspicions of eBay's investigations department; at the extreme, your account may be suspended if eBay suspects abuse of their system.

This is also where eBay's restrictions come into play: during the last 12 hours of an auction, you are not allowed to retract any bid placed *before* the final 12 hours.* Furthermore, if you bid in those last 12 hours, you can only retract your bid within one hour of placing it. Note that because of this restriction, sellers are not allowed to make certain changes to their auctions within the last 12 hours.

Getting Help from the Seller

If you find that you need to retract a bid but either don't want to or, due to eBay's restrictions, are unable to, you can still contact the seller and ask to have your bid canceled. A seller can cancel any bid on his auction at any time, and for any reason.

Keep in mind that you're asking a favor of the seller by requesting to have your bid canceled, so be especially polite and apologetic. Here are a few examples of good excuses:

- *"Would you mind canceling my bid? I just read your auction more carefully and discovered that I'll be unable to pay. I'm sorry for the inconvenience."* The last thing the seller wants is a deadbeat bidder, so make him feel it's in his best interest to cancel your bid. But try not to give the impression that you simply didn't read the description before you bid.
- *"Could you possibly cancel my bid on auction #3125058177? I made a mistake in my bid, but since there are fewer than 12 hours left in the auction, eBay won't let me retract."* eBay's bid retraction rules can be a little confusing, so don't be afraid to educate the seller on eBay policies.

The decision of whether to grant your request is completely up to the seller, and there are valid reasons why he may not agree. For example, if there's more than one bidder, canceling your bid may lower the current price. Or the seller may be desperate to unload the item, and if you're the only bidder, you're his ticket to freedom.

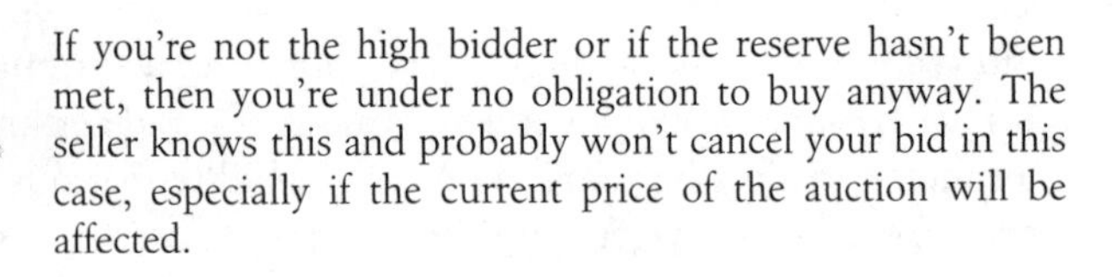

If you're not the high bidder or if the reserve hasn't been met, then you're under no obligation to buy anyway. The seller knows this and probably won't cancel your bid in this case, especially if the current price of the auction will be affected.

* The idea is to curb two different kinds of bidding abuse: *shill bidding* (where a friend of the seller bids to raise the price) and *bid shielding* (where a friend of the high bidder bids high and then retracts so the auction ends with an artificially low price).

The following excuses will probably just anger the seller, and should be avoided:

- *"I just bought another one of these from another seller on eBay, and I no longer need yours."* You should never bid on multiple auctions when you only intend to pay for one, and sellers know this. If you're currently the high bidder, the seller may let your bid stand just to teach you a lesson. (See "Snipe It Conditionally" [Hack #28] for a way to safely bid on multiple auctions.)
- *"I noticed another auction with a lower price, so I'd rather bid on that one."* This is a slap in the face, and a clear indication to the seller that you're wasting his time. Again, he may leave your bid intact out of spite alone.

Like much of using eBay, getting out of sticky situations requires diplomacy, careful wording, and an understanding that you won't always get your way.

Getting Out of Your Obligation

eBay is a community built on trust, as well as an understanding by buyers and sellers that successfully completed auctions are legally binding contracts. But it's also naïve to expect that all sellers are trustworthy and all transactions can go smoothly. Sometimes, you need to back out.

The easiest—and worst—way to back out of an auction is to simply not pay. Ignore all of a seller's emails and the eventual payment reminders and warnings from eBay. Do this once, and you'll get a nasty, negative feedback comment from the seller. Do this three times, and you'll be suspended from eBay indefinitely.

Only the seller can release you of your obligation to pay for an auction you've won, so it's typically a matter of delicate diplomacy to try to convince a seller to consider the auction void and not retaliate with negative feedback or nonpaying bidder alerts [Hack #89]. See the previous section for examples of some approaches that work and some that don't.

If you decide not to complete a transaction because you suspect fraud [Hack #25] or an illegal account takeover [Hack #25], the first thing you should do is contact the seller and express your concerns. For fear of eBay cracking down and possible legal consequences, the seller will probably just let it drop and not retaliate with negative feedback. At this point, you can contact eBay and ask them to investigate the seller. If the seller is suspended or the auction voided, the obligation will disappear, as will the seller's ability to leave feedback for you.

If, on the other hand, there is really nothing wrong with the seller or the auction, you should do everything you can to complete the transaction. If it turns out that you simply no longer need or want the item, you can always resell it on eBay, possibly for more than you paid!

HACK #33 Send Payment Quickly and Safely

Here are the best—and worst—ways to pay for an auction.

It's your money, and you can do anything you want with it. That said, I don't want to see any of you stuffing dollar coins up your nose or sending cash through postal mail.

Electronic payments have become the most popular method of paying for auctions on eBay, and for good reason—sending money online is by far the safest, quickest, and cheapest way to pay, for both buyers and sellers.

When deciding how to pay for an auction you've won, or when choosing an auction in the first place, look for any payment method that can be funded by a credit card. Although some people are downright terrified of the prospect of transmitting credit card numbers over the Internet, credit cards are indeed the safest way to pay online because you can dispute any charge on your statement.

You can dispute any unauthorized charge, any payment made to a seller who doesn't ship, or any payment that was not refunded after you returned an item. It's as simple as making a phone call to your credit card company, and is undoubtedly more productive than trying to find out what happened to a check you mailed six weeks ago. Some cards even offer extended buyer-protection services, such as replacement insurance.

Sellers choose which payment methods to accept, so make sure you review the seller's instructions *before you bid*. Once you bid, you're pretty much locked into whatever payment terms the seller has specified (although there are ways to get out of your obligation [Hack #32] if you find that you can't pay).

If the item you want is offered by several sellers, shop around for the listing with the best payment terms.

Avoid auctions by sellers with overly restrictive payment terms. A seller who accepts only Western Union money orders, for example, may be trying to rip you off (see [Hack #25]), or at least will be more of a hassle to deal with than a seller who accepts online payments. (Let this be a lesson to sellers, too: if you want more bids, give your customers more ways to pay.)

PayPal

PayPal allows you to send a payment to almost anyone with an email address, whether or not the payment is for an eBay auction. Payments are usually made instantly, allowing sellers to ship the same day you win an auction. See the "Signing Up with PayPal" sidebar if you don't yet have a PayPal account.

Signing Up with PayPal

To get a free PayPal account, just go to *www.paypal.com*, click Sign Up, and follow the instructions. They'll ask for the usual information, such as your name, address, email, and a username and password. What may not be clear, however, is that the amount of additional information you provide drastically affects your standing on PayPal, and thus your ability to send and receive auction payments.

First, there are three different types of accounts: Personal, Premier, and Business. A Personal account, the default, allows you to send and receive money at no charge, but comes with severe restrictions on the amount of money you can send and the types of payment you can receive. If you're serious about eBay, you'll need to upgrade to a Business or Premier account. Although the "upgrade" paradoxically means that PayPal will begin charging a percentage of all payments you receive, the restrictions will be lifted, and you'll be able to do things like accept credit card payments. And sending money will continue to be completely free, regardless of the type of account you have. (Note that Business and Premier accounts are essentially the same thing—the only real difference is the name seen by buyers and sellers with whom you conduct transactions.)

If at all possible, you'll want to link a credit card to your PayPal account. Not only will this allow you to pay for auctions with your credit card, but you'll be able to "confirm your address," a step required by many sellers (see "Protect Yourself While Accepting Payments" **[Hack #85]** for an explanation). You'll also want to link a checking account into which you can transfer money you've received from auction payments.

Once a serious competitor to eBay's now-defunct BillPoint system, PayPal is now owned by eBay, and their services are tightly integrated into eBay's checkout system. If a seller accepts PayPal payments, a PayPal logo will usually appear in the Payment section of the auction details or underneath the auction description, as shown in Figure 3-5.

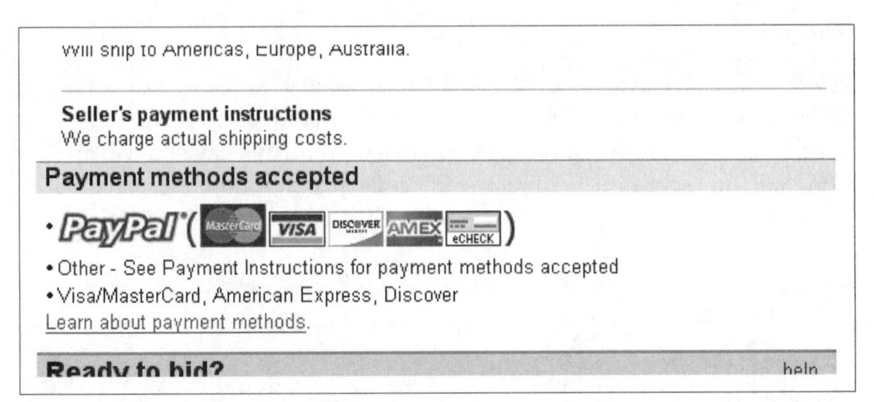

Will ship to Americas, Europe, Australia.
Seller's payment instructions
We charge actual shipping costs.
Payment methods accepted
PayPal
VISA
DISCOVER
AMEX
eCHECK
• Other - See Payment Instructions for payment methods accepted
• Visa/MasterCard, American Express, Discover
Learn about payment methods.
Ready to bid?
help

Figure 3-5. Look for the PayPal logo at the bottom of eBay listings if you want to pay for an item with PayPal

If you're the high bidder on a completed eBay auction (and the seller has elected to accept PayPal), simply click the Pay Now button **[Hack #64]** at the top of the auction page to go to the PayPal site (*www.paypal.com*) and complete the transaction. Or, to send a payment to anyone (without going through eBay), go directly to *www.paypal.com*, log in, click Send Money, and type the email address of the recipient and the amount to send.

PayPal automatically notifies sellers when they receive payments, but these emails can sometimes be delayed or even lost. Make sure to contact your sellers directly to be certain they're aware of your payment.

Note that if there's no PayPal logo on the listing page, it doesn't necessarily mean the seller doesn't accept PayPal payments, only that he or she perhaps didn't take the time to choose the correct options when constructing his auction. Look in the description itself or in the Payment Instructions box for clues; if in doubt, simply ask.

Your PayPal account has its own balance, like an ordinary bank account. Any payments you receive are added to your PayPal balance, which can then be transferred to a bank account or used to fund other auction payments.

But the beauty of PayPal is that you can pay for eBay items with a credit card even if the seller doesn't accept credit cards directly. You can also fund your PayPal payments with electronic bank account transfers, money in your PayPal balance, or PayPal *eChecks*. (You can even fund payments with airline frequent-flyer miles or other "partner" awards; see *anythingpoints.ebay.com* for details.)

If you have any money in your PayPal account, the default source of funds for payments is always your PayPal balance. If your balance is zero, the default is an electronic bank transfer. Either way, you can choose to fund your payment with a credit card **[Hack #35]** if you want the maximum level of protection.

Because PayPal offers three different types of accounts, a particular seller may have a restriction on what types of PayPal payments she can accept. New PayPal users with Personal accounts can receive all payments funded by a bank transfer for free (up to a limit), but will not be able to receive large payments or any payments funded by a credit card. More serious sellers upgrade to Premier or Business accounts (as described in the "Signing Up with PayPal" sidebar) so they can receive all types of payments, but pay a small percentage (about 3%) on all payments they receive.

Credit Cards

Sellers who are also credit card merchants **[Hack #85]** will be able to accept your credit card directly, without the use of an online payment system like PayPal. While paying directly has little advantage for buyers, it may be the best choice for sellers who don't accept PayPal.

If you frequently use your credit card online, you may wish to get a separate credit card only for online purchases. That way, if your credit card number is ever stolen, you'll still be able to buy groceries at the Piggly Wiggly down the street.

The main hurdle to paying directly with your credit card is finding a safe and convenient way to transmit your credit card number and expiration date to the seller. The seller may provide a web site address, but make sure the URL starts with *https://* (as opposed to *http://*) and the little yellow padlock on your browser's status bar is glowing and in the "locked" position (see Figure 3-6); these are your browser's ways of telling you that your connection to the server is secure and appropriate for transmitting sensitive information like credit card numbers. Also, look at the entire address of the page, and make sure you know where your information is going. While some sellers have their own secure web sites, many use third-party checkout services **[Hack #96]** such as Vendio (*www.vendio.com*) and Andale (*www.andale.com*). If you're not familiar with the company, look at their home page to learn more before you send any sensitive information.

You may also be able to phone or fax your order, if you still remember how to use such devices. Or, as a last resort, you can email your payment infor-

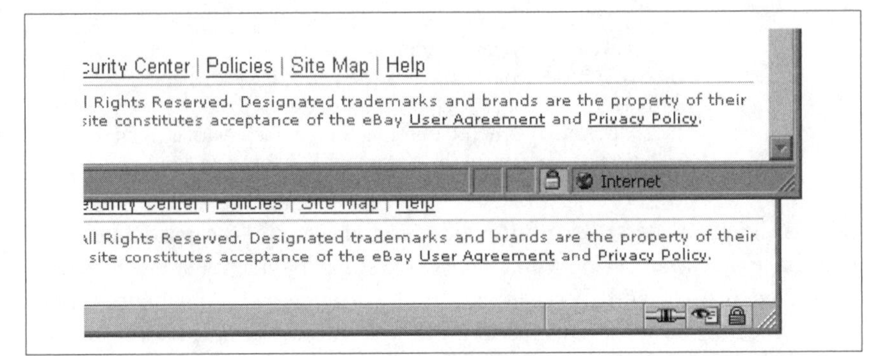

Figure 3-6. The little padlocks at the bottom of your browser window (both Internet Explorer and Mozilla shown here) tell you that you are using a secure connection

mation, but given that email is insecure, unreliable, and not even a little private, it's a poor choice. If you must use email, try breaking your number into multiple emails: send the first eight digits and expiration date in one message, then send the second eight digits in another message an hour later.

BidPay

BidPay (*www.bidpay.com*) allows you to use your credit card to purchase a Western Union money order online. This is great for the buyer who wants the protection offered by his credit card company, but has won an auction for which the only way to pay is to send a money order through postal mail.

There are drawbacks to BidPay, however. Sending payments through postal mail can delay shipment by several days (up to a week), and the buyer pays all fees (BidPay costs sellers nothing). Finally, BidPay can be used only to pay for eBay auctions, and is notorious for canceling payments without any explanation.

See Also

- See "Smooth Out International Transactions" **[Hack #37]** for additional ways to pay sellers in other countries, especially those that don't accept PayPal or credit cards.

HACK #34 Pay PayPal's Seller Fees

Make PayPal a no-cost option for sellers reluctant to part with 3% of the money you send them.

If you're a PayPal addict, you'll soon start avoiding listings in which PayPal isn't an available payment method. You can even have eBay filter search results to show only PayPal-enabled listings (click the Customize link in the

Search Options box if you don't see the Items Listed with PayPal option on search results pages). But that's a little excessive, isn't it? What if you see something you really want—something rare—sold by someone who won't accept PayPal?

Nearly all sellers who refuse online payments such as PayPal do so for one of three reasons. First, inexperienced sellers may simply not know how to accept such payments; in this case, you can politely offer to walk them through the process. Second, a previous bad experience may have turned a seller against online payment services, and it's unlikely that a single anxious buyer will change his mind. Finally, the seller may simply not want to pay the associated fees—this is where you have the most latitude.

Nothing speaks to people like money. PayPal takes about 3% of any payment a seller receives. Some sellers refuse PayPal payments merely to avoid paying the fees, despite the fact that the PayPal logo on their auctions will almost certainly get them more than enough additional business to make up for the fees. If this is the case, the seller may happily accept your payment if you offer to pay the fees yourself.

A Little Light Math

Not wanting to waste money, you'll want to calculate the amount to send so that the seller receives exactly the requested amount. Assuming PayPal takes 2.9% plus 30 cents for each transaction,* the total amount to pay is calculated as follows:

$$total = \frac{(subtotal + 0.30)}{1 - 0.029}$$

So, if you need a seller to ultimately receive $53.25 (the *subtotal*), you'd send a *total* of $55.15, or an additional $1.90. The seller is happy, and you get the additional security and convenience of paying online for less than two bucks.

Let PayPal Do It

If arithmetic is not your strong suit, PayPal has a little-known feature that lets you send payments while covering the fees yourself. The Mass Pay feature, designed to allow you to send payments to many different people at once, is admittedly a little cumbersome for only a single payee. But it also has one distinct advantage: the fees charged for Mass Pay are lower than standard seller fees!

* This is the standard rate charged to PayPal users with Business and Premier accounts. As always, your seller's mileage may vary.

At the time of this writing, the fee to send a Mass Pay payment is 2% of the payment amount, with a cap at US$1.00. (Compare this with the standard 2.9%, with no cap, charged to sellers.) Thus, it'll cost only 10 cents to send a US$5.00 payment, up to a maximum of only one dollar to send any payment of US$50.00 or more. (The catch is that Mass Pay fees are nonrefundable, even if the recipient returns the payment to you.)

To pay a seller with Mass Pay, follow these steps:

1. The funds for your payment must already be in your PayPal account; if you don't have a balance sufficient to cover the purchase and associated fees, go to your main PayPal account screen and click Add Funds.
2. In order to provide PayPal with the payment information, you'll need to prepare a special data file. Don't worry; it's easy. Open a plain text editor (e.g., Windows users can use Notepad), and type the recipient's email address, the amount of the payment, and the currency* (each separated with a tab), like this:

   ```
   dave@ebayhacks.com      $25      USD
   ```

   Make sure to include the dollar sign ($) and currency identifier (`USD`, in this case).
3. Save the file as *masspay.txt*.
4. Click the Mass Pay link at the bottom of any PayPal page.
5. Click the Make a Mass Payment! link.
6. Click Browse, and select the *masspay.txt* file you just created.

   (If you're using an older browser in Windows, you may have to select "All Files" from the "Files of type" list at the bottom of the Browse window before you'll see your file.)
7. Since the payment won't be automatically linked up with any specific eBay transaction, type a brief note to explain to the recipient what the payment is for.

If you're paying several people at once (which is the intent of this tool), this note will be included with all your payments. To send a different note to each recipient, type your notes in the fifth column (add two tabs after the currency type in the data file) of the data file before you upload it.

* The currency can be `USD` for U.S. dollars, `EUR` for euros, `GBP` for pounds sterling, `AUD` for Australian dollars, `CAD` for Canadian dollars, or `JPY` for yen.

8. Click Continue when you're done.
9. The next page, shown in Figure 3-7, shows the number of payments you're about to make (one, presumably), the total amount you're about to send, and the total fees assessed to your account. Click Send Money when you're done.

PayPal®

Log Out | Help

My Account | Send Money | Request Money | Merchant Tools | Auction Tools

Mass Payment

Secure Transaction

We've successfully read your file. Please confirm your Mass Payment.

Total Payments: 1
Payment Amount: $25.00 USD
Fee Amount: $0.50 USD
Total Amount: $25.50 USD

For confirmation, these are the first 5 and last 5 items in your Mass Payment file

Mass Payment File: dave@ebayhacks.com $25 USD

Email Subject: Because you're cheap
Note: Your note will retain its email format.

Send Money | Cancel

Mobile | Mass Pay | Money Market | ATM/Debit Card | BillPay | Referrals | About Us | Accounts | Fees | Privacy | Buyer Credit | Security Center | Contact Us | User Agreement | Developers | Shops | Gift Certificates/Points

PayPal, an eBay company

Copyright © 1999-2005 PayPal. All rights reserved.

Figure 3-7. Use PayPal's Mass Pay feature to send a payment while covering the seller fees yourself, and save money while you're at it

At this point, the payment makes its way to the seller just like any PayPal payment would, albeit after a short "processing delay." The recipient receives an email notification with details about your payment, and the payment appears in the recipient's account history. The big difference is that the fees are deducted from your account, not the seller's.

HACK #35 Use PayPal Without Depleting Your PayPal Balance

Temporarily zero your balance so you can choose how to fund your PayPal payments, even when you have money in your account.

Each time you make a payment with PayPal, the Source of Funds displayed on the Check Payment Details page (Figure 3-8) shows where the money will come from before you pay.

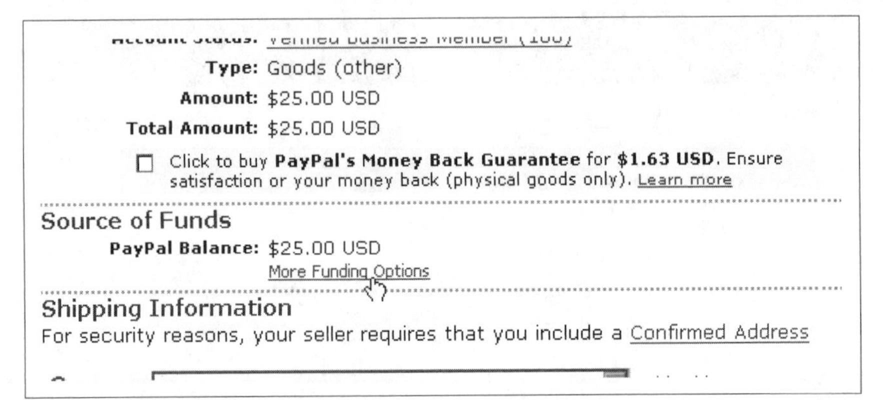

Figure 3-8. Always review where the money is coming from when you pay with PayPal

Click More Funding Options to display the Funding Options page, shown in Figure 3-9.

The choices shown depend on several factors, including which accounts you've added to your PayPal account, as well as a set of rules defining a hierarchy of payment methods:

PayPal Balance. If you have money sitting in your PayPal account (presumably from having sold something previously), your balance is always used first to fund your payment. Only if the amount of your payment exceeds your balance will you be able to choose from among the remaining sources to fund the remainder of the payment. (See the next section of this hack for a workaround.) The exception is the eCheck option, which can be used at any time.

Instant Transfer. Choose this option to draw the funds directly from your bank account. (This option is available only if you've linked a checking account to your PayPal account, a step required to become verified.)

Although PayPal doesn't actually get the funds from your bank for several days (thus, the transfer is not technically instant), the seller will get your payment immediately after you send it. To negotiate this, PayPal

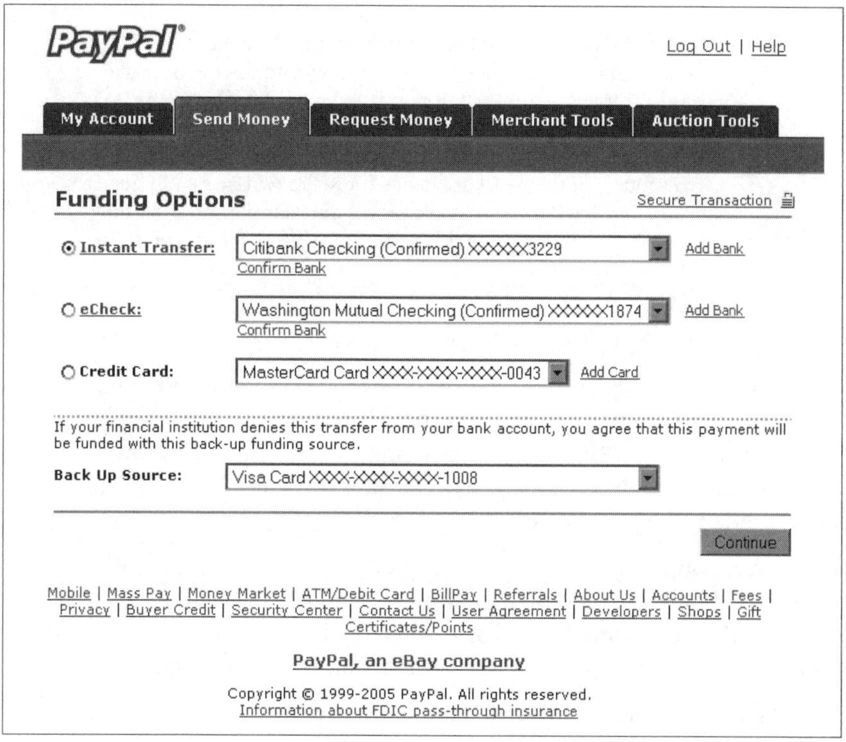

Figure 3-9. Choose a different funding source if you don't want to use the default when making a PayPal payment

requires a *backup funding source* be used in the event that the bank transfer fails (i.e., the transfer bounces). Your credit card (provided you have one connected to your PayPal account) is normally used as the backup funding source; without one, you might have to send an eCheck instead.

Credit Card. PayPal lets you pay with your credit card or debit card, but only if the recipient has a Premier or Business account with PayPal. If you're based in the U.S., you can pay with Visa, MasterCard, American Express, or Discover. In the U.K., Switch and Solo are also supported. See "Send Payment Quickly and Safely" **[Hack #33]** for an explanation of why payment by credit card may be preferable to the other options here.

eCheck. An eCheck is a noninstant bank transfer, for which your payment will remain pending until PayPal actually receives the funds from your bank. When the bank transfer clears, usually two to four business days, PayPal deposits the money in the recipient's account. eChecks are useful for large payments (greater than $1,000), since they can be used when other payment options aren't available (if, for example, you have maxed out your credit card).

The maximum fee assessed to an eCheck recipient is $5.00. This means that eChecks are a good way to lower your seller fees [Hack #68], at least for any payment of US$162.07 or more. Although you, as the buyer, will not directly benefit from this price advantage, you might be able to negotiate a discount on the purchase, since the seller will be saving quite a bit on PayPal transaction fees. For example, on a $1,000 purchase, the seller could stand to save $17.90 to $24.30 in transaction fees.

Paying Without Using Your Balance

If you have a balance in your PayPal account, you'll have no choice but to use it to fund your payments (at least until it has been depleted). As described in "Send Payment Quickly and Safely" [Hack #33], however, payments funded by a PayPal balance don't offer the same level of protection as those funded by a credit card.

Of course, you can withdraw your balance to your checking account to zero your PayPal balance, but you may want to keep it in place to fund other payments. So, here's a simple workaround that allows you to *temporarily* bring your PayPal balance down to zero before making your payment:

1. Make a payment to an email address that you control but that isn't registered with PayPal. Set the amount of the payment equal to the balance in your PayPal account. The status of the payment will be pending (or rather, "Unclaimed"), because it was sent to an email address that is not registered with PayPal, but the funds will remain tied up in the transaction.
2. Make your payment, and fund it any way you like (e.g., with a credit card or instant transfer).
3. When you're done, go to your payment history, find the Unclaimed payment you made to yourself, and click Cancel. The funds will be moved back into your PayPal account.

This way you can choose, for instance, to send balance-funded payments only to friends and people with whom you've previously done business, while still protecting yourself when transacting with strangers.

Access eBay from a Cell Phone or PDA

Use a variety of tools designed to work on that tiny screen.

How many times have you been walking down the street, hoping against hope that you could bid on that beautiful crystal rooster you saw on eBay earlier that morning? Okay, it probably doesn't happen that often, and if it does, you should really seek help. But isn't it nice to know you can access eBay just about anywhere?

If your cell phone or PDA supports *Wireless Application Protocol* (WAP) web sites (also known as *Wireless Web*), select Go to URL (or something similar), enter `wap.ebay.com`, and click OK.

As shown in Figure 3-10, eBay's WAP site lets you search, bid, browse categories, and manage your My eBay buying, selling, and watching lists, all from the tiny seven-line screen on your cell phone.

Figure 3-10. Use eBay's WAP-enabled web site to search current listings from your cell phone

Test any WAP site from your Windows PC with the Klondike WAP Browser (available free from *www.apachesoftware.com*) or the Openwave Mobile SDK (from *developer.openwave.com*). Although your PDA might have a web browser that supports real web sites, you can still access the fast, lean WAP sites mentioned in this hack with the WAPUniverse Mobile Internet Browser (*www.wapuniverse.com*) on your Palm. Or, if you're using a PocketPC, see *www.filesaveas.com/pocketpcwap.html* for help connecting to a WAP site with Mobile Internet Explorer.

eBay's WAP site is, unfortunately, rather spare. If you want richer wireless eBay content, check out Bonfire Media's Pocket Auctions (*www.bonfiremedia.com*) and Vindigo's AwayAuction for eBay (*www.vindigostudios.com*).

Let eBay Know You're on the Road

eBay can send an SMS text message to your cell phone or pager whenever you win or are outbid. To sign up, go to My eBay → eBay Preferences → Notification preferences → Add or change notification services → Subscribe. Then, enter the email address (provided by your wireless carrier) to which messages should be sent. Go to *pages.ebay.com/wireless* to learn more about eBay's support for wireless devices.

If you spend a lot of time with your cell phone, you may be interested in Wireless Rebidding (*www.rebid.com*), which offers outbid alerts and quick "rebidding" from your cell phone. Of course, with automatic sniping services [Hack #27] at your disposal, there's little reason ever to rebid on an auction, but it's nice to have the option nonetheless.

Send a PayPal Payment from the Road

Don't keep your sellers waiting; use your cell phone to send a PayPal payment to anyone. Just go to *www.paypal.com*, and PayPal's WAP site will automatically appear if you're using a WAP-enabled browser. Provided you already have a PayPal account [Hack #33], you can use your cell phone to send a payment or check to see if you've received a payment.

To request a payment with your cell phone, send an ordinary text message to the other person; just include `paypal.com` in the message, and the recipient will be able to select it to go to the PayPal WAP site.

With PayPal on your cell phone, you'll never be stuck at a garage sale without cash again!

Smooth Out International Transactions

Overcome the hurdles and gotchas associated with trading with members in other countries.

Everything gets a little more complicated when trading across international borders. Language barriers, currency confusion, payment hassles, and high shipping costs are all common problems. Here are some of the tools at your disposal to help simplify international transactions.

View Auctions on Your Native eBay

Although eBay has several international sites [Hack #19], all auctions are contained in the same global database. For example, if you're looking at an auction on the German eBay, like this one:

```
http://cgi.ebay.de/ws/eBayISAPI.dll?ViewItem&item=3128013702
```

You can simply change the domain from `ebay.de` to `ebay.com`, for example, and you'll see the auction details in more familiar terms:

```
http://cgi.ebay.com/ws/eBayISAPI.dll?ViewItem&item=3128013702
```

The currency used for the starting bid, current price, and minimum bid will all be automatically converted to your native currency. Additionally, the end time will be changed to your country's local time (e.g., Pacific time for *eBay.com* or eastern time for *eBay.ca*), and the payment and shipping terms will be translated into your native language. Almost every part of the auction page is changed—except for the auction description. See "Search Internationally" [Hack #19] if you want to convert an auction page back to its native language to enable access to its category.

Enter the Babel Fish

If the auction description is not in your native language, you'll have to translate it manually. The easiest way is to copy and paste the URL of the listing page (or a portion of the auction description) into an online translator, such as the following sites (all free):

AltaVista Babel Fish
: *babelfish.altavista.com*

Dictionary.com Translator
: *dictionary.com/translate*

FreeTranslation.com
: *www.freetranslation.com*

Google Language Tools
: *www.google.com/language_tools*

The languages supported by these tools, collectively, include Chinese (Simplified and Traditional), Dutch, English, French, German, Greek, Italian, Japanese, Korean, Norwegian, Portuguese, Russian, and Spanish.

Keep in mind that these automated translations are performed on-the-fly and are based primarily on strict definition conversions, and are therefore far from perfect. Still, they will help you get the gist of the description, and even translate your email messages to other members.

When emailing other eBay members in a language you don't speak fluently, be sure to include both your assisted translation and the original text in your native language. That way, the likelihood that your recipient will receive something like "bite the wax tadpole" will be somewhat more remote.

Paying and Shipping over Great Distances

Sellers in other countries are typically less likely to accept the payment methods used in your own country. For example, few sellers outside North America accept credit cards or PayPal, and virtually nobody outside Europe uses electronic bank account transfers. With fewer choices, you may have to resort to a less secure payment method.

Compound this with the other risks inherent in sending money to other countries (e.g., fluctuating exchange rates, flaky postal services, unfamiliar mailing addresses), and buying internationally becomes downright dangerous.

If the seller doesn't accept online payments or credit cards, your choices are pretty much restricted to the following:

International postal money order
: If you need to send a check or money order, probably the best choice is an international postal money order (as opposed to the no-postal kind), as the recipient will usually be able to cash it without any additional fees (which, of course, you'd have to pay). Although there's no practical way to retrieve your money once the check is cashed, you can at least get your money back if the money order is lost in the mail. You can buy international postal money orders from your local post office.

Electronic bank account transfer
: When buying from Germany and some other European countries, a bank account transfer is the fastest way to pay. Although it's secure in terms of the money safely reaching the recipient, buyers have virtually no protection if the seller doesn't ship. Unfortunately, electronic transfers are quite expensive in North America, making them impractical for small purchases. Contact your bank for details.

Interac email money transfer
: If you bank in Canada, or have a friend that does, you can send an electronic money transfer to a Canadian seller by going to *www.certapay.com*.

Credit card via Borderfree
: Borderfree (*www.borderfree.com*) works somewhat like eBay's Escrow service, but is intended for U.S.-based sellers who aren't quite comfortable or equipped to sell and ship internationally. Here's how it works: you send a request through Borderfree, and if the seller agrees, you pay

for your item (plus an extra fee) with your credit card. The seller ships the item to Borderfree, which then forwards your payment to the seller via PayPal [Hack #33], and ships the item to you.

Cash

A fool and his money are soon parted, a process that is significantly accelerated if you bring the postal service into the mix. Sometimes, though, it's your only option, but don't be surprised if the seller receives an empty envelope (or no envelope at all). If you insist on sending cash through postal mail (something the post office even discourages) make it look as much like an ordinary letter as possible by folding it between several pieces of paper and sealing it in a number-10 envelope. That way, it'll be less likely to be opened by customs.

Finally, give some thought to the shipping options (if any) offered by the seller, and don't just choose the cheapest one. For example, say you purchase a $300 item from a seller overseas, for which you can pay with an international postal money order. The seller has good feedback, but you don't want to take any chances. The shipping choices include surface shipping for about $50 and EMS (Express Mail) for $80; rather than go with the slower shipping option and risk the package arriving after you could leave feedback (Chapter 1) or file a dispute [Hack #41], it may be worth the extra $30 for the security of getting the package within a week.

Save Money on Shipping

Save the seller time, get your item sooner, and cough up less money for shipping.

I hate being ripped off, and one of the most common rip-offs on eBay is inflated shipping charges. The problem is that most sellers who overcharge for shipping don't even know they're doing it.

Sellers want to cover all their costs, so it's the buyer who ends up footing the bill for packing materials, shipping charges, insurance, and the bagel the seller ate while waiting in line at the post office. But even those who ask that you only cover legitimate shipping fees may still be charging too much, simply because they don't know a cheaper or more efficient shipping method.

If you don't know what method of shipping a seller will use, just ask. You have a right to know what you're paying for, and many sellers will be willing to use a cheaper (or faster) shipping option if you request it.

The problem is that most sellers don't care how much they spend on shipping because, in theory anyway, the buyer is the one paying for it.

A Little Knowledge Can Be Dangerous

Fortunately, every buyer has access to the same tools sellers use to estimate shipping costs. The first thing to do when quoted a shipping charge that seems a tad high is to look it up for yourself.

The three largest couriers in the U.S. are FedEx (*www.fedex.com*), UPS (*www.ups.com*), and the United States Postal Service (*www.usps.com*), and all three have online shipping-cost calculators. Most couriers in other countries have similar services **[Hack #37]**.

Typically, all you need for a shipping-cost quote are the origin and destination Zip Codes and the weight of the package.* The origin Zip Code can be found in the seller's mailing address, usually included with any payment instructions; if not, use Google to look up the Zip Code for the item location **[Hack #39]**. The destination Zip Code is simply your Zip Code, which you already know (hopefully). If you don't know the weight of the item, just take a guess. Make sure to include extras like insurance and residential delivery surcharges when choosing your shipping options.

Armed with the actual cost to ship your item, possibly from several different couriers, you now have two options (assuming your quote is better than the seller's). Either you can contact the seller and request a different shipping method, or better yet, you can offer to take care of shipping yourself.

Excuse Me While I Take Over

People are creatures of habit, and as such require a bit of careful persuasion before they'll change their routines. This is especially true of sellers, who won't want to spend any extra money or time on you or your package. If you want to save money to ship your package, you have to make it worth the seller's while.

As described in "Ship Cheaply Without Waiting in Line" **[Hack #86]**, the fastest and cheapest way to ship a package is almost always to use a prepaid shipping label. Using the same technique, you can create a shipping label addressed to yourself, and then email the label to the seller. Among other things, this ensures that you're not paying any unnecessary "handling" fees the seller might otherwise tack on.

* Some shippers also ask for the package dimensions, but these rarely affect the price quoted. If in doubt, just make an educated guess.

Before asking the seller to ship with your prepaid label, make sure there's a drop-off location nearby. Type the seller's Zip Code into your courier's online location finder to locate the closest drop-off box or counter. Most often, there will be one within a mile or two; if not, you may have to scrap your plan. Note that you can often schedule a pickup if there's no drop-off location close to the seller, but this may cost extra.

Before you snap into action, ask the seller if she would be willing to ship your way:

- "Would you be willing to use a prepaid shipping label I send you? All you'd have to do is affix the label to the package and drop it off. I'd save money, and you wouldn't have to fret about shipping details or wait in line at the post office. If this sounds OK, just email me the weight and dimensions of the package."
- "I have a shipping alternative that should save you time and save me money. All I need from you are the weight and dimensions of the package, and I'll do the rest. Simply affix the prepaid label I send you and drop off the package at a local courier counter. Let me know if that's all right with you, and I'll get started."

Diplomacy tip: don't make demands. You're asking the seller a favor, so be polite and encouraging, and make sure to let her know that she can refuse without any ill will. If the seller feels she has a choice in the matter, she'll be more likely to agree.

More often than not, the seller will agree, happy to save time by not having to put together a label and stand in line at the courier counter. (For sellers who refuse, you may still be able to give them your courier account number, or at least request a cheaper shipping method.)

The next step is to prepare a prepaid label [Hack #86]. But instead of printing the label on your own printer, you'll need to create a file that can be emailed to the seller. PDF files are perfect for this; see the "Turn Shipping Labels into PDF Files" sidebar for details.

Once you've created the PDF file with your shipping label, simply email it to the seller as an attachment. Include instructions in your email for obtaining the latest version of the Adobe Acrobat Reader from *www.adobe.com* in case she doesn't already have it. Make sure to specify one or two nearby drop-off

Turn Shipping Labels into PDF Files

The Portable Document Format (PDF), created by Adobe Systems, allows for the exchange of documents without losing formatting, and is ideal for creating shipping labels that can be emailed. Anyone can view a PDF file with the free Adobe Acrobat Reader software available at *www.adobe.com*; odds are you already have it installed on your system.

A PDF file can be created from any application, including your web browser (where you'll likely create your labels). Simply print as you normally would (File → Print...), but instead of printing to your printer, print to a PDF printer driver.

On any modern Mac, you can create a PDF file from your browser's Print dialog. But on any other platform, you'll need a PDF printer driver such as the full version of Adobe Acrobat (not the reader), a commercial product available at *www.adobe.com*.

Windows users can also create PDF files using the free Ghostscript software:

1. Start by installing Ghostscript (*www.cs.wisc.edu/~ghost/*) and GSview (*www.cs.wisc.edu/~ghost/gsview/*).
2. Install a free PostScript printer driver (*www.adobe.com/products/printerdrivers*) and make sure it's set to "print to file." Go to Control Panel → Printers → right-click the Postscript driver → Properties → Ports → click FILE:, and click OK.
3. Create your label [Hack #86] and print it to your PostScript printer driver. Choose a filename (such as *label.prn*) when prompted.
4. Start GSView and open the *.prn* file you just created. Go to File → Convert, select the *pdfwrite* device, choose a resolution of 600, and click OK. Choose a filename (such as *label.pdf*) when prompted.

Alternatives to Acrobat and Ghostscript include Create Adobe PDF Online (*cpdf.adobe.com*), a subscription-based service; JawsPDF (*www.jawspdf.com*); and PDFMail (*www.pdfmail.com*). All offer free trials.

locations, as obtained from your courier's online location finder, described earlier in this hack. Better yet, send a link to the courier's web site so the seller can see the map and any nearby alternatives.

If all goes well, the seller will print out the label, tape it to the package, and drop off the package as instructed. You'll be able to track the package from the courier's web site, and the seller will be out of the loop.

HACK #39

Estimate Transit Times

Use the courier's web site to calculate how long you'll have to wait for your package to arrive.

It's probably fair to say that impatience is a quality most eBayers have in common; sellers want their money right after their auctions end, and buyers want their stuff soon thereafter.

Before you bid on an item, it may be helpful to know when you'll have the package in hand. Fortunately, you have access to the tools you need to determine the transit time for almost any item on eBay.

First, you need to know the location of the item, which, in most cases, is the same as the location of the seller. If the seller has followed the rules when creating the listing, the Item Location is displayed near the top of the listing page, shown in Figure 3-11. Most of the time, this includes a city and state or province, as well as the country in which the seller is based.

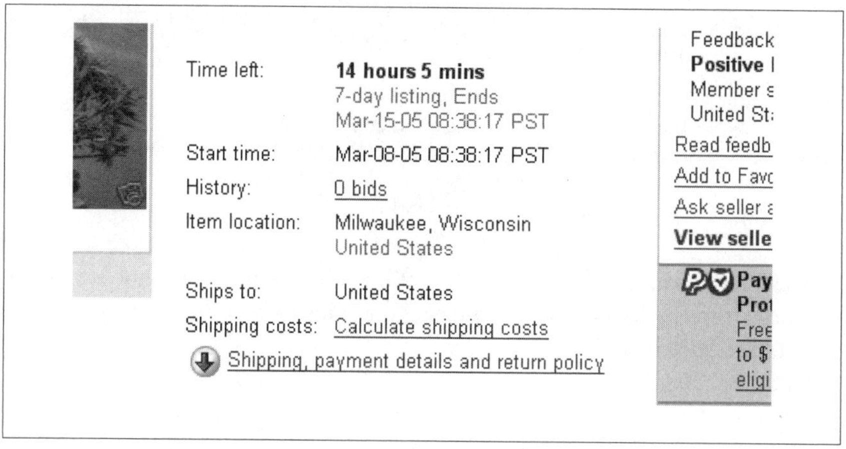

Time left:
14 hours 5 mins
7-day listing, Ends
Mar-15-05 08:38:17 PST
Start time:
Mar-08-05 08:38:17 PST
History:
0 bids
Item location:
Milwaukee, Wisconsin
United States
Ships to:
United States
Shipping costs:
Calculate shipping costs
Shipping, payment details and return policy
Feedback
Positive
Member
United St
Read feedb
Add to Favo
Ask seller
View selle
Pay
Pro
Free
to $
eligi

Figure 3-11. You'll need to know where in the world your item is located before you can estimate how long it will take to be shipped to you

But many sellers abuse this feature by writing things like "Bid Now!" or "Honest eBay Seller" in the space. This means you might have to look elsewhere to determine where the item is actually located. Possibilities include:

Payment instructions. Some sellers include a mailing address in the "Seller's payment instructions" box at the bottom of the listing page. If you see only a phone number, you can always search Google for the area code (include the phrase "area code" in your search) to find the city.

Sales tax. If the seller charges sales tax, there will usually be a clause somewhere in the description to the effect of "Sales Tax: 8.25% on orders shipped within California." If you're really sharp and have access to the state's sales tax tables, you might be able to localize it further.

eBay Shipping Calculator. If you see a Calculate Shipping box [Hack #59] at the bottom of the listing page, go ahead and type in your Zip Code and click Calculate. The page will indicate a typically imprecise "Estimated delivery time" for each of the available shipping methods. Furthermore, it may provide enough information to ascertain the approximate location of the item, at which point you can use the other tools described in this hack to get more information.

Ask. Of course, you can always choke it up and actually ask the seller where the item is located. Be precise here; make sure you request the actual location of the item, as opposed to the location of the seller, because some sellers *drop-ship* items from warehouses across the country when you place your order. Of course, it may take a day or two for the seller to respond (if he ever does), but it's your best bet if you can't find the information elsewhere.

Be wary of sellers who are reluctant to provide this information, as it may be an indication that they have something to hide, or at the very least, will be drop-shipping your item from the other side of the world.

At this point, you should know the location of the item. If you know the city (or state) but not the Zip Code, you can look it up with Google (or *zipinfo.com* for addresses in the U.S.).

Get Transit Times

Armed with both the origin Zip Code and the destination Zip Code (yours, presumably), the next step is to visit the courier's web site to use their online tools for calculating the delivery time. (For instance, if the seller uses FedEx, go to *fedex.com*, and then click Ship → Get Transit Times.)

Provided the seller ships right after you pay, you can figure out approximately when the package will arrive by adding the transit time to the date of the close of the auction. Thus, if a listing ends in the evening of Thursday, March 11th, the earliest the seller will be able to ship is the following day (Friday, March 12th); add, say, three business days for the package to travel across five state lines, and you can expect to have it land on your doorstep Wednesday or Thursday of the following week.

Search for Local Listings

If many sellers are offering the same item, you can narrow your search to local listings to reduce the transit time and get your item sooner.

Start by performing a search **[Hack #10]** and then sort the results by Time Left so that items ending soonest are shown first. Next, in the Search Options box to the left, place a checkmark next to the "Items within" checkbox. (If the option isn't available, click the Customize link at the bottom of the box, and move the "Distance to item" entry to the "Options you want to display" box.) Choose a distance (in miles or kilometers, depending on which eBay version **[Hack #19]** you're using), type your Zip Code in the box, and click Show Items.

The next page shows the results of your search, with far-away items filtered out and the distance to each item shown in a separate column. (To show the distance to each item on all your searches, click Customize Display in the upper right.) You can even sort by distance and isolate any items that might be as close as next door. Who knows; maybe the seller will even let you pick up the item yourself!

HACK #40 Deal with Disappointment: Getting Refunds

Get your money back when an item isn't all it was made out to be.

In some ways, eBay is no different from any other store. Whether it's a brick-and-mortar shop down the street or an online superstore across the country, sometimes you don't get what you were expecting and you want your money back.

Getting your money back requires three things: knowing what your rights are, understanding what policies and requests are considered "reasonable," and—most of all—knowing what tools you have at your disposal if the seller is less than cooperative.

> Sellers: see "Master Expectation Management" **[Hack #50]** for easy ways to reduce the likelihood of returns, and "Deal with Stragglers, Deadbeats, and Returns" **[Hack #89]** for tips on getting your eBay fees refunded if you allow a customer to return an item.

Diplomacy Tactics

It's the seller who sets the return policy for any given auction, so before you write the seller and complain, you'll need to check the auction description and the seller's About Me page (if applicable) to see if the seller has outlined a policy on returns. For instance, the seller might accept returns only under certain circumstances, or might not accept returns at all. Other sellers will be more understanding, accepting returns within three days of receipt, or offering refunds on everything except shipping.

Next, see if the problem (your reason for wanting a refund) is stated in the auction. For example, if the seller wrote in the description that the item is missing a wheel, then, of course, said missing wheel is not a valid reason for return. Sellers should not be held responsible for a bidder not having read the auction description.

Finally, contact the seller and let him know that you're not happy with the item you received. Your first email will set the tone for the entire conversation, so try to avoid sounding angry or unreasonable. Instead, be calm, understanding, and thoughtful. For example:

- *"I received the item yesterday; thanks for the quick shipping. Unfortunately, its condition was somewhat worse than described in your auction. Would you be willing to accept a return?"* This is friendly, even to the point of thanking the seller for something he did right. It also cuts to the chase and specifically outlines a valid reason for return. Also, it makes no demands, which will make the seller much more receptive to your request.

Including photos of the problem (including any damage or excessive wear) will help your case significantly. See Chapter 5 for information on taking good photos of items.

- *"I've been examining the item you sent, and it appears to be a different model than the one you advertised in your auction description. I'm afraid I'm going to have to return it."* This is a little more direct than the first example, but still contains an acceptable amount of level-headed diplomacy. It also leaves no room for interpretation; you're clear in what you want, and you're only awaiting return instructions. Naturally, this assumes that the seller's return policy allows returns in this case.
- *"The item I received is missing a few accessories, a fact that wasn't stated in the auction description. Would you be willing to accept a return, or at least offer a partial refund?"* This approach is extremely valuable, as it makes the seller feel empowered by giving him a choice. It also provides a solution (the partial refund) that both parties may prefer: the seller doesn't have to give you all your money back, and you don't have to hunt for another item.

Most sellers will be understanding and cooperative, especially if you were smart and bought only from those with good feedback profiles. But less scrupulous sellers will try any number of excuses to avoid having to give you some or all of your money back. For instance:

- *"I've sold plenty of these, and nobody else complained."* This response is common, but is easily defeated by responding with, "If you've had no trouble selling these items in the past, it should be equally easy to resell this one after I've returned it."
- *"I'm sorry, this is an 'as is' item, meaning no returns."* Although selling items "as is" is a tactic commonly used on eBay, it doesn't necessarily relieve the seller of all obligations. For instance, if the item was misrepresented in the auction or damaged in shipping, you are entitled to a refund even for an "as is" auction.
- *"Although the item isn't exactly what you expected, it should be every bit as good and work equally well."* Don't let a seller pull a bait-and-switch on you. You have every right to get what you paid for and to insist on a refund if you don't.
- *"I can give you a full refund, minus all shipping charges and eBay fees."* Most sellers understandably don't refund shipping charges, but you shouldn't have to pay to ship an item both ways if you're returning it due to the seller's mistake. Also, sellers can get refunds from eBay for final-value fees if the item is returned; if the seller is unfamiliar with this process, feel free to send instructions detailing how to get to eBay's Dispute Console **[Hack #89]**.

Sending Things Back

Assuming you can come to an agreement with the seller about the terms of your return and subsequent refund, the next step is to return the item to the seller. Here are a few tips:

Send it to the right place. Confirm the return address with the seller before you send it back. Don't use the return address on the package or the seller's payment address without first double-checking with the seller.

Don't dawdle. Don't sit on the package; get it out within 48 hours of contacting the seller.

Use a tracking number. Never send a package without a tracking number; see "Ship Cheaply Without Waiting in Line" **[Hack #86]** for details.

Communicate clearly. Tell the seller when you're sending the package back so that he knows to expect it. Make sure he understands that you expect a refund as soon as he receives the returned package. And if you use a tracking number, there will be no "misunderstandings."

If all goes well, you should have your money back shortly. See the next section if it doesn't go as planned.

When the transaction is complete, think twice about the feedback you leave for the seller. If the return was handled gracefully, reward the seller with positive feedback. Use neutral feedback only if the return was a hassle, and negative feedback only if you got no refund at all. This is important, because as a member of the eBay community, you want to reinforce—with all sellers—that accepting returns is in their best interest. If there's a stigma equating refunds with negative feedback, then no seller will ever accept a return. See "Withhold Feedback" [Hack #6] for ways to protect yourself from feedback retaliation.

If you've paid via PayPal, don't let the seller send you an ordinary payment in leu of a refund—otherwise, you and the seller will both pay the ~3% PayPal fees. Instead, make sure the seller knows to use PayPal's Refund feature [Hack #90].

If All Else Fails...

This is the part of the hack where I say, "You paid for this item with a credit card or PayPal, right?" And you say, "Yes, of course I did!"

As long as you used a credit card or PayPal [Hack #33] to pay for the item, you can, as a last resort, dispute the charge under the following circumstances:

- The item you received was not as the seller had described it in the auction, and the seller is uncooperative in accepting a return.
- You returned the item, you have proof the seller received it, but you have not yet received your money back.
- The item never arrived, and the seller is uncooperative.
- You suspect fraud [Hack #25] or some form of intentional misrepresentation.

Whether or not you're able to retrieve your money, you should file a dispute [Hack #41] with eBay to help ensure that the seller doesn't get off scot-free.

Of course, the real beauty of eBay is that, no matter what the circumstance, you can turn around and sell just about any item you'd otherwise be stuck with. And if you do it right, you'll probably get more than you originally paid!

HACK #41 File a Dispute

Try this last resort to get your money back.

Sometimes all the diplomacy in the world won't convince a seller to refund your payment [Hack #40]. In cases such as this, it's good to know there are other ways to get your money back.

Often, disputes are caused by nothing more than email problems (spam filters, full mailboxes, etc.). You may find that filing a dispute is the only way to get a message through to the seller [Hack #9].

If a seller misrepresented an item, never shipped it in the first place, or refuses to refund your money after you return an item, here are the tools you can use in your attempt to recover your money:

PayPal buyer complaint. If you paid for the item with PayPal, you can use PayPal's Buyer Complaint Form; log in to PayPal, go to Help → Contact Us → Contact Customer Service. Then choose Protections/Privacy/Security → Buyer Complaint Process. Unfortunately, PayPal's Buyer Protection Policy covers only purchases you never received.

Despite the presence of the "Item Not as Described" option, don't use it: it's a trap! If you select "Item Not as Described" during the process, PayPal will close the case and you won't be given a second chance.

eBay Dispute Console. At one time, eBay had a "nonpaying bidder" complaint form, yet no way to report a "nonshipping seller." In early 2005, eBay created the Dispute Console to take care of both tasks.

Go to My eBay → Dispute Console (*feedback.ebay.com/ws/eBayISAPI.dll?ViewDisputeConsole*) to file a dispute or to view a dispute currently in progress. Then, choose a dispute type by clicking Unpaid items (if you're a seller) or Items Not Received or Not as Described (if you're a buyer) from the box to your left.

In the case of an item you purchased but never received, as well as a misrepresented item, click Report an Item Not Received or Not as Described, respectively, to start a new dispute. Next, enter the item number [Hack #13] of the listing and click Continue. You can file a dispute at any time between 10 and 60 days after the close of a listing.

Note that eBay's buyer and seller protection services are available only to participants in officially completed auctions. This means that if you weren't the high bidder in an auction or if the reserve wasn't met, you won't have access to these services.

Then describe the problem to begin an unmoderated discussion between yourself and the seller in a private forum on eBay's site. In most cases, the structure of the discussion is enough to help both parties resolve the dispute without any help from eBay.

eBay fraud claim. If you fail to come to a resolution within 10 days of filing a dispute through the Dispute Console, you'll be given the option to escalate the dispute to a fraud claim. You fill out a special form that eBay provides, fax it to eBay along with proof of payment, and they mull it over for a few weeks. Then, if eBay determines that the other party is at fault, you may be entitled to a claim of up to US$175 ($200 minus a $25 processing fee). Naturally, this claim won't exceed the amount of your payment.

If you've paid for the item with a credit card, either directly or through PayPal, eBay asks you to dispute the charge with your credit card company.

Dispute the credit card charge. If you funded your payment with a credit card, you'll have to contact your credit card company and dispute the charge. You'll have to carefully explain the situation (providing relevant emails and all tracking numbers), but in most cases you should get a full refund whether the seller is cooperative or not. No other payment method offers this level of protection.

Don't dawdle when it comes to filing charge disputes, but don't file them frivolously, either. Although you'll typically have only 30–60 days in which to file a dispute, it's always better to handle it directly with the seller, so try to be patient. Sometimes filing a dispute is enough to convince a seller to cooperate, at which point the dispute can simply be canceled.

Squaretrade. You can also pursue a fraud investigation through SquareTrade (*www.squaretrade.com*), a separate company that offers dispute resolution services to eBay customers. (See "Remove Unwanted Feedback" [Hack #7] for another service provided by SquareTrade.) Squaretrade's free service works much like eBay's Dispute Console, but you can also get a professional mediator to help with your case for an extra fee.

Sleuthing Tools at Your Disposal

An eBay user who knowingly commits fraud will undoubtedly take steps to hide his or her true identity, but there are a few things you can do to learn more about who you're dealing with:

Start with the obvious. Check the user's feedback profile and look for a possible pattern of behavior. Next, contact other buyers and sellers with whom the user has completed a transaction. Use the buyer search and seller search to find relevant auctions in the last 30 days, or use the auction numbers in the user's feedback page to view auctions up to 3 months old.

Find contact information. Use the Find Contact Info form (from any eBay page, go to Advanced Search → Find Contact Information) and enter the user's ID and the auction number, and eBay will email you the phone number and mailing address on file for that user. The user will also receive a notice that you've requested the information. But don't be surprised if Mr. John Doe lives at 123 Fake St. in Springfield.

Whois search. If the user has an unusual domain name (as opposed to something common like *aol.com* or *hotmail.com*), the domain itself may provide more insight. Use a Whois tool, such as the one at *www.netsol.com/cgi-bin/whois/whois,* and find out who owns the domain behind the user's email address.

IP address. If you've received any email from the user, look for IP addresses in the email headers. For example, you might see something like this:

```
Received: from mx22.sjc.ebay.com (mxpool11.ebay.com [66.135.197.17])
```

where `66.135.197.17` is the IP address of one of the computers responsible for routing the email to you. In this case, the IP address is a machine at eBay, but if the user emailed you directly, his IP address would show up somewhere in the headers. If the machine name (here, `mxpool11.ebay.com`) doesn't appear next to the IP address, use the NSLookup tool to resolve the address.

NSLookup is included on most modern computers, such as those running Windows XP/2000, Unix, or Mac OS X. Just type `nslookup 66.135.197.17` into a terminal or command prompt window, and click OK. If you don't have NSLookup on your system, you can use an online NSLookup gateway (try *www.his.com/cgi-bin/nslookup* or *www.webreference.com/cgi-bin/nslookup.cgi*).

The computer name is often useful in determining the user's own domain, or at least his ISP (such as *aol.com* or *notmyrealdomain.com*). Use the Whois tool to find out more about the domain in the machine name.

Google. Try searching Google for the user's name, email address, postal address, phone number, Zip Code, or anything else you know.

eBay forums. Use eBay's forums [Hack #81] to reach out to other eBay users for help. You may even find someone else who has had dealings (negative or otherwise) with the seller, and can possibly offer some insight or advice.

CHAPTER FOUR

Selling

Hacks 42–69

People will buy *anything*. The old adage "one person's trash is another's treasure" has never been more true than on eBay. And for this reason, you'll find that people will *sell* just about anything. From handmade dolls to cell phone batteries, from computer components to human organs, from antique pottery to broken pieces of the Berlin Wall...to broken pieces of antique pottery, you'll find a rich assortment of junk and jewels at the world's largest flea market.

Selling on eBay [Hack #43] is a piece of cake. Just click the Sell button at the top of any eBay page and follow the prompts. When you're done, your listing will start, and other eBay users can bid on it.

The hard part, however, is the stuff eBay *doesn't* tell you, such as the fact that you should determine the market [Hack #42] for your item before you try to sell it. Nor does eBay explain which extra-cost listing upgrades provide the most bang for your buck or show you how to maximize the effectiveness of keywords in your listings. The hacks in this chapter are designed to show you the best ways to get more bids (and thus more money) for your items, as well as the fun stuff, like customizing your auction descriptions with JavaScript, HTML, forms, and other goodies.

What's It Worth?

Determine an item's current market value using eBay's Completed Items search and set your price accordingly.

On eBay, research is money. A seller who knows how much an item is worth will be able to choose the selling options more appropriately, and as a result, get more money. And a buyer who knows the worth of an item will more readily recognize a good deal and as a result, spend less money. Fortunately, there are tools at your disposal to help determine an item's worth in about 20 seconds flat.

Investigate the Market

Any item on eBay is worth only what someone is willing to pay for it. Fortunately, for almost every item sold on eBay, an identical or similar item will have been sold within the last month or two. And given the public nature of eBay's past auctions, it's easy to find out the health of the current market for your item before you list it.

Start with a standard search (see Chapter 2), and locate any auctions for items similar to the one you're selling. Click "Completed listings" in the Display box as shown in Figure 4-1, and then select "highest first" to sort the listing by final price in descending order. Note that eBay's Completed Listings search is a title-only search (descriptions of closed auctions aren't indexed), so you'll typically want to use simpler (broader) search queries than you'd use for active items.

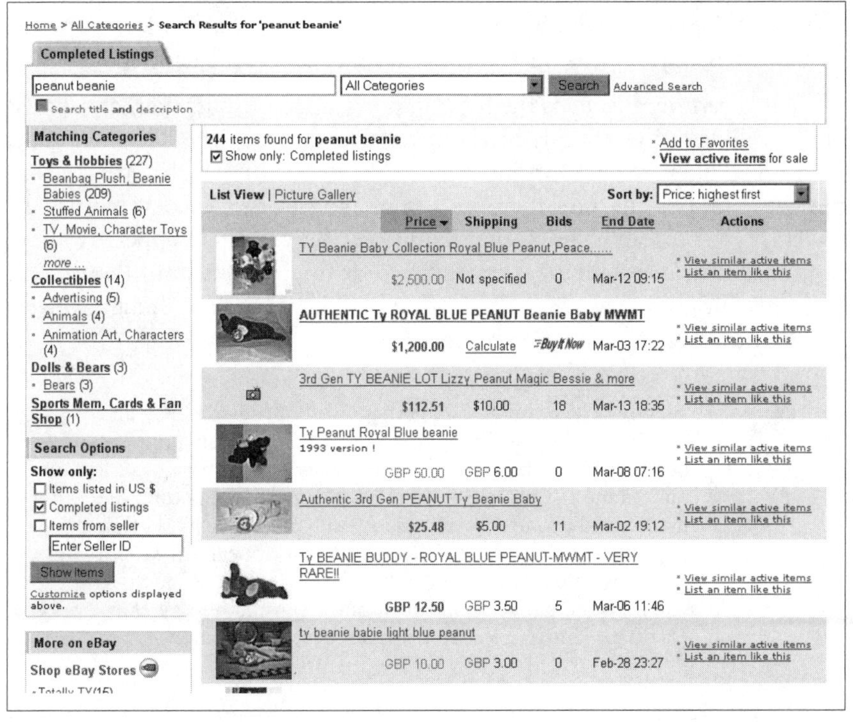

Figure 4-1. A quick search through recently completed auctions, sorted by price, gives you a good idea what your item is worth

Only the closing price of a successfully completed auction matters, so pay attention only to auctions that have received at least one bid. Even if the seller had a reserve that wasn't met **[Hack #45]**, the closing price will give you a picture of what buyers might be willing to bid for your item.

Completed auction listings are goldmines of information, and not just for finding closing prices. For example, you can find out how the top-selling completed auctions have been categorized [Hack #12] and titled [Hack #42] and build on past sellers' experiences. And if you're really determined, you can even track running auctions [Hack #29] for items similar to those you're selling, so you can see first hand when the market is good and when it's not.

It's important to realize that some markets will be more stable than others. For example, there's always an extremely healthy interest in laptops, PDAs, digital cameras, and other popular consumer electronics, especially since there are retail stores to help set prices. But markets for collectibles are typically more volatile, since the value of a given item is influenced more by its rarity and the people who happen to be visiting eBay that week than by the item's original price or its quoted value in some collector's handbook.

An item's *perceived value* is the most important factor in its market value. If you're selling a rare antique toy, and yours is the only one like it on eBay, then it will likely fetch a fortune. But during a week in which several examples of a supposedly rare item are being sold, its perceived value will be lower. If your research shows that the market for your item appears to have bottomed out, it usually pays to wait two or three weeks until those items currently on eBay have been sold off, and a new batch of hungry buyers makes their way to the auction block.

When you see a rare item getting a lot of bids on eBay and you have one just like it to sell, it's best to wait until the other auction ends before listing yours. Otherwise, you'll undermine the perceived value of your item by flooding the market and end up splitting bids with the other seller. Plus, if you time it [Hack #48] so that your item appears in search results within a few hours of the close of the other auction, you'll be the happy recipient of bids from the hungry eBayers disappointed at losing the other seller's auction.

The Empty Restaurant

Inexperienced sellers often make the mistake of setting the starting bid of an auction equal to the amount they expect—or hope—to get for their item. Other sellers forgo research and set the starting bid at a single dollar, relying on the market to set the price. Of the two, the second approach is the better choice for the lazy seller, because you're virtually guaranteed to sell your item.

The key is to remember the empty-restaurant syndrome. When strolling down the street looking for a good restaurant, are you more likely to enter an empty restaurant or a crowded one? If you're like most people, you'll go for the crowded restaurant, even if there's a wait.

Bidders on eBay think the same way. Consider two auctions for the same item, one starting at $20 and the other starting at $300. Assuming the market value of the item is at least $300, the first auction may receive 20 bids and close at $330 while the second may get only two bids and close at a measly $305. Why? Not only will the lower-priced auction attract more bidders early on and appear higher in search results sorted by price, its perceived popularity will buoy its perceived value toward the end of the auction.

The biggest mental block most sellers have when choosing a low starting price is the fear that the item will sell with too low a final price. But if you take the time to research the market for your item *before* you list it on eBay, you'll know how much money it will fetch even before the first bid is placed. Among other things, this means that if you find that the market for your item is weak, you can choose not to list it at all. Of course, you can always use a reserve price **[Hack #45]** to protect yourself, but that approach has drawbacks as well.

So, by that logic, should you start all your auctions at a single penny? Of course not. Instead, you'll want to temper this approach with the following concepts:

Limited appeal? When selling an item of limited appeal—when you might expect only one or two bidders to be interested—you'll want to set your opening bid much higher. Remember, if your starting bid is $5 and you get only a single bidder, the closing price will be $5, even if the buyer entered a maximum bid of $150.

Use Buy It Now. Use the Buy It Now listing upgrade **[Hack #46]** to set two prices for your auction: the artificially low starting bid price, and the full amount you'd like to get for your item. Hint: an especially eager bidder might be willing to pay a few extra dollars to get the item sooner.

Although the Buy It Now price disappears once the first bid is placed, there are ways to get around this. The most common method is to use a reserve price, which will keep the Buy It Now price visible until the reserve has been met. The problem with this is that your bidders may mistake the Buy It Now price for your reserve price, and as a result may simply be scared off.

Another workaround—which is *not* recommended—is to state your Buy It Now price in the auction description, instructing bidders to contact you directly if they're interested. Not only does this violate eBay policy, but it may also appear to bidders that you're trying to scam them **[Hack #25]**.

Of course, if you choose your Buy It Now price wisely, the need to keep it from disappearing won't be much of an issue.

Listing fee considerations. eBay's listing fees are based on the starting bid you choose: the lower the starting bid, the lower the cost to list. Fees are not calculated proportionally, however, but rather according to a tiered pricing structure. For example, a fixed fee of 30 cents is charged for all auctions under $10, which is why you see so many auctions starting at $9.99. The next cut-off is $25, so $24.99 is also a common starting price. Note that it rarely pays to use a lower starting bid just to save a few cents on eBay fees, however. Go to *pages.ebay.com/help/sell/fees.html* for descriptions of all current fees.

Be a little devious. Setting a starting bid of $1.00 or even $0.01 is a clear sign to the more experienced bidders that you expect heavy bidding for your item, and some bidders might pass it up as a result. Instead, a slightly higher, arbitrary starting bid like $20 might be a better choice. This is low enough to encourage healthy bidding, but *looks* like a starting bid entered by someone who doesn't know what he's selling. Auctions like these tend to catch the attention of advanced eBay members who will wait until the end of the auction to bid [Hack #26].

If nothing else, these examples illustrate why it's so important to know the market value of your item before you sell.

HACK #43 Create a Listing

Use the Sell Your Item form to create an auction or fixed-price listing and start selling on eBay in just a few minutes.

There's a bit of subtle (and not-so-subtle) strategy involved in creating a listing, from writing a catchy and concise title and adequately describing your item to choosing among the extra-cost listing options. The important thing is to take your time and have a little fun with it; attention to detail will pay off in the long run, while rushed listings cause nothing but problems.

Before you try to sell anything on eBay, take a moment to find out what it's worth [Hack #42]. That way, you'll know ahead of time if the potential payoff is worth your time.

When you're ready, click Sell at the top of any eBay page. If you've never sold on eBay before, you'll be asked to sign up for a Seller's Account; just follow the prompts and answer the questions; it shouldn't take more than a minute or two.

eBay makes most of its money in two ways: insertion (listing) fees and final value fees. You'll be charged an insertion fee when you list your item, regardless of whether or not it sells. The fees depend on the specific options you choose (discussed throughout this chapter); a summary of fees for each listing you create is shown at the end of the listing process.

If all goes well, you should see the first page of the Sell Your Item form, at which point you'll be given a choice as to the listing format:

Online Auction. Select this option to create a standard Chinese auction, wherein bidding takes place as described in the beginning of Chapter 3. You select the starting price, and optionally a Buy It Now price [Hack #31] and Reserve [Hack #45] and let bidders do the rest.

Fixed Price. If you have a feedback score of at least 10, you can use this option to set a firm price and, optionally, use eBay's Best Offer feature [Hack #66].

Fixed-price listings are nearly identical to auction listings, except that you specify only one price: the Buy It Now price. There's no starting bid (no bidding at all, actually), so if the item sells, you know exactly what it'll go for. There's no mystery and no suspense, which can be good if you just want to move your merchandise. But since this format doesn't have the excitement and uncertainty of a traditional auction, it's not such a great choice for collectibles and other items whose price is determined (and inflated) by your customers' frenzied bidding.

Store Inventory. Provided you've opened an eBay Store [Hack #91], you can create new fixed-price Store listings with this option. These are essentially the same as Fixed Price listings, except they last much longer (30, 60, or 90 days) and cost much less. The downside is that they won't show up in standard eBay searches or category listings.

Real Estate. The last option here is Real Estate, set aside as its own format because real estate is handled so differently from anything else on eBay. Essentially, you don't sell real estate on eBay; you advertise it. This is understandable, considering what's typically involved in purchasing a house or—if you live in California—a parking space.

Real estate listings last much longer than conventional listings (30 or 90 days) and are substantially more expensive. But since there's no bidding (and therefore no final value fees), the $150.00 insertion fee to advertise a quarter-million-dollar home for a full month suddenly doesn't sound so expensive.

You can list your real estate as a conventional auction, complete with bidding and a Buy It Now price, by choosing the "Sell at online auction" format and then choosing "Real Estate" for the category. This will also give you the option of a short 3-, 5-, 7-, or 10-day listing at a lower $35.00 insertion fee. As with 30- and 90-day real estate listings, eBay charges no final value fee for real estate listings.

Next to the Start a New Listing button, you might also see a Complete your listing link. If you didn't finish creating your listing the last time you used this form, you'll have the opportunity to pick up where you left off. Among other things, this means that you don't have to start over if the power suddenly goes out.

The rest of the Sell Your Item form is divided into the following five pages:

Category. This step involves choosing a category (or two [Hack #46]) in which to file your item. The best way to find the appropriate category for your item (particularly if you're not yet familiar with eBay's hierarchy of categories) is to search for completed listings [Hack #42] and see which categories [Hack #12] were used by the most successful listings.

Title & Description. Use these fields to type the title, subtitle, and description [Hack #47] your customers will see in search results and on the listing page itself. Note that most of the hacks in this chapter make use of HTML [Hack #52] and JavaScript (discussed in the Preface) code placed into the Description field.

Pictures & Details. Here, you indicate a price [Hack #42], duration [Hack #48], quantity [Hack #44], and location [Hack #39]. You can also specify one or more extra-cost upgrades [Hack #46] and even elect to have a counter [Hack #49] appear on your page. The most important thing on this page, however, is the picture, fully covered in Chapter 5.

Payment & Shipping. Here, you choose what types of payment you're willing to accept [Hack #85] and what parts of the world to which you're willing to ship. Then, choose either a flat shipping cost [Hack #86] or use eBay's optional Calculated Shipping feature [Hack #59]. Also on this page are boxes for your return policy and payment instructions [Hack #64].

Review & Submit. This last page shows a summary of the choices you made on the previous pages. At any point, you can return to an earlier step by clicking the step captions at the top of the page. (Avoid using your browser's Back button here, as this can cause eBay to lose information.) Finally, you'll see a summary of the insertion fees incurred by this new listing.

Click the Submit Listing button at the bottom of the page to start your listing; unless you've elected to have eBay schedule your listing [Hack #48], it starts right away. In most cases, it'll show up in search results within a few minutes, which you can confirm with the "Where is an item" feature [Hack #49].

HACK #44 To Bundle or Not to Bundle

Determine simply how and when to bundle items for sale.

One of the most common mistakes sellers make on eBay is selling too many things together as a *lot*. Sure, it's easier to list fewer auctions, but bundles are usually worth much less than the same items sold separately, and may even be less likely to sell.

One of my favorite eBay anecdotes involves a single auction for a large lot of model trains, for which I paid approximately $800. I then turned around and sold about *half* the collection, all told, for about $800. I estimated the value of the remaining items to be about $1,000, all of which I effectively got for free. (This is similar in concept to *arbitrage*, but relies more on skill than on simply taking advantage of inefficiencies in the marketplace.)

Obviously, the original seller of the collection would've earned quite a bit more money had he listed each item separately. But how could he have known?

The most direct approach is to compare the expected value of a collection with the total expected values of the separate items [Hack #42]. But this can take a lot of time, and you'll be hard-pressed to find another auction with exactly the same items.

So instead, just ask yourself this question: "How likely is it that any single bidder will want all of the items I'm selling?"

Bidders who buy large collections or lots typically do so with the intention of reselling some or all of the items. Since they'd only do this if there were profit in it, it's unlikely that anyone would pay the full value of such a collection. However, if there's a good chance that a single person will want to keep all of the items you're selling, then you very well may get what they're worth.

Never bundle unrelated or incompatible items. For instance, it wouldn't make sense to sell two camera lenses—each designed for a different brand of camera—in the same listing. Anyone who would bid on such a listing would likely be interested in only one of the lenses, and as a result wouldn't bid higher than that single lens is worth.

Accessories can go either way. Sometimes, adding $50 worth of accessories to an item will increase the desirability of the item by at least that much, if not more. Other times, it won't make a lick of difference.

Take, for example, a $300 handheld computer, sold along with a $40 flash memory card, $25 leather case, $10 screen protector, and $150 worth of software. Accessories such as used leather cases (at least the cheaper ones), used screen protectors, and especially the software are all pretty much worthless when sold separately, but will probably raise the value of the handheld if sold together. Why? Because it *is* likely that any single bidder will actually want all of those things, and that person might pay more to avoid having to buy them separately.

So, what if you have two or more *identical* items? Certainly, they're compatible with one another if they are indeed identical, but would anyone ever use them together? In the case of the aforementioned flash memory card, for instance, a single $40 card might raise the value of the handheld by $25 to $30. But if you have several memory cards, the odds are pretty remote that any single person would want them all. Instead, try including one of the cards in the same auction as the handheld PC and sell the rest separately.

Naturally, the market for your particular item will be different, but this should give you an idea of the methodology used to determine the practicality of bundling related items.

Leveraging Dutch Auctions

If you have a large quantity of an inexpensive item, you may be inclined to sell the entire lot in a single auction. But who is going to want 4,000 pairs of shoelaces, even if you do offer them all at the low, low price of only $200? Naturally, it also doesn't make sense to list them separately at 5 cents apiece, but there are other options.

Probably the best choice is a Dutch auction, but not necessarily the kind you might expect. The nature of a Dutch auction suggests that if you have 4,000 items, you enter a quantity of 4,000, wherein a single bid buys a single item. But then you'd be back where you started—handling up to 4,000 different customers at a nickel apiece.

Instead, try selling 400 bundles of 10 for $4.00 each; so a single bidder would be able to buy 10 pairs of shoelaces for $4.00, 20 pairs for $8.00, and so on. You'll have to build only one auction, you'll get 8 times as much money per shoelace, and you'll be much more likely to get any money at all for your bizarre collection.

Multiple Listings of Identical Items

So you have a bunch of identical items to sell, but you don't want to bury them all under a single Dutch auction listing? Rather than one listing with a quantity of 400, why not 400 individual listings? Apparently, you're not the first person to think of this.

eBay allows sellers to have a maximum of 10 identical listings running at any one time, mostly to keep sellers in your position from overwhelming search results and category listings with floods of identical items. This is also in your best interest, because buyers assess the value of an item [Hack #42] by its uniqueness; too many of an item only serves to make overly-common items unpalatable, to the point of forcing buyers to modify searches to exclude your listings [Hack #18]. But if you're creative about it, you can unload your burdensome inventory without breaking any rules:

Spread it around. Divide your 400 items into 10 identical Dutch auctions, each with a quantity of 40. Then, schedule your listings [Hack #48] so they're staggered throughout the week, and at least one ends and another starts each day.

Use shorter durations. The 10-listing limit applies only to concurrent listings, so if you have a lot of stuff to sell, you can move more product in less time by shortening your listing durations [Hack #48]. This allows you, for instance, to have up to 20 three-day listings or 70 one-day listings appear on eBay in any one-week period.

Add some variety. If you must work around the 10-listing limit, vary your offerings. If the items come in multiple colors, try 10 listings in aquamarine, 10 in chartreuse, 10 in viridian, and 10 in malachite. Or if there are accessories available, try some creative bundling: 10 listings with leather cases, 10 with car chargers, 10 with matching ear muffs, and 10 with all three (the infamous *superbundle*).

Make it someone else's problem. Sell your entire inventory as a *lot* by clicking the Lot tab when specifying the quantity to sell: specify `1` for the Number of Lots and then `400` for the Number of Items Per Lot. Then, hope that some enterprising young fellow—with more time on his hands than you've got—buys all your stuff for a single price and then, presumably, finds a way to resell the items [Hack #92] for a profit. Of course, if you feel particularly enterprising, you can seek out bargains like these by browsing any of the Wholesale Lots subcategories listed at *listings.ebay.com/aw/plistings/list/categories.html*.

See Also

- See Chapter 7 if you're running a business on eBay or simply a busy seller who needs to move a lot of product.

HACK #45 Reserve Judgment

Use a reserve-price auction for items with unknown value or limited appeal.

One of eBay's greatest strengths is the lengths to which its policies go to protect its millions of users, both buyers and sellers. One of the best-known policies is the reserve price, which consequently gets overused.

A *reserve price* is a dollar amount the seller specifies, below which he or she is under no obligation to sell. For example, you might want to sell a car for at least $15,000. But if you set the starting price [Hack #42] at $15,000, you might not get as many bids as with a starting price of $100. A reserve effectively allows you to start the bidding at $100 while protecting yourself from the auction closing with too low of a bid. If you list an item with a $15,000 reserve and no bids exceeding that amount have been placed by the end of the auction, then neither the seller nor the high bidder is under any obligation to complete the transaction.

Bidding on a reserve-price auction proceeds just like a normal auction, with two exceptions. First, a notice stating whether or not the reserve price has been met is shown next to the current price at the top of the auction page. Second, if a bidder comes along and places a bid that exceeds the reserve, the current price is automatically raised to the reserve price.

The bidding rules for reserve-price auctions in eBay Motors' Vehicles categories are different than the rest of eBay: when a bid has been placed on a reserve-price auction for a vehicle, and the reserve has not yet been met, the current price will rise to the high bidder's maximum bid.

The reserve is never made public, which is essential for it to work as intended. Keeping the reserve price secret allows the seller to decide whether to sell the item at the end of the auction at whatever price bidders have set.

The problem with a reserve price is that it can scare away bidders who feel that they have no chance of winning the auction, and as a result, the final price will often be lower than if there were no reserve at all. For this reason, you should use a reserve price only under these circumstances:

No guesswork. If you don't know the value of the item, a reserve still allows healthy bidding with minimal risk to the seller. However, in most cases you can determine the realistic market value of your item by using eBay's Completed Items search [Hack #42].

Limited appeal. For items of limited appeal for which you expect only one or two bidders, a reserve might help you get more money. For instance, consider an auction with a $1 starting bid and a $20 reserve, on which a single bidder enters a $25 proxy bid. Since eBay raises the current price to the reserve price when the reserve has been met or exceeded, the price will rise to $20 with that first bid. Without the reserve, the closing price would stay at $1. This approach might be useful if you're relisting an item that previously didn't sell with a high starting bid.

But that's about it. Sellers often use reserves for other reasons, most of which don't turn out to be terribly good ones. For example:

Artificial ranking. If there's a lot of competition, a seller might use a reserve to permit an arbitrarily low starting price, which would rank the auction more favorably in search results sorted by price. Unfortunately, any gains in visibility would likely be negated by the lower overall appeal of a reserve-price auction.

Buy It Now preservation. On nonreserve auctions, the Buy It Now price disappears once the first bid has been placed; on reserve-price options, it remains visible until the reserve is met. Some sellers add a reserve price simply to keep the Buy It Now option available longer.

The problem with this approach is that the Buy It Now price looks to bidders like the reserve price (even if it's not), which is likely to scare bidders away. If you want to set your reserve price equal to your Buy It Now price, it's best to use a fixed-price listing instead.

If you do end up using a reserve price in your auctions, you may want to explain a few things to your bidders. First, many less-experienced bidders don't really understand how reserve-price auctions work, so you might want to include something like this in your auction description:

> Attention bidders: don't let the reserve scare you. If you're interested in this item, just go ahead and bid as though there were no reserve. If your maximum bid is not over the reserve, you'll know right away, and you won't be under any obligation to buy. If your bid exceeds the reserve, the current price is automatically raised to the reserve price, and you'll have a shot at winning the auction!

You might also want to reassure your bidders that you're a serious seller by explaining that you might be willing to sell to the high bidder even if the reserve isn't met. In fact, you can use eBay's Second Chance Offer to do just that.

The Strategy of Listing Upgrades

Perform a simple cost/benefit analysis to determine which listing options offer the most bang for the buck.

An extra-cost listing upgrade pays for itself if it increases the auction's closing price by at least the cost of the upgrade. But no upgrade is a guarantee, and it can be difficult to predict which ones will be effective without first doing a little research.

For example, the Gallery option, which includes a tiny photo of your item in search results (shown in Figure 4-2), costs 25 cents. Gallery photos do a good job of increasing traffic to your listing, which can lead to more bids and a higher closing price. But it also takes time to prepare a proper Gallery image [Hack #82], and while 25 cents doesn't sound like much, listing fees add up fast. So, you may want to be selective with the Gallery and other listing upgrades you use.

Figure 4-2. The Gallery option is sometimes worth the cost and trouble if it ultimately raises the closing price

Table 4-1 lists the available listing upgrades, their costs, and recommended minimum prices for which they should be used. (Note that some of the fees are different for specialty items, such as autos and real estate.)

Table 4-1. Available extra-cost listing upgrades

Listing upgrade	Insertion fee	Recommended minimum item value	Affects search results	Affects listing page
Buy It Now	$0.05 and up	$0.00	✓	✓
Gallery	$0.35	$10.00	✓	
10-Day Listing	$0.40	$20.00	✓	✓
Subtitle	$0.50	$20.00	✓	✓
Additional Pictures	$0.15 each	$20.00		✓
List in Two Categories	2× listing fee	$35.00	✓	
Scheduled Listings	$0.10	$35.00	✓	✓
Bold	$1.00	$50.00	✓	
Picture Show	$0.25	$50.00		✓
Supersize Picture	$0.75	$50.00		✓
Gift Services	$0.25	$50.00	✓	✓
Reserve Price	$1.00 and up	$100.00		✓
Picture Pack	$1.00 and up	$100.00		✓
Listing Designer	$0.10 and up	$100.00		✓
Border	$3.00	$250.00	✓	
Highlight	$5.00	$500.00	✓	
Featured Plus!	$19.95	$500.00	✓	
Gallery Featured	$19.95 and up	$1,500.00	✓	
Home Page Featured	$39.95 and up	$20,000.00		

Whether or not any particular upgrade is appropriate for your item depends on several factors, as well as a certain degree of luck. With a little research (see the next section), you'll be able to make more informed decisions that will have greater impact on the success of your auction. But if you don't want to take the time, you can use the "recommended minimum item value" column in Table 4-1 as a quick-and-dirty guideline. For instance, if you expect your item to sell for about $40, there's little point in paying $20 for the *Featured Plus!* upgrade. By the same token, if you're selling a $1,500 item, that extra $20 doesn't sound like so much, because it might end up getting you an additional $100 for your item.

From time to time, eBay offers listing upgrade specials, such as **Free Bold Day** or *Gallery for a Penny*. Such deals are typically advertised above search results listings, on the Announcements board, and in the Messages area of My eBay, so keep your eyes open. See *pages.ebay.com/help/sell/fees.html* for the current standard insertion fees.

Statistics and Research

From time to time, eBay publishes statistics regarding the effectiveness of the more popular listing upgrades. For example, in February 2003, eBay estimated that the Gallery option, on average, increased bids by 13% and the final price by 11%. Likewise, the Bold option reportedly increased both the number of bids and the final price by 39%.

What these statistics *don't* say is that there were likely other factors that helped increase the closing prices of these auctions. For example, sellers who took the time to add the Bold or Gallery options to their auctions were probably also diligent enough to write proper titles and descriptions and take good photos. This doesn't necessarily mean that listing upgrades won't help you get more money for your items, but merely that any claims that a listing upgrade will increase the price of your auction should be taken with a grain of salt.

Since your item will likely be competing for bidders with other auctions, the upgrades you choose should depend largely on those used—and not used—by your competition. Start by performing a quick search for your item, as well as browsing the category in which your item will be placed, and see what other sellers are doing to promote their items (see Figure 4-3).

Increased competition usually results in increased use of listing upgrades. If you're selling a rare collectible or a one-of-a-kind item, you might find few sellers in your category using the Bold or Gallery upgrades. But for more common items, such as computers, just about every auction title will use Bold, and about a third will use Featured in Search or Featured in Category.

The best place to start is probably with a Completed Items search [Hack #42], in which you can see which upgrades were used in the most successful completed auctions for your item in the past month. You can also track the exposure of your own listings [Hack #49] to see the real-time effects of listing upgrades and other choices.

But that's all the help eBay will give you. If you want a little more analysis and summary, you'll have to go elsewhere.

Off-Site Research

Services like Terapeak (*www.terapeak.com*) and Andale Research (*www.andale.com*) allow you to analyze eBay's completed-item data in a variety of scenarios. For example, Figure 4-4 shows an analysis of data from a completed-listing search for "calculator" over the past 24 hours using Terapeak.

Home > All Categories > Search Results for 'eggplant'

All Items | Auctions | Buy It Now

eggplant | All Categories | Search | Advanced Search

Search title and description

Matching Categories

Clothing, Shoes & Accessories (283)
- Women's Clothing (163)
- Women's Shoes (37)
- Men's Clothing (31)
- more ...

Home & Garden (114)
- Gardening & Plants (24)
- Bedding (23)
- Home Decor (21)
- more ...

Collectibles (103)
- Decorative Collectibles (53)
- Housewares & Kitchenware (19)
- Advertising (11)
- more ...

See all categories ...

Search Options

Show only:
- Items listed in US $
- Completed listings
- Items from seller

Enter Seller ID

Show Items

Customize options displayed above.

More on eBay

708 items found for **eggplant** · Add to Favorites

List View | Picture Gallery Sort by: Price: highest first Customize Display

Featured Items

Item Title	Price	Shipping	Bids	Time Left
MARC JACOBS QUINN HOBO STYLE EGGPLANT COLOR NWT	$375.00 $600.00	$19.00	- Buy It Now	1d 13h 56m
100 LOREAL L'OREAL EYE SHADOW LINER SLATE EGGPLANT GOLD	$349.00 $350.00	--	- Buy It Now	2d 23h 51m
THIERRY MUGLER Couture Eggplant Wool Suit~No Reserve!	$35.00	--	5	4d 14h 43m

Optimize your selling success! Find out how to promote your items

Item Title	Price	Shipping	Bids	Time Left
RJC LARGE EGGPLANT AUTHENTIC NEW MARC JACOBS BAG	$687.77	$35.00	-	5d 15h 00m
Eggplant Purple CONTEMPORARY 8x11 AREA RUG Retro Carpet	$397.95 $399.95	$39.85	- Buy It Now	13h 08m
MARC JACOBS QUINN HOBO STYLE EGGPLANT COLOR NWT	$375.00 $600.00	$19.00	- Buy It Now	1d 13h 56m

Figure 4-3. If half your competition has paid extra to be Featured in search results, your item may be buried if you don't, and as a result, your auction will receive fewer bids

In an instant, you can see the how other listings similar to yours have fared using eBay's various upgrades, something you wouldn't be able to get yourself with "What's It Worth?" [Hack #42]. But what can you do with this information?

For starters, look at the overall success rate, shown in the upper-right of Terapeak's Research page (60.53% in Figure 4-4), which shows the percentage of all items that ended in successful sales. Then, compare this with the Sold % column in the listing features box; any number higher than the overall success rate shows a increase in the percentage of items that sold.

Keep in mind that these figures represent successful sales, not necessarily increases in final prices. Clearly, it's better (and more profitable) to sell your items than to pay fees on an unsuccessful sale, so in this regard, most of the upgrades represented in Figure 4-4 ended up being helpful. Presumably, any upgrade that boosts the success rate also increases traffic to the item and ends up raising the final price, but it's impossible to gauge this directly.

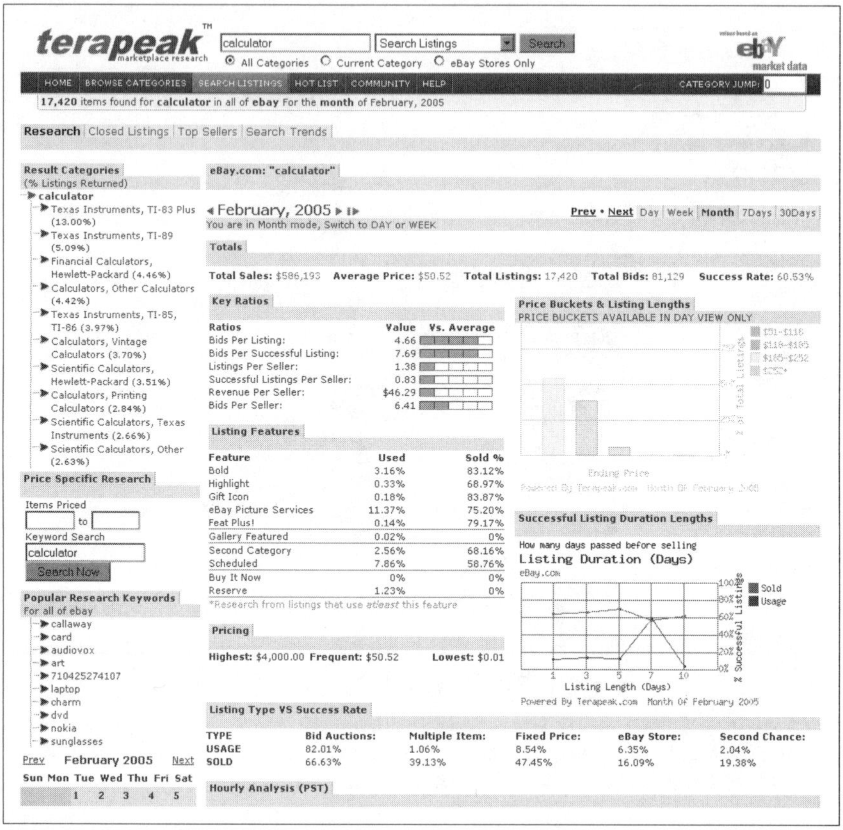

Figure 4-4. Terapeak provides a targeted summary of the success rate of completed items matching your search query, allowing you to gauge the effectiveness of certain listing upgrades

In this example, 83.12% listings with (at least) the Bold upgrade sold successfully, showing a 1/3 increase over listings without it! The success rates for the Highlight and Second Category upgrades, on the other hand, were much more modest, showing an increase of only a few percentage points. And the success rate for Scheduled listings [Hack #48] was actually lower than the average.

Also interesting is the Used column, which shows the percentage of all listings that had each particular upgrade. For instance, Figure 4-4 shows that a Reserve price [Hack #45] was used 1.23% of the time, but resulted in no successful sales at all. And 0.02% of the 17,420 total listings (about 3) used the Gallery Featured upgrade (at nearly $20 a pop), but none of them sold successfully.

Both Terapeak and Andale are subscription-based services; while Andale is marginally less expensive, Terapeak's tools are better integrated, offer more-thorough analysis, and even incorporate historical data. You can view success-rate comparisons to help you choose the best listing duration and start time

[Hack #48] or choose a listing format (i.e., fixed price versus bid auctions). And Terapeak's Search Trends tab shows fluctuations in the market for your item and lets you compare it with historical data to help you choose what to sell and when [Hack #92]. If you do it right, a subscription to a research service can pay for itself with a single successful sale.

Upgrade Analysis

Some listing upgrades are more effective than others, but the most expensive options don't always provide the biggest gains. As a rule, the most effective listing upgrades are those that affect your auction's visibility in search results, making them stand out from the rest. Here's a brief analysis of each of the extra-cost listing upgrades eBay has to offer:

Buy It Now. The Buy It Now feature allows you and a bidder to complete the transaction early at a price you set. But it can also be a very effective promotion tool, with the Buy It Now icon and price appearing in search results just below the opening price.

Set the Buy It Now price a little *under* the item's market value [Hack #42], and you'll likely make a sale to a shrewd buyer within a few hours of listing. Or set the Buy It Now price a little *over* the item's market value, and you might get a bite from a hungry bidder in a hurry. If nothing else, a carefully chosen Buy It Now price might subconsciously suggest a price to early visitors, even if they don't end up using it [Hack #31]. At only 5 to 25 cents (depending on the Buy It Now price you choose), it's not much of a gamble.

Gallery. Select this option to have eBay display a thumbnail photo next to your item in search results and category listings. Assuming you create a good gallery image [Hack #82], the Gallery option is one of the best and most cost-effective things you can do to promote your listing. The only downside (other than the 25-cent fee) is the time it takes to create good gallery images, but if you're preparing a bunch of images at once, the time required to create each gallery thumbnail decreases considerably.

If you let eBay host your photos, you'll have no choice but to use your first picture as the Gallery image. This means that you'll either have to live with a lousy gallery photo or consent to having the first picture your customers see be a postage-stamp-sized image of your item. For the best results with the Gallery feature, you should host your own photos [Hack #76].

10-Day Listing. eBay charges the same listing fee for 3-, 5-, and 7-day auctions, but a 10-day listing will cost an extra 40 cents. Since eBay prefers a quick turnaround, this fee is as much intended to dissuade you from using the 10-day option as to profit from the advantages it provides.

The theory is that the longer your listing is active on the eBay site, the more bidders will see it, and the more bids you'll get. In many cases, the extra exposure is easily worth the extra 40 cents. But its effectiveness is somewhat offset by the implied "urgency" of a short 3- or 5-day auction, which might encourage bidders to bid earlier—and higher. The best way to determine whether or not to use this option is to give some thought to the scheduling [Hack #48] of your listing.

Subtitle. For an extra 50 cents, you can display a second line of text (another 55 characters) underneath your title in search results and category listings, and on the listing page itself. The key to the Subtitle is that the words contained therein are only indexed in title-and-description searches, meaning that it'll have no effect on your listing's exposure in title-only searches.

Use this feature to add information or to attract attention to your listing without eating up title space that could be better-used for search keywords [Hack #47], such as the manufacturer and model number. For instance, if you're selling a camera, use the Subtitle to list any included accessories (e.g., lenses, carrying case, batteries) and to indicate the condition [Hack #17] of the camera itself, since bidders aren't likely searching explicitly for these things.

Additional Pictures. If you're having eBay host your photos, the first one is free, and additional photos cost 15 cents each. The problem is that eBay doesn't show all of your photos at once; your bidders have to click tiny thumbnails to see them.

Rather than wasting money on this feature, include only one photo and really make it count [Hack #70]. Or, better yet, host your own photos [Hack #76] and include as many pictures as you want at no charge.

List in Two Categories. It costs twice the normal listing price to include your item in two categories, so the risk increases with the starting bid and other upgrades you choose. Listing in two categories won't necessarily "double" your exposure, as eBay claims; for instance, it has no direct effect on search results, except possibly in cases where buyers narrow searches by selecting categories [Hack #12]. Only if there are two equally appropriate categories for your item is the upgrade usually worthwhile; otherwise, consider it unnecessary.

Scheduled Listings. The start time is an important factor in the amount of exposure your auction gets, since it affects when it shows up in Newly Listed and Ending First search results, as well as who's awake to see and bid on it. By default, a listing starts as soon as you complete the Sell Your Item form, but if you're up writing auction descriptions at 3:00 a.m., you may wish to pay an extra 10 cents to schedule your auctions [Hack #48] to start at a more reasonable time. Or, you can save your dime by using a listing tool [Hack #93] to prepare your auctions ahead of time.

Bold. The Bold option simply displays your listing title in a bold font in search results and category listings. To see how effective this upgrade is, try any search on eBay and see how the bolded listings stand out. Bold makes auctions harder to miss when there's a lot of competition. However, if most of your competition is already using Bold, you might need something more aggressive, such as Featured Plus!.

Picture Show. The Picture Show feature is an interactive slideshow, used to automatically (or manually) flip through the various photos you include with your listing.

Don't ever use the Picture Show option in your listings. Not only is it a waste of money, but its poor design can actually cause trouble later on. When a bidder clicks the preview image that appears at the top of the page, it opens a separate window in which your photos are shown full size, one-by-one. This means that your bidders will likely miss your description and payment details [Hack #54], thus increasing the likelihood of deadbeat bidders [Hack #68].

If you like the idea of having an interactive slideshow in your listing, include a little JavaScript in your description and make your own slideshow presentation [Hack #79] at no extra charge.

Supersize Picture. By default, each photo you host on eBay's picture server is shrunk to a cramped 400×300 pixels and then over-compressed to reduce its file size and download time (and consequently, unfortunately, its quality). If you select the Supersize upgrade, this doesn't change.

The only thing you get for your 75 cents is a tiny link beneath the photo, allowing any bidder who sees and clicks it to view an enlarged version (up to 800 pixels in the larger dimension). If you include multiple pictures in your listing (at 15 cents a pop), for each picture a bidder must first click each thumbnail and then click the Supersize link to view the larger versions. Include four pictures, and it will take *seven* clicks to see them all. Frankly, most bidders won't bother.

Large, dramatic photos will get you more money for your items, but not if bidders have to work to find them. Fortunately, you can include as many full-size photos as you like for free—right in your listing description—if you host the photos yourself [Hack #76]. Or, combine all your photos into a single collage [Hack #81] for a striking effect.

Gift Services. If you're willing to gift-wrap your item, include a gift card, use express shipping, or ship to a recipient other than the buyer, you can pay an extra 25 cents to advertise these services. Don't expect the little gift icon to get you any extra bids, though, except perhaps during the holidays. If you want to save money, you can simply say you'll gift-wrap your item in the subtitle or description.

Reserve Price. See "Reserve Judgment" [Hack #45] for tips and pitfalls of this overused, but sometimes necessary feature.

Picture Pack. This is a bundle of three listing upgrades (Gallery, Supersize Picture, and Additional Pictures) offered at a discounted price.

Listing Designer. For an extra 10 cents, you can use one of eBay's predesigned templates for your auction. But with a little knowledge of HTML and some imagination, you can create a unique look for your auctions [Hack #56] without paying any extra fees.

Border. Choose this upgrade to wrap a purple border around your listing title in search results and category listings. Like the Bold upgrade, the Border feature attracts attention to your listing, necessary only if there's a lot of competition in your item's category. Despite the fact that it's less expensive, it's actually a bit more noticeable than the Highlight upgrade, described next.

Highlight. The Highlight feature changes the background color behind your auction title in search results and category listings. In most cases, though, it's barely noticeable, and hardly worth the $5 fee. But if most of your competition is already using the Bold and Featured upgrades, then Highlight might give you enough of an edge to pay for itself.

Featured Plus! The "Featured" upgrades (Featured Plus! and Gallery Featured) are the only ones that actually affect your *ranking* in search results. If your item normally appears on a particular search results page or category listing page, then it will also appear in the Featured section at the top of the page, as shown previously in Figure 4-3.

Featured Plus! is a particularly effective way of promoting your item, which you probably already know if you've ever performed a search on eBay. At nearly $20 per listing, it isn't cheap, but it's a no-brainer if it gets you another $100 on your $1,500 item.

Gallery Featured. This is basically the same as the Featured Plus! upgrade except that it affects only the Picture Gallery view of search results and category listings (whereas Featured Plus! affects only the List View). But since the Picture Gallery isn't the default view, you'll get less bang for your buck with Gallery Featured than you would with Featured Plus!.

Home Page Featured. If you choose to throw away $40 for this upgrade (or twice that if you're promoting a multiple-item listing), your auction *might* appear in the small Featured Items box on the eBay home page—but there is no guarantee that your item will *ever* actually appear in this list, and even if it does, the odds that the person who sees it will actually be interested enough to bid are so astronomical that the option is a gamble at best. It might be worth the cost if you're selling real estate or promoting a pyramid scheme; otherwise, it's a complete and utter waste of money.

See Also

- If you're interested in promoting all your listings, consider advertising in search results [Hack #99].

HACK #47 Use Keywords Effectively

Strategically place keywords in your title and description to increase your exposure without violating eBay's keyword spamming rules.

The title is the single most important part of your auction, as it is the only basis for standard searches on eBay. You have 55 characters with which to simultaneously describe your item and include as many search keywords as possible, so don't waste them.

Say you're selling a camera, and you want to attract as many bidders as possible to your auction. To construct the best possible title, start by including the full manufacturer name, product name, and model number, like this:

```
Nikon F100
```

If you were to put only "Nikon" in the title, any searches for the model name ("F100" in this case) would fail to bring up your item. Next, state what the item actually is:

```
Nikon F100 35mm Camera
```

One of the more common mistakes sellers make is never stating what the item *is* in the title or even in the description. Think about it: without the word "camera" in the title, searches for "nikon camera" wouldn't bring up your item.

eBay goes to great lengths to help sellers describe their auctions. If you're not familiar with a certain category, check out eBay's seller's guide for the section. For instance, eBay's Art Seller's Guide (*pages.ebay.com/artsellersguide*) suggests that the word "art" is consistently one of the top five search terms.

Next, you'll want to compensate for common variations by including them right in the title:

```
Nikon F100 F-100 35mm Camera 35 mm
```

This means that searches for "F100" and "F-100", as well as "35mm" and "35 mm" (with the space), will bring up this item. Note that some variations, such as "tshirt" and "t-shirt" are considered equivalent, thanks to eBay's support for fuzzy searches [Hack #11], so you don't have to waste space by including both.

The order of the keywords in your title is also important, because some bidders search for phrases [Hack #10]. Here, "35 mm" (with the space) appears after "camera" so that the phrase "35mm Camera" remains intact. For the same reason, you wouldn't want to type something like "F100 Nikon". This is also acceptable:

```
Nikon F100 F-100 35 mm 35mm Camera
```

Next, if the manufacturer is known by other names (or other spellings), include them as well:

```
Nikon F100 F-100 35mm Camera 35 mm Nikkor
```

Finally, if there's room, think about other things your bidders might be looking for. Remember, the title not only seeds search results; it must also compel bidders to view your item when they see it listed in search results and category listings. For instance, if your item comes with extras, say so right in the title:

```
Nikon F100 F-100 35mm Camera 35 mm 2 Nikkor Lens Lenses
```

Again, multiple variants are included ("lens" and "lenses"). Now, after a simple test [Hack #11], you'll find that eBay considers these two words equivalent, so both are not strictly necessary. But you may want to leave them in to catch searches for the phrase "Nikkor Lens," which paradoxically does not find the same items as "Nikkor Lenses."

In this last example, the number "2" was used instead of "two," which saved two characters for other keywords. This kind of abbreviation is okay because nobody will be searching for the word "two." But if there's space, "two" is a little more eye-catching and easier to scan (read quickly), and may be worth dropping the second "35 mm" variant:

```
Nikon F100 F-100 35mm Camera TWO Nikkor Lens Lenses NEW
```

This change also makes room for the word "NEW," something for which many customers will actually be looking.

> Be judicious with your use of capital letters. In most cases, putting the entire title in ALL CAPS is unnecessary, and actually may turn off bidders. But a few choice words in all capitals will not only emphasize those words, but will help separate them from other words in the description without having to resort to unnecessary punctuation and prepositions like "with." A good mix of upper- and lowercase will stand out better than an otherwise homogeneous title.

Naturally, your ability to squeeze more words into the title will vary with the item being sold and which words you think people are likely to use in searches. If you run out of room, you'll have to start prioritizing. Remove the less common words, phrases, and monikers and embed them in the subtitle or description, discussed later in this hack.

Title Don'ts

eBay's support for fuzzy searches [Hack #11] is very limited, so in most cases, only exact matches will bring up your auction in search results. For this reason, never abbreviate:

```
Nikon F100 Cam. with two lns. & other xtras brand new
```

For the same reason, be careful not to misspell the name of your item, or nobody will find it. This, of course, doesn't include *intentional* misspellings you might include to accommodate your spelling-challenged bidders (e.g., "Nikkon").

Next, avoid wasting space with prepositions ("with"), conjunctions ("and"), and punctuation (commas, periods, semicolons, and quotes). In most cases, nothing more than a single space is needed to separate words in your titles. But don't take it too far; a lot of sellers make the mistake of squishing all their words together, like this:

```
NikonF100with2lensesextrabatteriesbrandnewsowhywait
```

This auction won't show up in any searches, ever, and is so difficult to read that few people will bother opening it in category listings. Do this only if you want to completely hide your auction from your customers.

Don't abuse keywords by using them to spam search results. A common practice is to include the word "not" followed by other manufacturer names, like this:

```
Nikon F100 Camera not Canon Olympus Minolta
```

The idea is to increase the item's visibility by having it show up in a wider variety of searches, a plan that usually backfires for several reasons. First, anyone searching for a different manufacturer is very unlikely to be interested in your item. Second, this is in violation of eBay's keyword-spamming rules, and is grounds to have your item removed (yes, they actually delete listings for this). Third, this practice will probably end up annoying the very customers you're trying to attract. Finally, these superfluous keywords are a total waste of space that could otherwise be used to include relevant keywords that will attract bidders who might actually bid on your item.

Here's an especially bad title:

```
°º¤ø,¸¸,ø¤º°`°º¤ø,¸¸,ø¤º° * * Nikon F100 * * @_@ LOOK @_@
```

Obviously, all this fluff is a total waste of space, consuming precious characters that could otherwise be used to include more keywords. And when was the last time you searched for the word "LOOK" anyway? But a lot of sellers do this; a recent title-only search on eBay for the word "LOOK" actually generated 79,533 results.

In the rare case that you have space to spare, fill it with an acronym [Hack #17] or two. And if you want to attract attention to your listing, eBay's listing upgrades [Hack #46] do a much better job than ASCII art, and easily pay for themselves if you use them appropriately.

Make Space with a Subtitle

A relatively new addition to eBay's extra-cost listing upgrades, the subtitle is another 55 characters of text that appears beneath your title in search results, category listings, and on the item page itself. The key is that words in the subtitle are included only in title-and-description searches, whereas only words in the title are included in title-only searches.

Use the subtitle to include extra information or eye-catching phrases for which your customers would be less likely to search. For instance, instead of this lone title:

```
Nikon F100 F-100 35mm Camera TWO Nikkor Lens Lenses NEW
```

you could use this title-subtitle combination:

```
Nikon F100 F-100 35mm Camera 35 mm Film Nikkor Lens NEW
Brand new setup w/ two Nikkor lenses & extra batteries!
```

This new title regains all the keywords that were removed to make room for higher-priority ones, and even has space for "Film" (presumably to catch searches for "film camera"). The subtitle need not be as efficient and can, rather, focus on a selling point or two to help grab attention in a crowded market.

The Description

The description is used (obviously) to describe your item. But it's also the only other part of your auction that is indexed by eBay's search, so make sure to insert any relevant search terms that you weren't able to fit in the title or subtitle.

Since there's no size limit for the description, you can use as much space as you like with keywords, variations, alternate spellings, and anything else you can think of. The catch, of course, is that description text comes into play only in title-and-description searches.

The only big "don't" when it comes to writing auction descriptions is keyword spamming, which essentially involves listing a bunch of search keywords unrelated to the actual item being sold. As in the title, keyword spamming is grounds for removal of your listing.

> As a seller, you have something at stake when other sellers flood category listings and search results with irrelevant auctions. Not only does this practice annoy potential customers, but the increased competition can make it harder for bidders to find your listings. What's worse is that more-adept bidders may feel it necessary to narrow their searches as a result, using exclusions [Hack #10] that might inadvertently exclude your listing as well. If you suspect that a seller is keyword spamming, you have every right to report the listing by going to *pages.ebay.com/help/contact_inline*.

To avoid *looking* like you're keyword spamming (whether you are or not), you'll want to embed your keywords in your descriptions rather than blatantly listing them somewhere. This is a much better way to "hide" keywords than, say, making them invisible with white text [Hack #52] or including them with `<meta>` tags.

For instance, consider an auction for a used camera. Here's a paragraph that surreptitiously hides intentional misspellings, variations, specific phrases, and other keywords, all of which have been set apart in **bold**:

> You are bidding on a like-**new Nikon F3 35mm camera**, complete with all the original paperwork, three **Nikkor** lenses (a 28–80 mm **zoom lens**, a 55mm **macro** lens, and a 105mm **Nikon lens**), and the original **Nikkon warranty** card. I've had the **F-3** for only a few months, during which time I've only used **FujiChrome 35-mm film** with it. Of all the **cameras** I've used, including a **Canon EOS**, this has been my favorite. I'm selling because I'm shooting mostly **digital** these days. Being a **photo** nut, I also have some other **photographic** equipment for **sale** this week, such as two **Olympus cameras** and a bunch of **Kodak TMAX** black and white film, so check out my other listings.

As you can see, many of the keywords come from subtle advertising of other listings in the description [Hack #60]. Of course, since description searches also include titles, you don't have to go out of your way to duplicate keywords in your description that already appear in your title.

Item Specifics

Lastly, don't forget to take advantage of the specialized *Item Specifics* fields available for certain categories. For instance, if you're selling a pair of women's shoes, you'll be given the opportunity to fill out a handful of related fields, such as Style (e.g., athletic, boots, flats, sandals, etc.), Size, Main Color, Heel Height, and Condition. Not only do these choices show up in a dedicated box just above your description, but your customers will be able to find your listing by filling in the corresponding Item Specifics fields on eBay search pages. Among other things, any selections you make here may allow you to drop a word or two from the title to make room for any more-vital keywords.

Schedule Your Listing for Optimal Exposure

Choose the best day of week and time of day to start and end your listing.

Timing is as important in online auctions as it is in comedy. Most of your customers will see and bid on your listing during its last day—and particularly, in its last few minutes—on the auction block. So it stands to reason that you should favor end days and times that are most popular with your customers.

When creating a listing [Hack #43], you're given the opportunity to select a listing duration and, for an extra fee, a start time and day, but what you should really be thinking about is the day and time your listing *ends*.

Choosing a Duration

With an assortment of durations at your fingertips, you have the ability to choose almost any day of the week to end your listing. If only celebrity boxing was this accommodating.

You can choose a 1-, 3-, 5-, 7-, or 10-day listing. eBay charges the same insertion fee for 1-, 3-, 5-, and 7-day listings, but imposes an extra fee [Hack #46] if you want your listing to last 10 days. The duration is important for two reasons: it determines how long your listing is active on eBay (and thus how many customers see it) and, when taking the start day into account, what day of the week your listing ends.

Conventional wisdom holds that the longer the duration, the better. The theory is that the more time a listing is active on eBay, the more bidders will see it, and the more bids you'll get. In most cases, the extra exposure afforded by the longest duration—especially for rare items—is easily worth the added expense.

But there's also the implied "urgency" of a short 3- or 5-day auction to consider, which might encourage bidders to bid earlier—and higher. Plus, many sellers feel that longer auctions just unnecessarily postpone the inevitable bidding frenzy on the last day—particularly for common items—and that a duration of 5 or 7 days is just as good as 10, if not better.

1-day listings, while seemingly pointless for getting the attention of a lot of bidders, are great for time-sensitive listings, such as event tickets and travel tickets. Note that 1-day listings are available only if you have a feedback rating of at least 10 or if you're ID-verified [Hack #8].

You also may want to choose a shorter listing duration if you're not going to be around when a 7- or 10-day listing would end, or if you want last-minute buyers to be able to complete the transaction and receive the product before an upcoming holiday.

The duration you choose is ultimately up to you and should be based on your own experience, patterns, and knowledge of your markets. For instance, if you list a lot of similar items, you'll want to stagger them so they don't all end on the same day, both to avoid flooding the market and to preserve your own sanity. Or perhaps you'll simply settle into a weekly routine of listing on Tuesdays, collecting payments on Saturdays, and shipping on Mondays.

The Best Day to End Your Listing

Now, if you start a five-day listing on a Wednesday, it'll close on the following Monday. The start day is important, because that's when your listing will appear at the top of search results sorted by time listed. But the end day is even more important, not only because of when it will appear at the top of ending-soonest searches, but because it will affect snipers [Hack #26] who will kindly drive up the price of your item at the last minute.

Here's a breakdown:

Sunday. Sunday is widely considered to be the best day to end an auction, as Jane eBay and Joe Bidder are more likely to be sitting in front of their computers at home with time to shop. Many people also use Sunday-and to a lesser extent, Saturday—as "get things done" days, including searching and bidding on eBay. Avoid holidays and long weekends, though, as those same customers will probably be taking the opportunity to get outside and take in some fresh air (as should you).

Monday. Monday is also good, because many eBayers only have Internet access at work and might spend some time shopping before resigning to the fact that they eventually have to get back to work after a weekend of loafing. Plus, if you start a 10-day auction on a Friday, it will span an entire week plus two weekends, and end the Monday after next.

Wednesday. Wednesday, on the other hand, is probably the worst day to end your auction, presumably because more people will be preoccupied with work or too tired to shop when they get home. Friday is a similarly poor choice, mostly because the approaching weekend means that customers are less likely to expect immediate service from eBay sellers, and hence, feel less urgency to bid.

Obviously, all this involves a little psychology and a lot of conjecture. As you build your own experience, you'll find that some end days indeed work better than others for your market or even just your style. See the research section later in this hack for more help in choosing a good day to end your listing.

Choosing a Start Time

Separate from the duration, the time of day at which you begin your listing determines the time of day it ends. This means that a seven-day listing that you start at 3:42:01 on a Tuesday afternoon ends precisely at 3:42:01 p.m. the following Tuesday.

As described in the previous section, the first few hours—and more importantly, the last few—are the periods during which you'll see the most active bidding on your listings. Thus it pays to begin (and therefore end) your auctions at an hour when your customers are more likely to be awake and sitting in front of their computers.

eBay claims that the hours between 4:00 p.m. and 9:00 p.m., Pacific time, constitute their busiest time of day, presumably because so many bidders do their shopping after they come home from work. This roughly translates to early-to-midevening hours (7–9 p.m.) in each of the four time zones of the United States (eBay's biggest market). Obviously, if your customer base is elsewhere, you would do well to target the evening hours of your customers' time zones.

A Little Research Goes a Long Way

As you might expect, optimal end days and times vary by market, seller, and prevailing winds. But there are a few sure-fire ways to predict the patters of your market and adjust your selling accordingly.

If you're new to a market, start with an off-site research tool like Terapeak (*www.terapeak.com*) or Andale Research (*www.andale.com*) and perform a search here as though you were looking for completed listings [Hack #42]. (If you're using Terapeak, click the Month tab to view data accumulated from a larger period than the default of a single day.)

Terapeak's Research tool, illustrated in Figure 4-4 [Hack #46] provides all sorts of interesting data, but the most relevant items for scheduling purposes can be found here:

Successful Listing Duration Lengths. This box, shown in Figure 4-5, contains a five-point line chart that illustrates the usage rate and success rate for each of the five listing durations. What's particularly interesting is how much these statistics change with the particular search that is performed.

For instance, the search for pocket calculators in Figure 4-4 shows an almost inverse relationship between usage and success, while Figure 4-5, which shows results for model trains, shows a very different picture. In this example, the 7-day listing is the most popular, but the 10-day listing has the highest success rate.

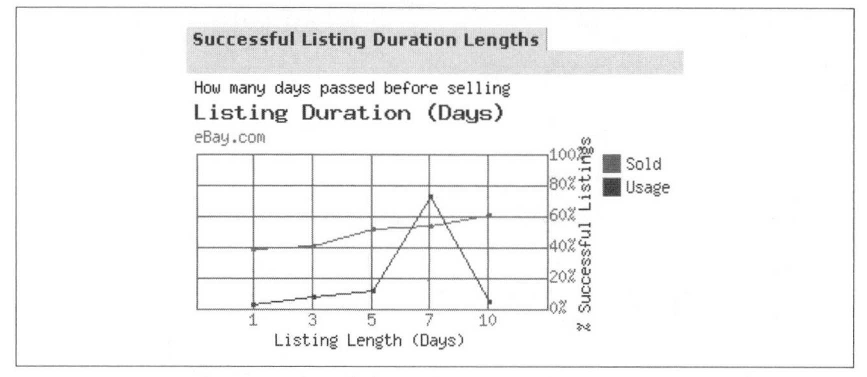

Figure 4-5. Terapeak's research tool shows the usage and success rates of different listing durations

Hourly Analysis. As explained earlier in this hack, most activity happens in the evening hours. But the upper chart in Figure 4-6, which shows total listings as well as the percentage of those listings that were successful listings, tells an interesting story.

The peak shows that the largest percentage of listings closed at approximately 5 p.m. Pacific time. But the number of *successful listings* is higher at 6 p.m. The *success rate*, which is the number of successful listings divided by the total number of listings, is indicated by a higher percentage of blue to gray (dark to light) in each bar. In this example, the highest success rates appear to be at 4 a.m. and 7 p.m. (7 a.m. and 10 p.m. eastern time), while the success rate clearly bottoms out at 2 p.m. and 10 p.m. (5 p.m. and 1 a.m. ET).

The lower chart in Figure 4-6 brings closing prices into the mix, showing the average price of successful listings for each of the 24 one-hour periods. In this example, you can clearly see a gentle dip in the middle of the day (despite the spike at noon) and higher average closing prices late at night and early in the morning.

Search Trends tab. Although neither Andale nor Terapeak offer analyses comparing success rates or closing prices based on days of the week (i.e., Monday versus Sunday), there is a way to infer this information from Terapeak's Search Trends tool, shown in Figure 4-7.

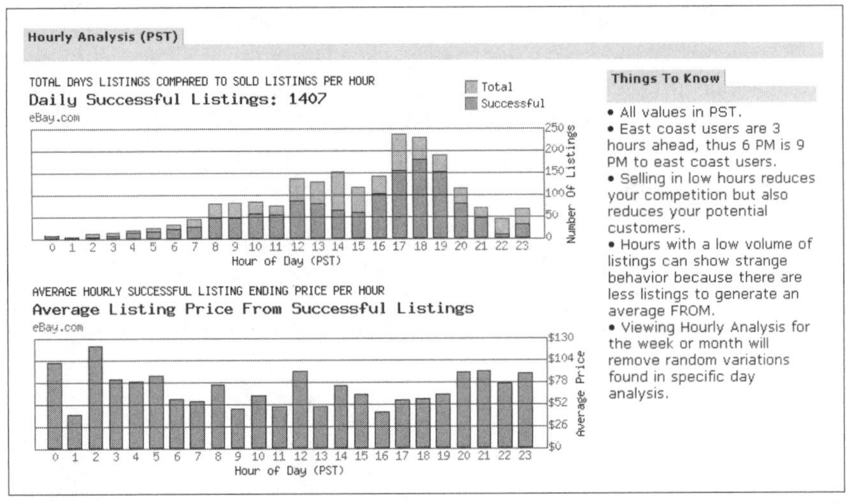

Figure 4-6. Use Terapeak's Hourly Analysis tool to see which times of day are best to end your listing

The most useful report for this purpose is Total Sales, broken down by day over a one-month period. In the example in Figure 4-7, you can clearly see massive spikes on the Sunday of each week, both in total sales and in successful listings. And the lowest points consistently seem to fall on Wednesday, which, ironically, is known as hump day.

If you want to see what days of the week your customers are viewing your listings, you can measure this data by tracking your exposure **[Hack #49]**.

HACK #49

Track Your Exposure

See how findable your listings are and use this information to improve future sales.

You have at your disposal all the tools available to your bidders, which means that you should be able to locate any of your listings in only a few seconds. If you can't, neither can they.

Figure 4-7. Use Terapeak's Search Trends tab to view a running tab of daily total sales over the past month

Although listing upgrades such as Bold, Highlight, and Featured Plus! [Hack #46] can make your listing more visible (and thus easier to find), they can also double or triple the cost of your insertion fees. Unless you can measure their effect, however, it's hard to determine if your money has been well spent.

Start by doing a quick search, not only for the specific keywords in your title but for anything your customers might type to find items like yours. If your item doesn't appear when it should, return to your listing [Hack #65] and take a moment to add any necessary keywords [Hack #47].

Where Is an Item?

eBay provides another handy tool that is used for locating a single item in eBay's various category listings. Go to Site Map → Where Is an Item, select the "Find location of item" option, and enter the item number of the auction you wish to track.

The results, shown in Figure 4-8, show the category and the page number on which the item currently appears. If the item is newly listed or due to close soon, or if you paid for the Gallery upgrade [Hack #46], you'll also see entries indicating your item's locations in these specialized searches.

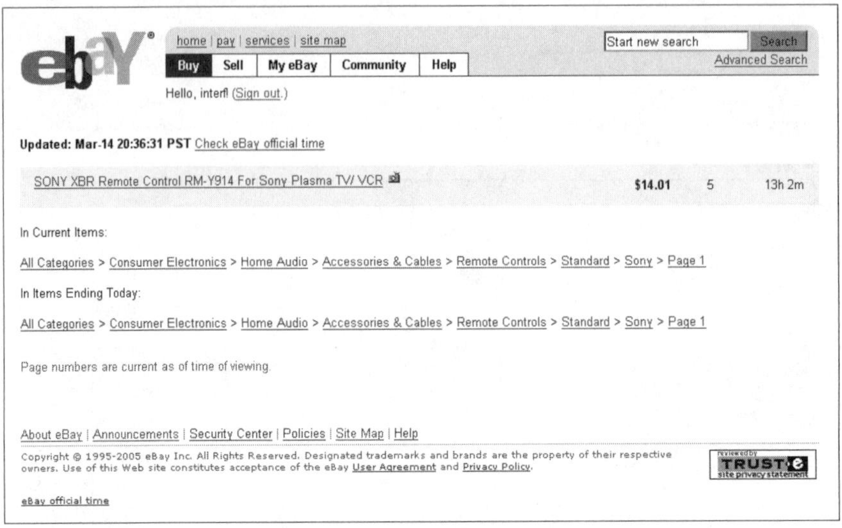

Figure 4-8. Use the "Where is an item" tool to see where your item is listed

The category links shown on the "Where is an item" page will take you right to your item in the listings, automatically scroll down the page as necessary, and highlight your listing in bright yellow.

The striking yellow highlight makes your item easy to spot, but it doesn't exactly give you an accurate picture of how your listing appears to others. To remove the yellow stripe, you'll need to modify the URL [Hack #13], which should look something like this:

```
http://clothing.listings.ebay.com/Sunglasses_Revo_
WOQQsacatZ79733QQsaitmZ8174267035QQsocmdZListingItemList#findit
```

If you look closely, you can find your item number (*8174267035* in this case) buried in the URL. Just break the item number by inserting an extra character (e.g., **x**) in the middle of it, like this:

```
http://clothing.listings.ebay.com/Sunglasses_Revo_
WOQQsacatZ79733QQsaitmZ8174x267035QQsocmdZListingItemList#findit
```

Press Enter to refresh the listing and show it as it appears to your customers.

Count Traffic

If you want to see the number of people who have viewed a single item, add a *counter* to your page. A counter is simply a dynamically generated image residing on a server that keeps track of the number of times the image is requested.

You can show the counter in the form of an odometer right on the page, or you can select the "hidden" counter so that only you can view the statistics. Counters in eBay listings are provided by Andale; you can view your counter totals, choose a different visual style, and even reset your counters by going to *www.andale.com*.

On its own, a counter isn't much more than a curiosity, but when used on a variety of listings with different listing upgrades, they give you a pretty good idea how well your extra-cost upgrades [Hack #46] are working.

Try creating three listings [Hack #43], each identical except for the selected listing upgrades. Buy a Bold upgrade for one, add a Gallery photo to another, and use no special upgrades on the third. Assuming all three auctions start and end at the same time, the counters on each auction should reflect the differences in each item's visibility, and the eventual closing prices should show you the bottom-line results.

Analyze Your Own Traffic

If you host your own photos [Hack #76], you may be able to obtain usage statistics from your own server. Start by isolating your auction photos so they don't share a domain name or IP address with another web site; otherwise, the traffic from the other site will pollute your statistics.

Install some traffic analysis software, such as the excellent Webalizer (available for free from *www.mrunix.net/webalizer*), on the server. This software works by gathering data from server logs and generating reports in HTML format that you can view with any web browser.

If you're renting space on someone else's server, you may have to ask the administrator to set this traffic analysis software up for you. The good news is that most commercial servers will already have some sort of traffic statistics package installed; contact your ISP for details on accessing the reports it generates.

Analysis can take a long time, so don't plan to run the program each time you need it. Schedule the analysis program to generate a report in the middle of the night (when traffic is lowest) using *cron* (for Unix) or Scheduled Tasks (for Windows), as described in "Create a Search Robot" [Hack #21]. Also, for best results, configure Webalizer to save historic data by setting the `Incremental` variable to yes in Webalizer's configuration file. Then, clear the server logs immediately after running the report so that Webalizer can start with a clear slate the next day.

Configure Webalizer to save its reports to a public folder so you can view them by going to an address like *www.your.server/webalizer*. Once Webalizer has accumulated statistics for a few weeks, you should see (among other things) a graph that looks something like the one in Figure 4-9.

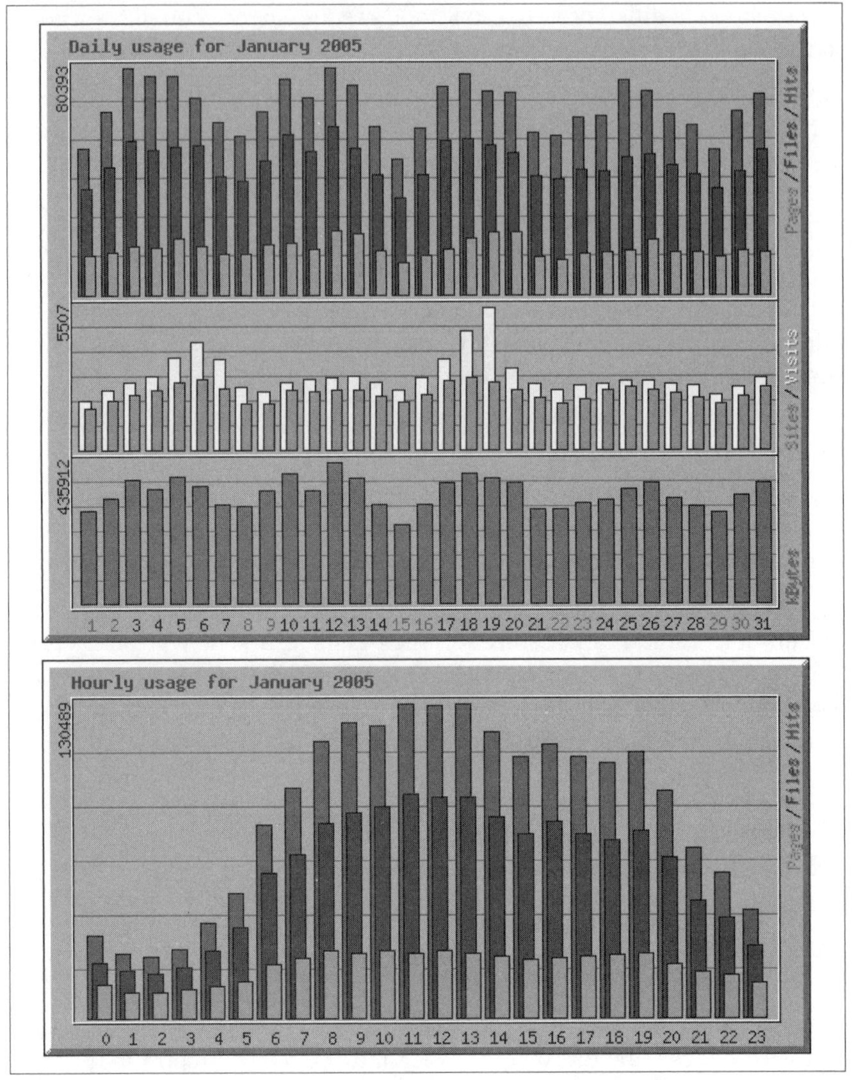

Figure 4-9. Use Webalizer to analyze the traffic to your own listings

Once Webalizer has accumulated statistics for a few weeks, look for trends, such as the peaks in the top-most chart that indicate popular days of the week, or the humps in the bottom chart that indicate the times of day your customers are looking at your listings.

Watch the Watchers

Possibly more useful than the number of visits your listing has gotten is the number of people who are actively interested in it.

Just go to My eBay → All Selling and look at the "# of Watchers" column to see how many people are currently watching [Hack #23] each of your listings. (If you don't see a "# of Watchers" column, click the Customize link in the upper-right corner of the Items I'm Selling box.)

Hot items may get over a hundred people watching, while items of limited appeal may get only one or two. One of the handiest uses for this statistic is to help gauge whether or not it will get a healthy amount of last-minute bidding [Hack #26]. Even though an item may have few bids early on, you can rest assured that it will fetch a good price if there are a lot of watchers, and spend less time and money on extra-cost listing upgrades [Hack #46] or making other changes [Hack #65].

HACK #50 Master Expectation Management

A few carefully chosen words in your auction descriptions will help avoid unhappy buyers, returns, and negative feedback.

If you lend someone $20 and never see that person again, it was probably worth it.

Most sellers would agree that an eBay transaction can be considered successful if the bidder pays promptly, leaves positive feedback, and then disappears. Naturally, this happens when the bidder is happy. Unhappy bidders, on the other hand, have complaints, want refunds, leave nasty feedback, and, all told, make themselves a general pain in the neck.

When a bidder is displeased, it's usually because of a failure by the seller that occurred long before the customer even placed a bid. It's the seller's job to describe the item so that the eventual buyer will be pleased with it, even if it means pointing out the item's flaws.

Think about it: every time you're happy or unhappy with a transaction, it's because the experience either met or failed to meet your expectations. The higher the expectations, the harder it is to meet them. The key is to strike a balance between making your product look good and setting reasonable expectations. Consider the following when writing your auction description:

How new is it? If you would like to categorize an item as "like new," say it's in "mint condition" instead. The phrase "like new" means "indistinguishable from brand new." No matter how good it looks to you, the person who's just laid down $1,500 of her hard-earned money will expect more than you'll probably be able to deliver.

Is it used? If the item has been used, say so; don't expect your bidders to realize this simply by scrutinizing your blurry photos or noticing that you set a low starting bid.

How used is it? Mention all flaws, regardless of how seemingly insignificant: whether or not the flaws are important is beside the point. Rather, it's the blunt honesty that will win the trust of your bidders, and ultimately get you more money for your items (and happier bidders to boot).

Where has it been? If you're selling something on behalf of someone else, say so. Otherwise, your bidders will expect *you* to have full knowledge of its history and will hold you accountable for any flaws you don't specifically mention up front. Anything you know about the item's history (such as previous owners, repairs, or accidents) should be mentioned in the description, along with the current condition of the item. Or, if the item has had a relatively cushy life—surviving no accidents and requiring no repairs—then say so.

Is it broken? Selling broken equipment [Hack #51] can actually be profitable, if you do it right. Make sure your bidders clearly understand what's wrong with the item, as a few bucks in profit from a misrepresented item is never worth negative feedback.

If it's dirty, clean it. If you don't want to take the time to clean it, say that it's dirty in the description. Or, better yet, say something like "With a good cleaning, this item will be as good as new!"

Smoker? If you're selling clothing, stuffed animals, dolls, camping gear, or anything else that can trap odors, be sure to mention whether the items were kept in a smoke-free environment. Your nonsmoking customers will thank you either way.

Measuring tapes are cheap and plentiful. Be sure to include the dimensions of your item, especially if you're not that familiar with it. This is not so much for the bidder's convenience, but rather to help ease (or confirm) your bidders' fears that you might have miscategorized your item. For instance, if you're selling your grandfather's model trains and you're not sure of the scale (HO, N, Z, etc.), then you run a pretty good chance of getting it wrong. If you include the dimensions, your bidders can be sure of what they're buying, long before they receive it and have to send it back.

NWT, MIB. Don't forget to mention the inclusion (or exclusion) of the original box, manuals, accessories, cables, warranty card, paperwork, price tags, or anything else your bidders might expect to get with your item. This is important enough that many sellers take the space to include this information with common abbreviations [Hack #17] in listing titles.

Focus, please? Take a good photo [Hack #70] to simultaneously make your item look good and inspire trust in those who are considering paying you for it.

Don't say "the photo says it all." The photo *never* says it all.

Be clear. Take the time to explain exactly what's included in your auction and what types of payments you accept [Hack #54], which is especially useful in keeping out deadbeat bidders [Hack #68]. And, when appropriate, include answers to your customers' questions [Hack #67] right in the description.

Be nice. Finally, your tone sets an expectation with your bidders as to what you'll be like to deal with. Be inviting and friendly, and answer inquiries from interested bidders—and write in complete sentences.

Although it may sound trite, honesty is indeed the best policy. By selling on eBay, you are joining a community. By dealing fairly and honestly, you will build a good reputation, attract more bidders, and contribute positively to that community. This will, in turn, improve your reputation and attract more bidders. Plus, you'll make lots of cash.

HACK #51 Sell a Broken VCR on eBay

Unload your nonfunctional merchandise on eBay guilt-free, and help save the planet while you're at it.

With DVDs all the rage these days, VCRs are going the way of 8-track tapes, fuzzy dice, and honest politicians. As you might expect, eBay is the perfect way to unload that old machine that has been blinking 12:00 for as long as you can remember. It won't be worth very much, but some lucky bidder will be happy to get a bargain, and you don't have to be responsible for adding it to a landfill.

But what if it's broken? If a *working* machine isn't worth much [Hack #42] on eBay, why even bother trying to sell one that doesn't work? As you spend more time on eBay, you'll begin to understand that for every item, there's a market. All you need is a little time, creativity, and knowledge of the item you're trying to sell.

The VCR, for instance, is essentially an obsolete technology. DVDs look and sound better, and DVRs (such as TiVo) are easier to use and do a better job recording TV programs than VCRs. Thus the market for new VCRs has bottomed out, leaving only the cheapest units available for retail purchase.

Now, VCRs are mechanical devices, and as such, do have a habit of breaking down, which means that there's a steady supply of people who want to replace or repair their old units, if for no other reason than to watch old tapes of *Fantasy Island*. As you might expect, sending these old units back to the factory is out of the question, because replacement parts, if they're even available, usually cost more than a new machine. So these customers turn to eBay.

When creating the listing [Hack #43] for your broken VCR, you can take one of two approaches: either describe it as a "Sony SLV-799HF with a functionality disorder" or market it as "Parts for the Sony SLV-799HF." Of these two approaches, the second one is usually the best choice. Here's how you do it.

First, include the word "parts" in your title [Hack #47]. Then, make sure the first thing you write in the description is that this unit doesn't work. Go ahead and explain the problem [Hack #50]. Then take a sentence or two to explain what *does* still work: this is critical, because that's what your buyers will be looking for.

For instance, your VCR may eat tapes, but the display works, and you still have the remote control and all original accessories. Any owners of the identical VCR may then bid on your listing to get a cheap replacement for a broken display or motor, to get a spare remote control, or even just to get the manual.

Assuming you get a bite, you've just recycled an old VCR, helped someone else save some money, and earned a few bucks for yourself. Good for you!

A Case in Point

This approach works for almost anything. PDAs (Personal Digital Assistants, a.k.a. Palm Pilots or handheld computers), for instance, are plentiful on eBay, and there's usually strong demand for the newer models.

Most PDAs share the same design: a small tablet with a large, glass screen. The most common form of irreparable damage is a crack in the screen, which breaks the digitizer, the sensor that reads the taps of your stylus or fingernail. (If nothing else, let this be a lesson to avoid storing your PDA in your back pocket.)

I came upon just such a PDA not too long ago; it was an older model, typically selling for about $25 in working condition on eBay. So, I searched Google, and seconds later I had disassembly instructions for my particular model. After cracking the unit open, I found a gold mine of spare parts.

The screen was useless, so I threw it out. But the battery was still good, and it subsequently fetched about $20 on eBay. The motherboard fetched another $15, and the keypad ended up being worth about $8. In all, I got $43 for a broken PDA, when a working model was only worth $25.

Why Bother?

eBay isn't just about bargains and profits; it's a regime that facilitates recycling on a global scale. Rather than throwing something away and adding to the world's growing landfills, or letting it accumulate dust in your attic, you can use eBay to find a buyer who will put it to good use.* And who knows; maybe someone is just about to take apart *his* VCR, and extract just the part *you've* been looking for.

HACK #52 Format the Description with HTML

Use HTML tags to turn a drab block of text into an interesting, attractive, and effective sales tool.

As a seller on eBay, you're expected to wear a lot of hats: diplomat, market researcher, salesperson, and yes, even web designer. Since eBay auctions are web pages, your description area can be decorated with the same fonts, colors, images, links, and tables found on any other web site.

If you're already familiar with HTML, you'll probably want to skip this primer or perhaps just use it as a quick reference as the rest of the hacks in this chapter contain more meaty HTML code.

Now, if you're using Internet Explorer, the Sell Your Item form [Hack #43] includes a rudimentary HTML editor (below the Standard tab on the Describe Your Item page), as shown in Figure 4-10. (You'll see only an ordinary text box here if you're using Mozilla or Firefox.)

Here, you can select a font from among four standard Windows typefaces, a font size, and even a color. You can bold, italicize, or underline your text, change the justification, indent, and format bulleted and numbered lists. And at any time, you can click the "Enter your own HTML" tab to view the code for the text you've typed so far. (You'll see something similar if you're building your listings with Turbo Lister [Hack #93].)

But if you want to include images, tables, JavaScript, or any of the other advanced tags used throughout this book, you'll have to type the HTML by hand or import it from another program [Hack #53].

* If you can't find a buyer—or just don't want to take the time to write up a listing—you can always recycle or donate your computer, cell phone, or other consumer electronic component. Visit *www.ebay.com/rethink* for an extensive directory of recycling and donation resources near you.

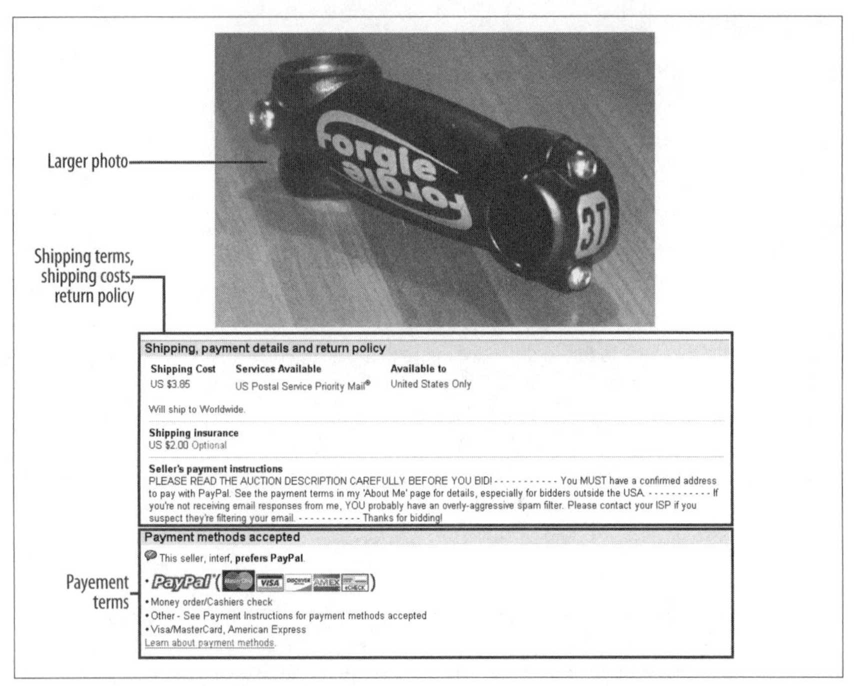

Larger photo
forgie
3T
Shipping terms, shipping costs, return policy
Shipping, payment details and return policy
Shipping Cost
US $3.85
Services Available
US Postal Service Priority Mail®
Available to
United States Only
Will ship to Worldwide.
Shipping insurance
US $2.00 Optional
Seller's payment instructions
PLEASE READ THE AUCTION DESCRIPTION CAREFULLY BEFORE YOU BID! - - - - - - - - - - - You MUST have a confirmed address to pay with PayPal. See the payment terms in my 'About Me' page for details, especially for bidders outside the USA. - - - - - - - - - - - If you're not receiving email responses from me, YOU probably have an overly-aggressive spam filter. Please contact your ISP if you suspect they're filtering your email. - - - - - - - - - - - Thanks for bidding!
Payment methods accepted
This seller, interf, prefers PayPal.
PayPal (VISA DISCOVER AMEX eCHECK)
Payement terms
• Money order/Cashiers check
• Other - See Payment Instructions for payment methods accepted
• Visa/MasterCard, American Express
Learn about payment methods.

Figure 4-10. Use eBay's standard description editor (IE only) if you're not comfortable entering your own HTML code

Rapid HTML Primer

For many sellers, the introduction to HTML comes in the disappointment of seeing a carefully arranged description seemingly mutilated by eBay. For example, this text:

```
Antique steam shovel toy:
     real working treads
     working shovel, turn crank to raise
     glossy red lacquer
in immaculate condition!
```

will look like this when viewed on an eBay auction page:

```
Antique steam shovel toy: real working treads working shovel, turn crank to
raise glossy red lacquer in immaculate condition!
```

The fault lies not with eBay, but with the way web browsers interpret plain text. All spacing, alignment, and line breaks are effectively ignored in favor of the HTML code that is the basis of formatting in all web pages.

HTML (HyperText Markup Language) consists of plain text interspersed with markup tags. A *tag* is a special formatting keyword enclosed in pointy brackets (also known as carets or greater-than and less-than symbols). For instance, simply place the <br> tag in your text to insert a line break, or <p> to insert a paragraph break. For example:

```
real working treads<br>working shovel, turn crank to raise<br>glossy red
lacquer
```

Tags that modify text actually require two parts: a tag to turn the formatting on and another to turn it off. For example, the <center> tag, used to center justify text and images, requires a corresponding </center> tag later on to stop center justification and restore the default left justification. Other tags that work like this include <b>bold</b>, <i>italics</i>, and the <table> </table> structure, all described in the next few sections.

HTML Quick Reference

Table 4-2 shows some more of the tags* you'll use in your auction descriptions, and how they'll appear on the auction page.

Table 4-2. HTML tags that affect spacing and alignment

Goal	HTML code	What it will look like
Line break	First line Second Line	First Line Second Line
Paragraph break	First line<p>Second Line	First Line Second Line
No break	My <nobr>red steam shovel</nobr>	My red steam shovel
Horizontal line, centered	First section<hr>Second section	First section ———————— Second section
Center-justify	<center>In the middle</center>	In the middle
Right-justify	<p align=right>way over</p>	way over
Indent	<blockquote></blockquote>	*See the next table*
Bulleted list (unordered list)	<ul><li>item A<li>item B</ul>	• item A • item B
Numbered list (ordered list)	<ol><li>item A<li>item B</ol>	1. item A 2. item B

Display preformatted text with all line breaks and spacing	<pre>Color: Red
	Size: Small
	Age: Really old</pre>
		Color: Red
		Size: Small
		Age: Really old

Display text in a scrolling marquee	<marquee>Bid Now!</marquee>	w! Bid No

* For a complete listing of HTML tags, consult an HTML reference such as *www.w3.org* or *HTML & XHTML: The Definitive Guide* (O'Reilly).

Using some of these tags, you can fully reproduce the steam shovel description as intended:

HTML code	What it will look like
Antique steam shovel toy: <blockquote>real working treads working shovel, turn crank to raise glossy red lacquer</blockquote> in immaculate condition!	Antique steam shovel toy: real working treads working shovel, turn crank to raise glossy red lacquer in immaculate condition!

Better yet, use bullets:

HTML code	What it will look like
Antique steam shovel toy: <ul><li>real working treads<li>working shovel, turn crank to raise<li>glossy red lacquer</ul> in immaculate condition!	Antique steam shovel toy: • real working treads • working shovel, turn crank to raise • glossy red lacquer in immaculate condition!

Note that the individual tags don't have to be on separate lines, but it sure makes the code easier to read. Table 4-3 shows the commonly used HTML tags that affect the appearance of text.

Table 4-3. HTML tags that affect fonts and appearance

Goal	HTML code	Preview
Bold	`Shipping is <b>Free</b>`	Shipping is **Free**
Italics	`it's <i>really</i> important`	it's *really* important
Subscript	`Drink H<sub>2</sub>O`	Drink H_2O
Superscript	`Turn 180<sup>o</sup>`	Turn 180°
Set the font	`<font style="font-family:courier">Mono-paced</font>`	`Monospaced`
Set the font size	`<font style="font-size:120%">Big</font> or <font style="font-size: 80%">small</font>`	Big or small
Set the font color	`It's <font style="color:white">invisible</font>!`	It's !

Tags can be combined to achieve just about any effect. Take care when nesting HTML tags, however, so that structures do not improperly overlap. For example, this is wrong:

```
The <i>coldest <b>winter</i></b> I ever spent
```

But this is correct:

```
was <i>a summer in <b>San Francisco</b></i>
```

Essentially, tags that are opened *first* should be closed *last*.

If you want to test your HTML code before placing it into your auction, simply type it into a plain text editor. Save the file with the *.html* filename extension and open it in your favorite web browser. Reload/refresh to see changes as they're made.

Images

An image of any size, from a tiny icon to a full-size photo of what you're selling, can be inserted anywhere in your text using the <img> tag, like this:

```
<img src="http://pics.ebay.com/aw/pics/navbar/ebay_logo_home.gif">
```

In this case, the image URL points to a GIF file on eBay's *pics.ebay.com* server that happens to be the eBay logo itself. If you want to put your own photos in your listing, you'll need to host them yourself [Hack #76].

By default, the image will appear inline with the text, which typically doesn't look very professional. Instead, you can left justify or right justify the image, and the text will wrap around it:

```
<img src="http://pics.ebay.com/aw/pics/navbar/ebay_logo_home.gif"
align=right hspace=4 vpsace=7 border=1>
```

Also shown in this example are the `hspace` and `vspace` parameters, which specify invisible horizontal and vertical margins in pixels, and the `border` parameter, which places a black line around the image with the thickness also specified in pixels.

Links

Hyperlinks are created by placing the <a> (anchor) structure around ordinary text, like this:

```
<a href="http://www.ebayhacks.com/">click here</a>
```

Here, the text "click here" will automatically appear blue and underlined in your auction; anyone who clicks it will be taken to the URL *http://www.ebayhacks.com/*. Make sure to include the closing </a> tag that ends the hyperlink.

Always test each and every one of your links before placing them into your auction descriptions. The last thing you want is 20 confused bidders emailing you because you mistyped a URL in one of your links.

Because you don't want your bidders to click a link and leave your auction, never to return, just have the link open in a new window, leaving your auction description window intact. Include the target="_blank" parameter:

```
<a href="http://www.ebayhacks.com/" target="_blank">click here</a>
```

Of course, you can also place an <img> tag inside of a <a> structure to make clickable images [Hack #77].

Tables

Tables are easy to create and are a great way to organize information in your auction descriptions. A table is defined with a single <table></table> structure with one or more <tr></tr> and <td></td> structures contained therein. For instance, this code defines a simple table with two rows and two columns:

```
<table width=90% border=1>
  <tr>
    <td>Color:</td>
    <td>red lacquer with chrome trim</td>
  </tr>
  <tr>
    <td>Dimensions:</td>
    <td>3 inches high, 4 inches long</td>
  </tr>
</table>
```

Each <tr></tr> structure defines a row in the table, and each <td></td> structure defines a single table cell inside that row. Once a row is complete, another row begins. The resulting table looks like this:

Color:	red lacquer with chrome trim
Dimensions:	3 inches high, 4 inches long

Better yet, add align=right inside the first <td> tag in each row to align the colons in the left column:

Color:	red lacquer with chrome trim
Dimensions:	3 inches high, 4 inches long

Note that text and images in tables should never be placed outside the <td> tags. Use indents, like in the example above, to make the code more readable and to help you keep track of your rows and columns.

Using nested tables, you can create a nice-looking box to highlight important information:

```
<table border=0 cellspacing=0 cellpadding=0 width=40% bgcolor=#2D775D>
  <tr><td>
    <table width=100% border=0 cellspacing=1 cellpadding=3>
      <tr><td bgcolor=#BAF9DB align=center>
```

```
        <b>Condition of this item</b>
      </td></tr>
      <tr><td bgcolor=white>
        Brand new in the original box with all original paperwork.
        <br>Batteries are not included.
      </td></tr>
    </table>
  </td></tr>
</table>
```

which should look something like this:

Condition of this item
Brand new in the original box, with all original paperwork. Batteries are not included.

The bgcolor parameter in the <td> tag sets the background color using a six-digit code **[Hack #55]**. Boxes like this are particularly useful for highlighting payment and shipping terms **[Hack #54]**.

Tables are also often used to make simple bars and stripes. For example, to include section headers that match those on eBay auction pages, use this code:

```
<table width=100% border=0 cellpadding=0 cellspacing=0>
<tr><td bgcolor=#9999CC>
  <img src="http://pics.ebay.com/aw/pics/x.gif" width=1 height=1>
</td></tr>
<tr><td bgcolor=#EEEEF8 nowrap>
  <img src="http://pics.ebay.com/aw/pics/x.gif" width=6 height=1>
  <font face="Arial" size=3><b>
    Your Title Goes Here...
  </b></font>
</td></tr>
</table>
```

Table cells with background colors set with the bgcolor parameter can be fine-tuned with transparent, single-pixel images (like *x.gif* here) used as spacers.

Another use for tables is to add whitespace to text, making it easier to read and more pleasant to look at. For example, enclose your description with this simple table:

```
<center>
<table width=85% border=0>
<tr><td>
   Your description goes here...
</td></tr>
</table>
</center>
```

Your text will appear in a stylish column, centered on the page, with 7.5% of the window's width devoted to whitespace on either side. Or, if whitespace is too plain for your tastes, you can use a decorative table to frame your description [Hack #56] without having to resort to eBay's listing designer.

Prepare Your Listings with a Web Page Editor

Use a standalone HTML editor or word processor to format your listing descriptions.

Sometimes, the only way to achieve a desired effect in a listing description is to hand-code the HTML [Hack #52], or so they would lead to you believe.

If you're a WYSIWYG purist (as opposed to an ASCII purist or a sushi purist), you may prefer to create your complex page layouts with a dedicated graphical web page editor, such as Mozilla Composer (free as part of Mozilla Suite, *www.mozilla.org*), HTML-Kit (free from *www.chami.com/html-kit*), or a full-blown commercial product like Dreamweaver (*www.macromedia.com*). Or, if you're most comfortable using a good ol' word processor (e.g., Wordperfect or Word), you can output to HTML as long as you're using a recent release of the software.

The problem is that web page editors are designed to generate complete HTML pages rather than snippets to be inserted into other pages. This means that you'll need to modify the generated HTML code before inserting it into one of your listings. Otherwise, your page may not display correctly and may even interfere with people's ability to bid on your item.

To avoid such display problems, open the generated HTML file in a plain text editor (e.g., Notepad in Windows) so you can see the HTML tags. The actual body of the page is contained within a `<body></body>` structure, so all you need to do is delete everything before the opening `<body>` tag and everything after the closing `</body>` tag, as well as the tags themselves. Then, select everything that's left (Ctrl-A), copy it to the clipboard (Ctrl-C), and paste it (Ctrl-V) into the description field on eBay's Sell Your Item form [Hack #43] or into the description box in Turbo Lister [Hack #93].

Obviously, this process can be a little cumbersome, especially if you're creating a few dozen listings at a time. To speed up the process, use "Extract HTML page content," a component of Creative Element Power Tools (*www.creativelement.com/powertools*; free demo and $18 thereafter). After saving in your web page editor, right-click the HTML file and select Extract Page Content. The tool will automatically extract the necessary code and copy it to the clipboard, at which point you can paste it right into eBay's description field. No editing necessary!

Fixing Broken Images

Most web page editors don't do a very good job of discriminating between files on your hard disk and files that will eventually be on web servers. Case in point: you use a graphical editor to place a photo in your auction description, but when you upload it to eBay, your customers complain that the image is broken.

What likely happened is that your editor generated code that looked like this:

```
<img src="file:///C:/Documents%20and%20Settings/Dave/My%20Documents/
                                        auctions/bowling%20ball.jpg">
```

As you can see, the <img> tag [Hack #52] references a file on your hard disk (*C:/Documents and Settings/Dave/My Documents/auctions/bowling ball.jpg*) rather than a file on a web server [Hack #76] (the %20 codes in the examples represent the spaces in the pathname). Of course, you have access to your hard disk, so it looks fine when you view the listing; but to anyone else who doesn't have a photo of a bowling ball in the same place on her own hard disk, the image will appear broken. To fix this, you'll have to replace the folder name with the URL of the file on your server [Hack #76]. While you're at it, remove the space from the filename. When you're done, the link should look like this:

```
<img src="http://www.your.server/auctions/bowlingball.jpg">
```

Your customers will finally be able to see the bottle cap stuck in the middle finger hole.

Unclogging Microsoft Pages

If you generate a page with a Microsoft Office application such as Word, Excel, or Powerpoint, the resulting HTML will be clogged with tons of extraneous codes that should be removed before you use it in an eBay listing.

The easiest way to do this is to use the Microsoft Office 2000 HTML Filter 2.0, available for free at *www.microsoft.com/downloads*. (Despite the name, it works with all versions of Office, including Office XP and Office 2003.) To clean your Office HTML documents, open the filter, click Add to select one or more files, and then click Apply.

Clarify Your Payment and Shipping Terms

Reduce the chances of deadbeat bidders and unhappy customers by overcoming the limitations in eBay's listing page design.

There's a great deal of comfort in familiarity. For example, I find solace in the knowledge that there's always a butter knife in the first drawer on the right, allowing me to stumble into my kitchen at 1 a.m. for a snack without having to undertake a full-scale utensil search. Move the knife—or worse yet, the drawer—and I'll spend many subsequent nights cursing the change, even if the new location is ultimately more convenient when I'm actually awake.

I find that computer software invokes the same feelings, which is, I think, why people are often reluctant to upgrade (and give up all the bugs they've gotten used to in favor of a bunch of new ones). But visitors to web sites such as eBay don't have that luxury; when a change is made to the site, it immediately affects everyone who uses it.

A few years ago, eBay completely redesigned the standard auction page, the page that shows the price, photos, description, and other details of any particular item you happen to be selling or bidding on. Most of the changes were significant improvements, such as the preview photo [Hack #70] and the adaptive title block [Hack #64] that shows different information to the seller than to, say, the winning bidder, or to the unlucky bloke who was just outbid.

But there were also sacrifices; problems with the design that remain to this day. For example, shipping and payment terms, once displayed near the current bid price at the top of the page, are now buried deep beneath the auction description and photos, as shown in Figure 4-11. Only after the auction is over does eBay display this essential information in the checkout box [Hack #64] at the top of the page where it belongs.

Without clear payment and shipping information in a place your customers can see it, you're just asking for a flood of deadbeat bidders [Hack #68] who bid and find out later they can't meet your terms (i.e., pay).

Getting into the Heads of Your Customers

So why is the placement of your payment and shipping terms so important?

Take another look at Figure 4-11 and then imagine the sequence of events leading up to a bid:

1. The bidder finds the item while searching or browsing category listings, clicks the title, and is shown the top of the auction page. Without scrolling, the bidder can see—at most—the eBay logo, the header block, the seller information box [Hack #1], the preview photo [Hack #70], the current price, the location of the item [Hack #39], and perhaps the first line or two of the description, if viewed on a large screen.
2. If the bidder is interested in your item, she might click the preview photo (or simply scroll down) to view the auction description, a larger version of the top photo, and any additional pictures.

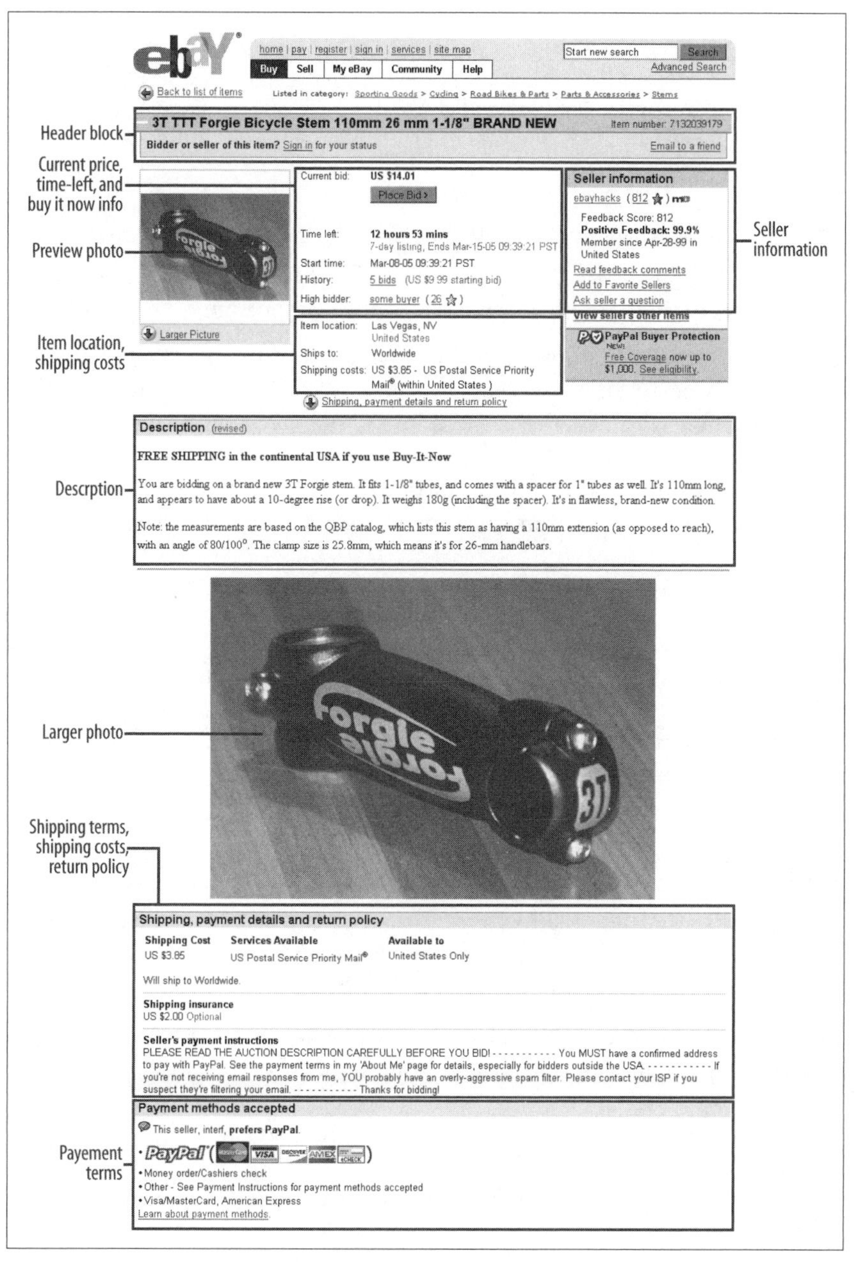

Figure 4-11. The layout of a standard auction page, and where to find the important stuff

If you've purchased the Picture Show listing upgrade [Hack #46], a new window appears with larger versions of your photos when the bidder clicks the preview photo. As you can imagine, this could mean that bidders skip your description altogether.

3. The customer will likely scroll back *up* to look at the price again.
4. Once the bidder decides to bid, she clicks the Place Bid button (or Buy It Now) to jump to the bidding box at the very bottom of the page.

You'll notice that the shipping and payment terms are effectively bypassed in a bidder's hasty purchase. This can pose a problem for a bidder with a post office box who never sees the note in your payment terms explaining that you ship only with UPS (which won't deliver to P.O. boxes). Or, perhaps a bidder outside the United States will never see that you only accept PayPal payments [Hack #85] from customers *inside* the United States.

The Solution

The number-one rule of selling on eBay is that your customers will never read your auction description, at least not thoroughly...or at least not the part you wish they'd read when it comes time to collect payment. So the key is to make this important information more prominent rather than burying it in the single paragraph that makes up your listing description.

Now, your instinct might be to do what most people do when they don't feel listened to: yell. And in Internet "netiquette," yelling means TYPING IN CAPITAL LETTERS, possibly embellishing with large, bright red text. But yelling sends a hostile tone to your customers, and will likely drive many of them away. Plus, it will bully the rest of the text around it so that other information—important details—might be lost in the shuffle.

Instead, use a little carefully placed HTML [Hack #52] to clearly distinguish between your item description and your terms. For instance, here is the most basic approach:

```
You are bidding on...
<P>
<B>Condition:</B> The condition of this item is...
<P>
<B>Payment terms:</B> I accept PayPal and cash, in pennies.
<P>
<B>Shipping terms:</B> I proudly ship with the Pony Express. Shipping is
fixed at $4.00.
```

Paragraphs are separated with <P> tags, and each starts with a section header set apart in bold text using the <B></B> structure. This is simple, and best of all, it works.

Another, possibly more effective way of setting apart your payment and shipping terms right in the auction description involves putting each in its own little table:

```
<table cellspacing=8 cellpadding=0 width="100%" border=0>
<tr><td valign=top width="30%">
 <table cellspacing=0 cellpadding=0 width="100%" bgcolor=#2D775D border=0>
 <tr><td>
     <table cellspacing=1 cellpadding=3 width="100%" border=0>
     <tr><td bgcolor=#BAF9DB>
         <b>What's Included</b>
     </td></tr>
     <tr><td bgcolor=#ffffff>
         One toy car, original box, original manual
     </td></tr>
     </table>
 </td></tr>
 </table>
</td><td valign=top width="30%">
 <table cellspacing=0 cellpadding=0 width="100%" bgcolor=#2D775D border=0>
 <tr><td>
     <table cellspacing=1 cellpadding=3 width="100%" border=0>
     <tr><td bgcolor=#BAF9DB>
         <b>Payment Terms</b>
     </td></tr>
     <tr><td bgcolor=#ffffff>
         I accept PayPal and cash, in pennies.
     </td></tr>
     </table>
 </td></tr>
 </table>
</td><td valign=top width="30%">
 <table cellspacing=0 cellpadding=0 width="100%" bgcolor=#2D775D border=0>
 <tr><td>
     <table cellspacing=1 cellpadding=3 width="100%" border=0>
     <tr><td bgcolor=#BAF9DB>
         <b>Shipping Terms</b>
     </td></tr>
     <tr><td bgcolor=#ffffff>
         I proudly ship with the Pony Express. Shipping is fixed at $4.00.
     </td></tr>
     </table>
 </td></tr>
 </table>
<td valign=top></td></tr>
</table>
```

In addition to payment and shipping terms, there's a third box to combat the other big problem with most auction pages, namely that most sellers don't take the time to clearly spell out what's included in the auction. This box, not surprisingly, is entitled "What's Included," and is illustrated with the others in Figure 4-12.

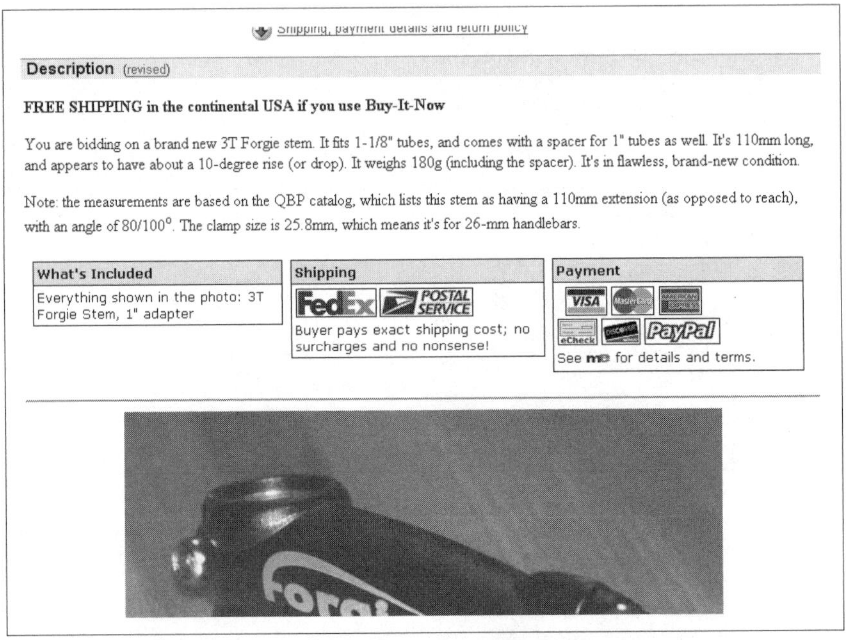

Shipping, payment details and return policy

Description (revised)

FREE SHIPPING in the continental USA if you use Buy-It-Now

You are bidding on a brand new 3T Forgie stem. It fits 1-1/8" tubes, and comes with a spacer for 1" tubes as well. It's 110mm long, and appears to have about a 10-degree rise (or drop). It weighs 180g (including the spacer). It's in flawless, brand-new condition.

Note: the measurements are based on the QBP catalog, which lists this stem as having a 110mm extension (as opposed to reach), with an angle of 80/100°. The clamp size is 25.8mm, which means it's for 26-mm handlebars.

What's Included	Shipping	Payment
Everything shown in the photo: 3T Forgie Stem, 1" adapter	FedEx POSTAL SERVICE Buyer pays exact shipping cost; no surcharges and no nonsense!	VISA MasterCard AMERICAN EXPRESS eCheck DISCOVER PayPal See me for details and terms.

Figure 4-12. Putting important information in boxes helps set it apart from the description without burying it at the bottom of the page

Notice how these boxes stand out! Put something like this in your auction, and you'll get fewer deadbeats, less negative feedback from displeased bidders (fewer displeased bidders, actually), and fewer dumb questions **[Hack #67]** while the auction is running.

Jump to the Description

As described earlier in this hack, a visitor to your listing can miss your description entirely by clicking the preview photo at the top of the page. If you like, you can solve this problem by redirecting the preview photo to any other position on the page.

Here's how it works. Unless you're using the Picture Show listing upgrade **[Hack #46]**, the small preview photo is linked to a *named anchor* lower down on the page, immediately above the full-size photo. The link looks something like this:

```
http://cgi.ebay.com/ws/eBayISAPI.dll?ViewItem&item=5974611839#ebayphotohosting
```

The #ebayphotohosting suffix in the URL points to the ebayphotohosting anchor, which is located immediately above the full-size photo. Click the little photo, and the browser scrolls the page—past your description—so that the full-size photo is positioned at the top of the window.

To redirect the link, just place a second anchor—with the same name—at the beginning of your description, like this:

```
<a name="ebayphotohosting"></a>
```

Thereafter, whenever visitors click the preview photo in your listing, their browsers will jump to the beginning of your description, and they'll be less likely to miss anything important.

HACK #55 Customize Auction Page Backgrounds

Make your item stand out with a little personalization of the auction page using JavaScript.

Although the description area occupies only a portion of the auction page, it's possible to include code that affects the entire page.

Why would you want to do this? Well, as the theory goes that a more distinct auction will get more attention from bidders. However, anyone who looks at your auction has already given you her attention, so the effect will not be earth-shattering. Still, a little tweaking may make your auction look nicer, or at least let you express your own personal style and have a little fun with your auctions.

Never build an auction that will be rendered inoperable if a bidder has disabled JavaScript. For instance, if you place white text on a dark background but the background remains white due to the nonworking JavaScript code, then all you'll have is white text on a white background and a very frustrated bidder.

This code, when placed anywhere in your auction description, will change your auction's background color:

```
<script language=javascript><!--
  document.bgColor='blue';
--></script>
```

Basic colors include aqua, black, blue, fuchsia, green, gray, lime, maroon, navy, olive, purple, red, silver, teal, white, and yellow. For fancier colors, use an HTML color code chart, like the one at *www.computerhope.com/htmcolor.htm*. Or for more control, you can use RGB (red-green-blue) color coding like this:

```
document.bgColor='#C5D0EE';
```

The six-digit color code (here, C5D0EE) is comprised of three pairs of hexadecimal numbers, ranging from 00 (zero, no color) to FF (256, full color). Each pair represents the amounts of red, green, and blue to be used, respectively. For instance, #FF0000 is solid red (no green or blue components), and #FF00FF is purple (red and blue, but no green). Likewise, #000000 represents solid black and #FFFFFF represents solid white.

If you have Adobe Photoshop, you can mix colors in the Photoshop color picker, and the corresponding hex code will appear right next to the red, green, and blue values. See *www.utexas.edu/learn/html/colors.html* for a hex-based color code table.

Unfortunately, the eBay logo and menu bar that appear at the top of auction pages aren't intended to be used with colored backgrounds; they have an unsightly white matte background instead of the ideal transparency. If you don't like the effect, you can still use these colors to paint the cells of HTML tables [Hack #52].

To change your auction's background wallpaper image, insert this code into your auction description:

```
<script language=javascript><!--
document.body.background='http://www.ebayhacks.com/pictures/stone.gif';
--></script>
```

Simply replace `http://www.ebayhacks.com/pictures/stone.gif` with the full URL [Hack #76] of the background image you wish to use.

If you're interested in changing the appearance of the eBay listing page, you might as well go all the way and change the look of all the text [Hack #57] on the page as well.

HACK #56 Frame Your Listings

Use tables and carefully aligned images to place decorative frames around your auction descriptions.

A little extra decoration will give your customers that warm, fuzzy feeling they need to open their wallets and bid a little higher, or so the theory goes. At the very least, frames may help your auctions look more polished and inviting.

For a fee, eBay's Listing Designer upgrade [Hack #46] will do this for you. But using the predesigned templates everyone else uses is not exactly the best way to make your listings look unique. Instead, take a few minutes to design your own and save the fees for buying more stuff on eBay.

The Table

It all starts with a single table, which positions the frame across the top, bottom, and sides, holding your content snugly inside. While you're designing the table, turn on the border by placing `border=1` in the `<table>` tag so you can see more clearly what's going on.

```
<table style="width:100%" cellpadding=0 cellspacing=0 border=1>
<tr>
  <td width=25>top-left</td>
  <td>top-middle</td>
  <td width=25>top-right</td>
</tr>
<tr>
  <td width=25>left side</td>
  <td>

Your content goes here...

<br><br><br><br><br><br><br><br><br>

  </td>
  <td width=25>right side</td>
</tr>
<tr>
  <td width=25>bottom-left</td>
  <td width=25>bottom-middle</td>
  <td width=25>bottom-right</td>
</tr>
</table>
```

The resulting table shown in Figure 4-13 is a placeholder for the eventual design. Note the `width=25` parameters in the left- and righthand columns, which can be changed to accommodate whatever images are eventually placed inside.

Early versions of Internet Explorer and Netscape are notorious for improperly resizing table cells and trying to automatically adjust the cell widths based solely on content. If your table doesn't appear to be responding to the `width=25` parameters as it should, try filling the center cell with lots of text, which should give it the "bulge" it needs to squeeze the sides into position.

The Images

In most cases, you'll need eight images (one for each corner, and one for each side), all hosted on an off-site server [Hack #76].

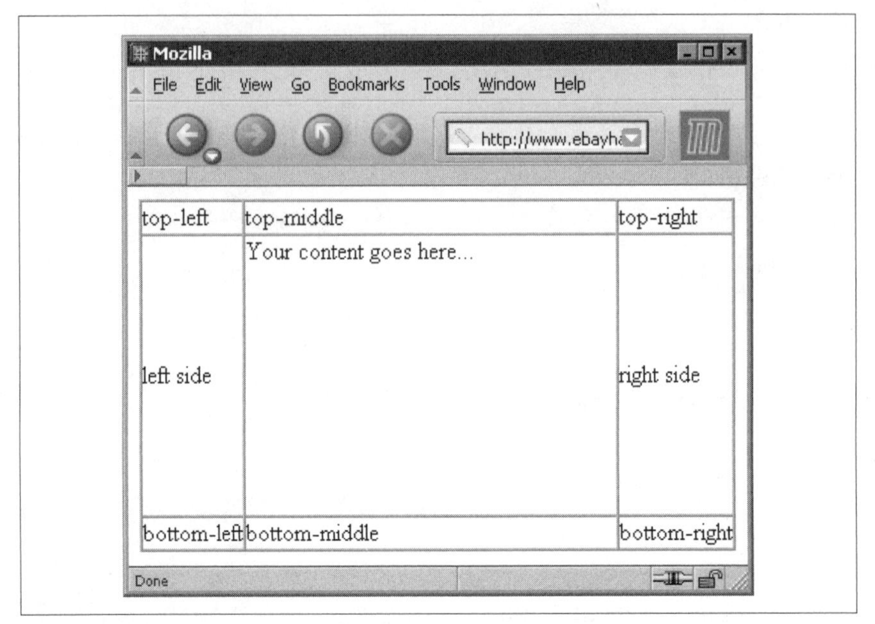

Figure 4-13. This simple table provides the structure for a decorative frame around an auction description

The corner images stay put, but since the width of the browser window and the height of your content cannot be taken for granted, the side images (top, bottom, left, and right) should be designed so that they are either stretchable or repeatable.

To make an image stretch to fill its container (in this case, a table cell), specify `100%` for the `width` if it's a top or bottom piece, or for the `height` if it's a left- or righthand piece. For example, place this in the top-middle cell:

```
<td><img src="http://www.my.server/top_image.jpg" width=100% height=25></td>
```

Since the image will be stretched, you'll want to do this only with images comprised of solid colors, and that won't look bad if distorted in one direction.

Make sure not to leave any spaces between the opening `<td>` tag and the `<img>` tag or between the `<img>` tag and the closing `</td>` tag; otherwise, those spaces will manifest themselves as gaps between the pictures.

On the other hand, you may want to have a single image repeat like wallpaper, which is accomplished by modifying the `<td>` tag and dumping the `<img>` tag altogether, like this:

```
<td background="http://www.my.server/top_image.jpg"> </td>
```

Naturally, repeating images should be designed as such, with an edge that provides a smooth transition to the adjacent image. Note the use of the ` ` code (nonbreaking space) here to convince browsers that there's content to display; otherwise, the cell (and its background) might not show up at all.

Putting It Together

For the full effect, the theme of your decorative border should relate to the item being sold. When selling photographic equipment, for instance, a film-based theme, as in the example that follows, would be appropriate.

Uncut film makes an excellent border because it's comprised entirely of a very simple, repeating pattern, so the image need contain only a single frame, and the browser will do the rest. Figure 4-14 shows a completed border with four film canister images and film extending down the sides of the auction, accommodating long and short descriptions with ease.

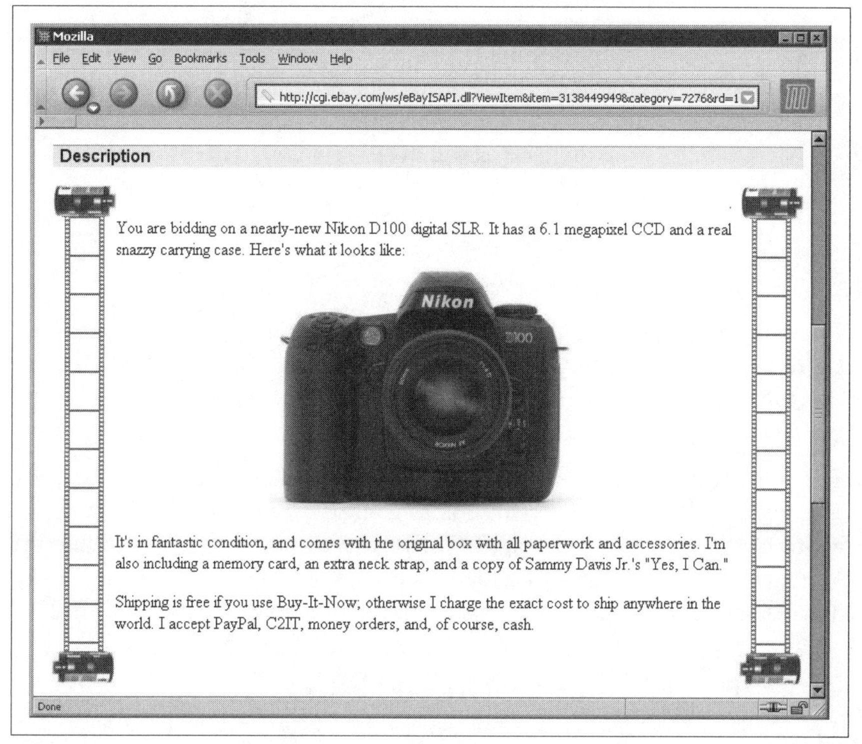

Figure 4-14. The completed frame with four film canister images and a single film frame image repeated down both sides

Here's the code for this frame:

```
<table style="width:100%" cellpadding=0 cellspacing=0 border=0>
<tr>
  <td width=60><img
    src="http://www.ebayhacks.com/pictures/film_canister_top.jpg"></td>
  <td></td>
  <td width=60><img
    src="http://www.ebayhacks.com/pictures/film_canister_top.jpg"></td>
</tr>
<tr>
  <td width=60 background="http://www.ebayhacks.com/pictures/film.gif"
               width=60> </td>
  <td>

Your content goes here...

<br><br><br><br><br><br><br><br><br>

  </td>
  <td width=60 background="http://www.ebayhacks.com/pictures/film.gif"
               width=60> </td>
</tr>
<tr>
  <td width=60><img
    src="http://www.ebayhacks.com/pictures/film_canister_bottom.jpg"></td>
  <td></td>
  <td width=60><img
    src="http://www.ebayhacks.com/pictures/film_canister_bottom.jpg"></td>
</tr>
</table>
```

The canister images, `film_canister_top.jpg` and `film_canister_bottom.jpg`, are referenced by the `<img>` tags in the corner cells, providing a weird *scroll* effect. You could also replace two of the canisters with jagged film edges for more realism, if that's the effect you're after.

The film strip, `film.gif`, appears as the background of the two side cells. The widths of the left and right columns are set at 60 pixels to match the width of the film canister images. To get the 38-pixel-wide film to line up, 11 pixels of whitespace was added to each side. Make sure to get all the dimensions right, or unsightly gaps or misalignments could ruin the effect.

HACK #57 Override eBay's Fonts and Styles

Use Cascading Style Sheets to change the look of more than just the description.

The `<font>` tag [Hack #52], allows you to set the font for any block of text. But it won't have any effect on text outside the `<font></font>` structure, which means you can never use it to control the appearance of any text outside the description area (e.g., the rest of the auction page). Instead, you'll have to use *Cascading Style Sheets* (CSS) if you want to apply your styles to the entire page.

CSS purists may balk at the presence of the following <style></style> structure inside the body of an HTML page. If you had control over the entire page, the technique used in this hack would not be entirely proper, but since you only have control over a portion of the body, you'll have to break from good practice to hack the listing page.

The following code, for instance, will turn all text on the page green:

```
❶ <style>
❷ BODY,FONT,TD,A {
      font-size: 10pt !important;
    font-family: Verdana,Arial,Helvetica !important;
❸         color: green !important;
   }
   </style>
```

Here's how it works. First, the `<style></style>` structure ❶ sets apart your CSS definitions, which will take effect regardless of where the code is placed on the page. Next, a single CSS definition ❷ lists the HTML tags to modify with your new styles. In this case, you're applying your styles to all `<body>` text, as well as to any text inside `<font></font>` tags, `<td></td>` tags (used for tables), and `<a></a>` tags (used for links). If you don't want to modify link colors, for instance, just remove `,A` from line ❷.

The actual styles applied are listed between the curly braces { }, separated one per line for clarity. This includes the font size, the typeface, and, of course, your glorious green color ❸. The `!important` keywords ensure that your styles override any styles defined elsewhere in the page, which is why even the section headers and the light gray text in the "Time left" section are overpowered by your choice.

If you feel that making all text the same color is a little drastic, you can customize it further:

```
<style>
BODY,FONT,TD {
  font-family: Verdana,Arial,Helvetica !important;
        color: blue !important;
}
A {
  font-family: Verdana,Arial,Helvetica !important;
        color: orange !important;
}
</style>
```

This sets all ordinary text blue and links to orange (which will look pretty awful, by the way). Note the absence of the `font-size` style, which ensures that the original size of all text is preserved.

For a complete list of all the CSS styles you can use, you'll need dedicated CSS documentation such as *Cascading Style Sheets: The Definitive Guide* (O'Reilly), or the official W3C CSS specification (*www.w3.org/Style/CSS/*).

You can also use this technique to alter other aspects of the page. Don't like the blue shading section headers? Well, try something like this:

```
<style>
TD { background-color: white !important; }
</style>
```

You may find this particular solution somewhat extreme, since it removes the shading used in every table on the page. But it will give you a taste of the power of CSS.

While you're at it, try playing around with the background [Hack #55] as well.

Override Other Sellers' Hacks

You'll eventually encounter an auction that has been hacked up pretty well, possibly by a seller with worse taste than yours. Fortunately, you may still have some control over the pages you view with your own browser.

Have you ever opened a page with a text/background combination that rendered the page nearly impossible to read? Here's a quick fix: just press Ctrl-A to highlight all text on the page. This makes all text appear white on a dark blue background, which will likely be a significant improvement.

You can set your browser preferences to favor your own color choices over those made by web site designers, but this can be a pain to turn on and off as needed. Instead, you may wish to set up a user stylesheet, a set of carefully constructed preferences and rules that will trump any crazy code like the stuff at the beginning of this hack. User stylesheets are supported by Mozilla, FireFox, Netscape 6.x and later, and Internet Explorer 5.x and later.

See Also

- Probably the best source for information about user stylesheets is Eric Meyer's "CSS Anarchist's Cookbook" at *www.oreillynet.com/pub/a/network/2000/07/21/magazine/css_anarchist.html*. There, you'll find ways to "wreck" tables, disable banner ads, and render font coding pretty much useless, all worthwhile pursuits for the anarchist in each of us.

HACK #58 Use Media in Your Listings

Entertain bidders with video and animation in your listings or drive them away with background music and sound effects.

Your listings don't have to be static brochure-like pages; they can be interactive multimedia extravaganzas! Okay, I hear your groans. But there is still a place for media on eBay if you are subtle about it.

Video Killed the Radio Star

Video clips, or "mov-ies," as some people like to call them, are a great way to show how your product works when a static photo just won't cut it.

There are several ways to include video clips in your listings, each with it's own intended purpose. Before you can put video in your listings, you'll need to upload your clip to a web server [Hack #76] and reference it with a URL like this:

```
http://www.your.server/videos/penguin.mpg
```

where *http://www.your.server* is the URL of the server, */videos* is the folder name, and *penguin.mpg* is the filename of the clip.

Most modern computers can play MPEG (*.mpg*) files and Apple Quicktime (*.mov*) files. AVI (*.avi*) files also work, but aren't recommended, because they can't be played until they've finished downloading. And Windows Media (*.wmv* and *.asf*) files, while popular on Windows PCs, won't work on many Macs or Unix systems without extra software.

The first method involves the `<embed>` tag, like this:

```
<embed src="http://www.ebayhacks.com/videos/penguin.mpg" autostart=false
      loop=true type="video/x-ms-asf-plugin" width=368 height=333></embed>
```

which places a video box right in your listing, complete with standard video controls as shown in Figure 4-15. The `width` and `height` specify the size of the *box*, not the size of the video, so make sure to add an extra 45 pixels to the height to accommodate the video controls.

Figure 4-15. Put a video clip right in your listings to show how your product works

Note that if you're embedding an Apple Quicktime movie, you'll have to instruct the browser to use a different plug-in, like this:

```
<embed src="http://www.ebayhacks.com/videos/penguin.mov" autostart=false
      loop=true type="video/quicktime" width=368 height=333
      pluginspage="http://quicktime.apple.com"></embed>
```

The problem with the `<embed>` tag is that it doesn't always work, although it shouldn't cause any serious problems other than a blank box in the middle of your listing. An alternative is to simply link to the video in your listing, like this:

```
<a href="http://www.ebayhacks.com/videos/penguin.mpg">play the movie</a>
```

or, better yet:

```
<a href="http://www.ebayhacks.com/videos/penguin.mpg"><img src="http://www.
ebayhacks.com/videos/penguin.jpg" width=368 height=288></a>
```

Instead of using a text link, place a still photo from the movie in your listing and link it to the video. Your bidders then click the photo to play the video; include the `target="_blank"` parameter in the `<a>` tag to have the movie open in a new window.

The last way to put video in your listings is to convert your video clip to an animated GIF file and then place the GIF in your description as though it were any other image. It's a low-tech solution, with no controls, no audio, and poor video quality. But since GIFs work in any browser on any platform, and without any special plug-ins, they're a good choice for simple videos of no more than a few seconds long.

> If you're like most people and find animated GIFs annoying, you can disable them. In Internet Explorer, go to Tools → Internet Options → Advanced tab → Multimedia and turn off the "Play animations in web pages" option. In Mozilla/Firefox, type *about:config* into your address bar, double-click `image.animation_mode` in the list, it and set its value to "none."

To create an animated GIF, you'll need a media converter application that can import AVI or MPG movies, such as Adobe ImageReady (*www.adobe.com*) or Ulead GIF Animator (*www.ulead.com*). Once you've converted your video, you can reference it in your description like any ordinary image:

```
<img src="http://www.ebayhacks.com/videos/penguin.gif" width=368 height=288>
```

The clip will play automatically as soon as someone views your listing.

Some Call It Elevator Music

Sound can be useful when text and photos just won't do. For example, if you're selling a music box, you may want to include a clip of the music it plays, especially if you don't know the name of the song. Or, if you're selling a product that modifies sound (such as a car exhaust silencer), your customers will appreciate being able to hear, first-hand, what it sounds like with—and without—your product. And obviously, if you're selling music on CD, tape, record, or DVD, you may want to include a short clip to entice your bidders.

> Although I despise sound in web pages, I feel compelled to show you how to do it properly so you don't pick up any bad habits on the street. The number-one rule to remember when including sound or music in web pages is to provide a means of turning it off. Otherwise, your bidders will eventually discover the workaround themselves…and they probably won't come back.

You can insert background music (in either *.wav* or *.midi* format) into your auction with this line of code:

```
<bgsound src="http://www.ebayhacks.com/files/aah.wav" loop=1>
```

where the `loop` parameter specifies the number of times to play the sound. The problem is that the `<bgsound>` element has no controls: no way for your customers to turn off the sound or adjust the volume. In other words, it's a poor choice.

The more general-purpose `<embed>` tag can do everything `<bgsound>` does, but it also includes a controller box:

```
<embed src="http://www.ebayhacks.com/files/aah.wav" hidden=false
                                    autostart=true loop=true></embed>
```

The `loop=true` parameter can be replaced with `playcount=3` to play the sound a specified number of times and then stop. Go to *www.htmlcodetutorial.com* for further documentation on embedded objects.

The actual audio controller that appears on the page depends entirely on the browser plug-in currently configured to handle sound objects. (Note that users without an appropriate plug-in installed will just see an empty box and won't hear any sounds at all.) Instead of using the default controller, which is usually large and rather clumsy, you can integrate the controls into your auction description quite nicely.

First, modify the `<embed>` tag to hide the default controller, turn off the `autostart` feature, and give it a name, `mySound`, that you can reference with JavaScript:

```
<embed src="http://www.ebayhacks.com/files/aah.wav" hidden=true
autostart=false loop=false name="mySound" mastersound></embed>
```

Since it's now hidden, it doesn't strictly matter where you put the `<embed>` tag. In most cases, it's probably best to place it at the end of the auction description so browsers load the rest of your auction before the sound file. Next, include these links in your text to control the audio:

```
<a href="javascript:document.mySound.play( );">Listen</a>
to the music made by this music box. When you're done, you can
<a href="javascript:document.mySound.pause( );">Pause</a> or
<a href="javascript:document.mySound.stop( );">Stop</a> the music.

( Volume: <a href="javascript:document.mySound.setVolume(33);">Soft</a> |
<a href="javascript:document.mySound.setVolume(66);">Medium</a> |
<a href="javascript:document.mySound.setVolume(100);">Loud</a> )
```

The "controller," in this case, will simply appear as ordinary text links in your auction description. The text links can also be replaced with images to make a fancier controller.

If you find that a controller in your description is overkill, you can simply link to your audio files directly, like this:

```
<a href="http://www.ebayhacks.com/files/aah.wav">Listen</a> to the music
made by this music box.
```

The problem is that about a third of your bidders will get a download prompt and nothing else, and will probably not know where to go from there. If you choose this solution, you'll want to include a bit of instruction, telling them to save the file on their desktop and then double-click the icon that appears.

HACK #59 Put a Shipping Cost Calculator in Your Listing

Use a variety of tools to allow your customers to determine shipping costs without having to bother you.

A shipping cost calculator, placed right in your auction description, will allow you to avoid setting a single, fixed shipping cost (which can scare away frugal bidders), and still avoid the burden of having to quote shipping costs to everyone who asks [Hack #67].

Probably the easiest way to provide self-service shipping cost information is to include your Zip Code and the weight of your item right in your auction description, and then link [Hack #52] to your courier's web site (e.g., *ups.com* or *fedex.com*). Your bidders can then punch that information and their own Zip Codes into the courier's shipping cost calculator and get an accurate cost to ship, as well as any available shipping options (insurance, overnight, etc.).

Of course, there's no way to include shipping surcharges, and the likelihood that a bidder will make a mistake or choose the wrong shipping options is pretty high. Fortunately, there are more streamlined solutions you can use in your listings.

eBay's Calculated Shipping

eBay offers sellers its own shipping calculator. When listing your item [Hack #43], just choose the "calculated shipping" option. Specify your Zip Code, the weight and dimensions of your item, and one or more shipping methods you're willing to use, and eBay will allow your bidders to determine shipping costs on their own. You can even add a shipping surcharge to cover your packaging costs.

Here's how it works: a box like the one in Figure 4-16 is shown in the shipping details box towards the bottom of your listing. A potential customer enters her Zip Code into the little box and clicks Calculate to view her personalized shipping cost quotes in a separate window.

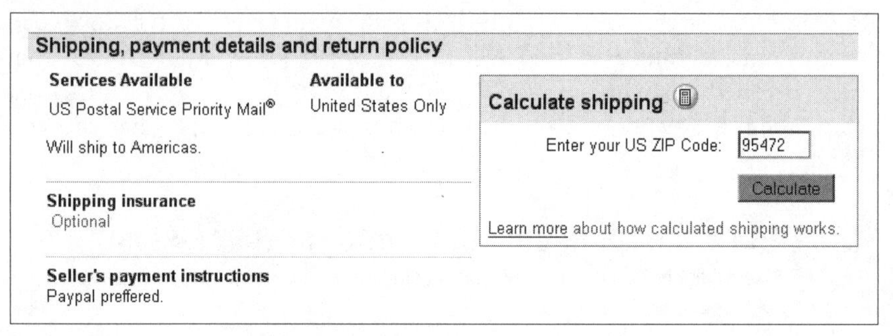

Figure 4-16. Use eBay's Calculated Shipping option to allow your customers to see how much shipping will cost—without bothering you

The Calculate Shipping box can be hard to spot, especially for newbies who don't know where to look. If you're taking the time to include your shipping terms in your description [Hack #54], you can link to the Calculate Shipping box like this:

```
To find out how it will cost to ship this item, please use
the <a href="#ShippingPayment">Calculate Shipping</a> box.
```

The calculated shipping feature, however, is rather limited. First, it uses software provided by Connect Ship, a UPS company, so only UPS and U.S. Postal Service rates are supported. Second, it works only for buyers and sellers in the continental United States. Finally, any insurance you specify won't show up in the Shipping Calculator pop-up window, meaning that customers may view your $6.00 insurance requirement as a "hidden fee" when they finally discover it in the checkout process [Hack #64].

The biggest advantage to Calculated Shipping is probably also its biggest drawback. For the convenience of the bidder and the seller, the calculated shipping cost is automatically inserted into the winning bidder's invoice. This allows the customer to use check out [Hack #64] to send payment without any post-auction input from you, the seller, even if the shipping quote is incorrect.

Calculated Shipping can also combine shipping costs for multiple auctions won by the same bidder, although the accuracy of the calculation should never be taken for granted. As the seller, you may want to take an active role in helping your bidders complete transactions by sending accurate totals and payment instructions promptly. Otherwise, you'll be deluged with complaints from impatient bidders who have sent incorrect payments and who blame you for their mistakes.

Third-Party Shipping Calculators

Whether or not eBay's Calculated Shipping option is sufficient is entirely up to you. But if you're outside the continental United States, if you need to ship internationally, or if you use a courier other than UPS or USPS, you may want to pursue a different solution, such as any of these third-party calculators:

Zonalyzer. The free Zonalyzer calculator doesn't utilize any external web sites, but rather encapsulates all of the rate tables and functionality in an HTML form you can paste in your listing descriptions. Of course, since including rate tables for all locations would make the script needlessly complicated, only the rate tables that apply to your location are included. To generate your custom code, go to *www.zonalyzer.com* and follow the prompts. Note that courier rate tables do change, so you may have to regenerate your calculator code from time to time.

Paid ShipCalc. For a subscription fee of $14.95 per year, you can use Paid ShipCalc (*www.auctioninc.com*) to provide UPS, USPS, FedEx, and DHL quotes to all your bidders. They also offer a free version that works only with USPS, as well as an international add-on module for the ShipCalc package.

ShipScript. ISDN*tek's ShipScript supports FedEx in addition to UPS and USPS. Go to *www.isdntek.com/shipscript.htm* to download the software (Windows PCs only) and generate custom HTML forms from your desktop.

FreightQuote. For shipping heavier items, such as furniture and appliances, you can use FreightQuote, a free shipping cost calculator available at *www.freightquote.com*. Although it isn't self-contained, it's still fairly compact and rather professional-looking. Just make sure you're able to ship with one of their affiliated shippers before you insert their calculator into your auctions.

.netShip. If you're looking for a more flexible solution and have your own Windows-based web server, you can use a product such as .netShip (*www.dotnetship.com*) to build your own custom shipping cost calculator that ties into your product database [Hack #114].

Among other things, the HTML forms for these third-party tools can be placed in a prominent position [Hack #54] in your listing description, allowing bidders to find and use them more easily. And no matter how you specify your shipping costs, make sure to take the time to choose an appropriate checkout method [Hack #64] so your customers can pay you the correct amount without a hassle.

Pre-Filling Calculator Forms

If a bidder who has used eBay's Shipping Calculator at least once visits your listing, his Zip Code will automatically appear in eBay's shipping cost calculator form. If you decide to use one of the third-party calculators discussed in the previous section, however, your bidder will have to type his Zip Code manually.

With a little JavaScript, though, you can pre-fill your shipping cost calculators with your bidders' Zip Codes, saving them a step and making it easier for them to get accurate shipping quotes.

First, take a look at the generated HTML code for your third-party calculator, and get the id of the text field into which your bidders are supposed to type their Zip Codes. If you're using Zonalyzer, for instance, the <input> tag looks something like this:

```
<input type="text" id="ZzIp" style="font-size:12px;width:50px">
```

In this case, the id of the field is ZzIp.

Next, include this bit of JavaScript anywhere *after* your custom shipping cost calculator:

```
<script>
document.getElementById('ZzIp').value =
                             document.shippingcalcbox.destinationZipCode.value;
</script>
```

and replace *ZzIp* with the id you found in the previous step.

To use the script, create a listing [Hack #43], and paste both your custom calculator form and the little snippet of JavaScript into your listing description. Make sure you select the "calculated shipping" option when choosing your shipping preferences (otherwise, eBay's form won't appear on your pages), and then start your listing. When a customer views your page, his Zip Code will automatically appear in both eBay's shipping calculator and your own custom calculator.

HACK #60 Advertise Your Other Listings in Your Description

Capitalize on an auction's popularity by using it to promote your other items.

Visibility is one of the biggest factors in any particular listing's success. The more people that see your listing, the more bids it will get, and the more money you'll make. Assuming this goal interests you, it's easy to use any listing to promote your others.

The first thing you'll want to do is tell your customers that they can save money (in the form of shipping expenses) by purchasing multiple items from you at the same time, which is a great way to increase sales. Probably the simplest and most effective way to do this is to place the following HTML code your auction descriptions:

```
<a href="http://cgi6.ebay.com/ws/eBayISAPI.dll?
                         ViewSellersOtherItems&userid=my_user_id">Check out
my other auctions</a> - bid on multiple items and save on shipping!
```

where *my_user_id* is your eBay member ID. This link is effectively no different from the "View seller's other items" link that eBay provides, except that your message suggests to customers that they have something to gain by clicking through.

Specific Product Links

The next step is to actually link to specific auctions in your description. This is most useful if you're selling an item and related accessories separately. For example, an auction for a PDA might contain this HTML code:

```
Note that I'm also selling a genuine leather case for this PDA <a href=
"http://cgi.ebay.com/ws/eBayISAPI.dll?ViewItem&item=3116521524">here</a>
and a travel charger <a href=
"http://cgi.ebay.com/ws/eBayISAPI.dll?ViewItem&item=3116521523">here</a>.
Bid on multiple items and save on shipping!
```

Then, in the auction description for the aforementioned travel charger, you might include something like this:

```
Note that I'm also selling the PDA that uses this charger <a href=
"http://cgi.ebay.com/ws/eBayISAPI.dll?ViewItem&item=3113167823">here</a>.
Bid on multiple items and save on shipping!
```

The resulting links, shown in Figure 4-17, are much more convenient and conspicuous than the simple list of auctions hidden behind the "View seller's other items" link. Your bidders can quickly flip between your related auctions, and you'll probably get more bids as a result.

There is one catch, however. The item numbers in the links are assigned when the listings begin, so you can't include complete links to auctions that haven't started yet. Instead, just type your links without the auction numbers, like this:

```
<a href="http://cgi.ebay.com/ws/eBayISAPI.dll?ViewItem&item=">here</a>
```

Then, once the auctions have started, go back and revise the descriptions **[Hack #65]**, inserting the corresponding auction numbers as needed.

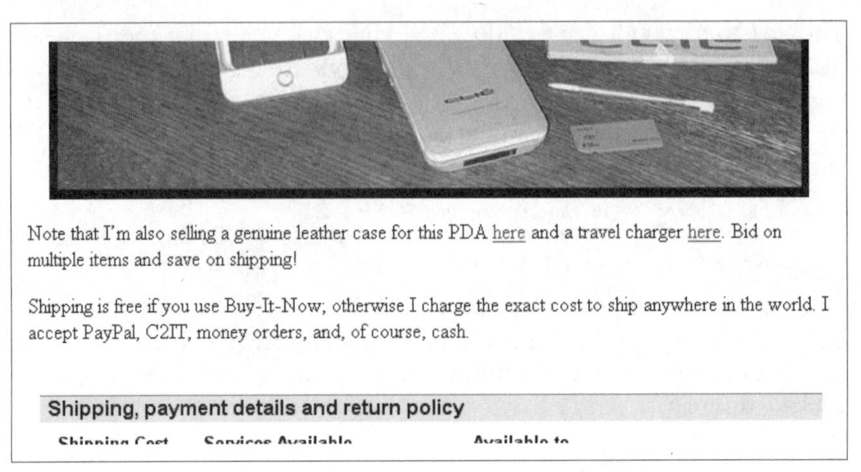

Note that I'm also selling a genuine leather case for this PDA here and a travel charger here. Bid on multiple items and save on shipping!
Shipping is free if you use Buy-It-Now; otherwise I charge the exact cost to ship anywhere in the world. I accept PayPal, C2IT, money orders, and, of course, cash.
Shipping, payment details and return policy

Figure 4-17. Place links to related auctions right in your auction descriptions to increase the likelihood that buyers will purchase multiple items from you

Cross-Promotion

Although the targeted links described previously are often the most effective method for linking to your other auctions, they do require a good amount of extra time and attention for each auction in which they're used. If you're particularly busy, you may benefit from a more automated solution.

eBay's own See More Great Items From This Seller box, shown in Figure 4-18, shows the titles of up to four other concurrent listings, along with their gallery images [Hack #46] and current prices.

Figure 4-18. Use eBay's free cross-promotion feature to advertise a few of your other listings to your customers

There are two ways to get the cross-promotion box in your listings:

eBay Stores. Once you open an eBay Store [Hack #91], eBay automatically places the "See More Great Items From This Seller" box in each of your running listings, and at the top of the page whenever someone places a bid on one of your items, just beneath the description and photos.

Checkout. Whether or not you have an eBay Store, eBay displays the See More Great Items From This Seller box only underneath the checkout box [Hack #64] on each of your completed listings, and at the top of the bid confirmation page whenever someone bids on your items (but never in the description unless you have an eBay store).

To enable cross-promotion for your listings, go to My eBay → eBay Preferences, scroll down to the Seller Preferences section, and click the Change link next to "Participate in eBay cross-promotions."

While you're at it, check out the "Unsuccessful bidder notices" and "End of Auction and Transaction emails," also found in the Seller Preferences section. Among other things, these two features allow you to further advertise your other listings.

eBay automatically chooses the four items displayed in your cross-promotion box, based on the categories in which they're filed. (For Store inventory items, eBay uses your custom Store categories.) For instance, if you've created seven individual listings for autographed baseball cards and a dozen listings for other items, the cross-promotion ads in each of your baseball card listings will point only to other baseball cards you're selling.

eBay shows only currently running listings in the See More Great Items From This Seller box. If you've used a listing tool such as Turbo Lister [Hack #93], there's a good chance that all your listings started (and will end) at precisely the same time, meaning that unless you have an eBay Store, nobody will ever see your cross-promoted items on the checkout page. To make better use of the cross-promotion feature, stagger your listings to end at different times, so there will be something to advertise when your first few listings end.

If you want to choose how specific items are cross-promoted, open any of your listings and click "Change your cross-promoted items" at the top of the page. On the next page, click "Change to manual selection" and then make your selections.

Occasionally, some of your running listings won't appear on the manual selection page. To specify a listing that doesn't show up on the list, you'll have to manually assemble a URL that works. Right-click one of the listings on this page, and select Copy Shortcut or Copy Link Location (in Internet Explorer or Mozilla/Firefox, respectfully). Then, paste the URL into a plain text editor (e.g., Notepad in Windows) and replace the item number in the link with the item number of the listing you want to promote. When you're done, paste the link into your browser's address bar and press Enter.

Java-Based Galleries

eBay's cross-promotion box only shows up in running listings if you have an eBay Store, and then only shows up to four other listings. If you'd like to promote more than just four other items, or don't want to have to open an eBay store, you may instead prefer to use a third-party interactive gallery in each of your listing descriptions.

Several companies offer subscription-based galleries you can place in your listings. For instance, the Andale Gallery (*www.andale.com*), shown in Figure 4-19, is an interactive, scrolling browser that allows your customers to browse through your other items without leaving your auction page.

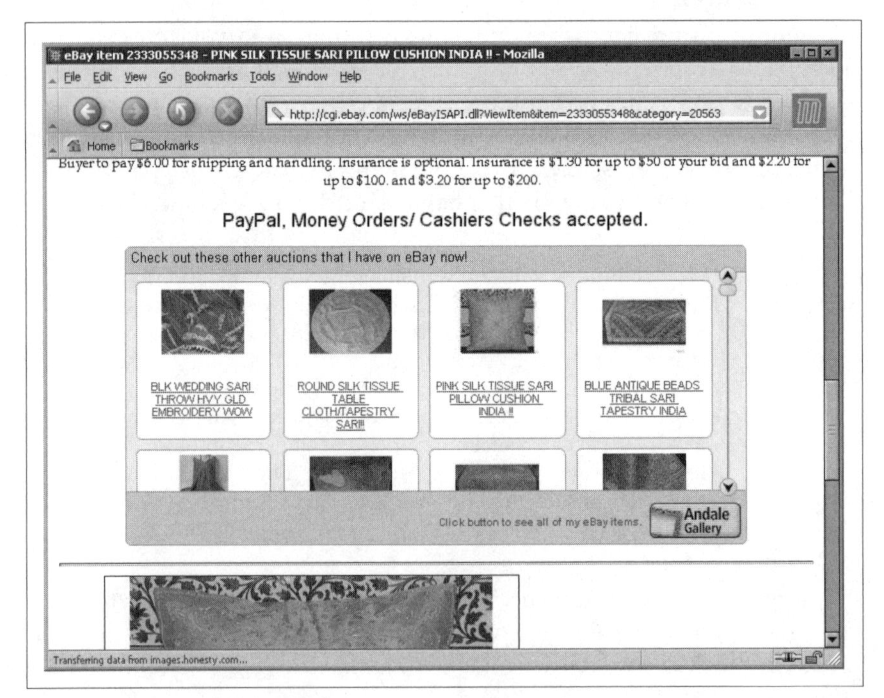

Figure 4-19. Include the Andale Gallery in your auction descriptions

If you have a lot of items, AuctionLynxx (*www.auctionlynxx.com*) offers a more complex three-pane browser, allowing your customers to thumb through your various categories and even sort your listings, all without leaving the original item page. If you can live with its somewhat cluttered interface, it's a great way to let your customers find specific items more quickly than using eBay's search tools, while helping ensure that subsequent sales go to you rather than one of your competitors.

These third-party galleries aren't free, but if you're selling a lot of items, you'll likely make back the monthly fee with a single sale.

Advertise Your Listings Elsewhere

There are lots of ways to promote your listings outside of eBay, such as affiliate links [Hack #98] and eBay's Editor Kit and Merchant Kit [Hack #99], all of which will earn you money each time someone uses those links and subsequently registers with eBay or bids on an item.

HACK #61 Allow Visitors to Search Through Your Listings

Put an HTML search form in your auction description to make it easier for your customers to find other items you're selling.

People have short attention spans. This is never more clear than when you're searching eBay and...wait, what was I talking about?

The "View seller's other items" link that appears at the top of each of your listings allows customers to see other items you're currently selling using standard eBay search pages. This means that people viewing your item can click the link and then search through your listings [Hack #18] on the next page, provided they remember how they got there in the first place.

Instead of taking the risk of losing your customers to some other page, you can include a search box, shown in Figure 4-20, in each of your listings to help keep your customers on track.

Shipping is free if you use Buy-It-Now; otherwise I charge the exact cost to ship anywhere in the world. I accept PayPal, C2IT, money orders, and, of course, cash.

Search This Seller

Search

Search title **and** description

Shipping, payment details and return policy

Figure 4-20. A search-by-seller box in your auctions helps promote your other items

The Code

To put this box in your auction, simply place the following code somewhere in your auction description:

```
<table border=0 cellpadding=0 cellspacing=0 width=200>
<tr>
  <td colspan=4 bgcolor=#FFCC00><img
       src="http://pics.ebaystatic.com/aw/pics/s.gif" width=1 height=1></td>
</tr><tr>
  <td width=1 bgcolor=#FFCC00><img
       src="http://pics.ebaystatic.com/aw/pics/s.gif" width=1 height=1></td>
  <td colspan=2><table cellpadding=0 cellspacing=0 border=0 width=100%>
    <tr>
      <td bgcolor=#FFE684 width=100%><table cellspacing=0 cellpadding=0
                                                    border=0 width=100%>
      <tr>
        <td height=22 width=4 background=
        "http://pics.ebaystatic.com/aw/pics/listings/subHdrOrange_4x22.gif"
        ><img src="http://pics.ebaystatic.com/aw/pics/s.gif" height=22
        width=4></td><td height=22 width=4><img src=
         "http://pics.ebaystatic.com/aw/pics/s.gif" height=22 width=4></td>
        <td><b>Search This Seller</b></td>
      </tr></table></td>
      <td bgcolor=#FFE684><img src=
          "http://pics.ebaystatic.com/aw/pics/s.gif" height=1 width=15></td>
    </tr><tr>
      <td colspan=2><img src=
          "http://pics.ebaystatic.com/aw/pics/s.gif" height=5 width=1></td>
    </tr></table></td>
  <td width=1 bgcolor=#FFCC00><img src=
          "http://pics.ebaystatic.com/aw/pics/s.gif" width=1 height=1></td>
</tr><tr>
  <td width=1 bgcolor=#FFCC00><img src=
        "http://pics.ebaystatic.com/aw/pics/s.gif" width=1 height=1></td>
  <td width=4><img src="http://pics.ebaystatic.com/aw/pics/s.gif"
        width=4 height=4></td>
  <td>
❶    <form name="advsearch_form" style="display:inline"
                   action="http://search.ebay.com/ws/search/SaleSearch">
    <nobr>
❷    <input type="text" name="satitle" maxlength=300 size=20 value="">
    <input type="submit" value="Search">
    <br></nobr>

❸    <input type="checkbox" name="fts" value="2">
    Search title <b>and</b> description

    <input type="hidden" name="fsop" value="1&amp;fsoo=1">
    <input type="hidden" name="fcl" value="3">
    <input type="hidden" name="frpp" value="200">
    <input type="hidden" name="seller" value="1">
```

```
❹     <input type="hidden" name="sass" value="my_ebay_id">

❺     </form>
    </td>
    <td width=1 bgcolor=#FFCC00><img src=
        "http://pics.ebaystatic.com/aw/pics/s.gif" width=1 height=1></td>
  </tr><tr>
    <td width=1 bgcolor=#FFCC00><img src=
        "http://pics.ebaystatic.com/aw/pics/s.gif" width=1 height=1></td>
    <td colspan=2><img src=
        "http://pics.ebaystatic.com/aw/pics/s.gif" width=100% height=15></td>
    <td width=1 bgcolor=#FFCC00><img src=
        "http://pics.ebaystatic.com/aw/pics/s.gif" width=1 height=1></td>
  </tr><tr>
    <td colspan=4 bgcolor=#FFCC00><img src=
        "http://pics.ebaystatic.com/aw/pics/s.gif" width=1 height=1></td>
  </tr></table>
```

The only thing you have to do before you use this form in your own listings is replace *my_ebay_id* on line ❹ with your own eBay member ID to confine the search results to your own running auctions. The code can otherwise be used exactly as is.

Since this box has a genuine eBay look, complete with the yellow lines and even the "Search title and description" checkbox, it's somewhat more complicated than it otherwise would need to be. In fact, the actual search form is comprised only of the code between lines ❶ and ❺. But the official eBay appearance will make your bidders more comfortable using it, as well as make your listing look more professional.

Hacking the Hack

Here are some things you can use to customize the search box:

Custom table. Naturally, you can customize your search box to suit the style of your auctions by replacing all the code above line ❶ and below line ❺ with a custom table [Hack #52]. Just be careful not to disturb the code within the `<form></form>` structure.

Right-justify. As it is, the box will appear left-justified in your listing. To right-justify it, add the `align=right` parameter to the `<table>` tag on the very first line, like this:

```
<table border=0 cellpadding=0 cellspacing=0 width=200 align=right>
```

Or, to center the table, use this:

```
<table border=0 cellpadding=0 cellspacing=0 width=200 align=center>
```

Open in a new window. Don't let your bidders forget where they came from. Instead of the search results appearing in the same window, you can have the search open a new window simply by adding the target="_blank" parameter to the <form> tag on line ❶, like this:

```
<form name="advsearch_form" style="display:inline" target="_blank"
        action="http://search.ebay.com/ws/search/SaleSearch">
```

Enable descriptions by default. To turn on the "Search title and description" checkbox by default, which will likely increase the number of search results your bidders see (thus increasing the exposure of the corresponding auctions), just add the checked parameter to the <input> tag on line ❸, like this:

```
<input type="checkbox" name="fts" value="2" checked>
```

Default search. Finally, if you have a lot of different auctions running at once, you may want to show your customers results that are more likely to interest them. For instance, if the form is appearing on a wireless phone accessory, pre-fill the satitle field ❷ with the search word "wireless," like this:

```
<input type="text" name="satitle" maxlength=300 size=20 value="wireless">
```

Thus, the customer need only click the Search button to view a listing of relevant listings.

The search box can help sell multiple items to buyers who would otherwise purchase only a single item from you. Another way to promote your other products is to place links to your listings in your description [Hack #60].

Put a Floating Contact Link in Your Listings

Make it easier for your customers to contact you by using JavaScript to ensure that a Contact Seller link is always visible.

The easier it is for your customers to contact you, the more likely they'll do it. Of course, the thought of getting deluged by more stupid questions [Hack #67] probably makes you want to run screaming for the hills, but stop and consider the benefits first. When customers ask questions, there are fewer misunderstandings [Hack #54] and fewer deadbeat bidders [Hack #68]; if nothing else, the ever-visible link helps inspire trust [Hack #8] in your customers that you are a seller who cares about customer service.

The Code

To put a floating Contact Seller link in your listings, place this code in the beginning of your listing description:

```
<script language="JavaScript"><!--
function MoveBox( ) {
  if (document.getElementById&&!document.all) {
    BoxLayer = document.getElementById('ContactSeller');
    if (BoxLayer.style.top != pageYOffset) {
```

```
      BoxLayer.style.top = pageYOffset;
    }
  }
  else if (navigator.appName == "Microsoft Internet Explorer"
                    && navigator.appVersion.substring(0,1) >= "4") {
    if (ContactSeller.style.top != document.body.scrollTop) {
      ContactSeller.style.top = document.body.scrollTop;
    }
  }
  setTimeout ('MoveBox()', 50);
}
setTimeout ('MoveBox()', 50);

function contactSeller() {
  for (var i=0; i < document.links.length; i++) {
    if (document.links[i].href.indexOf('ShowCoreAskSellerQuestion') > 0) {
      window.open(document.links[i].href);
    }
  }
}

//--></script>

<div id="ContactSeller" align=right
          style="position: absolute; width: 99%; z-index: 0; clip:auto;">
<a href="javascript:contactSeller();">Ask seller a question</a>
</div>
```

When you load the page, a small link appears in the upper right of your description. As soon as you scroll the page, the link jumps to the upper-right corner of the window, and stays there.

One of the nice things about this script is that you don't need to modify it with your eBay member ID or the current listing number. Instead, the link uses the URL of the existing "Ask seller a question" link, thus preserving all the information contained therein.

Hacking the Hack

The "Ask seller a question" link is an ordinary HTML hyperlink [Hack #52] placed on a transparent, floating <div> layer. Because it's transparent, your bidders will always be able to see what's behind it. To take full advantage of this transparency, you may want to replace the "Ask seller a question" text with a semitransparent image like the one shown in Figure 4-21.

The transparent image you use can be any GIF or PNG file, but JPG files are not suitable because they don't support transparency. (Just about any image editor [Hack #74] supports transparent images.) Once you've prepared the image, reference it in your listings by replacing the text link with this line:

```
<a href="javascript:contactSeller();"><img
             src="http://www.ebayhacks.com/pictures/contactseller.gif"></a>
```

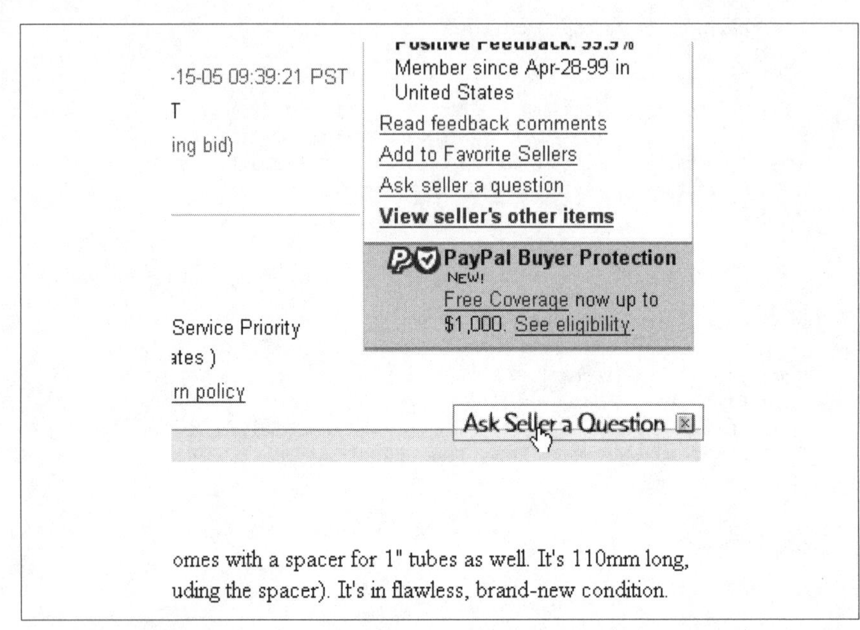

Figure 4-21. This floating "Ask seller a question" link is always visible, encouraging customers to contact you

where *http://www.ebayhacks.com/pictures/contactseller.gif* is the full URL of the image hosted on your web server **[Hack #76]**.

Some bidders may find the floating link annoying, so it might be helpful to provide a way for them to turn it off. To do this, add the following link immediately after the "Ask seller a question" link:

```
[<a href="javascript:hideBox();">X</a>]
```

and then place the following code inside the `<script></script>` structure:

```
function hideBox() {
  if (document.getElementById&&!document.all) {
      BoxLayer.style.visibility = 'hidden';
  } else {
      ContactSeller.style.visibility='hidden';
  }
}
```

If you'd rather use an image than a text link, you can incorporate the close button with your image, like the one shown in Figure 4-22. To do this, either use two different images, like this:

```
<nobr><a href="javascript:contactSeller();"><img
src="http://www.ebayhacks.com/pictures/contactseller.gif"></a>
<a href="href="javascript:hideBox();"><img
src="http://www.ebayhacks.com/pictures/close.gif"></a></nobr>
```

or, use a single image with an image map, like this:

```
<map name="contactseller">
<area shape=rect coords="1,1,143,23"
            href="javascript:contactSeller();">
<area shape=rect coords="145,1,166,23"
            href="href="javascript:hideBox();">
</map><img usemap="#contactseller">
src="http://www.ebayhacks.com/pictures/contactseller.gif">
```

All the bidder has to do is click X, and the "Ask seller a question" link will disappear completely until the page is reloaded.

Make Good Use of the About Me Page

Set up a static page on eBay for stuff that would otherwise clutter your auction pages.

Many sellers make the mistake of including pages and pages of payment and shipping terms, only to supplement it with a single sentence about the item itself. No wonder bidders never read descriptions!

I hate clutter, whether it's on one of my own auctions or someone else's. I like to reserve the space in my auction descriptions for information about the item being sold, mostly because bidders have a limited attention span, and I, as a seller, have a limited amount of time to prepare my auctions.

eBay allows any seller to build a static page right on the eBay web site—separate from their listings—with whatever content he wants to make public. Although any eBay member can put together an About Me page by going to Site Map → About Me, it's sellers who benefit most from this feature.

> Since the About Me page is separate from listings, its content can be modified [Hack #65] at any time, even after your auctions have received bids.

Although you can maintain your own web page on any off-eBay site, there are significant advantages to using the About Me feature. For one, the information on the page will appear more trustworthy to your bidders because it looks like part of the eBay site, complete with the eBay logo and menu bar. Second, a link to your About Me page will appear next to your user ID whenever your ID appears on eBay. And finally, you'll be able to insert dynamic, eBay-specific content in your page, as described next.

Just Say No to Templates

When you use the About Me feature for the first time, eBay presents a selection of templates you can choose from to frame your page. The next step involves filling in about a dozen fields with your personalized information (see Figure 4-22), such as a title, welcome message, something called "another paragraph," and some of your favorite links. You can also choose to display recent feedback and a list of your items for sale, right on the page.

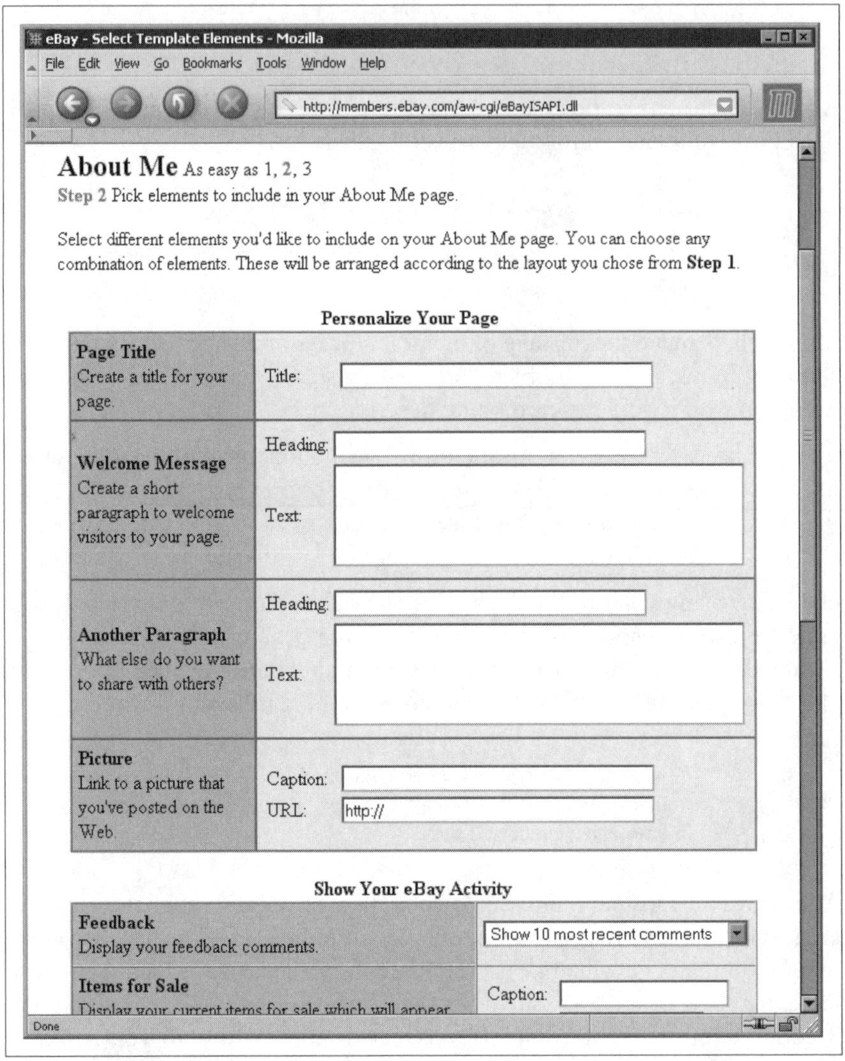

Figure 4-22. The About Me setup page is the first thing you see when you build an About Me page, but it doesn't afford the flexibility of the optional HTML editor interface

If you want full control over the look of your page, skip the setup page by clicking Preview at the bottom of the page. Then, on the next page, click "Edit using HTML." You'll then be shown a single edit box, prefilled with the HTML code [Hack #52] from your current About Me page. You can proceed to modify or replace this code as you see fit, including employing the services of a standalone graphical web page editor [Hack #53].

Once you leave the template interface, you won't be able to go back without "starting over," which effectively deletes your page and returns you to the blank slate provided when you first started. For this reason, you should always keep a copy of your custom About Me page in a text file on your computer. Just highlight all the text in the edit box (Ctrl-A), copy to the clipboard (Ctrl-C), and paste into your favorite text editor (Ctrl-V). To make sure your backup remains current, do this every time you modify your page.

Since the page is hosted on the eBay site, you'll have access to features not otherwise available if you were to host the page yourself. Using specialized HTML tags, you can insert eBay-specific content, such as recent feedback or a list of your running auctions. The following five tags are available, each with a selection of options to further customize your page:

`<eBayUserID>`
: Instead of putting your email address in your About Me page, you can take advantage of eBay's privacy features. Having your bidders contact you through the Contact an eBay Member form will reduce the spam and other nuisance emails you might otherwise get. For example:

```
<ebayuserid nofeedback nomask>
```

The `nofeedback` and `nomask` options remove the feedback in parentheses and the icons that would normally appear after your user ID. If you want more flexibility, include a hard-coded link [Hack #13] to the same page, like this (all on one line):

```
<a href="http://cgi3.ebay.com/aw-cgi/eBayISAPI.dll?
                              ReturnUserEmail&requested=user_ID">contact me</a>
```

`<eBayFeedback size=n>`
: Use this tag to include a table with some recent feedback you've received; specify `size=15` to show the last 15 comments. You can further customize the table with the following additional options:

`alternatecolor=red`
: The color [Hack #55] of the *upper* line of each comment

`color=white`
: The color of the *lower* line of each comment

`border=1`
: The width, in pixels, of the table border

`tablewidth=100%`
: The width of the table, as a percentage of the width of the browser window

`<eBayItemList>`
: This tag places a table with a list of your running auctions right in your text, similar to the "View seller's other items" page. You can customize the table with these options:

  `sort=`*n*
  : Where *n* can be `8` to show newly listed auctions first, `2` to show the oldest auctions first, `3` to show the auctions ending first, or `4` to show the lowest-price items first.

  `since=`*n*
  : Include a positive number for *n* to show completed items, up to `30` days old.

  `category=`*n*
  : Restrict the listing to items in a single category; see "Tweak Search URLs" [Hack #13] for more information on the category number to include here.

  `border`, `tablewidth`, *and* `cellpadding`
  : See `<eBayFeedback>`, described previously.

`<eBayMemberSince>`, `<eBayTime>`
: These two tags display the date you first registered and the current date in eBay time, respectively.

  You might use `<eBayMemberSince>` like this:

```
eBay member since <ebaymembersince format="%B %d, %Y">
```

  and you'd see something like "eBay member since May 31st, 2003" in your About Me page. The idea is to imply a certain level of trustworthiness, corresponding to the length of time you've been buying and selling on eBay. But since this date never changes, there's no reason you can't simply type it directly onto your page.

  Since `<eBayTime>` doesn't necessarily show either the seller's local time or the bidder's local time, but rather only the current time in eBay's time zone (Pacific time, GMT-8:00), its usefulness on this page is pretty limited.

  The codes used in the `format` string are as follows. To format the date, include `%A` for the day of the week (`%a` to abbreviate), `%m` for the month number, `%B` for the month name (`%b` to abbreviate), `%d` for the day of the month, and `%Y` for the year (`%y` for only two digits). Likewise, to format the time, type `%I` for the hour (`%H` for 24-hour clock), `%M` for the minute, `%S` for the second, and `%p` for the appropriate "a.m." or "p.m." text. (Note that the codes are case-sensitive; `%Y` is different from `%y`.)

Referencing the About Me Page

Once you've built an About Me page, a little "me" icon will appear next to your user ID (right after the feedback rating) wherever your ID appears on the eBay site. Another user can simply click the icon to view your About Me page. But you can also link directly to your About Me page in your auctions using this simple URL:

```
http://members.ebay.com/aboutme/user_ID/
```

If you want eBay's little "me" icon to appear in your link, use this code:

```
See <a href="http://members.ebay.com/aboutme/user_ID/" target=_blank><img
src="http://pics.ebay.com/aw/pics/aboutme-small.gif" border=0></a> for
payment and shipping terms.
```

If your About Me page is complicated or lengthy, you may want to divide it up with named anchors. For instance:

```
<a name="shipping"></a>
My Shipping Terms...
<p>
<a name="payment"></a>
My Payment Terms...
```

You can then jump to any anchor on the page by placing a # sign at the end of the URL, followed by the anchor name. For example, you may want to place this code in your auction description:

```
Please read my <a href="http://members.ebay.com/aboutme/user_ID/#shipping">
shipping terms</a> and my <a href="http://members.ebay.com/aboutme/user_ID/
#payment">payment terms</a> before you bid.
```

This creates two links, each to a different part of your About Me page.

HACK #64 Customize the Checkout Process

Keep the personal touch in your transactions by disabling eBay's controversial Checkout feature.

The direct communication between buyers and sellers is one of the main reasons eBay works as well as it does, and one of the things that makes eBay fun. Way back in 2001, eBay took an unfortunate step toward circumventing that communication by introducing the Checkout feature, which angered and alienated (at least temporarily) many of its most loyal members.

Originally, Checkout was intended to accomplish two things. First, eBay felt that both buyers and sellers could benefit from an integrated, unified system to handle the completion of transactions. Second, eBay wanted to funnel more business into eBay's now-defunct BillPoint auction payment system (and away from its rival, PayPal). The problem was that the Checkout system wasn't optional for sellers, and even went so far as to give buyers the impression they could pay with BillPoint even when sellers didn't accept BillPoint payments. Well, it seems that fate is not without a sense of irony: within six months, BillPoint was history, and eBay had acquired PayPal. And while eBay has since improved the Checkout system quite a bit, making it less aggressive and more customizable, some problems do still remain.

One of the biggest problems with Checkout is that it allows the winning bidder to complete the transaction without having to wait for the seller to send payment instructions. For example, a bidder in another country can pay for an auction for which the seller has specified a fixed shipping charge intended only for domestic shipments. The result is a frustrated seller and a confused bidder, not to mention a transaction that has to be redone.

Avoid including your postal address in your listings. In addition to privacy concerns, this allows your buyers to mail their payments without waiting for input from you. This possibility is especially troublesome because a payment sent via postal mail is much more difficult to rescind than an electronic payment like PayPal. And bidders who have to re-send payments typically blame sellers for the hassle.

Figure 4-23 shows what your customers see at the top of completed item pages when the Checkout feature is in full force.

MZZ Lanz Bulldog Tractor Z-Scale Unpainted — Item number: 5580082198

Email to a friend

You won the item!

Pay Now > or continue shopping with this seller

Click the **Pay Now** button to confirm shipping, get the total price, and arrange payment through: PayPal; money order; credit card; other.

Other actions for this item:

You can manage all your items in My eBay and do the following:

- Request total payment amount from the seller.
- Mark payment sent for this item.
- Leave feedback for this item.
- Contact seller about this item.

Additional Options:

- To view other items from this seller, view seller's other items.
- If this listing is similar to an item you want to sell, list an item like this.
- You may add this seller to your Favorite Sellers in My eBay.
- To report that this item hasn't been received, you can report the item as not received.

Figure 4-23. Your customers see this page when you enable eBay's Checkout feature

Since eBay doesn't let you prioritize your payment methods or link to off-site Checkout services (introduced later in this hack), PayPal will always be shown more prominently than any other payment method.

Checkout Options

Although it isn't obvious by any stretch of the imagination, Checkout is indeed optional for sellers. Whether you decide to use it depends on your needs and how the Checkout system fits with the way you like to do business.

To customize various aspects of the Checkout feature, go to My eBay → eBay Preferences, scroll down to the Seller Preferences section, and click the Change link next to Payment Preferences.

Next, on the Payment & Shipping Preferences page, you'll have several options:

Use Checkout. Turn this off to remove the Pay Now button normally displayed at the top of your completed listings. Note that this setting has no effect for any listing in which you offer PayPal [Hack #85] as a payment option.

Offer PayPal as a payment method in all my listings. Enable this option if you know you'll always want to accept PayPal payments. Since you can also elect to accept PayPal when creating a listing [Hack #43], this option has little more than symbolic value.

Tell buyers that I prefer PayPal payments. If you enable this option, the PayPal logo appears twice in the "Payment methods accepted" box at the bottom of your listings and on the Checkout page. Otherwise, it has no effect on the checkout process (although it's sometimes used as a requirement to participate in some PayPal promotions). If you want to emphasize that you prefer PayPal payments, take the time to clarify your payment terms in your listing descriptions [Hack #54].

Show my buyers low monthly payments. Select this option to help PayPal advertise the Buyer Credit program [Hack #96]. Since this is a service offered by PayPal, it won't actually affect payments you receive—you'll still get all your money at once—but its presence in your listings may make your potential customers more comfortable bidding on expensive items.

Include my items when buyers pay all their sellers at once. As a convenience to buyers, PayPal allow bidders to pay all outstanding bills at once. If you enable this option, it'll be easier for your customers to pay you without reviewing your payment terms beforehand (especially since the transactions are handled on the PayPal web site). If you disable the option, however, your customers will have to complete your checkout process separately from the rest of their transactions and, as a result, may take longer to do so. But since few people actually use this feature, it probably doesn't matter what you choose here.

Allow buyer to edit total. Enable this option to add a text box to the Checkout page, enabling your customers to add or subtract from the payment they're about to send you. Although you might think the last thing you want is for customers to be able to knock a few bucks off their own bills, this feature is not often abused. Instead, it's effectively the only way you can give your customers discounts or sell them additional merchandise [Hack #66] without hassling with refunds or separate payments made from the PayPal web site.

Payment Address. Unless you want your customers to be able to send you payments through postal mail without contacting you first, you should remove your postal address from this page. Instead, change the City and State fields to "Nowhere" and the Address 1 field to something like "Please Ask." That way, you'll be able to make sure your customers send you the correct amount and can use a payment method you can accept [Hack #85] before they lick any stamps.

UPS Shipping Rates. Select the Daily Rates option only if you:

- Have a UPS account
- Prefer to ship via UPS
- Use eBay's Calculated Shipping feature [Hack #59].

As you can see, most of these options are for fine-tuning the way payments are sent. If you want to disable the Checkout option entirely, you'll have to remove PayPal from your listings.

Disabling PayPal

The Pay Now button will be visible on all completed auctions for which PayPal is an accepted payment method, even if the Checkout option (discussed in the previous section) is disabled.

Although PayPal can be very convenient for both buyers and sellers, there are situations where it can't—or shouldn't—be used, at least not until the bidder and seller have worked out the details of the transaction.

Since PayPal protects only sellers who accept payments from certain buyers, you may wish to restrict PayPal sales to customers in the United States [Hack #85]. Unfortunately, the Pay Now button gives all winning bidders the impression that they can pay with PayPal, regardless of their location or ability to complete the transaction. See the next section of this hack for other settings that can further restrict who is allowed to bid on your items.

At this point, the only way to get rid of the Pay Now button—and put all payment methods on equal footing—is to remove the PayPal option from your listings. You can do this in the Sell Your Item form as well as the Revise Your Item form **[Hack #65]**.

Turning off the PayPal option doesn't mean that you can't accept PayPal payments; it simply disables the link between PayPal and eBay and removes the PayPal logo from the "Payment methods accepted" box at the bottom of the page. One unfortunate consequence of this, however, is that your auctions won't be included in searches for PayPal-only items. To help compensate for this, you may wish to place a PayPal logo prominently in your auction description **[Hack #54]**.

When both the Checkout and PayPal options have been disabled, your completed auctions will look like the one in Figure 4-24.

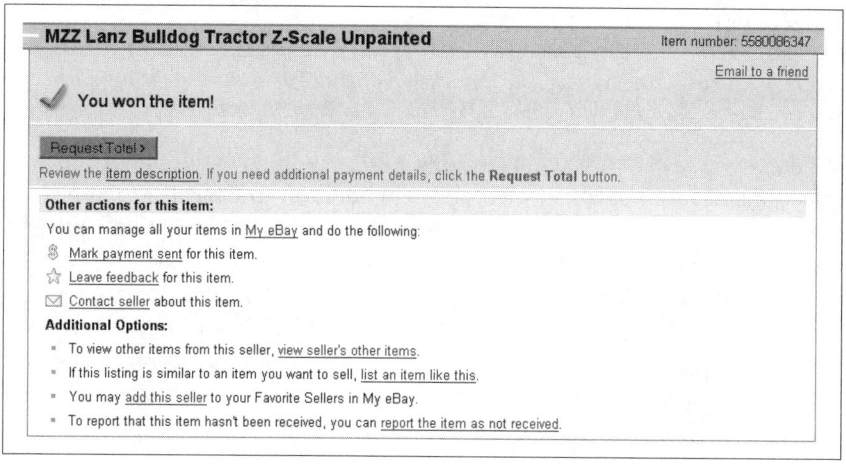

MZZ Lanz Bulldog Tractor Z-Scale Unpainted
Item number: 5580086347
Email to a friend
You won the item!
Request Total >
Review the item description. If you need additional payment details, click the Request Total button.
Other actions for this item:
You can manage all your items in My eBay and do the following:
Mark payment sent for this item.
Leave feedback for this item.
Contact seller about this item.
Additional Options:
To view other items from this seller, view seller's other items.
If this listing is similar to an item you want to sell, list an item like this.
You may add this seller to your Favorite Sellers in My eBay.
To report that this item hasn't been received, you can report the item as not received.

Figure 4-24. Your customers will see this when you've both disabled Checkout and removed PayPal as an official payment option

This scenario—with neither Checkout nor PayPal in effect—is probably the most convenient for sellers who wish to use any of the off-eBay checkout services **[Hack #96]**. But with no automated way for a bidder to pay you directly through eBay, this is the *least*-convenient setup for customers.

At this point, you can try re-enabling Checkout, while leaving the PayPal option inactive; the resulting page now looks as it did before, complete with the Pay Now button. But a customer who uses Pay Now will be able to send nothing more than her mailing address and intended method of payment with the page shown in Figure 4-25. This is effectively the best choice if you don't want to receive payments until you have sent your bidders payment instructions, but also want to take advantage of eBay's automated Checkout system.

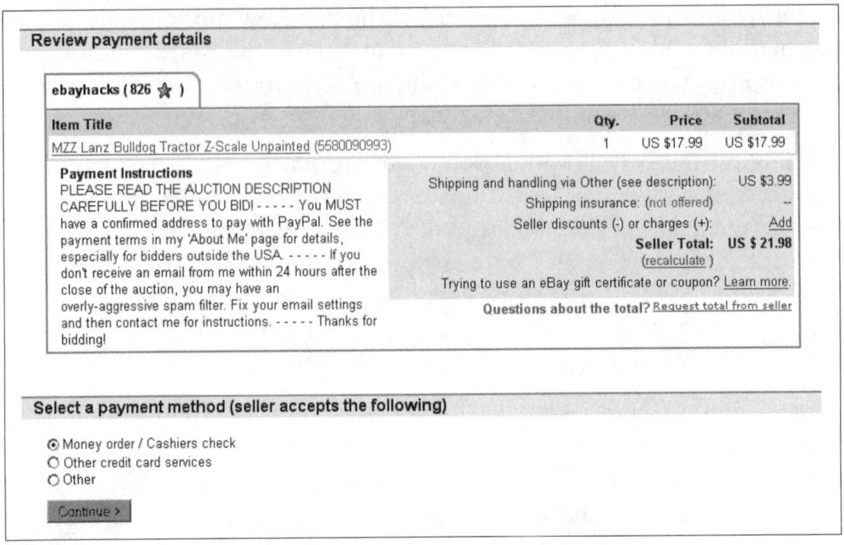

Review payment details

ebayhacks (826)

Item Title	Qty.	Price	Subtotal
MZZ Lanz Bulldog Tractor Z-Scale Unpainted (5580090993)	1	US $17.99	US $17.99

Payment Instructions
PLEASE READ THE AUCTION DESCRIPTION CAREFULLY BEFORE YOU BID! - - - - - You MUST have a confirmed address to pay with PayPal. See the payment terms in my 'About Me' page for details, especially for bidders outside the USA. - - - - - If you don't receive an email from me within 24 hours after the close of the auction, you may have an overly-aggressive spam filter. Fix your email settings and then contact me for instructions. - - - - - Thanks for bidding!

Shipping and handling via Other (see description): US $3.99
Shipping insurance: (not offered) --
Seller discounts (-) or charges (+): Add
Seller Total: US $ 21.98
(recalculate)
Trying to use an eBay gift certificate or coupon? Learn more.
Questions about the total? Request total from seller

Select a payment method (seller accepts the following)

- Money order / Cashiers check
- Other credit card services
- Other

Continue >

Figure 4-25. Your customers will see this when they click Pay Now on a listing in which you've enabled Checkout, but removed PayPal as a payment option

When you create individual listings [Hack #43], you'll have the opportunity to select one or more payment methods—in addition to PayPal—to appear in the "Payment methods accepted" box at the bottom of the listing page and on the checkout page shown to your high bidder. If you have a merchant account [Hack #96] and are able to accept Visa, Mastercard, Discover, or American Express cards, you should enable the respective options in the Sell Your Item form to display their logos in the "Payment methods accepted" box. Of course, to accept credit cards directly, you'll have to provide your own checkout page [Hack #96], as eBay doesn't offer any way to capture a customer's credit card information securely.

Other Settings That Affect Checkout

Go to My eBay → eBay Preferences, scroll down to the Seller Preferences section, and click the Change link next to "Buyer requirements." This handy page lets you block bids from customers you know you won't be able to serve:

Buyers in countries to which I don't ship. This setting ties in with the "Ship-to locations" options on the Sell Your Item form [Hack #43]. Basically, this allows you to indicate that you only ship to your home country, plus block bids from anyone registered in a different country. Use this only if you're sure you don't want to handle any international transactions.

Buyers with a negative feedback score. This won't block bidders with a high percentage of negative feedback comments, which ironically are the ones most likely to be deadbeat bidders [Hack #68], but rather will block those with an overall feedback score less than zero. This penalizes new eBay members who may be nothing more than victims of their own inexperience.

Buyers with Unpaid Item strikes. If a buyer has two Unpaid Item strikes [Hack #68], it means she was the high bidder on two separate items, yet did not follow through and pay the sellers of either listing. One Unpaid Item strike may be nothing more than a consequence of a communication breakdown [Hack #9], but two strikes in a 30-day period is a real problem. You should definitely enable this setting.

Buyers without a PayPal account. Choose this setting if you only accept PayPal payments [Hack #85]. This option will definitely decrease your sales, because it will block even bidders who might otherwise be willing to sign up with PayPal in order to complete the transaction.

The options you choose will likely be the result of your own past negative experiences with problematic customers. Before you go ahead and enable all the options on this page, take a moment to review some of the more-effective ways you can keep out deadbeat bidders [Hack #68].

Payment Instructions

Regardless of the checkout configuration you choose, you should explain to your bidders exactly what they need to do to complete the transaction, both in the auction description and in the special Payment Instructions box. For example:

> Please read the auction description and the payment terms in my About Me page carefully, and make sure you can pay before you bid. – – – Winning bidders will receive payment instructions via email. If you're the high bidder, and you don't receive an email from me within 24 hours after the close of the auction, you may have an overly aggressive spam filter. Adjust your email account settings and then contact me for instructions. – – – Thanks for bidding!

Since you're limited to 500 characters in the Payment Instructions box and you're not permitted to use HTML [Hack #52] here, you'll need to be concise and a little creative to communicate the most important information to your winning bidders. For instance, notice the repeating dashes to help separate paragraphs.

Although this information appears near the bottom of your listing page, it's biggest asset is that it's shown to your high bidder during the checkout process. Since you can also clarify your payment terms in the description [Hack #54], you should focus these Payment Instructions to high bidders. This comes in particularly handy when your payment instructions email [Hack #84] doesn't reach the high bidder due to a full mailbox or overactive spam filter [Hack #9].

Make Changes to Running Auctions

Keep your auctions looking and performing their best with post-listing revisions.

We all misspell words from time to time, but where auction titles and descriptions are concerned, innocent typos can adversely affect sales. eBay allows you to modify your auctions once they've been started, but certain revisions may not be allowed, depending on when you submit them and whether the item has received any bids.

For example, eBay understandably doesn't let you change the description once someone has bid on your auction, even if you cancel the member's bid [Hack #68]. But eBay does allow you to submit additions to the *end* of your listing description, accompanied by a date and timestamp, making it clear to your bidders exactly what you added and when. And since eBay doesn't allow bidders to retract their bids [Hack #32] within the last 12 hours of an auction, normal revisions otherwise available to sellers are prohibited during that time. Thus the policies governing revisions to running auctions can be rather confusing.

Table 4-4 shows possible revisions to a running auction; a checkmark indicates when each revision is allowed.

Table 4-4. When the components and features of alisting can be changed

Revision	Before first bid	After first bid	Last 12 hours	Completed items
Best Offer (fixed-price listings only)	✓			
Bold	✓	✓ (nonrefundable if removed)	✓ (nonrefundable if removed)	
Buy It Now	✓	Vehicles with a reserve price only		Only using second-chance offer
Calculated shipping	✓			Change in invoice only
Cancel bids		✓	✓	
Categories	✓	✓ (add second category only)		
Counter	✓	✓	✓	
Description	✓	Add to only	Add to only, unless it has also received a bid	
Duration	✓	Only by ending early		

Table 4-4. When the components and features of alisting can be changed (continued)

Revision	Before first bid	After first bid	Last 12 hours	Completed items
End listing	✓	✓		
Featured	✓	✓ (nonrefundable if removed)	✓ (nonrefund-able if removed)	
Gallery	✓	✓ (nonrefundable if removed)	✓ (nonrefund-able if removed)	
Gallery photo	✓	✓	✓	
Gift services	✓	✓ (nonrefundable if removed)	✓ (nonrefund-able if removed)	
Highlight	✓	✓ (nonrefundable if removed)	✓ (nonrefund-able if removed)	
Item location	✓			
Listing format (auction vs. fixed-price)	Auctions only, using Buy It Now			
Item Specifics	✓			
Payment details	✓	Add to only		Change in invoice only
Payment instructions	✓			Change in invoice only
PayPal email address	✓			
Pictures (if hosting on eBay)	✓	Add to description only		
Pictures (if hosting yourself)	✓	✓	✓	✓
Private auction	✓			
Quantity	✓			
Reserve price	✓	Vehicles only, can be removed or lowered once		Vehicles only, use second-chance offer
Shipping details	✓	Add to shipping destinations only		Change in invoice only
Starting price	✓			
Subtitle	✓			
Title	✓			

Most revisions can be made by clicking the "Revise your item" link at the top of the auction page, or by going to Site Map → Revise my item and entering the auction number. There are a few exceptions, such as "Fix my gallery image," all of which appear in the "Manage My Items for Sale" section of the eBay site map.

If you find that a revision you need to make is prohibited by eBay policy, your final resort is to go to Site Map → End My Listing, cancel all bids, end the auction early, and relist the item. eBay will refund your listing fees (minus any listing upgrade fees) from the first auction if the relisted auction sells, so it should ultimately cost you nothing but time.

Sneaking in Changes

There are a few legitimate ways to sneak around eBay's auction revision policies, of course, as long as you don't do anything egregious like changing what the auction is for after the high bidder has bid:

Photos. If you host your own photos [Hack #76], you can change them at any time, even after the auction has ended. All you need to do is make sure you don't change the photo filenames.

Text. This restriction is probably the most aggravating for sellers; if you don't notice a particularly serious mistake in your listing until after it receives a bid, you have to end the listing and create a new one [Hack #43] to fix the problem. About the only way to change the description once a listing has started is to create one or more images *containing* text, and then reference them [Hack #52] using HTML. Since they're stored on your own server [Hack #76], you can change them at any time. But unless you limit this practice to things like payment or shipping terms, it usually isn't worth it because the graphical text won't get picked up in searches.

About Me. Your About Me page [Hack #62] is separate from your auctions and can be modified at any time, regardless of the status of your auctions. This makes it ideal for your payment and shipping terms, contact information, and details about your business.

Answer questions. If a bidder contacts you through eBay's "Ask seller a question" link, you'll have the opportunity to add both the question and your reply [Hack #67] to the end of your listing description.

And that's about it. Obviously, it pays to review your listings before you start them. One of the best ways to do this is by using an off-site listing tool, such as Turbo Lister [Hack #93] that allows you to view full previews of your listings, and even edit them in place.

Ending Your Listing in the Last 12 Hours

eBay has instigated a new, rather draconian rule with respect to ending listings early. Just as most types of changes are disallowed in the last 12 hours of a listing's lifespan (provided it has received bids), eBay now prohibits sellers from ending their listings in these final hours. This is unfortunate, as the "End my listing" feature (Site Map → End my listing) has been the last bastion for any seller who didn't want to be forced to let a doomed auction run its course.

If you lose or break an item, or merely discover that it's been miscategorized, misspelled, or misrepresented, you should be allowed to cancel the listing at any time. Of course, eBay doesn't want sellers canceling their listings simply because they aren't getting bid up high enough, but that should be your prerogative as well. (Many people use a Reserve Price [Hack #45] for this purpose, but this isn't always a good choice.)

Now, there is still a way out, but eBay doesn't make it easy. If there are fewer than 12 hours left in your listing, you can still manually cancel any bids it has received. Go to Site Map → Cancel Bids on My Item, enter the item number, the member ID whose bids you wish to cancel, and a reason for cancellation. (If you don't know what reason to use, you can always type a generic message like "bid cancelled.") The catch is that you have to do this manually—one at a time—for each bidder who has bid on your item; if 8 people placed a total of 12 bids, you'll have to fill out the cumbersome "Cancel Bids on My Item" form 8 times.

Obviously, you won't have time to cancel 8 bids if you wait until the last 30 seconds, which is something you might be tempted to try if you wanted to allow last-minute snipers [Hack #26] to give your listing's current price the boost it needs. Thus, be sure to allow several minutes to cancel bids and assess your remaining options. If you have a lot of bids to cancel, use your browser's Back button to reuse the data in the "Cancel bids on my item" form without having to start from scratch each time.

With no bids remaining, you might expect to be able to end your listing, but eBay will have none of it. What's worse is that with all revisions still prohibited at this point, there's very little you can do to prevent new visitors from bidding on it.

About the only thing you can do is take down all your pictures for the listing, which will be possible only if you're hosting your own photos [Hack #76]. Better yet, replace your images with rasterized text [Hack #75] that clearly instructs visitors not to bid.

Of course, this won't stop bidders who've set up automatic snipe bids [Hack #27] ahead of time, and thus may not revisit your listing before placing their bids. You can try to cancel those bids as they come in, but it'll be difficult to cancel a bid placed seven seconds before the end of the listing. If any bids do make it through, and you end up with a high bidder despite your best efforts, your only recourse is to do a little damage control [Hack #88] and explain to the bidder that you've lost the item. Put on your best diplomacy hat, because the high bidder will be within his rights to leave you negative feedback if he feels like you're trying to cheat him out of a legitimate win.

To lessen the risk of losing money to this policy, you may want to place a disclaimer in all your listings—ahead of time—that says something to this effect:

> Seller isn't responsible for mistakes in this listing. Listing will be considered null and void if any problems are discovered after the point that it can no longer be cancelled.

HACK #66 Let's Make a Deal

Handle impatient bidders without losing customers and without getting kicked off eBay.

From time to time, bidders will contact you with special requests, such as those suggested in "Manipulate Buy It Now Auctions" [Hack #31] and "Retract Your Bid Without Retracting Your Bid" [Hack #32]. How you respond to such requests and how you decide to conduct business is entirely up to you, but you'll want to be careful about some of the steps you take. As a seller on eBay, you'll have to walk a fine line between protecting yourself from dishonest bidders, not upsetting your *honest* bidders, not violating eBay policy, and not wasting large amounts of your time.

> See who you're dealing with by taking a moment to look at the feedback profiles [Hack #1] of those who contact you [Hack #67]. That way, you'll know whether you should trust the bidder or cancel his bids and add him to your Blocked Bidder list [Hack #68].

For instance, an impatient bidder might want to use Buy It Now on one of your auctions, even though the item has received bids and the option has disappeared from the page. The following are a few different approaches to dealing with this type of request, each with its own advantages and disadvantages:

Forget it. Assuming you know the value of your item [Hack #42], you should be able to look at the current bids—as well as the relative success of your competition—and predict how much you're ultimately going to get for your item. Your auction may indeed be on track to fetch a higher amount than your original Buy It Now price, in which case you'll want to politely tell the bidder that you prefer to let the auction run its course. Naturally, you run the risk of not getting as much as the bidder is offering, or, at the very least, driving the bidder away by making him wait.

Cancel bids. If you cancel all bids on an auction, the Buy It Now price will reappear, and the bidder in question can buy the item. Unfortunately, this approach is not without risks. First, you'll need to get the timing right; if the bidder isn't quick enough, someone else may place a bid and the Buy It Now price will once again disappear. But what's worse is the possible flight risk: if the bidder doesn't end up using Buy It Now, you've essentially canceled a bunch of honest bids on your item for no reason.

Wink, wink. You may be tempted to make an under-the-table deal with the bidder, agreeing to end the auction early for a certain dollar amount. But this, too, is fraught with peril. First, eBay may consider this to be a violation of their "fee avoidance" policy, and as a result may suspend your account. Second, since it is an off-eBay transaction, it won't be covered by eBay's fraud protection policies, and neither you nor the bidder will be able to leave feedback. And worst of all, some bidders who pursue this may be trying to rip you off **[Hack #69]**.

> As a seller, you should never solicit an off-eBay transaction from your bidders, either in your auction descriptions or in any eBay-related emails. There are several reasons for this, not least of which is that it's a common practice of scammers and spammers **[Hack #25]** and may unsettle otherwise-interested customers. It would also violate several eBay policies put in place to protect both buyers and sellers. This doesn't mean that you should never entertain such requests from bidders, only that you should be very careful about how you proceed.

Second Listing. Probably the safest approach is to create a second listing, identical to the first. When it's ready, send the URL to the bidder and instruct him or her to use the Buy It Now option promptly (before anyone else bids). Only when that auction has closed successfully should you cancel bids on the original auction and end it early. This way, you and the bidder can complete the transaction officially and enjoy the protection of eBay's buying and selling policies. And if the bidder backs out, you can simply end the superfluous listing or modify it to accommodate a different item.

Best Offer. eBay is well aware of these types of requests, mostly because any off-eBay transactions rob them of the final value fees they'd otherwise collect from a successful listing. As a result, eBay provides the Best Offer feature, essentially allowing a particularly anxious buyer to make you an offer through official channels, at which point you can accept or decline the offer (again, through official channels).

Ironically, the Best Offer feature is available only for fixed-price listings, suggesting that someone at eBay has a loose interpretation of the meaning of the word "fixed." If you're using the more-popular auction format, you'll have to resort to one of the other solutions in this hack.

You can select the Best Offer option when creating a fixed-price listing [Hack #43], or you can add it when revising your listing [Hack #65]. Then, the bidder views your listing, clicks the "Submit your Best Offer" link at the top of the page, and makes you an offer.

As you might expect, this feature is intended to be used when you otherwise might post an ad with the phrase "40 dollars or best offer." Of course, this is pretty much the whole point of the auction format and the Buy It Now option [Hack #31].

Although the preceding example is the most common request of this sort, it's not the only one you'll receive. Bidders often contact sellers to ask for alternative colors, versions, etc., as well as related items and accessories, and a cooperative seller can stand to make quite a bit of extra money. Just be careful about how much you reach out to bidders.

If you're selling shoes, for example, it's generally acceptable to mention that you have other sizes and colors, either in other auctions [Hack #60] or for sale in your online store [Hack #91]. But this is different from posting a "dummy" auction whose purpose is to simply direct customers to your off-eBay store. Bidders won't buy it, and eBay won't tolerate it.

HACK #67 Diplomacy 101: Answer Dumb Questions

Handle communications with seemingly lazy or dimwitted bidders.

No matter what you do, you'll never get all your bidders to read your auction descriptions, shipping terms, or payment instructions as carefully as you'd like them to, if at all. As a result, you'll occasionally get a bidder who looks at an auction entitled "Antique Royal Blue Vase," sees the large photo of a royal blue vase, and then writes you to ask what color the vase is.

OK, it's not usually that bad, but sometimes it seems like it is. The first thing to remember is how easy it can be to miss even the most obvious piece of information. Instead of antagonizing your bidder with the all-too-familiar, "It's blue, like it says in the description," try one of the following:

- "The vase is a deep royal blue that looks almost purple in low light. The glaze seems a little darker at the bottom." Not only does this answer the bidder's question respectfully, it presumes that the bidder was looking for more information than simply, "it's blue."

- "The vase is royal blue. The photo in the auction actually has a pretty good reproduction of the color, so please let me know if it doesn't come through." This not only (kindly) reminds the bidder that there is a photo, but it helps inspire trust that the photo is accurate, a fact the bidder may not have wanted to take for granted. It also suggests a legitimate reason for the bidder asking the question in the first place; namely, that the photo might not have loaded properly on the bidder's computer.

Instead of driving your customers away, you'll be sending them the message, so to speak, that a transaction with you will be a pleasant one, that you're trustworthy, and that your item is as you've described it. Keep in mind, also, that your customers may be contacting you simply to see that you really have the item and are not trying to rip them off [Hack #25].

Next, remember that for every bidder who writes you with a question, there will be 10 potential bidders who don't bother. Either they bid without asking, only to be disappointed later, or they move on and bid on someone else's auction instead. Since neither scenario is desirable, it pays to be a little proactive.

When someone contacts you via the "Ask seller a question" link in one of your currently running listings, you'll have three different ways to respond:

Revise the description. If a bidder asks a question that isn't answered in your description, and no bids have been placed, go ahead and revise the listing [Hack #65] to include the extra information. If the listing has received bids, you can either add a note to the end of the description or respond publicly , described next.

Respond publicly. In each of those "Question for item #..." email messages, there will be a link immediately following the bidder's question. Click the link to go to eBay's web site and write your reply. At this point, you'll have the option of adding the bidder's question and your reply to the item description, the result of which is shown in Figure 4-26.

Respond privately. Use your email program's Reply feature to respond to the message directly. Make sure the customer's original question appears in your message; that way, the bidder doesn't receive an email that simply says "Yes," with no further clue as to what question you're answering. (Strangely, this simple bit of "netiquette" is basically ignored by even the most experienced sellers—don't be one of them.)

In most cases, there's no reason you can't do all three. In fact, if you send your response both publicly *and* privately, you'll increase the odds that the recipient will actually receive your message [Hack #9].

Questions from other buyers

Q: Is this for 26 or 31.8 bars? Thanks — answered on: Feb-01-05
A: The clamp size is 25.8mm (for 26mm bars).

Q: What is its clamp size? Thanks — answered on: Feb-01-05
A: Bar: 25.8mm (slightly adjustable, perhaps down to 23mm)
Stem: 28.8mm or 25.4mm

Ask seller a question

Figure 4-26. You can have eBay show customers' questions and your replies at the bottom of your item description, which can help reduce the number of subsequent questions your customers will have

Finally, as a seller on eBay, it's often your job to act as a teacher, instructing your bidders on basic bidding concepts, your payment terms, and some of the more confusing eBay policies. After all, a bidder's first dumb question is not likely to be the last.

HACK #68 Keep Out Deadbeat Bidders

A little diplomacy will help keep out deadbeats and still allow healthy bidding on your auction.

Good judgment comes from bad experience, and a lot of that comes from bad judgment.

One of the most frustrating aspects of selling on eBay is dealing with winning bidders who don't pay. Not only are nonpaying bidders a waste of the seller's time and money, they end up ruining honest bidders' chances of winning the auction.

You can always tell a seller has been recently burned by a deadbeat from the harsh warnings in their auction descriptions:

- "Don't bid if you don't intend to pay!"
- "Serious bidders only."
- "If you have zero feedback, email before bidding or your bid will be canceled!"
- "A nonpaying bidder will receive negative feedback, lots of threatening email, and a note to your mother."

The problem with all of these is that they typically do more harm than good. For example, you should *never* tell visitors not to bid on your item, regardless of your intentions. The tone is angry and threatening, and sends a message (even to honest bidders) that dealing with you will likely be a less-than-pleasant experience. Besides, your average deadbeat bidder probably won't read your description anyway.

Instead, start by thinking about why someone may not pay after winning an auction, and then find a diplomatic way to weed out such bidders.

In most cases, it will be new eBay users—with a feedback rating of less than 10 or so—who end up bidding and not paying, a fact due largely to their inexperience rather than any kind of malice. For instance, new bidders will often wait until after they've bid to read the auction description and payment terms (if they read them at all). Or, a bidder might bid and later discover that she no longer needs or wants your item. And since inexperienced eBay users typically don't know how to retract bids [Hack #32] or communicate with sellers [Hack #62] nor do they understand that they can simply resell something they don't want, they just disappear, hoping that the problem will go away if they ignore a seller's emails.

Naturally, there are also those clowns who bid with no intention of paying. This is actually quite uncommon, and such abusers of the system don't last long on eBay. If you suspect that someone with a vendetta against you might bid on one of your auctions just to leave feedback, you may want to update your Blocked Bidder List, described later in this hack.

So how do you tell the difference between honest bidders and dishonest deadbeats? Go to Advanced Search → Items by Bidder, enter the bidder's member ID, and click Yes to include completed items. If the user's bidding history seems reasonable (a few bids, all along the same lines), then she is probably a legitimate bidder. However, if the user is bidding as though it were going out of style, seemingly trying to buy up as many high-priced items as possible, then you've likely found yourself a deadbeat.

An Ounce of Prevention

Since the problem of deadbeat bidding is most often caused by a lack of experience, any notes of warning in your auction description should instead be welcoming and instructional. Think of it as educating your bidders on eBay basics. For example:

- "Attention new bidders: please read the auction description carefully and make sure it's what you want before you bid."
- "Please read my payment and shipping terms to be sure you can complete the transaction before you place your first bid."
- "If you have any questions about this auction, please contact me before you bid."

Not only do these examples encourage bidders to bid on your auctions, they enforce the practices that help ensure that they're happy [Hack #50] once they have paid and received their items, which will reduce the likelihood of negative feedback and having to deal with returns.

Finally, to avoid misunderstandings that can lead to nonpaying bidders, take steps to make sure your payment and shipping terms [Hack #54] are as clear as humanly possible. And don't be afraid to create an About Me page [Hack #63] to remove clutter or to make good use of HTML [Hack #52] to format your description so important points are easy to spot and understand.

Being Proactive Behind the Scenes

Probably the best approach to preventing deadbeats is to be a little sneaky about it. Instead of relying on bidders to censor themselves (which they won't), simply let them bid freely. After all, only the intentions of the *high bidder* count; all lower bids—even those placed by deadbeats in the making—only serve to raise the final auction price.

Check back and review the status of your running auctions every day or two. If you see an eBay user with zero feedback or the little "new user" icon next to his user IDs, just send him a quick note to verify that he's serious. If you don't get a reply within 24 to 36 hours, cancel his bids and let him know why. Explain that if he's serious about your item, he can always bid again.

Now, if any of your auctions has a high bidder with a *negative* feedback rating (less than zero) or a feedback profile [Hack #1] with excessive negative comments, don't hesitate to unceremoniously cancel the member's bids and block any future bids.

Canceling Bids and Blocking Bidders

Canceling bids is easy...and fun! With the ability to cancel a bid at any time and for any reason, a seller wields tremendous power (over his own running listings, anyway).

To cancel a bid, go to Site Map → Cancel Bids on My Item, and follow the prompts. All bids placed by the specified bidder will be canceled, and the auction price will be adjusted accordingly. (You can also cancel all bids on an auction in one step by ending your listing early [Hack #65].)

Once a member's bids have been canceled, you'll have the opportunity to add that member's ID to your Blocked Bidder List, available at Site Map → Blocked Bidder/Buyer List. The list is simply a textbox with the eBay member IDs of all the bidders you don't want to be allowed to bid on your listings, separated by commas. This feature is particularly useful for blocking bids by possibly disgruntled bidders (or sellers) with whom you've dealt previously.

Although blocking a user prevents the user from placing any future bids on your auctions, it has no effect on any open bids placed by that user on any running auctions, so you may want to check your running auctions when you're done for any remaining bids that need to be canceled.

> You can also modify your Buyer requirements [Hack #64] to block bids by members with negative feedback ratings, excessive Unpaid Item strikes, or residences in countries to which you don't ship. But use this feature sparingly; after all, every eBay user has to start somewhere. Don't assume every new user is going to be a deadbeat, but don't expect new users to understand all the ramifications of bidding, either. If you get stuck with a deadbeat bidder, he'll usually shape up with a little diplomacy and motivation [Hack #89].

Timing is important when canceling bids. Canceling a bid too early is usually pointless, since the user is likely to be outbid by someone else, and the cancellation would just lower the final price needlessly. Canceling *too late* is also not a good idea, because it would keep the final price artificially high close to the end of the auction, possibly dissuading last-minute bidders from sniping [Hack #26]. A good window in which to cancel bids is typically about 20 to 30 hours before the end of the listing.

Regardless of the timing, there's usually no benefit to canceling bids of a user who isn't currently the high bidder, with two small exceptions. First, unless you block a bidder, she can place additional bids and become the high bidder. Second, if higher bidders retract their bids [Hack #32], a once-trailing bidder can take the lead without doing anything. Of course, bidders cannot retract their bids in the last 12 hours of an auction [Hack #65], so that threat is minimal.

HACK #69 Avoid Buyer Scams

Spot the red flags associated with buyers who try to rip you off.

Just as there are sellers out there trying to scam buyers [Hack #25], there are unscrupulous *bidders* on eBay trying to take advantage of unsuspecting sellers. Here are some of their more common tactics:

Beware bidders offering to overpay. Someone contacts you and offers to send a $4,000 money order for a $2,000 item. Then, you're supposed to ship the package and send back the difference. Only *after* you've parted with your item and $2,000 in cash do you find out the original $4,000 money order is a fake.

Hello seller. Most of your customers will be ordinary people with ordinary needs. But once in a while, you'll see a particularly formal message, in which the author has assembled an utterly plausible, yet needlessly complicated scenario. Invariably, these messages begin like this:

> Hello seller
>
> Am elisabeth jones, i deal with exporting of goods to African countries
>
> But to start with, we will like to ask some general questions concerning
>
> the item and the transaction:
>
> (1) Do you accept western union auction payments (bidpay)also called money order in which they will bring the money cas to ur doorstep and they are very trustworthy in case of handling money and cash.
>
> (2) Will you be able to release the package for FEdEx express as soon as you get the payments confirmation letter from western union??
>
> (3) How many of this items you have readily available instock??
>
> (4) Whats is your best prices?
>
> i am buying this because its urgently needed and i wount need u to reply by force and u can only reply if u are ready to do this transaction neatly and safely. am very longing to hear from you so...

Next, this mysterious customer—who happens to write worse than an 11-year-old with an attention deficit disorder—asks for your name, address, city, state, social security number, shoe size, and any other details presumably necessary for this urgent transaction. And just when you're ready to dismiss this message as spam, you notice the following at the bottom:

```
This request is related to item # 5748850091.
```

As it happens, `5748850091` is the item number of one of your currently running listings, so you look closer. Although the message loosely resembles an official eBay "Ask seller a question" email, there's no sign of the author's eBay member ID, and the links in the email all point to *ebay.sg* or *ebay.ph* (as opposed to *eBay.com* **[Hack #19]**). This is a con, plain and simple. Just throw it out, and don't lose any sleep (or money) over it.

It arrived damaged, did it? Shipping damage occurs from time to time; it's part of the cost of doing business online. Thus, a customer might contact you immediately after receiving an item you've shipped, informing you that the item arrived damaged or is nonfunctional in some way. Now, depending on the circumstances, this may be perfectly plausible, but there's a scam that's been around as long as shippers have been drop-kicking fragile packages.

Here's how it starts: someone owns something that is broken—say, a slide projector—and has been out of warranty for years. Either the owner can throw out the damaged item, have it repaired at a cost likely to exceed the value of the item, or try to get it replaced for free on eBay. This is where you come in.

You just happen to be selling exactly the same slide projector. An eager bidder wins the auction, pays right away, and happily thanks you for your quick shipping. Your fully insured, well-packed package [Hack #86] arrives fully-intact on the customer's doorstep, at which point the customer removes your functional projector from the box, puts the broken one in its place, and then kicks the package a few times for good measure. As far as you—and the courier's insurance investigators—know, it's the same projector, and the damage took place during shipping.

Here's how you should handle this situation:

- Ask the customer to email you a photograph of the item, clearly showing the damage. Knowing how thoughtfully you packaged the item, you are understandably suspicious when it looks like it was crushed by Godzilla.
- Ask the customer to ship the item back to you, at the customer's expense. Explain that if you can determine that the damage was your fault (or the fault of the shipper), you'll refund the purchase price *and* the customer's shipping expenses. Most bidders will give up at this point, not wanting to risk losing more money on the item.
- If you sell a lot of used merchandise, find a way to make a unique, yet inconspicuous mark on each item before you ship. If a customer then returns the item, look for the mark to confirm that it is actually the same item.

Unfortunately, there's not a whole lot else you can do in this situation; as always, your best defense is your common sense. Be diplomatic and patient, but don't let your customers push you around. And to help ensure that you're not penalized for your customer's dishonesty, make a habit of withholding your feedback [Hack #6] until the matter is resolved.

Check Out Your Customers

When an unfamiliar eBay user contacts you or a past customer complains, you may want to take a moment to do a little research and find out who you're dealing with before you reply.

For example, if your auction states that you won't ship internationally, and someone from Iceland* is inquiring about your item, you'll want to let her know that you can't ship to her. But how do you know where these bidders are located? Well, you'll have a pretty good clue if someone asks, "How much to ship to Iceland?" but otherwise you'll have to do a little investigating.

* For my beloved readers in Iceland, please substitute *Greenland* here.

Start by going to Advanced Search → Find a Member, type the bidder's user ID, select "Feedback profile," and click Search. (For a shortcut, just open any member's feedback page and replace the user ID in the URL [Hack #13] with that of the member you're investigating.) The country in which the member is registered is shown right in the summary box at the top of the feedback profile page [Hack #1].

> While you're at it, take a look at the member's feedback rating. If the member has an excessive number of negative comments, now may be an excellent time to make sure that bidder can't bid on your items [Hack #68]. Also, if you take a look at the feedback this person has left for other sellers, you'll get an idea of exactly how much trouble this customer is likely to be.

The country specified on the Feedback page is not foolproof, however. If you're suspicious, just look at the bidder's email address, which will appear at the top of the email they've just sent you. Unless the bidder's domain is *.com*, *.net*, *.org*, or *.edu*, the TLD (top-level domain) will contain a country code (such as *.uk* for the United Kingdom, *.de* for Germany, or *.ca* for Canada). If the country indicated by the TLD doesn't match the country in which the member is registered, this may be a sign that something isn't right.

The feedback profile itself is not foolproof either. For instance, while account takeovers [Hack #25] are usually perpetrated for selling fraud, it's not unreasonable to expect some scammers to use these hijacked accounts for buying fraud, too.

The best way to find out what more about another member is to search for items he or she has bought (or tried to buy) in the last 30 days. Go to Advanced Search → Items by Bidder, type the bidder's user ID, turn on the "Include completed listings" option, and click Search. Then, do another search to see what the person has sold [Hack #18] in the last 30 days.

If you see any inconsistencies [Hack #25] or other causes for suspicion, don't hesitate to ignore the member's requests, cancel and block the member's bids [Hack #68], and get on with your day. After all, there are plenty more where this person came from.

Working with Photos

Hacks 70–82

There are no two ways about it: a photo can make or break an auction.

Attractive, clear, well-composed photos will excite your customers and get you more money for your items. Poor photos, however, will make your item —and therefore your auction—less desirable. And, not surprisingly, having no photo is tantamount to auction suicide (aucticide?).

But there's more to photos than the basic mechanics of transferring photos to your computer [Hack #73], preparing the files, and putting them in your auctions. First, there's proper composition and lighting [Hack #70], something made easier if you assemble a makeshift studio [Hack #72], and then there are the nuances of close-up photography [Hack #71]. But the real fun begins when you start coming up with creative ways to put photos in your listings and make them dance with a little JavaScript.

HACK #70 Keep Your Item from Looking Pathetic

Use this simple approach to take great photos of your items.

Simply put, good photos will get you more bids and more money. An attractive, clear, well-composed photo will excite customers and inspire trust in your bidders that you're selling what you say you're selling.

On the other hand, if your photos are blurry, poorly lit, too small, or too cluttered with junk, your bidders will not be nearly as impressed. Not surprisingly, bad photos will make your item look pathetic, and as a result your item will get fewer bids and less money, if it sells at all.

Background

Start with a neutral background, like an empty table or section of the floor. A little texture (like wood or fabric) can be nice, but don't overdo it. A single piece of printer paper is a good backdrop for small items; use a solid-color bedsheet, placed on a hard surface, for larger items.

Avoid carpet, which can make your item look dirty and shabby. And nobody is going to want something that is shown literally sitting in the dirt, so avoid taking photos in the back yard whenever possible. If you're photographing a bicycle, car, or other outdoor object, use pavement as a backdrop by standing on top of a chair or ladder and shooting down at your object.

Your item will be lost in the photo if it's in front of a busy pattern or other high-contrast background. Instead, make sure most of the contrast in your photo comes from the boundary between your object and the background, as shown in Figure 5-1. To further de-emphasize your background, try reducing the depth of field [Hack #71].

Figure 5-1. The item is lost in the high-contrast background on the left; the sold color on the right is much better

For more backdrop tips, check out "Construct an Auction Photo Studio" [Hack #72].

Composition

First things first: always make sure the photo is in focus. Most digital cameras let you zoom in to inspect the detail of your shots using the built-in LCD screen, giving you instant feedback. But don't be afraid to shoot a few extra backup shots so you don't have to set up your shot more than once.

Most cameras focus on the object in the center of the screen, so if you find it difficult to get your item in focus, try centering it; increasing the depth of field [Hack #71] also helps. Most higher-end cameras will let you choose the part of the frame targeted by the auto focus, and the best will let you focus manually until it's perfect.

Next, shoot from an angle to illustrate that you're selling a three-dimensional object. An object photographed slightly askew will look much better than if it's perfectly centered and aligned with the edges of the photo. Figure 5-2 shows the same object shot at two different angles, one of which looks much better than the other.

If possible, frame your photo so the entire object is visible in at least one of your photos. (Nothing is more frustrating to bidders than to try to imagine what an object looks like when the seller only includes a handful of "fractional" photos.) Proper framing can be difficult when photographing large objects, such as furniture or cars, so you may have to move the object to get a better shot. If you shoot a lot of large objects, consider getting a wide-angle lens (24 mm equivalent or shorter).

Figure 5-2. Photograph your items from an angle to make them look more attractive

Finally, it should be crystal-clear to your customers exactly what they're bidding on, so remove all unnecessary clutter from the photo. Moving the detritus out of the way *now* will prove easier than trying to crop it out [Hack #74] later.

Photographing Collections

If you're selling a collection of items, or if there are included accessories, include at least one photo showing the entire collection together. Figure 5-3 shows a handheld computer (PDA), together with a bunch of included accessories. The group shot makes your bidders feel like they're getting a lot for their money, and it clearly illustrates exactly what is included with the auction.

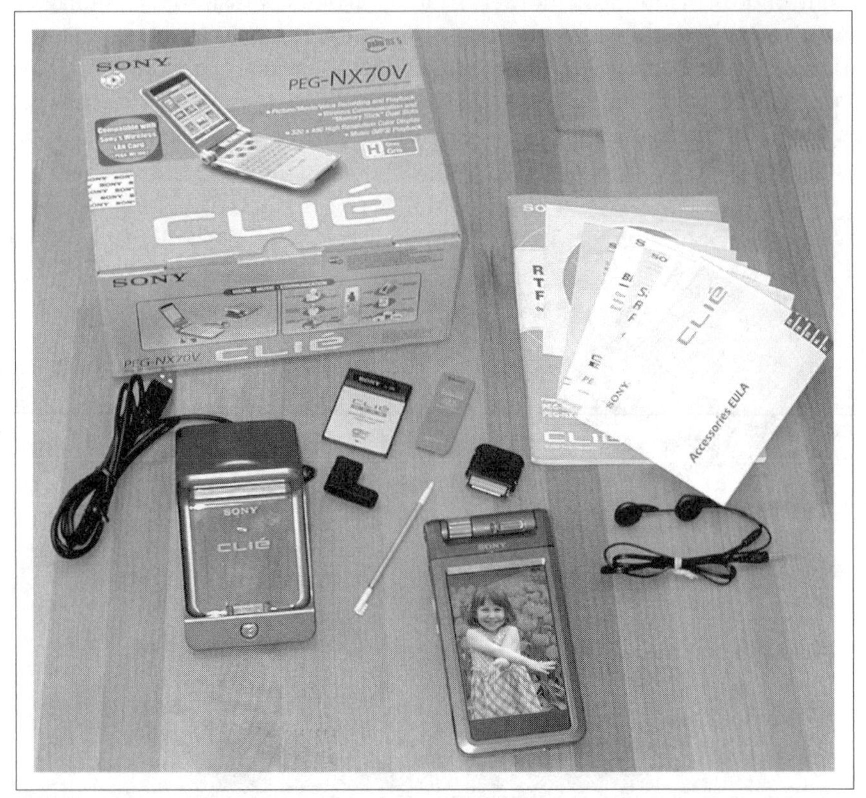

Figure 5-3. A carefully aligned group shot shows bidders exactly what they're getting

If the item comes apart, show the entire item—fully assembled—in at least one photo, preferably the first. Don't open it or take it apart unless you feel it's important to show an internal feature or to illustrate the way the item goes together.

Case in point: Not too long ago, I purchased a toy car on eBay from a seller who included only a single, rather small photo of the item. To illustrate that one of the wheel bolts was missing, the seller physically removed one of the wheels and placed it underneath the vehicle to prop it up. The photo made it look more like a pile of junk than a car, and as a result, I got it for less than half the price the model typically fetched. When the car arrived, I simply attached the wheels and reveled at the great deal I had gotten. Although the seller was probably just trying to set a reasonable expectation [Hack #50], he went too far, and his car simply looked pathetic.

Lighting

Don't underestimate the importance of proper lighting [Hack #72] for your item, even if you're just taking a handful of shots. If your item is improperly lit, your photo won't have sufficient contrast and will have excessive shadows, two things that will make your item look particularly pathetic.

Of course, too much light can cause problems, too. You'll lose all the detail in shiny items if there are too many reflections, so consider diffused light, a polarized filter, and a lens hood to reduce reflected light and lens flares.

Take time to learn about close-up photography [Hack #71], not only to take better detail shots, but to get the tools you need to more easily control what's in focus and what's not.

Finally, if you're taking multiple photos, shoot each one as if it will be the only thing your bidders see. Given how unreliable Internet connections can be, any single photo might indeed be the only thing a bidder sees!

HACK #71 Master Close-up Photography

Control the depth of field to get a perfect close-up every time.

Nothing does more than close-up photos do to compensate for the fact that bidders can't see your item in person. A good close-up photo will show detail (a really good close-up will show the texture of the paint), and will even allow you to adequately explain any flaws or damage. Different ways of shooting close-up photos yield different results.

Understanding depth of field is the key to shooting good close-ups. Depth of field is the distance between the closest object in focus and the furthest object in focus, as illustrated in Figure 5-4.

Several things affect the depth of field:

Distance from the object. The further the distance between the camera and the object, the closer your lens will be focused to infinity, and the wider the depth of field will become. Bring the camera closer to the object to narrow the depth of field.

Focal length. A wide-angle lens will increase the depth of field, and a telephoto lens will decrease it. This means that if your camera lens has an optical zoom (as opposed to a *digital* zoom), you can zoom *out* to put more of your object in focus, or zoom *in* to throw more of your object out of focus.

As you zoom out, hoping to increase the depth of field, you might be inclined to walk toward your object to keep the frame full. Unfortunately, these two actions work against one another. Instead, let the object get smaller in the frame and simply crop the photo [Hack #74] later.

Aperture. If you're using an SLR (digital or film), you'll likely have control over the f-stop. A smaller aperture (larger f-stop) increases the depth of field, and a wider aperture (smaller f-stop) decreases the depth of field. This allows you to adjust what's in focus without zooming or moving the camera.

Extension tube. Although it's almost certainly overkill for auction photos, an extension tube inserted between an SLR camera and the lens will increase the macro (close-up) capability of your lens and reduce the depth of field to almost zero. The wider the angle of the lens, the closer you'll be able to focus. For example, a 40mm lens mounted on a 55mm extension tube will allow you to focus on the *dust* on the lens glass!

So how does depth of field come into play when taking close-up photos? First, when composing an ordinary detail shot, the depth of field will likely be too small, and it will seem nearly impossible to get all of your item in focus. So, all you have to do is move *away* from the object to bring more of it into focus, as described previously. Then, simply crop out the excess with an image editor [Hack #74].

Figures 5-4 and 5-5 show the same object with a narrow and a wide depth of field, respectively. The only difference was the position of the camera and the f-stop.

If you're shooting a shiny or reflective item, or your object is in front of a reflective backdrop [Hack #72], you'll want to *reduce* the depth of field. That way, any objects reflected in your item will be thrown out of focus, and your bidders will be able to see the subject more clearly.

Finally, if you're shooting a sculpture or other large object with a complex shape, you might have a particularly hard time getting everything in focus without bringing in too much of the background. In this case, you'll want to move the object further away from the backdrop and fine-tune the depth of field so that the entire subject is in focus, but nothing else.

Figure 5-4. Depth of field is the width of the plane in which your subject will be in focus

HACK #72 Construct an Auction Photo Studio

Save time and improve the look of your pictures by setting up a dedicated area in which to take all your eBay photos.

If you sell regularly, you're probably getting tired of repeatedly setting up your camera, backdrop, and lighting equipment every time you want to snap a few more shots. So why not set aside a small space in your office, attic, or apartment for a simple studio, and have the convenience of zero setup time?

Figure 5-5. Increase the depth of field to bring more of an item into focus

So that your studio consumes the least amount of space possible, use the corner of a room. The amount of space you need depends on the size of the items you'll be photographing; if you sell jewelry, for instance, you probably won't need anything larger than a 12in×12in (30cm×30cm) square. For larger items, like dolls, camera equipment, or pottery, set aside 2ft–3ft (0.5m–1m) square.

Next, find a small wooden box or a shallow foot stool, and place it in the middle of your studio. This will allow you to elevate your items above the ground and help throw the background out of focus [Hack #71].

Use a tripod with your camera so you can shoot items from any angle and at any height without having to hold the camera by hand. A pistol-grip camera mount like the one shown in Figure 5-7 will allow you to make quick adjustments without having to loosen and tighten a bunch of little wheels: just squeeze the grip to release the camera, aim, and let go to lock the position. Also, a crank on the tripod makes height adjustments quick and painless.

Backdrop

You'll need to put something behind or underneath your object; a solid, neutral color is a good choice, as it will mask the walls without stealing contrast from the object you're photographing. Naturally, the backdrop you choose depends on what you're selling, the mood you're trying to convey, and, of course, your personal tastes. Here are a few examples:

Jewelry. Earrings, rings, and necklaces look nice on black velvet. For artisan pieces, consider sand (think Japanese rock garden) or even dry rice.

Dolls. Plain, off-white fabric is a good, neutral background, and will emphasize the colors in the doll's clothing. A postcard propped up behind the doll showing some sort of landscape or small town is a cute touch and helps emphasize the scale.

Electronics. Plain white paper is a nice base for photographic equipment or other consumer electronics with optical elements. Items with a lot of black in them look nice in front of light-colored wood, as shown previously in Figure 5-3 **[Hack #70]**.

Toys. To make a toy look rugged, place it on a hard surface, such as a wood or Corian-like table. Model trains, for instance, can be photographed right on the rails, but usually look better on a shiny, clean, reflective base, like a mirror, a piece of glass, or the top of a silver file cabinet.

When using a reflective backdrop, a shallow depth of field **[Hack #71]** will throw any unwanted background reflections out of focus, while allowing your item to remain crystal-clear.

Clothing. Clothing looks best on a human-shaped figure (preferably a human, but barring that, a mannequin): just avoid hangers or laying clothing flat. Note that clothing is one of the few things can be photographed outdoors without appearing washed out.

If you're not sure how you'd like your item to look, you have an excellent resource at your disposal: do a quick search on eBay, and make note of the backdrops other sellers are using to make their items look good.

Lighting

Don't rely entirely on your camera's flash to sufficiently illuminate your object, because half your item will appear in shadow. You don't need professional quality studio lighting; a desk lamp or overhead light will serve as a second light source. But if there's too much light, detail in the item might be washed out. Figure 5-6 shows the same item photographed with different amounts of light.

Figure 5-6. More detail is visible if the object is lit from at least two sources

Indirect light helps avoid reflections: try bouncing stronger lights off the walls or ceiling—or if you really want to go pro, try an umbrella-style reflector.

If you have a detachable flash that clips onto the top of your camera or rests on its own tripod, LumiQuest (*www.lumiquest.com*) makes excellent, low-cost reflectors and diffusers. For instance, the LumiQuest Promax Softbox/Mini Softbox attaches to your flash with Velcro, and softens the light quite effectively. Better yet, point your flash towards the ceiling and use the LumiQuest Promax 80-20 to direct 20° of the light towards your object while the remaining 80° bounces off your ceiling and lights your object from above. In other words, with a simple attachment, you can light your item from two different angles with a single light source!

The Whole Megillah

Figure 5-7 shows a completed studio setup.

The white backdrop covers the walls and base (just a box) and can be secured with tape or pins. A variety of surfaces can be placed on top of the box, depending on what is being photographed. The camera, sitting on a lightweight tripod, is positioned so the edges of the backdrop are outside the frame, yet can always be moved to adjust the depth of field [Hack #71].

You'll be surprised how easily you can achieve good results with a little time, creativity, and about four square feet in the corner of a room.

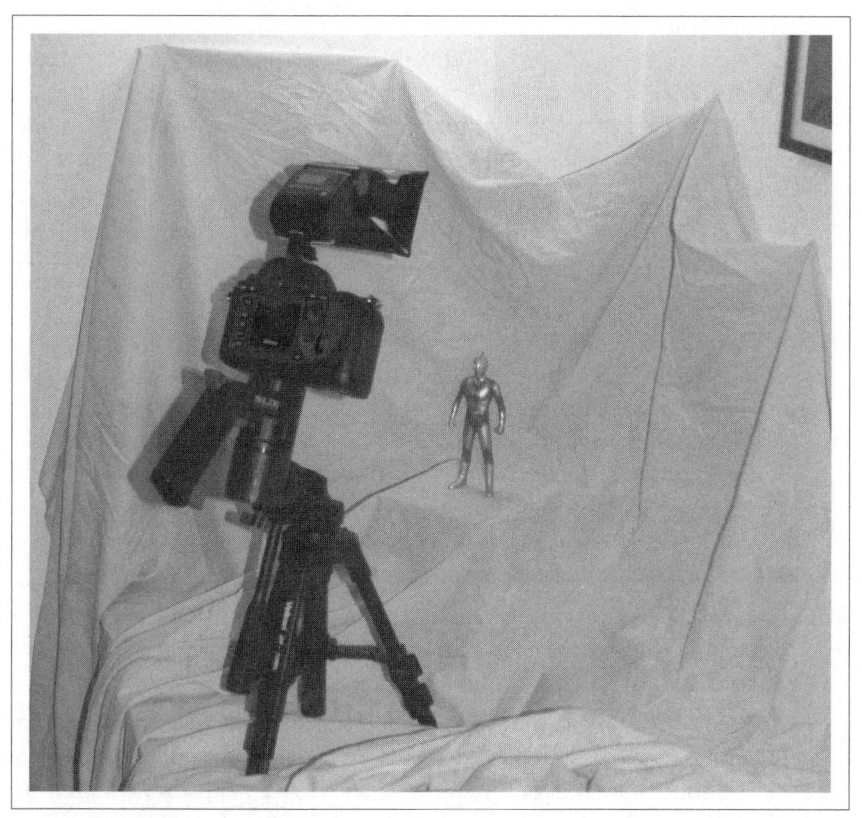

Figure 5-7. A simple studio is sufficient to photograph most items for auction

HACK #73 Get Photos into Your Computer

Prepare your photos for eBay in a few simple steps.

Probably the biggest hurdle most sellers face is getting photos into their computers. In most cases, this involves an investment, not only of money for equipment, but of time taking photos and preparing them properly. If you do it right, though, the investment will more than pay for itself in a very short time.

The first step involves taking the photos [Hack #70], which, naturally, requires a camera. In this department you have several options:

Digital camera. Easily the best choice for taking auction photos, a digital camera allows you to see your results immediately and get your photos online quickly.

Better digital cameras have better optics and take higher-resolution photos (more megapixels); the one you choose depends on your budget and your needs. But since the largest auction photos are typically no bigger than about 800×600 pixels, which translates to only about 0.5 megapixels, the camera's maximum resolution is ultimately not that important. If you're shopping for a camera specifically for shooting auction photos, look for one with a good macro (close-up) lens.

If a digital camera seems like an expensive investment, consider that the extra money you'll get for your items by having good photos will more than pay for a digital camera—which, of course, you can also buy used on eBay!

Video-conferencing camera. A cheap alternative to a real digital camera is a garden-variety video-conferencing camera, the kind that sits on top of your monitor and connects directly to your USB port. Since they have no internal memory, no LCD screens, and no optics to speak of, these cameras are remarkably cheap (with prices starting at under $10), and most support taking snapshots of at least 640×480. Make no mistake, however—the quality is pretty lousy, so it should be used only if you have no other choice at the moment.

Film camera. Never fear: film purists among us will not be left out in the cold. Flatbed scanners are cheap and relatively easy to use, and allow you to transform any print into an image file in about a minute.

Furthermore, many film-developing services include CDs with film processing, sometimes at no additional cost. The quality is nothing to write home about, but it's convenient nonetheless. You can also send your undeveloped film to an online photo service, such as Kodak's Easyshare Gallery (formerly Ofoto; *www.kodakgallery.com*) or Shutterfly (*www.shutterfly.com*). In a few days, you'll be able to download high-quality scans from the company's web site.

Any way you do it, however, you'll be subject to the limitations of film photography, namely the film and developing costs and, of course, the wait. With digital, you know right away if the picture came out, which can otherwise be difficult to predict when taking close-up auction photos.

Downloading Images into Your PC

Assuming you're using a digital camera, you'll need to transfer the images to your hard disk. All digital cameras come with cables for this purpose; refer to your camera's documentation for details.

Often, however, a digital film reader will be quicker and more convenient. Look for a USB-based memory card reader that accepts all major memory card formats, including CompactFlash, SecureDigital, Memory Stick, Memory Stick Pro, SmartMedia, and xD Picture cards. Just plug the reader into your computer, insert the flash memory card from your camera, and the photos will appear in a new drive letter (if you're using Windows) or a new folder on your desktop (if you're using a Mac). Just drag and drop the photos to a folder on your hard disk.

Preparing Images for eBay

Before you put any photos in your listings, you'll need to open them in an image editor [Hack #74] and do the following:

1. *Crop.* Crop the image [Hack #74] to remove anything that isn't for sale.
2. *Resize.* If you're using eBay's Picture Services [Hack #76] to host your photos, the image shouldn't be any larger than 400×300 (or 800×600 if you're using the Supersize option [Hack #46]). Although eBay will shrink your photo for you, it will turn out better if you do it yourself—plus, you'll have less data to send when it's time to start the listing.

   If you have access to a web server and can host your own photos [Hack #76], you have more freedom as to the size of your photos, but it's still a good idea to keep your images no larger than 800×600; otherwise, your bidders may be annoyed by photos that take too long to load and run off the sides of their screens.

> If you're using Windows XP, try Microsoft's free Image Resizer utility, which is available at *www.microsoft.com/windowsxp/pro/downloads/powertoys.asp*, to resize a bunch of photos in a single step. Or, if you have a recent version of Adobe Photoshop (on any platform), you can use Photoshop's Batch command to automate almost any kind of change.

3. *Touch up.* If necessary, touch up the photos [Hack #74] to adjust the lighting, remove unwanted distractions, or add text [Hack #75].
4. *Save.* Save your photo as a JPG file. See the "Dialing in the JPG Compression" sidebar for compression setting advice, and the next section for more information on file formats.
5. *Upload.* When your photos are ready to go, the last step is to put them on the Web so they will appear in auction photos. The easiest way to do this is to use eBay's Picture Services, which allows you to upload the files to eBay as part of the Sell Your Item form. If you want more control, however, you may want to host your own photos [Hack #76].

Image File Formats

Of all the different image file formats, the only one you should ever use for your photos is the JPG (pronounced "jay-peg") format. JPG files support

Dialing in the JPG Compression

The JPG file format supports adjustable "lossy" compression, which means that some information is lost when the image is compressed. The higher the level of compression, the more data is thrown away, and the worse the resulting photo will look. Conversely, a lower compression level will provide crisper photos, but at a cost: the resulting files are larger and take longer to load.

A good compromise is somewhere in the middle, with a slight bias toward better quality. The confusing part is that different programs represent compression levels differently. For example, the *quality* setting in Adobe Photoshop ranges from 0 to 12, with 7 typically being a reasonable compromise. In Paint Shop Pro, the *compression factor* ranges from 1 to 99, with 15 being a good compromise. And digital cameras typically have three settings: Fine, Normal, and Basic, with Normal often being the best compromise.

You may wish to perform a few experiments before settling on a single compression level. For instance, one of the example 300×225 photos in this chapter saved with the lowest quality setting (representing the highest level of compression) produced a 17 KB file and a miserable-looking image. Conversely, the same image saved at the highest quality setting (and least compression) produced a 50 KB file. While the high-quality image looked excellent, it was virtually indistinguishable from the same image saved with a medium-quality setting of 7, which topped out at only 27 KB (roughly half the size).

Naturally, your mileage will vary with the photos you take and the software you use. Note that eBay's Picture Services **[Hack #76]**, tends to overcompress photos, which may be reason enough to host them yourself.

24-bit color, which is sufficient to reproduce all the hues you'll ever need for auction photos. JPG files also support compression (discussed in the previous section), which means that they will be smaller and will load more quickly than the same images stored in most other formats.

Other image file formats you might encounter include:

GIF. GIF files support only 8-bit color (256 shades with an adaptive palette), which makes for pretty lousy photos. But GIF also has "lossless" compression (as opposed to the lossy compression used by JPG), which means that it's a better choice for logos, drawings, and text. GIF images are supported by all web browsers.

BMP. The Windows Bitmap format is the default format used by MS Paint, the rudimentary image editor included with Microsoft Windows. Not all web browsers support BMP files, and with good reason—the BMP format doesn't support compression, so even the smallest photos consume huge amounts of data. Never put BMP images in web pages.

TIF (or TIFF). TIFF is the default file format for many flatbed scanners. If your scanner supports JPG but your JPG scans look bad, it's because your scanner software doesn't allow you to adjust the JPG compression, explained in the previous section. In this case, your best bet is to save your scans as TIFF files and convert them with a suitable image editor [Hack #74].

PNG. The PNG format has all the advantages of JPG with some of the added features of GIF (such as animation and transparency). Unfortunately, the format was established years after the web browser, so many older browsers don't support it. You're probably safe using PNG files in your listings, but if you don't need the extra features they support, you're better-off sticking with JPG for the time-being.

Any decent image editor [Hack #74] should be able to convert files between any of these image file formats.

HACK #74 Doctor Your Photos

Fix up your photos after they've been taken.

There's more to image preparation than simple crops and rotations. When presentation really matters, you may want to take a few extra minutes to make your auction photos look perfect.

Be careful not to doctor the photo so much that it misrepresents the item being sold. Try to strike a balance between making your photos look professional and setting a reasonable expectation [Hack #50] with your bidders.

Regardless of how you take your photos [Hack #70] and get them into your computer [Hack #73], you'll eventually end up with one or more image files. But before you send them to eBay or upload them to your web server [Hack #76], you'll need to prepare your images, and for that, you'll need an image editor.

Image Editors

A good image editor will be able to do the following:

- Read, write, and convert all popular image file formats [Hack #73]
- Basic image manipulation, such as crop, resize, and rotate
- Basic touch-up, including clone, line, and text tools
- Basic color adjustments, such as contrast, brightness, and color balance
- Batch processing (converting or modifying a group of files in one step)

Here are some of the image editors currently available, including both free and commercial applications:

Adobe Photoshop (www.adobe.com). Easily the best photo editor available, Photoshop will do just about anything you'll ever need when it comes to processing auction photos. The Windows and Macintosh versions are practically identical, meaning that the Photoshop-specific instruction in this book (which covers Version 7) should be easy to follow. The down side is that Photoshop is rather expensive, and is probably overkill for most eBay sellers.

Adobe Photoshop Elements (www.adobe.com). Essentially a scaled-down version of Adobe Photoshop, Photoshop Elements offers many of the basic functions—without the sophistication or the steep learning curve—of its older cousin at a fraction of the price.

Jasc Paint Shop Pro (www.jasc.com). Although not nearly as capable as Photoshop, Paint Shop Pro's strengths lie in its support for every conceivable image format and its ability to easily and quickly convert between them. Supports Windows only.

The Gimp (mmmaybe.gimp.org). A free image editor for Unix, Windows, and Mac OS X, The GIMP (GNU Image Manipulation Program) is probably the most full-featured freeware image editor you can get, although the learning curve may be a little steeper than some of the other products discussed here.

VicMan's Photo Editor (vicman.net/vcwphoto). A free image editor with a good assortment of tools. Supports Windows only.

IrfanView (www.irfanview.com). Also free, IrfanView is a basic image viewer with some image manipulation tools.

iPhoto and MS Paint. iPhoto and MS Paint are free image editors that come with Mac OS X and Windows, respectively. Although they support only rudimentary functionality, these programs have the significant advantages of being free and already installed on your computer.

Most of the specific instruction in this chapter covers Photoshop and, where applicable, Paint Shop Pro. Although most image editors work similarly to these programs, the usage and location of the various features will likely be a little different. Refer to the documentation included with your favorite image editor for details on its tools and capabilities.

Tools

The following tools are available in most of the more capable image editors, but their names and usage may vary slightly:

Crop. Use the crop tool to draw a box on your image, as shown in Figure 5-18 [Hack #82]. Most image editors allow you to drag the corners of the box to fine-tune your selection. When you're done, click the crop tool button again (or go to Image → Crop) to remove the excess.

Clone tool. Use the clone tool to copy one part of an image to another part, useful for removing dust and unwanted reflections.

Start by choosing an area to clone. In Photoshop, click while holding the Alt key. In Paint Shop Pro, click while holding Shift. Then, start drawing on a different part of the image. The horizontal and vertical distance will be held constant, so if you move a half-inch to the left, you'll be cloning the area a half-inch to the left of the spot you originally selected. Figure 5-8 shows an image doctored with the clone tool.

Figure 5-8. Use the clone tool to touch up small areas of your images; here, the table edge and a few scratches in the table surface were removed with cloning

Skew, Distort, and Perspective tools. Photoshop supports a variety of linear distortion tools, useful for fine-tuning the perspective of your item. This can be particularly useful if you're photographing artwork from an angle; just use the Perspective tool to correct the perspective and square the object with the edges of the image.

Start by selecting a portion of your image (or the entire image), and then go to Edit → Transform → Perspective. Drag any of the eight handles with your mouse to distort the selection, and click any tool in the toolbox to commit (or reject) the change. The Skew and Distort tools work the same way, but the distortions they permit vary slightly.

Drop shadows. Although somewhat old-school, drop shadows are handy for making small photos stand out, especially thumbnails [Hack #77]. Although Photoshop has a feature to automatically add a drop shadow to any layer, here is a more general procedure that will work in any image editor:

1. Start by floating the layer containing your image. Press Ctrl-A to select all, Ctrl-X to cut, and Ctrl-V to paste the image into a new layer.
2. Enlarge the canvas of your image slightly, enough to accommodate the shadow; say, 20 pixels on the right side and bottom.
3. Duplicate the layer by going to Layer → Duplicate Layer, and then move the lower layer down and to the right slightly.
4. Go to Image → Adjustments → Brightness/Contrast, and turn both the brightness and contrast all the way down. The lower layer will turn completely black.
5. Finally, perform a Gaussian blur (Filter → Blur → Gaussian Blur) on the lower layer; adjust the radius to achieve the desired effect.

Auto levels. Most image editors allow you to adjust the individual levels of red, green, and blue, as well as the brightness and contrast of an image. If all you want to do is make the image look more balanced, you can let your image editor do all the work by using the Auto Levels tool (in Photoshop, go to Image → Adjustments → Auto Levels or press Shift-Ctrl-L). It's nothing more than a mathematical operation so it's not always perfect, but most of the time it does a pretty good job.

When you're done doctoring your photos, save the new versions under different filenames so you can compare them side-by-side with the originals to see if your changes were actually improvements.

Protect Your Copyright

Prevent other sellers from stealing your photos.

Taking a good-quality photo of each and every item being sold can be extraordinarily time consuming, not to mention practically impossible for items still in their boxes or not in the seller's immediate possession. As a result, many sellers resort to hijacking other sellers' photos for use in their own auctions.

The problem is that photo theft can be extremely damaging, and not so much because of mere copyright law (though it does apply).

A big part of any item's desirability is its perceived uniqueness. The more uncommon an item appears to bidders, the more valuable it becomes. When bidders see the exact same photo in two different auctions, not only are the implied scarcity and value of the item severely weakened, but the integrity of both sellers becomes suspect. And unless it's painfully obvious, most bidders won't distinguish between the thief and the seller whose photos were pilfered; a single theft of an image will hurt both sellers.

Protecting Your Image

My inspiration for this solution was a hot-dog vendor in my college town. On a shelf next to the broiler sat an old black-and-white television set, with the words "Stolen from Top Dog" written in permanent marker on its side.

The idea is to mark your photos so that they're unusable by other sellers, but in a way that doesn't adversely affect your own auctions. This is accomplished, quite simply, with a bit of text carefully superimposed on your photos.

The text should be carefully placed so that it neither obscures the subject nor can be easily removed by the thief (such as with the clone tool [Hack #74]). Often the easiest way to do this is with large, translucent text right over the center of the image, as in Figure 5-9.

The specific text you use is up to you, but it should include a copyright symbol (©) and your eBay user ID. The user ID is important, as it indicates that the photo belongs in *your* auction and no one else's.

Disabling Right-Click

The right mouse button is what most people use if they want to save an image on a web page. If you want to take an aggressive stance on image theft, you can disable your customers' right mouse buttons for your auction photos. Just include this code* somewhere in your auction description:

```
<script language="JavaScript1.1"><!--

function lockout( ) {
  for (var i=0; i < document.images.length; i++) {
➊   document.images[i].onmousedown = norightclick;
➋   document.images[i].oncontextmenu = nocontextmenu;
```

* Based on code snippets by Martin Webb (*irt.org*).

Figure 5-9. Tagging your photos with your eBay user ID is an effective deterrent against image theft

```
    }
  }

  function norightclick(mousebutton) {
    if (navigator.appName == 'Netscape' &&
                (mousebutton.which == 3 || mousebutton.which == 2)) {
❸     alert("Please don't steal my pix.");
      return false;
    }
  }

  function nocontextmenu( ) {
❹   event.cancelBubble = true;
    event.returnValue = false;
    return false;
  }

❺ if (document.layers) {
    window.captureevents(event.mousedown);
    window.onmousedown=norightclick;
  }

  // --></script>
❻ <body onLoad="lockout( );">
```

Here's how it works. The `lockout` function sets two rules for the page: any time a user clicks an image on the page, the `norightclick` function is run ❶, and any time a user opens a context menu on an image, the `nocontextmenu` function is run ❷. Later on, the `<body>` tag ❻ calls the `lockout` function only when the page has completely loaded, otherwise, the `for` loop would miss any images that haven't yet finished loading.

The `norightclick` function then blocks the right click with a warning message ❸, but only for Netscape and Mozilla browsers. The `nocontextmenu` function disables the context menu with no warning ❹, but only for Internet Explorer. The two browsers are handled differently because only Internet Explorer supports the `oncontextmenu` event. (And, to cover all the bases, there's a bit of code to handle older versions of Netscape ❺.)

This code is by no means foolproof. Any knowledgeable or determined user can disable JavaScript, or view the page source, perform a screen capture, or simply drag and drop images off the page (for browsers that support it). But most users who steal images do so because they don't know any better, and this script gets the point across.

Other Ways to Protect Your Copyright

Here are a few other ways to protect your images from being stolen:

Take 'em down. If you're hosting your own photos, take them down right after your auctions close to reduce the window during which other sellers might find and steal your images. But this could arouse the suspicions of your winning bidder, and would weaken the marketing power of any photos in your completed auctions that might otherwise help drive bidders to your current listings.

CopySafe Pro. If you're really concerned about image copyright, you can use CopySafe Pro (available at *artistscope.com*), a Java-enabled image viewer. It may be overkill for simple auction photos, and it's not foolproof, but it may be the additional security you're looking for.

Watermark. Some image editors, like Photoshop, support invisible watermarking, a method by which images can be marked and later identified for copyright infringement. Image thieves won't ever know it's there, but it can be useful for proving that theft has taken place.

Reporting Image Thieves

The most effective means of protecting your images is to simply report any auctions in which another seller has used one of your images without permission.

> You can try contacting the offending sellers directly, but you may not get far. A few sellers have gotten downright hostile after I asked them to remove photos they've stolen from me. Plus, if their auctions have received bids, they may not be able to change the photos [Hack #65] (or may simply not know how).

To report the theft of one of your images or any of your text content, go to *pages.ebay.com/help/contact_inline/*. On the Contact Us page, select Report a listing policy violation → Copying of your listing → Your picture was copied. Click Continue and then click the Email link on the next page. Finally, specify the offending item number in the first box, the item number of your original listing in the second box, and explain the offense in the third box.

eBay typically takes two or three days to investigate and respond to claims. In the case of content theft, eBay will simply remove the offending auction and explain the situation to the seller (assuming you've sufficiently proven your case).

HACK #76 Host Your Own Photos

Bypass eBay's photo restrictions by hosting auction photos on your own server.

Any photos that appear in your auctions must be stored on a web server somewhere; which one you use is up to you. When you use eBay's Picture Services, you're instructing eBay to store your photos on their own dedicated picture server and link them to your listing automatically. While this is the easiest and most convenient way to host photos, it's also fraught with limitations.

Hosting photos off-eBay has tons of advantages over using eBay's Picture Services (ePS). For instance, you can have:

More photos. Include as many photos as you like in any listing at no additional charge.

Larger photos. Include photos of any size with no "supersize" fees. With ePS, photos are limited to 400×300 pixels, or 800×600 for an additional fee [Hack #46].

More photos at once. Large photos are more striking and show much more detail than small ones, and will end up getting you more bids. The problem with eBay's supersize photos is that they appear only when bidders click the Supersize Picture links beneath the thumbnails. If you host your own photos, you can put the large versions right in the auction (as many as you like), so your bidders don't have to click to see them. This is especially helpful if you choose to create a photo collage [Hack #81].

Better quality photos. Control the quality (compression) settings of your JPG photos. ePS has a tendency to over-compress photos, which reduces detail and increases fuzziness.

Different shape photos. Use very long or very wide images that don't conform to the standard 4:3 aspect ratio. These would otherwise be shrunk beyond recognition to conform to eBay's 400 × 300 size limit.

More flexible photos. Place your photos directly in the text of your auction descriptions or use a more creative photo presentation, such as thumbnails [Hack #77], a custom photo album [Hack #79], or even a rotating 360° view of your item [Hack #80].

Photos that can be changed. Make changes [Hack #65] to photos while an auction is running, even after it has received bids. You'll also have control over how long the images remain in your auctions after they've closed.

Photos that can be recycled. Reuse the same photos for multiple auctions without having to upload them repeatedly.

Photos that aren't necessarily photos. Include logos and section headers right in your text.

All that's required to host your own auction photos is access to a web server on which you have an account. If you don't have access to your own server, see the "Looking for a Good Home" sidebar.

Sending Photos to the Server

In most cases, an FTP program is required to transfer your images from your computer to your web server. (The exception is when you're using a dedicated picture hosting service that requires you to upload photos through a web page.)

Although nearly every modern computer comes with a command-line FTP client, you'll probably want something a little friendlier and more streamlined. Popular FTP programs include Fetch for the Mac (*fetchsoftworks.com*) and WS_FTP for Windows (*ipswitch.com*). All you'll need is the host name (the name or address of the server), your username and password, and the full path of the public folder in which to store the files.

Users of most modern versions of Windows (Me, 2000, and XP) can also access FTP servers right from Explorer by typing this URL into Explorer's address bar:

```
ftp://my_server.com
```

Looking for a Good Home

If you want to host your auction photos outside of eBay, but you don't have access to a web server, never fear—there is always help for those who need it.

Start with your ISP. Most Internet providers offer free web space to their customers, so you might have 20 MB or so of space with your name on it (literally). However, some ISPs specifically lock out image hosting, so if your photos don't load in your auctions, that's probably why.

If your ISP turns you away, you have other options. There are a number of companies that offer space (for a fee) specifically for hosting auction photos, such as *pixhost.com*, *boomspeed.com*, *inkfrog.com*, *eaph.com*, and *andale.com*. But since one of the goals of this hack is to save money by hosting the photos yourself, you may want to look elsewhere.

Some sites that offer free auction picture hosting include *freepicturehosting.com*, *photobucket.com*, *easypichost.com*, and *villagephotos.com*. Each site works a little differently, so make sure to read the fine print.

When selecting a site to host your images, there are a few things to look for. First, make sure the images can be placed in your auctions; you don't want your customers to have to click a link to see your photos (because they won't). Second, since most free sites are advertising-supported, you'll want to make sure the ads don't interfere with your auction (and never pay for image hosting with ads). Finally, the site you choose shouldn't impose the same (or worse) restrictions on your photos that eBay does (see the beginning of this hack).

If you're resigned to paying for image hosting, consider paying for *web* hosting instead. Simple, no-frills web space is often the best choice, whether you pay for it or get it free with your Internet connection. You'll not only be able to insert photos into your auctions with none of the nonsense that accompanies most image hosting services (ads, logos, restrictions), but you'll also be able to use this space to host an entire web site, including the CGI programs detailed in the Preface and several other hacks in this book.

where `my_server.com` is the host name or IP address of your FTP server. If you want Explorer to log you in automatically, include your username and password in the URL, like this:

```
ftp://username:password@my_server.com
```

The FTP server then acts like any ordinary folder, where files can be drag-dropped, deleted, renamed, or moved into subfolders.

Filename Requirements

When hosting your own photos, be sure to choose appropriate filenames for your image files; otherwise they may not work as expected. Make sure the filenames are all lowercase and have no spaces whatsoever. Avoid special characters, such as #, @, and %. Also, the images should use the JPG format [Hack #73], except for logos and animated images, which work best as GIFs.

If you sell a lot of the same stuff repeatedly on eBay, you'll probably want to leave your images on the server for the long haul. To make image management easier down the road, try to be consistent when naming your files. For instance, say you sell bonsai trees and pruning tools. The filenames of your tree photos might be *tree_apple.jpg*, *tree_juniper.jpg*, and *tree_elm.jpg*, while your photos of tools might be named *tool_shears.jpg* and *tool_stakes.jpg*.

Placing Photos in Your Listings

The most direct way to include a photo in one of your auctions is eBay's Sell Your Item form [Hack #43]. On the Pictures & Details page, click the "Your own Web hosting" tab, and in the "Picture Web address" field, specify the full URL of your photo, like this:

```
http://my_server.com/my_folder/image.jpg
```

where *image.jpg* is the filename of the photo, *my_folder* is the public name of the folder in which the image file is stored, and *my_server.com* is the host name. No HTML is required to specify your photos this way, which makes it especially convenient; your images will simply appear beneath your auction description.

Avoid the Picture Show option [Hack #46], which presents multiple self-hosted photos in a slide-show format. Although it allows you to specify more than one self-hosted photo, it circumvents some of the advantages of hosting the photos yourself, such as being able to show multiple full-size photos side-by-side. Another drawback—depending on your perspective—is that eBay opens a new window when a bidder clicks the preview photo at the top of the page, which means new bidders may never see your payment and shipping terms [Hack #54].

If you want to include multiple photos in this space, one of the best ways is to consolidate them into a photo collage [Hack #81], and then specify the URL of the collage in the "Picture Web address" field.

If you have more than one photo or if you prefer to place your photos directly in your auction text, use the <img> HTML tag [Hack #52] to reference them, like this:

```
<img src="http://my_server.com/my_folder/image.jpg">
```

You can include as many pictures as you like with the <img> tag, but it's up to you to present them in an attractive and efficient manner using the <img> tag's alignment and text-wrapping parameters [Hack #52]. Figure 5-10 shows some photos placed right in the text, one right-aligned and one left-aligned.

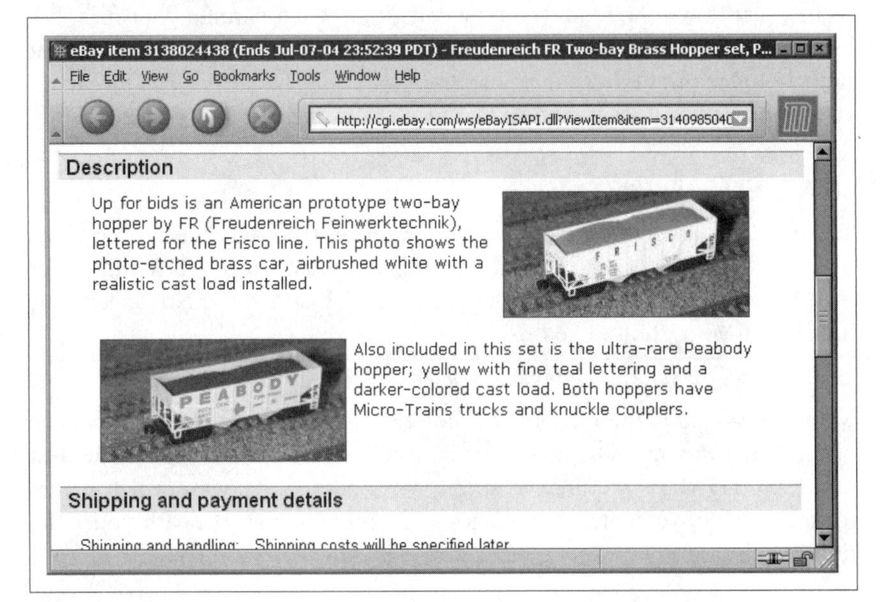

Figure 5-10. A self-hosted photo appears beneath the auction description unless you insert it directly into the description text with HTML

Ordinary inline images are only the beginning; if you want to have a little fun with the presentation of your self-hosted photos, you can make clickable thumbnails [Hack #77], construct an interactive photo album [Hack #79], and show a 360-degree view of your item [Hack #80].

The Preview Photo

The preview photo is the small picture that normally appears at the top of your listing, as shown in Figure 4-11 [Hack #54], and is one of the first things your customers see when they view the page. The preview photo is linked so that bidders can click it to jump to the full-size version shown beneath your description. If you like, you can redirect this link [Hack #54], which will help ensure your bidders read your description and see your shipping terms.

When you specify the URL of a self-hosted photo in the aforementioned "Picture Web address" field, eBay uses it for the preview photo. (Or, if you're using eBay Picture Services, eBay uses your first photo.)

For this reason, avoid leaving the "Picture Web address" field blank, which you may be tempted to do if you want all your photos to appear inside the listing text. Instead, there's no reason you can't put photos *both* in the description and in the "Picture Web address" field. If you *do* decide to put your photos exclusively in the description text, make sure to check the box that says, "The description already contains a picture URL for my item," when constructing your listing [Hack #43]. This ensures that the little green "picture" icon appears next to your listing in search results and category listings, unless, of course, you specify a Gallery photo [Hack #82], which appears in this space regardless.

HACK #77 Make Clickable Thumbnails

Use thumbnails for professional-looking auction photos that load quickly.

If you're hosting your auction photos [Hack #76], you have the freedom to include as many full-size, high-quality images as you like at no additional charge. But you're also responsible for inserting those photos into your auctions and presenting them in a way that is efficient and appropriate.

Now, large photos are more dramatic and eye-catching than small ones, but they also take longer to load, and including a lot of them will overwhelm the rest of the auction page (especially on small screens).

For some perspective, an average eBay auction page is about 45 kilobytes in size, not including any photos you might include. (There's also about 215 KB of JavaScript code and 18 KB of eBay images, but these will be quickly cached and ultimately loaded only once.) The size of a single, medium-sized JPG file is usually 50–60 KB; include eight or nine such photos, and each bidder will have to download at least a half-megabyte of data just to look at your listing.

Thumbnail photos are much smaller than their full-size equivalents, both in physical dimensions and in the amount of data that must be transferred. This means that by replacing several full-size photos with thumbnails, your auction will not only appear tidier but will load faster as well.

Preparing the Images

Thumbnails are nothing more than smaller versions of full-size images, so you'll need to make two versions of each photo.

Don't even think about using the `width` and `height` parameters of the `<img>` tag to "shrink" down large photos. Not only will your images look awful, but they'll load much more slowly than true thumbnails.

Start by duplicating each of your image files. In Windows, for example, highlight all the images you wish to duplicate, drag them with the *right* mouse button to another part of the same folder window, and select Copy Here.

Next, rename your thumbnails appropriately. For example, if one of your images is named *front.jpg*, name the thumbnail image something such as *front.small.jpg* or *front_thumb.jpg*. Remember to follow the naming conventions outlined in "Host Your Own Photos" **[Hack #76]**.

If you're using a recent version of Windows, an easy way to quickly rename large groups of files is to use Power Rename, a component of Creative Element Power Tools (*www.creativelement.com/powertools*). Among other things, Power Rename allows you to add or replace text in any number of filenames simultaneously, and to create duplicates in the process.

Finally, open the newly created duplicates in your favorite image editor or batch-resizing utility **[Hack #74]** and shrink them down. A good size for thumbnails is 150 pixels in the larger dimension, but you can certainly make them smaller or larger as you see fit. Anything smaller than 50 or 60 pixels, however, will be too small to be practical, and anything larger than 300 is likely to be unnecessarily large.

In most cases, your thumbnails will look best if they're all the same size, which can be a bit of a challenge if they have different aspect ratios or orientations. If you're placing them side by side, you might want them to be all the same height; if you're stacking them, you might want to make them all the same width. But probably the most effective approach is to pick a size to use for each photo's larger dimension.

When your images and corresponding thumbnails have been prepared, upload them all to your server **[Hack #76]**.

Putting Thumbnails in Your Listings

To put a single thumbnail image in your auction description, use the following bit of HTML **[Hack #52]**:

```
<a href="http://www.ebayhacks.com/pictures/view1.jpg"><img
    src="http://www.ebayhacks.com/pictures/view1_small.jpg"></a>
```

Replace `http://www.ebayhacks.com/pictures/view1_small.jpg` with the URL of the thumbnail image, and replace `http://www.ebayhacks.com/pictures/view1.jpg` with the URL of the full-size image.

To right-align or left-align your thumbnail in the description so that the surrounding text wraps neatly around it (as shown in Figure 5-10 [Hack #76]), include either the `align=right` or `align=left` parameter, respectively, in the `<img>` tag, like this:

```
<img src="http://www.ebayhacks.com/pictures/view1_small.jpg" align=right>
```

You can use tables [Hack #52] to group a bunch of thumbnails together. Not only does this impose some structure on your images, but it permits captions, which require the alignment only tables can afford. For instance, the following code displays four thumbnails—and their captions—aligned in a simple 2×2 table:

```
<table cellpadding=10 cellspacing=0 border=0>
<tr><td align=center>
  <a href="http://www.ebayhacks.com/pictures/front.jpg" target="_blank">
       <img src="http://www.ebayhacks.com/pictures/front_small.jpg"></a>
  <br>The front of the car
</td><td align=center>
  <a href="http://www.ebayhacks.com/pictures/glovebox.jpg" target="_blank">
       <img src="http://www.ebayhacks.com/pictures/glovebox_small.jpg"></a>
  <br>The spacious glove compartment
</td></tr>
<tr><td align=center>
  <a href="http://www.ebayhacks.com/pictures/fender.jpg" target="_blank">
       <img src="http://www.ebayhacks.com/pictures/fender_small.jpg"></a>
  <br>The dent in the fender
</td><td align=center>
  <a href="http://www.ebayhacks.com/pictures/dog.jpg" target="_blank">
       <img src="http://www.ebayhacks.com/pictures/dog_small.jpg"></a>
  <br>The dog I found in the back seat
</td></tr>
</table>
```

The resulting table is shown in Figure 5-11.

Hacking the Hack

There are plenty of ways you can customize your thumbnails:

Pop-up windows. The `target=_blank` parameters in each of the `<a>` tags in the preceding example force the full-size images to open in new windows, thus leaving the original auction page intact. This is important, as it helps keep customers on your page, whereas otherwise they might get lost and return to eBay without revisiting your listing. For a slicker presentation, use JavaScript to create custom pop-up windows [Hack #78].

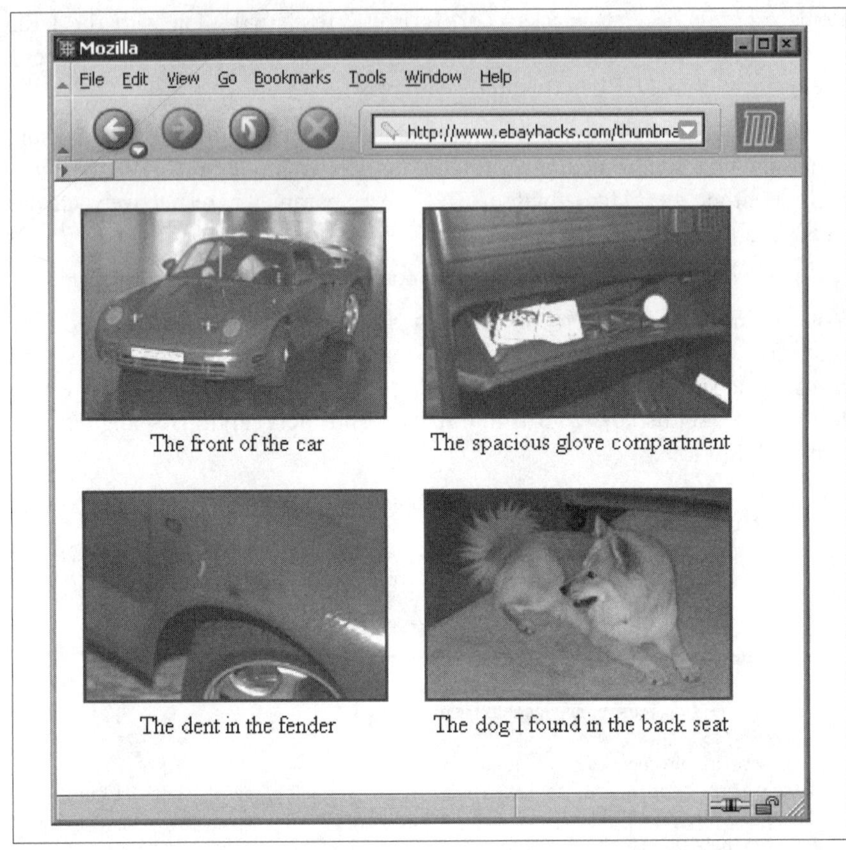

Figure 5-11. A simple table helps you align thumbnail images and their captions

No windows. If you'd rather have the full-size images appear right in the description, rather than in separate windows as with photos eBay hosts, use an interactive photo album **[Hack #79]**.

Custom borders. By default, images placed inside `<a>` tags are given a 2-pixel border in blue (or purple for previously visited links). You can change the border width of the thumbnails by placing the `border=n` parameter in each `<img>` tag, where *n* is the number of pixels. A 1-pixel border (`border=1`) often looks sharper than the default, but you may prefer no border (`border=0`) if your thumbnail images already have borders or if you've added drop-shadows **[Hack #74]**.

You can also add a border to the table, which, among other things, can make it easier to work with while you're building and previewing it. Just change the `border=0` parameter in the `<table>` tag to specify any other pixel size (i.e., `border=3`). Or, if you want more control over the look of the table, use Cascading Style Sheets **[Hack #57]**.

Whitespace. Make your listing look less cramped by adding whitespace around your thumbnails. Just add the hspace and vspace parameters [Hack #52], to each of your <img> tags. If you don't know where to start, try eight pixels on each side and four each on the top and bottom, like this:

```
<img src="...dog_small.jpg" hspace=8 vspace=4>
```

Any border will hug the image and won't be affected by any whitespace you add.

Window dressing. Further enhance the table containing your thumbnails (or perhaps enhance each individual thumbnail) by adding a decorative frame [Hack #56].

HACK #78 Customize Pop-up Image Windows

Have your thumbnails open slick, customizable pop-up windows.

There are times when it pays to have a compulsive personality, which you probably like to call "attention to detail."

On eBay, for instance, "attention to detail" makes your listings look more professional and will likely compel you to more carefully describe and photograph your items, both of which are good ways to inspire trust with your bidders [Hack #8] and set a proper expectation [Hack #50]. But why stop there?

If you're including clickable thumbnails [Hack #77] or video clips [Hack #58] in your listings, you can customize the pop-up windows that appear using JavaScript.

Unfortunately, this is not as easy as it sounds. On most other web sites, you could do this quite simply with the window.open JavaScript statement, but as described in the Preface, eBay displays the "Your listing cannot contain JavaScript" error if you try to submit a description containing the window.open statement in any context.

The Code

Instead, a slightly more complex script is needed. Start by placing the following JavaScript code in the beginning of your listing description:

```
<script language="JavaScript">
❶   var w = window;
    var whack = w.open;
    function ohack(url, name, attributes) { return (new Object()); }
❷   w.open = ohack;

    var objImage = new Image();

    function showpic(url) {
```

```
❸      objImage.src = url;
       width = objImage.width;
       height = objImage.height;

       if (width == 0) {
         retry = 'showpic("' + url + '")';
         setTimeout(retry, 300);
       } else {
❹        var flags = "width=" + width + ",height=" + height +
                ",resizable=no,scrollbars=no,menubar=no,toolbar=no" +
                ",status=yes,location=no,alwaysraised=yes" +
                ",innerHeight=0,innerWidth=0";

❺        var contents="<html><head><title>Photo Viewer</title></head>" +
                "<body topmargin=0 leftmargin=0 rightmargin=0 " +
                "bottommargin=0 marginwidth=0 marginheight=0><img src=" +
                url + "></body></html>";

❻        popup = whack('', "mywindow", flags);
❼        popup.document.write(contents);
       }
     }
   // --></script>
```

Then, set up each of your thumbnails [Hack #77] to call the script, like this:

```
<a href="javascript:showpic('http://www.your.server/bigphoto.jpg');"><img
            src="http://www.your.server/thumbnailphoto.jpg"></a>
```

where *http://www.your.server/thumbnailphoto.jpg* is the full URL of the thumbnail image and *http://www.your.server/bigphoto.jpg* is the full URL of the full-size version.

Running the Hack

To try it out, just click the thumbnail image. The full-size version will appear in a slick, minimalist window—perfectly sized to fit the image—like the one in Figure 5-12.

How It Works

The first thing the script does (lines ❶ to ❷) is fabricate a new function, `whack`, which is merely an alias for the `window.open` statement. This allows the script to work in eBay listings.

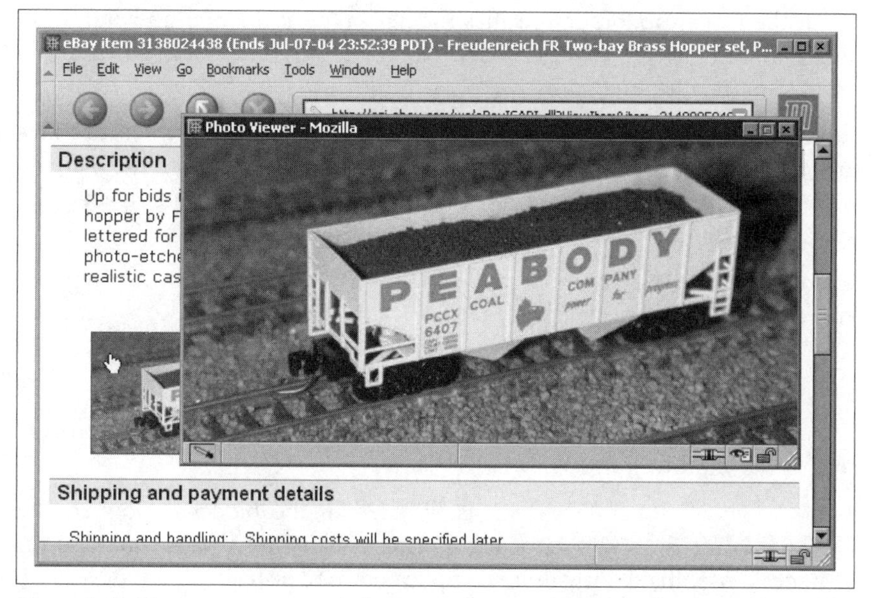

Figure 5-12. Use custom pop-up windows to make your pictures look more professional

> By the time you read this, eBay may have modified their JavaScript policies in such a way as to prohibit some or all of the code employed by this hack. (Such is the nature of hacking.) Now, these policies, not surprisingly, are in place to help reduce the kinds of abuse that are rampant elsewhere on the Internet (in this case, pop-up ads). If this happens, please take a moment to contact eBay and ask them to reduce the restriction. If they get enough such requests, perhaps they'll set up a registry of sorts, allowing honest sellers to apply for the right to include unrestricted JavaScript in exchange for promising to use that right responsibly. In the mean time, check *www.ebayhacks.com* for any necessary revisions to this, or any other code in this book.

The rest of the script consists of the `showpic` routine, called whenever someone clicks one of your images.

In order to size the window properly, the code pre-loads the image into the `objImage` object ❸, and then sets the `width` and `height` variables to the dimensions of the image. Since the image may take a second or two to load, the script checks the `width` variable before continuing; if `width` is zero, the code retries the `showpic` routine roughly three times per second until `width` is nonzero, indicating that the image has loaded successfully. (A nice side-effect of this is that the window will never open if the image is missing or corrupt.)

Next, the `flags` variable ❹ specifies the attributes of the pop-up window so that it's not cluttered with toolbars, menus, or scrollbars, and so that it is sized to fit the image.

Rather than just opening the window to the provided URL, the script creates a little page on the fly to hold the picture ❺. This allows all the margins to be set to zero, which ensures that the image appears snug against the sides of the window.

At long last, the code opens a new window ❻ and fills it with the prepared content ❼.

Hacking the Hack

There are a bunch of different things you can do to customize the link, as well as the window it opens:

Make it fool-proof. If JavaScript is disabled in the bidder's browser, the link won't do anything at all. To make your links idiot-proof, so-to-speak, use this slightly more complicated code instead:

```
<a href="http://www.your.server/bigphoto.jpg" target="_blank"
        onClick="showpic('http://www.your.server/bigphoto.jpg');return
        false;"><img src="http://www.your.server/thumbnailphoto.jpg"></a>
```

This version of the link is similar to the original, except the `href` parameter now points directly to the full-size image and the JavaScript code is called from the `onClick` event. Notice the `return false;` statement, which tells the browser to ignore the `href` parameter. If JavaScript is disabled, however, it works like one of the ordinary thumbnail links in **[Hack #77]**.

Title the window. You can specify a title to appear at the top of the pop-up window by replacing the text "Photo Viewer" on line ❺ with something else. Here might be a *great* place to attribute *eBay Hacks* (hint, hint).

Construct an Interactive Photo Album

Use JavaScript to save money and get a better photo album to boot.

eBay provides a "photo album" feature to accommodate more than one photo in your listings, provided you're using eBay's Picture Services **[Hack #76]** to host your photos. If you're hosting your own photos, all you need is a little JavaScript to accomplish the same thing.

The Code

The first thing you need to do is create thumbnail versions **[Hack #77]** of each of your photos. Then, place this code in your listing description:

```
<table cellpadding=10 cellspacing=0 border=1>
<tr><td>
```

```
❶     <img src="view1.jpg" border=0 name="view">
   </td></tr>
   <tr><td align=center>
❷    <img src="view1s.jpg" border=1
              onClick="document.images['view'].src='view1.jpg';">
❸    <img src="view2s.jpg" border=1
              onClick="document.images['view'].src='view2.jpg';">
   </td></tr>
   </table>
```

This creates a simple, two-cell table, shown in Figure 5-13. The upper cell contains the first of several images and the lower cell contains the thumbnails for all images.

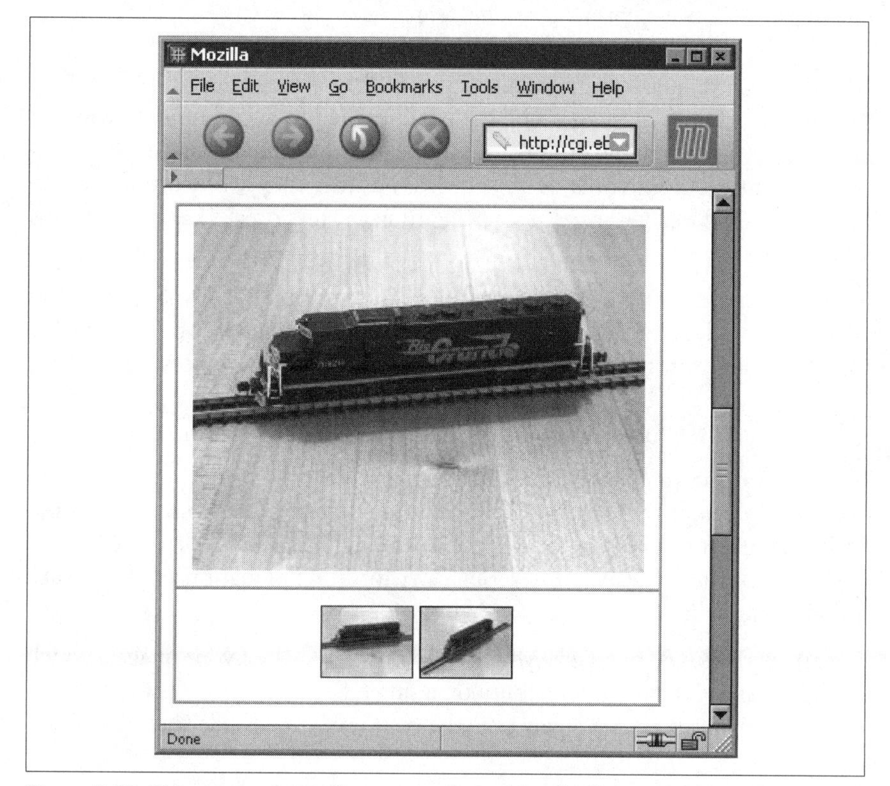

Figure 5-13. This simple photo album gives photos hosted off eBay a classy presentation

Lines ❷ and ❸ specify the two thumbnails, but they're not linked to their larger counterparts with <a> tags as in "Make Clickable Thumbnails" **[Hack #77]**. Instead, the following JavaScript code—activated by the `onClick` event—changes the image ❶ in the upper cell:

```
document.images['view'].src = 'view2.jpg';
```

The code is simple enough, but its greatest strength is its flexibility.

Hacking the Hack

Of course, you'll want to put your own images in the photo album. Start by replacing `view1.jpg` on line ❶ with the full URL of the first image you wish to appear in the album. Then do the same for each of the thumbnails, `view1s.jpg` and `view2s.jpg` on lines ❷ and ❸. Finally, specify the full URLs for the corresponding full-size images, replacing `view1.jpg` and `view2.jpg`.

In theory, your full-size images can all be different sizes, but it won't look particularly good, and may even cause problems on some browsers. To allow your bidders to view all the images properly, make sure all your JPGs have the same orientation and pixel dimensions.

You can have as many thumbnails as you'd like—simply duplicate line ❷ or ❸ for each additional image. The table is designed to accommodate without modification a virtually unlimited number of thumbnails; for instance, if there are more thumbnails than will fit on a line, they will simply wrap to the next line. If needed, use the `<br>` tag to insert line breaks between groups of thumbnails.

As it is, this photo album will not function if support for JavaScript is disabled in a bidder's browser. To make the hack work even if JavaScript is disabled, change your thumbnail code (lines ❷ and ❸) to the following:

```
<a href="view1.jpg"><img src="view1s.jpg" width=60 height=45 border=1
      onClick="document.images['view'].src='view1.jpg';return false;"></a>
```

This works because of the added `<a>` tag that links the thumbnail image to the full-size image [Hack #77]; it also has the side-effect of showing bidders the little "hand" cursor that indicates the thumbnails can be clicked. See "Customize Pop-up Image Windows" [Hack #78] for an explanation of the `return false;` statement.

For an extra fee, eBay will give you a slide show [Hack #46] of your images, which is nothing more than a photo album on a timer. See "Show a 360-Degree View of Your Item" [Hack #80] for a way to make your own timed slide show.

HACK #80 Show a 360-Degree View of Your Item

With a few photos of your item and a little JavaScript code, you can wow your customers with that snazzy showroom feel.

One of JavaScript's greatest strengths is its ability to manipulate images on a web page, allowing you to turn an otherwise static auction page into an interactive selling tool. In addition to being much cooler than eBay's built-in slide show feature, it's completely free and limited only by the amount of time you want to spend preparing your images.

Taking the Photos

The most challenging part of creating an interactive 360-degree view of your item is taking the photos, which really isn't all that difficult. The goal is to take photos of all sides of an item so that when they're viewed consecutively, like frames in a movie, it looks like the object is spinning. In most cases, you won't need more than four or five images. Having more frames will produce a smoother effect, but will also take a little longer to load.

There are two basic approaches to taking the photos:

Stationary camera. To produce a "spinning" effect, simply mount your camera on a tripod and point it at your item. Take a photo, rotate the item 30 degrees, take another photo, rotate it again, and so on. For a smoother effect, place your item on a turntable or lazy susan, commonly available at hardware and houseware stores.

Stationary object. If you're photographing a large item, like a car or piece of furniture, or if you simply want that "walkaround" effect, then you can literally walk around your item and photograph it from each angle. For the best effect, use a tripod to keep the height and angle consistent, and use a ruler or measuring tape to maintain a consistent distance from the edge or center of the object.

Either way you do it, you'll want your photos to be as evenly spaced as possible. If you're taking only four frames, each photo should be 90 degrees apart (72 degrees for five frames, 60 degrees for six frames, 45 degrees for eight frames, and so on). Figure 5-14 shows four sides of an object photographed with a stationary camera.

If you don't have a tripod, do your best to keep the angle, height, and distance from the object as consistent as possible—otherwise, your object will "jump," and the rotation will look sloppy. Also, don't mix portrait and landscape shots.

Preparing the Images

The more consistent your images are, the better the animation will look. For instance, the object you're photographing must appear to be the same size in each photo. If you use a tripod to take the photos, this will be a snap; otherwise, you may have to crop and resize the photos to make them all proportional.

The lighting **[Hack #72]** should also be consistent; you can correct slight aberrations in exposure by using your image editor's Auto Levels tool (in Photoshop, go to Image → Adjustments → Auto Levels). If you're doing a walkaround, attach your lighting equipment to the camera so that your object is always lit from the same angle.

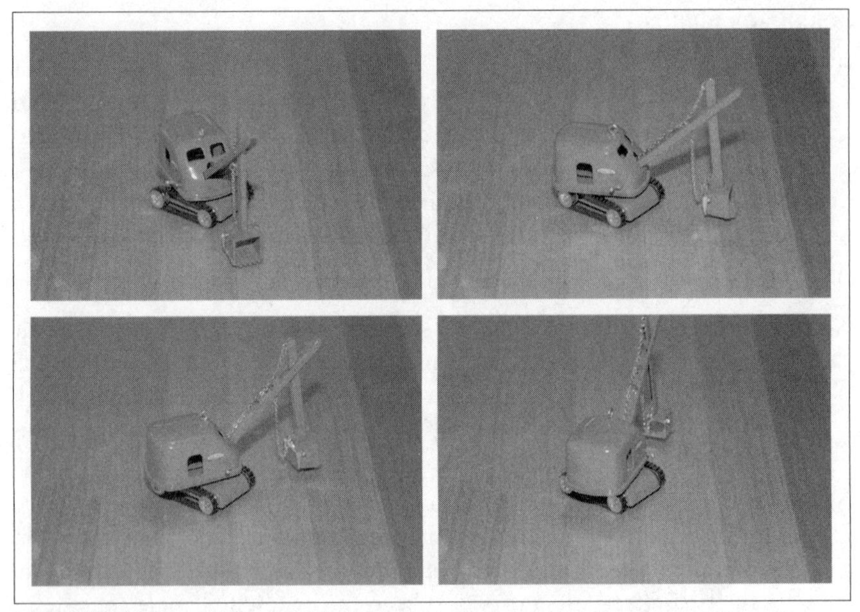

Figure 5-14. Photograph four sides of an object with a stationary camera for a "spinning" effect

All your images must have the same pixel dimensions. To allow the animation to run smoothly, your images should be small, so that they load quickly. Don't bother making them bigger than 400 pixels wide (for the larger dimension); 300 pixels is even better. See "Doctor Your Photos" **[Hack #74]** for an easy way to resize a batch of pictures.

When you're done, upload all the photos to your web server **[Hack #76]**.

The Code

Simply place this code in your auction description to include an interactive 360-degree view of your object:

```
<script language="JavaScript"><!--
var lastimg = "1";
var width = 300;
var height = 225;

❶ view1 = new Image(width, height);
view2 = new Image(width, height);
view3 = new Image(width, height);
view4 = new Image(width, height);
view5 = new Image(width, height);
view6 = new Image(width, height);
view7 = new Image(width, height);
```

```
❷  view8 = new Image(width, height);

    filenameprefix = "http://www.ebayhacks.com/pictures/view";

❸  slider = new Image(20,20);
    thumb = new Image(20,20);
    slider.src = "http://www.ebayhacks.com/pictures/slider.gif";
❹  thumb.src = "http://www.ebayhacks.com/pictures/thumb.gif";

    function rotate(img) {
❺    document.images['view'].src = filenameprefix + img + ".jpg";
❻    document.images[lastimg].src = slider.src;
❼    document.images[img].src = thumb.src;
❽    lastimg = img;
    }
    // --></script>

    <table width=300 cellpadding=10 cellspacing=0 border=1>
    <tr><td>
❾    <img src="http://www.ebayhacks.com/pictures/view1.jpg" width=300
                                          height=225 border=0 name="view">
    </td></tr>
    <tr><td align=center>
      <nobr>
❿    <img
        src="http://www.ebayhacks.com/pictures/slider.gif" width=20
          height=20 name="1" onMouseOver="rotate('1');"><img
        src="http://www.ebayhacks.com/pictures/slider.gif" width=20
          height=20 name="2" onMouseOver="rotate('2');"><img
        src="http://www.ebayhacks.com/pictures/slider.gif" width=20
          height=20 name="3" onMouseOver="rotate('3');"><img
        src="http://www.ebayhacks.com/pictures/slider.gif" width=20
          height=20 name="4" onMouseOver="rotate('4');"><img
        src="http://www.ebayhacks.com/pictures/slider.gif" width=20
          height=20 name="5" onMouseOver="rotate('5');"><img
        src="http://www.ebayhacks.com/pictures/slider.gif" width=20
          height=20 name="6" onMouseOver="rotate('6');"><img
        src="http://www.ebayhacks.com/pictures/slider.gif" width=20
          height=20 name="7" onMouseOver="rotate('7');"><img
        src="http://www.ebayhacks.com/pictures/slider.gif" width=20
          height=20 name="8" onMouseOver="rotate('8');">
      </nobr><br>
        Move the slider to rotate the object
    </td></tr>
    </table>
```

How It Works

A two-cell table holds the first frame of the animation ❾ and, beneath it, a series of identical images ❿ that make up the slider bar. As the mouse is moved across each section of the slider bar, the JavaScript code replaces the big image with the corresponding view of the object, as shown in Figure 5-15.

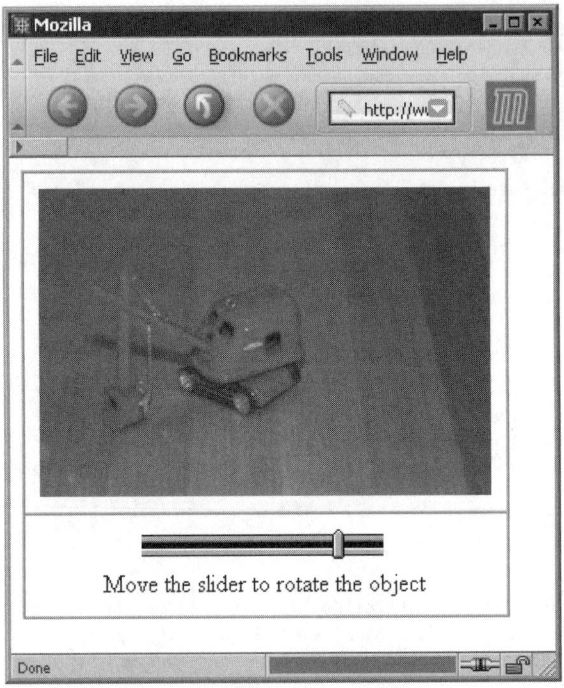

Figure 5-15. Move your mouse over the slider to flip among views of your item

The bulk of the JavaScript code simply preloads the images: the eight frames in this example appear (lines ❶ to ❷), followed by the two images used for the slider bar (lines ❸ to ❹). You'll need to replace the URLs in these lines with the addresses of your own images, and then change the `width` and `height` variables at the beginning of the script to match the dimensions of your frames. If you have fewer or more than eight frames, you'll need to adjust lines ❶ to ❷ accordingly, as well as change the number of slider bar segments on line ❿.

The `rotate( )` function does all the work. First, on line ❺, a new photo is placed into the `view` image (so named on line ❾). The script knows which photo to use because of the `img` variable, passed to the function from the `onMouseOver` event in each slider bar section on line ❿.

Further down, on line ❼, the current section of the slider bar is "highlighted" by replacing the "empty" slider bar section (*slider.gif*) image with a "full" slider image (*thumb.gif*). Finally, the current position is recorded into the lastimg variable ❽ so that the next time the function runs, it can make this section "empty" again, as it does on line ❻.

Hacking the Hack

Ultimately, the photo album produced by this code is similar to the one in "Construct an Interactive Photo Album" [Hack #79]. The only things that make the image "rotate" are the collection of photos you use and the fact that the images are preloaded for more responsiveness. If you want a photo album instead, but prefer the approach in this hack to the aforementioned photo album hack, you can simply replace the slider bar segments with thumbnails.

The sample code rotates the object as the mouse moves over the slider. If you prefer to have the slider move only when clicked, replace each instance of onMouseOver on line ❿ with onClick, like this:

```
<img src="http://www.ebayhacks.com/pictures/slider.gif" width=20
                                    height=20 name="3" onClick="rotate('3');">
```

To have the image rotate automatically, add this code immediately above line ❶:

```
setTimeout('autorotate()', 500);

function autorotate() {
  img = lastimg + 1;
  if (img > 8) { img = 1; }
  rotate(img);
  setTimeout('autorotate()', 500);
}
```

where 500 is the number of milliseconds to wait between frames (about a half second). Specify 200 for a fifth of a second, 1000 for a full second, and so on.

HACK #81

Create a Photo Collage

Combine multiple photos into a single image for convenience and dramatic effect.

When you choose to host your own photos [Hack #76], eBay allows you to specify only a single image URL to appear beneath your auction description. If you have any additional photos, you'll have to include them directly in the description with HTML [Hack #52]. But you also have the option of combining all your photos into a single image file, thus completely eliminating the need to use thumbnails [Hack #77] or a photo album [Hack #79] to organize multiple pictures.

A single collage of your photos is easy to build, and may ultimately require less work to insert into your auctions than hand-coding HTML or JavaScript. A collage also provides a good amount of control over the presentation of your photos, allowing you to easily emphasize the most important pictures.

You don't have to host your own photos to take advantage of this hack. However, if you use eBay's Picture Services to host your photos, you'll be limited to their cramped 400×300 standard size, which is much too small for a photo collage. And while the Supersize upgrade [Hack #46] would remedy this, your customers won't see it full size unless they click the Supersize link underneath the smaller version.

To build a collage, start with the most prominent photo of your item, properly cropped and resized [Hack #74]. Then, use your image editor to increase the canvas size to accommodate additional photos. Most people are accustomed to scrolling web pages up and down, rather than side to side, so you'll need to orient your photos vertically rather than horizontally. For example, if you're combining three 600×450 photos, make the canvas at least 700×1400.

Next, place your additional images on the newly enlarged canvas. In most image editors, you can do this via copy-and-paste. First, open one of the images you want to place in the new canvas, select the entire image area (Ctrl-A), and copy the image to the clipboard (Ctrl-C). Then, paste the image into your new canvas (Ctrl-V) and use the mouse to position it. (See the next section for some shortcuts for Photoshop users.)

Figure 5-16 shows a completed photo collage. Here, a black background was used to make the collage a bit more striking. You can use white if you want the photos to blend in more smoothly with the surrounding auction. Try to avoid brightly colored backgrounds, however, as they can be hard on the eyes.

When you're done, crop out any unused background (except perhaps for a nice thin border), and, if needed, shrink down [Hack #74] the collage, so it's no larger than 600 to 800 pixels in its larger dimension. Save it as a JPG file, upload it to your server [Hack #76], and you're ready to go!

Photoshop Shortcuts

Adobe Photoshop has a few nice features that can make collages much easier and quicker to create. First, you can create an *action* (a.k.a. macro) to increase the canvas size and turn the original photo into a floating layer. (You can also download this action at *www.ebayhacks.com*.) Here's how to do it:

1. Open a sample photo in Photoshop. Any file will do, as long as it's smaller than 1000×1000 pixels. (If you need to work with larger photos, modify the numbers in step 7.)
2. Show the Actions palette by going to Window → Actions.
3. Record a new action by clicking the arrow button at the top-right of the Actions palette, type a name like "Increase Canvas Size," and click Record.

Figure 5-16. A photo collage combines several photos into a single image file, producing a rather striking effect

4. Click the little black/white icon below the color swatches to reset the colors to black and white.
5. Press Ctrl-A to select all.
6. Press Ctrl-X to cut the selection to the clipboard.
7. Go to Image → Canvas Size, type arbitrarily large numbers for the new width and height (try 1000 and 1000), and click OK. (You can use larger numbers if you think you'll need them.)
8. Press Ctrl-V to paste the image back into the newly enlarged canvas.
9. Press the square Stop button at the bottom of the Actions palette.
10. Click the little arrow button at the top-right of the Actions palette and select Button Mode.

From now on, to increase the canvas size and float the image, all you need to do is click the Increase Canvas Size button on the Actions palette.

Once the canvas size has been increased, the next step is to paste other images onto the collage. Photoshop has a shortcut for this, too: just open the other photos and use the Move tool to drag them from their own document windows onto the newly enlarged canvas (no fussing with copy-and-paste).

You can then press Ctrl-T to begin a free transform and resize the photo in place (hold the Shift key to preserve the aspect ratio). When you're done, select any tool on the toolbox to commit the free transform.

Finally, go to Layer → Flatten Image to combine all the floating layers so that the collage can be saved into a JPG file. Or, to preserve the floating layers, go to File → Save for Web (Photoshop 7.x and later only).

HACK #82 Create a Good Gallery Photo

Prepare your gallery photos to use the postage stamp–sized area to its fullest potential.

The Gallery upgrade [Hack #46] displays a small thumbnail photo next to your item in search results and category listings. All that's required (aside from the small fee) is that you provide eBay with an image to use.

When your listing goes live, eBay automatically processes the photo by performing the following tasks:

Converted
: The image file is converted to the JPG file format.

Resized
: The photo is resized so that the larger dimension is 80 pixels.

Hosted
: The image file is hosted on eBay's server, making it accessible at:

```
http://thumbs.ebaystatic.com/pict/31354034868080_0.jpg.jpg
```

where *3135403486* is the item number of the corresponding listing. (This URL comes in handy, for instance, if you want to hack the Search Robot [Hack #21] to email you photos of the listings it finds.)

> The closer your photo is to eBay's current final size of 80×80, the less of a hatchet job eBay's servers will have to do, and the better your gallery photo will look. From time to time, however, eBay changes the size of gallery photos. Fortunately, it's easy to get the current size by performing an ordinary a search on eBay. Then, right-click one of the gallery images in the search results, and select View Image (in Mozilla/Firefox) or Properties (in Internet Explorer).

The best auction photo [Hack #70] will not necessarily be the best gallery photo, so you'll most likely want to prepare two different images.

For starters, your gallery photo should be square and without any superfluous background or borders. Figure 5-17 shows a few examples of gallery photos, both good and bad.

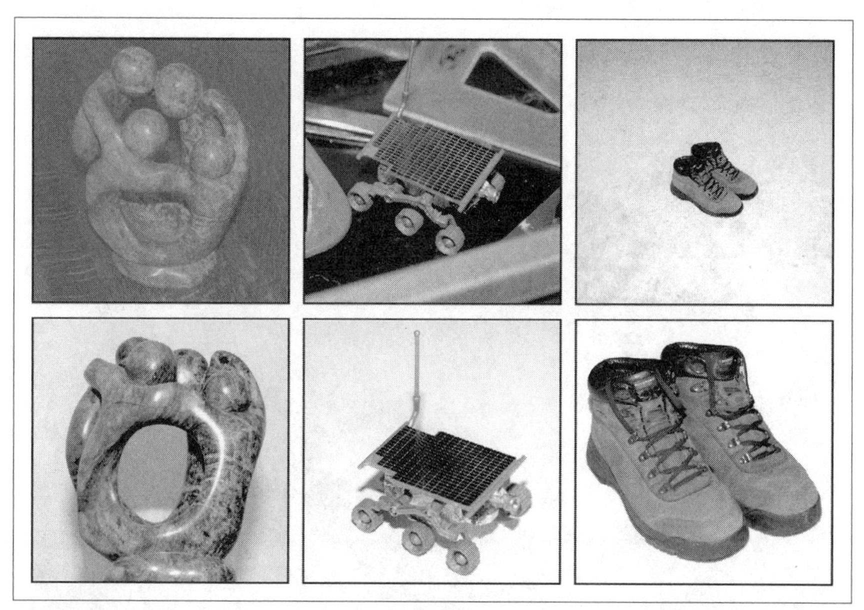

Figure 5-17. Bad gallery examples are shown on the top row, with good counterparts beneath them

The easiest way to create a good square image is to use the rectangular selection tool of your image editor software [Hack #74] and specify a 1:1 aspect ratio. Then, simply draw a box around your image, and the software will automatically impose a square shape.

It's likely that your photo will not fit perfectly into the square shape. In this case, it's better to slightly crop your object than to leave extra space around it, because the resulting object will be bigger and more compelling as it appears to break out of the bounding box. If your final image is a perfect square, you'll make better use of the space provided than if it's rectangular.

Figure 5-18 shows a well-drawn selection rectangle around an object—before cropping—in Adobe Photoshop.

When you're happy with the box you've drawn, just crop the image to your selection (Image → Crop in Photoshop, or Image → Crop to Selection in Paint Shop Pro) and resize the image to 80×80 pixels. When you're done, save it as a JPG file.

Finally, you'll need to host the photo on a web server [Hack #76], and then specify the gallery image URL when listing your item [Hack #43]. Unfortunately, if you use eBay Picture Services to host your photos, you'll have no

Figure 5-18. Your gallery photo looks best if you crop it to a perfectly square shape

choice but to use your first auction photo as the gallery photo, in which case you probably don't want to make it the size of a postage stamp.

CHAPTER SIX

Completing Transactions

Hacks 83–90

When a listing ends, it's the seller's job to guide his customers through the rest of the transaction. The hacks in this chapter cover your various tasks as a seller after each of your listings closes.

Simple transactions typically involve one or more email messages to the high bidder [Hack #84], the acceptance of some form of payment [Hack #85], and the packing and shipping of the item [Hack #86]. If you're running a business on eBay, see Chapter 7 for ways to streamline these tasks, so you can handle more volume.

HACK #83 Keep Track of Items You've Sold

Use a simple spreadsheet or database to record the details of closed auctions.

eBay is not your keeper. They won't pick up your room, they won't do your homework, and they won't keep permanent records of your completed auctions.

If you sell on eBay, you'll need to keep some semblance of records of all the items you've sold. You should track your high bidders, whether they've paid, and whether you've shipped. It's very easy to do, and all that's required is a spreadsheet or database (suitable applications include Microsoft Excel and Microsoft Access, respectively. If you're not sure which one to use, see the "Spreadsheet or Database?" sidebar.

If you're diligent about it, you'll never forget to send payment instructions again. You'll always know who has paid (and who hasn't), and you'll know at a glance which items still need to be packed up and shipped.

Spreadsheet or Database?

Both spreadsheets and databases represent data in tables, a convenient format for keeping track of your auctions. But each type of application has strengths and weaknesses, so you should choose the one that best suits your needs.

First, if it's too difficult to keep records, you won't do it. So make sure to choose an application with which you're familiar and comfortable. If you use Excel every day but fear databases, that comfort level trumps the rest of the considerations (at least for the time being).

A spreadsheet requires minimal setup; just type the column headers across the top and start entering the details of your auctions. Spreadsheets are flexible in that they impose few limits on the structure or type of data you enter. For instance, you can drag and drop rows to rearrange them, placing multiple auctions won by the same bidder together.

A database is more rigid, enforcing strict rules on the types of information you can place in the various fields. But that rigidity affords certain perks that aren't available with a spreadsheet. For instance, you can run queries on a database to view sales trends, total spent on eBay fees, and so on, or run reports to make mailing labels. And databases can be much more easily linked to applications (see Chapter 8), making them more scalable. Setup is a little more involved, but if you're comfortable using a database, it's probably the better choice.

My eBay

eBay provides a ledger of your current and recently completed listings, as well as some tools to help you keep track of some of the more important details. Go to My eBay → All Selling → Sold to view the Items I've Sold page, shown in Figure 6-1. Here, the high bidder, sale price, and sale date are shown for each of your listings that has closed within the past 60 days. To the far right, eBay provides icons to indicate the following:

Dollar sign. The customer has sent payment.

Box. You've shipped the item.

Star. You've left feedback for the customer.

Bubble. The customer has left feedback for you.

eBay automatically changes the status icons for your listings when appropriate, such as when a customer completes the checkout process **[Hack #64]** or when you leave feedback for a customer. But you can also change the Paid and Shipped icons manually by clicking the little arrow in the Action column and selecting Mark as Paid or Mark Shipped, respectively. (And

Figure 6-1. The Items I've Sold list, found in My eBay, lets you track your recently completed listings, but doesn't provide a way to keep permanent records of your sales

although you can disable the Shipped status by selecting Mark Not Shipped, there's no similar feature to change the status of a listing to "not paid.")

> You can add custom notes to the listings on this page. Click the Customize link at the top-right corner of the list, turn on both the My Notes and eBay Notes options, and click Save. If eBay has any notes, such as, "This user is no longer registered on eBay," they'll show up as yellow stripes underneath the respective listings. To add your own note, click the checkbox next to the listing and then click the Add Note button* at the top. This can be particularly useful for keeping track of payments due to arrive via postal mail or customer complaints you haven't yet resolved.

The big problem with the Items I've Sold page is that completed listings appear for no more than 60 days. This means that if you want to keep a permanent archive of your past sales, you'll have to manually record completed listings into a spreadsheet or database on your own computer.

* Be careful not to click the Remove button, which is right next to Add Note. See "Keep Track of Auctions Outside of eBay" **[Hack #29]** for help retrieving accidentally-removed listings.

Building the Tracking System

Start by creating a spreadsheet with the following columns (or a database with the following fields):

Field name	Data type	Description
End Date	Date	Closing date of the auction.
Item Number	Text	Auction number. In Excel, you can paste the full URL of the auction here, and it will create a hyperlink automatically. Next, remove everything *except* the item number. Click the item number to view the auction page.
Title	Text	Auction title or brief description.
Closing Price	Currency	The exact amount of the winning bid, not including shipping or any other fees or charges.
Shipping Cost	Currency	The estimated cost to ship, as quoted to the bidder. If the actual cost to ship is different, include the difference in the "Fees" column; see [Hack #86] for a way to make sure this never happens.
High Bidder	Text	The user ID of the high bidder. If it's a Dutch auction [Hack #44], and you have more than one bidder, include a separate entry (row) for each bidder.
Email Address	Text	The email address of the high bidder. It's important to record this separately from the bidder's user ID, especially if the customer uses a different address than the one registered with eBay.
Contacted?	Yes/No	Mark with a ✓ when you've sent payment instructions [Hack #84].
Wrote Back?	Yes/No	Mark with a ✓ the first time the bidder writes you.
Have Address?	Yes/No	Mark with a ✓ as soon as you have the bidder's mailing address.
Paid?	Currency	The full amount of the bidder's payment. It should equal "Closing Price" + "Shipping Cost," but you could subtract any applicable PayPal fees, for instance, so you have a record of exactly how much money you've taken in. Or use the "Fees" field.
Shipped?	Text	Paste the tracking number here once you ship the package.
Fees	Currency	Optional. Any applicable fees imposed by eBay, PayPal, your credit card merchant account, etc.
Notes	Memo	Any applicable notes, such as the method of shipping, the customer's Zip Code, any special requests made by the customer, or a reminder of the expected arrival date of a pending payment. Also handy for recording the date of a nonpaying bidder alert [Hack #89] so you know when you can apply for a refund of eBay's final value fees.

If you're using a spreadsheet, you can set the data type of a field by first selecting the entire column by clicking the column header, and then going to Format → Cells → Number tab. If you're using a database and want to print mailing labels, you'll also want to add fields for the customer's name, address, city, state/province, Zip Code, and country. Refer to your database documentation for details on reports and how they can be used to make mailing labels.

How to Use It

Every time one of your auctions ends, add a row to your spreadsheet or database and fill in the details of the auction. Keep track of the progress of the transaction: place a ✓ in the "Contacted?" column when you send payment instructions, another in the "Wrote Back?" column when the bidder first contacts you, and yet another in the "Have Address?" column when you receive the bidder's full shipping address. Do the same for the "Paid?" and "Shipped?" fields. See Figure 6-2 for an example of how it should look.

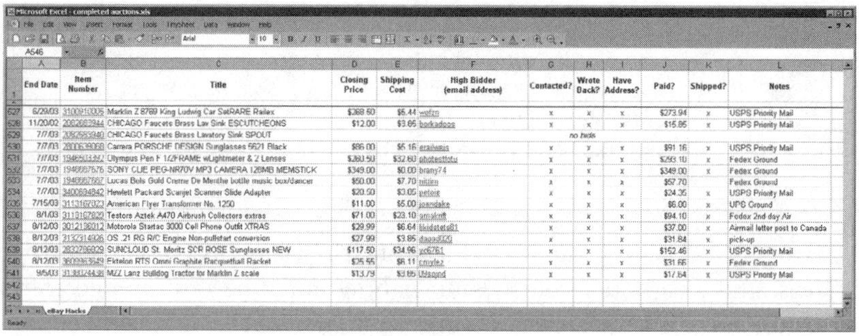

End Date	Item Number	Title	Closing Price	Shipping Cost	High Bidder (email address)	Contacted?	Wrote Back?	Have Address?	Paid?	Shipped?	Notes
6/29/03	3100810005	Marklin Z 8769 King Ludwig Car SetRARE Railex	$268.50	$5.44	wofzn	x	x	x	$273.94	x	USPS Priority Mail
11/20/02	2002683944	CHICAGO Faucets Brass Lav Sink ESCUTCHEONS	$12.00	$3.85	borkadoos	x	x	x	$15.85	x	USPS Priority Mail
7/7/03	2082583940	CHICAGO Faucets Brass Lavatory Sink SPOUT					no bids				
7/7/03	2800639068	Camera PORSCHE DESIGN Sunglasses 5621 Black	$86.00	$5.16	eraiheis	x	x	x	$91.16	x	USPS Priority Mail
7/7/03	1946503342	Olympus Pen F 1/2FRAME wLightmeter & 2 Lenses	$260.50	$32.60	photesttofu	x	x	x	$293.10	x	Fedex Ground
7/7/03	1946887676	SONY CLIE PEG-NR70V MP3 CAMERA 128MB MEMSTICK	$349.00	$0.00	brany74	x	x	x	$349.00	x	Fedex Ground
7/7/03	1946887667	Lucas Bols Gold Creme De Menthe bottle music box/dancer	$50.00	$7.70	nittin	x	x	x	$57.70		Fedex Ground
7/7/03	3400694842	Hewlett Packard Scanjet Scanner Slide Adapter	$20.50	$3.05	peteie	x	x	x	$24.35	x	USPS Priority Mail
7/15/03	3113167823	American Flyer Transformer No. 1250	$11.00	$5.00	joandake	x	x	x	$6.00	x	UPS Ground
8/1/03	3113167829	Testors Aztek A470 Airbrush Collectors extras	$71.00	$23.10	amaknft	x	x	x	$94.10	x	Fedex 2nd day Air
8/12/03	3012138012	Motorola Startac 3000 Cell Phone Outfit XTRAS	$29.99	$6.64	likidstets81	x	x	x	$37.00	x	Airmail letter post to Canada
8/12/03	3132314926	OS .21 RG R/C Engine Non-pullstart conversion	$27.99	$3.85	dagad320	x	x	x	$31.84	x	pick-up
8/12/03	2832796829	SUNCLOUD St. Moritz SCR ROSE Sunglasses NEW	$117.50	$34.96	yc6761	x	x	x	$152.46	x	USPS Priority Mail
8/12/03	3600983649	Ektelon RTS Omni Graphite Racquetball Racket	$25.55	$6.11	cmylez	x	x	x	$31.66	x	Fedex Ground
9/5/03	3138024438	MZZ Lanz Bulldog Tractor for Marklin Z scale	$13.79	$3.85	UVsqind	x	x	x	$17.64	x	USPS Priority Mail

Figure 6-2. Keep track of the status of all your closed auctions

Automation

At first, it may seem like a royal pain in the keister to have to record all this stuff, but it'll quickly get easier. Plus, you'll find that the time you save by keeping your records up-to-date will compensate for the time you spend, because you'll no longer have to wade through your email to figure out who hasn't yet sent payment.

For very busy sellers, the task of keeping the spreadsheet or database up-to-date will quickly get out of hand, and you'll want something less cumbersome **[Hack #97]**. But if you're a hacker—and I think that you are—you'll probably want to bypass the commercial solutions in favor of something you build yourself **[Hack #112]** with the eBay API.

HACK #84 Send Payment Instructions

Communicate essential information to your bidders and avoid misunderstandings.

When an auction ends, it is your responsibility as the seller to guide your bidders through the rest of the transaction. Although eBay, by default, will send a notification email to bidders when they've won an auction, you may not want to rely solely on that email—or your auction description, for that matter—to communicate all the information your bidder needs to know to send payment. When you email your customers, you'll need to communicate each of the following:

Thanks. Thank the customer for bidding on and purchasing your item. Include the title and item number of the auction your customer won.

Shipping cost. Tell the customer how much shipping will cost (even if it's already specified in the auction) and explain exactly which shipping method you'll be using. (Your customer has a right to know what he's paying for.)

You can get the winning bidder's location (and Zip Code for addresses in the U.S.) from the checkout box [Hack #64] at the top of the completed listing page, allowing you to determine the shipping cost before waiting for the bidder to send his street address.

Total to pay. Calculate the total, including shipping, tax, and any handling fees, and clearly tell your customer how much he is supposed to pay. Don't make your customer do any math, because he'll most likely get it wrong. In most cases, you'll have all the tools you need to calculate a customer's total before you send the email.

If your customer has purchased more than one item from you and you're willing to ship them together, add these in as well, and make it clear that you're doing so.

Payment methods. Even if it's noted elsewhere, carefully explain the types of payment you accept [Hack #85]. It's important to be clear on this point; otherwise, your bidders may try to send you something you can't accept, or worse, won't send payment at all [Hack #68].

Your contact information. Instruct your customer to email you with any questions. As much as you probably don't need to be bothered with lots of stupid questions [Hack #67], the last thing you want is for your customers to leave negative feedback rather than writing you first.

Now, you can rely on eBay to send this information for you, you can customize the email eBay sends (next), or you can send your own separate email to get your point across (later).

Customize eBay Notifications

eBay lets all its members choose whether or not to receive most automated notifications by going to My eBay → eBay Preferences → Notification preferences. But one of the few notifications for which members have no choice is the "Notify me when a listing ends and I am the winning buyer" option.

The "eBay Item Won!" email looks something like this:

```
------------------------------------------------------------------
Congratulations - You Are The Winning Buyer!
------------------------------------------------------------------
Dear ebayhacks, you have committed to buy this eBay item from ebayseller.

Click here to confirm shipping, get total price, and arrange payment
through: PayPal; personal check; money order.

------------------------------------------------------------------
LISTING DETAILS
------------------------------------------------------------------
Item name:          BRAND NEW Tonka Pickup Truck
Item number:        7171516323
Seller:             ebayseller (R. U. Done - Cincinnati, OH United States)
End date:           Aug-28-05 17:47:28 PST
Buyer:              ebayhacks
Buyer email:        mailto:dave@ebayhacks.com

------------------------------------------------------------------
PAYMENT DETAILS
------------------------------------------------------------------
Sale price:         US $86.02
Quantity:           1
Subtotal:           US $86.02

Shipping and Handling
- Standard flat rate shipping service         US $4.00
- Insurance per item:                         (not offered)
```

As you can see, the most important information—the amount to pay—is nowhere to be found in this message. This omission may seem trivial, as it's not terribly difficult to add $86.02 and $4.00, but as soon as customers start sending payments for only $86.02 or $86.42, you'll discover you need a way to make things clearer.

"Standard flat rate shipping service" appears only if you've specified flat-rate shipping [Hack #86]; if you're using eBay's Calculated Shipping feature [Hack #59], the customer sees the shipping cost only when she returns to eBay and completes the checkout process [Hack #64]. And if you didn't specify a shipping cost when you listed the item [Hack #43], you'll need to click Send Invoice at the top of the listing page to include the cost before the customer tries to check out.

Now, if PayPal [Hack #85] is one of your accepted payment methods, you can somewhat customize this email with a personalized message and a logo, if you have one.

Customizing the Notification Email

Start by logging into your PayPal account [Hack #33]. (You can also customize the notification email on the eBay site by going to My eBay → eBay Preferences → End of Auction and Transaction emails, but since you might need to go to PayPal anyway, you might as well do it all at the PayPal site.)

Under the My Account tab at *PayPal.com*, click Profile, and then in the Selling Preferences section, click Auctions. Any linked eBay accounts appear here; if yours isn't listed, click Add.

On the Auction Accounts page, click the link (either On or Off) in the Customize End of Auction Email column, and you'll see a page that looks something like the one in Figure 6-3. If you haven't done so already, select On where it says "Select your preference to customize End of Auction emails."

At this point, you'll be able to type a message (up to 2000 characters) to be included in the End of Auction email eBay/PayPal normally sends. Although you can't use HTML [Hack #52] here, you can litter your message with any of several AutoText variables, into which PayPal will insert pertinent information for each transaction. The variables you can use, each of which is in ALL CAPS and surrounded by {curly braces}, are as follows:

Variable	Meaning
`{BUYERUSERNAME}`	The customer's eBay Member ID (e.g., `ebaybuyer`). It's important to include this to help differentiate your message from the spam that invariably starts, "dear ebay user."
`{FAVORITES_LIST}`	Provides a link so the customer can add you to his My eBay Favorite Sellers list.
`{ITEM#}`	The eBay item number [Hack #13] of the listing.
`{S_EMAIL}`	Your email address.
`{SELLERUSERNAME}`	Your eBay Member ID.
`{TITLE}`	The title of the listing or auction.
`{TOTAL$}`	Total price to pay, including shipping and insurance.

Use these placeholders like this:

```
Congratulations, {BUYERUSERNAME}!

You're the high bidder for the {TITLE} (eBay #{ITEM#}). With Priority Mail
shipping, your total comes to ${TOTAL$}.

The types of payment I accept are listed in the auction description and on my
"About Me" page at eBay. Payment can be made in any of the following ways:

- If you have a free PayPal account, you can pay with your credit card or
with an electronic bank account transfer. Unfortunately, I cannot accept
PayPal payments from buyers outside of the United States.
```

```
- If you'd like to pay directly with your Visa, Mastercard, or American
Express, you can use my private, secure server at:
https://www.ebayhacks.com/checkout.html

- Although it will delay shipment by several days, you can also send a money
order or cashier's check (sorry, no personal or business checks) to:
    Acme Auctions
    123 Fake Street
    Springfield, 90125

Either way, please send a confirmation email to {S_EMAIL} and let me know
how you intend to pay as soon as you get this message. Thanks for bidding!

Sincerely,
{SELLERUSERNAME}
```

Naturally, the details of your auction and the terms you choose will be different, but the methodology is always the same. Here, the tone is friendly, and an effort has been made to make the instructions as clear as possible. Separate paragraphs and hyphens as makeshift bullets are especially helpful, since not all your recipients will be able to view HTML-formatted email messages.

Note also that the final price of the auction is nowhere to be found in this letter—only the cost to ship and the total amount to pay are specified. This is an effective way to prevent customers from mistakenly (or intentionally) omitting the shipping cost when sending payment.

If you don't accept PayPal, or you just want to handle communications on your own, you can write a program to send an email [Hack #95] using the same template.

Protect Yourself While Accepting Payments

Reduce your odds of getting burned by setting firm policies about the types of payments you accept.

Just as bidders must be cautious when sending money [Hack #33], sellers need to be careful about the payments they receive. A little common sense is all that's required to avoid fraudulent payments, payments that can be reversed, and payments that require excessive fees to process.

Fortunately, it's the seller who sets the rules, at least when it comes to payment terms. Before you start selling, and especially before you send payment instructions to your customers, you'll need to develop a strict policy regarding the types of payments you'll accept.

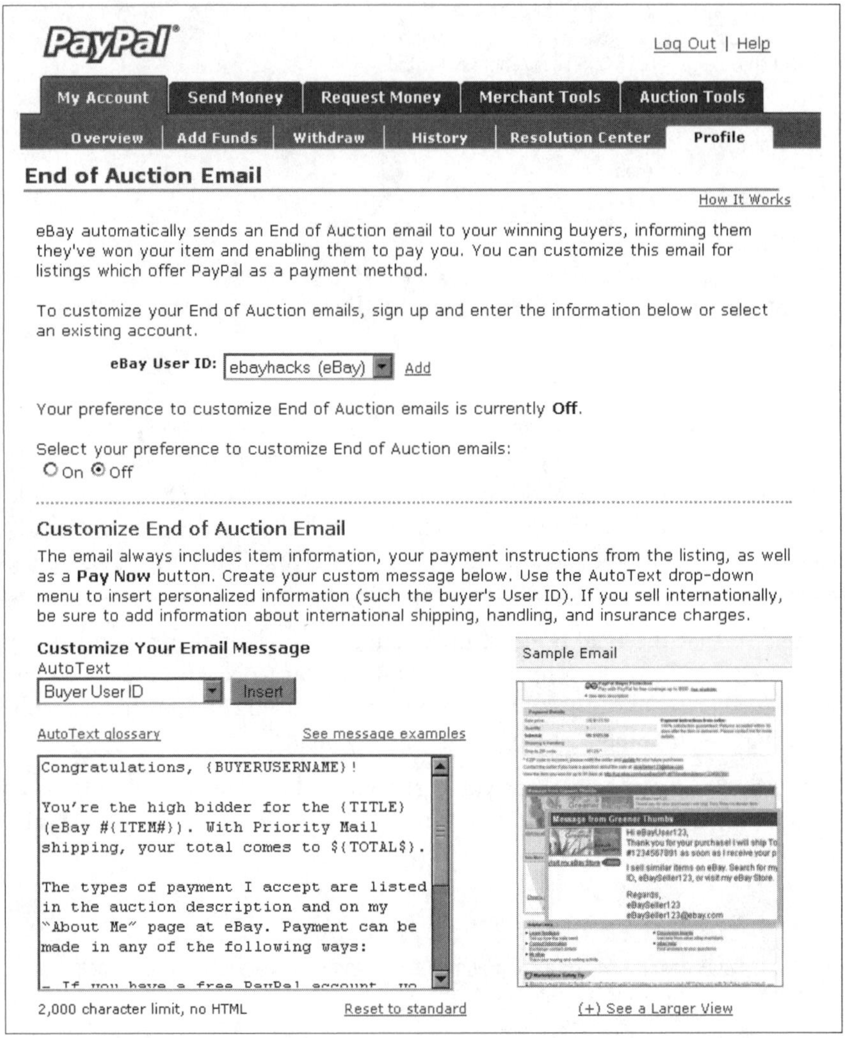

PayPal®

Log Out | Help

My Account | Send Money | Request Money | Merchant Tools | Auction Tools

Overview | Add Funds | Withdraw | History | Resolution Center | Profile

End of Auction Email

How It Works

eBay automatically sends an End of Auction email to your winning buyers, informing them they've won your item and enabling them to pay you. You can customize this email for listings which offer PayPal as a payment method.

To customize your End of Auction emails, sign up and enter the information below or select an existing account.

eBay User ID: ebayhacks (eBay) Add

Your preference to customize End of Auction emails is currently **Off**.

Select your preference to customize End of Auction emails:
On Off

Customize End of Auction Email

The email always includes item information, your payment instructions from the listing, as well as a **Pay Now** button. Create your custom message below. Use the AutoText drop-down menu to insert personalized information (such the buyer's User ID). If you sell internationally, be sure to add information about international shipping, handling, and insurance charges.

Customize Your Email Message

AutoText

Buyer User ID | Insert

AutoText glossary | See message examples

```
Congratulations, {BUYERUSERNAME}!

You're the high bidder for the {TITLE}
(eBay #{ITEM#}). With Priority Mail
shipping, your total comes to ${TOTAL$}.

The types of payment I accept are listed
in the auction description and on my
"About Me" page at eBay. Payment can be
made in any of the following ways:
```

2,000 character limit, no HTML | Reset to standard

Sample Email

(+) See a Larger View

Figure 6-3. Customize PayPal's End of Auction email message to include essential information

PayPal

PayPal goes further than just about any other payment service to protect its sellers from fraudulent payments (such as those made with a stolen credit card). But if you don't follow the rules spelled out in PayPal's Seller Protection Policy, and the payment is disputed or turns out to be fraudulent, PayPal will yank that money out of your PayPal account faster than you can say "incontinence."

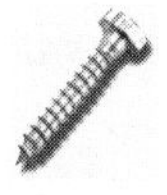

Often the reason a particular seller might refuse to accept PayPal is that he has been previously burned by a fraudulent payment, most likely as a result of not having bothered to read the fine print of the Seller Protection Policy.

To qualify for PayPal's Seller Protection, you'll need to do each and every one of the following:

Get a Business account. If you still have a Personal account [Hack #33], you'll need to upgrade to either a Premier or Business account. Yeah, it means that PayPal will start charging you fees (about 2.9% of the money you receive), but you'll be able to accept payments funded by credit cards. The extra business this gets you will more than make up for the higher costs.

Verify your account. Verification involves nothing more than linking an ordinary bank account with your PayPal account and confirming it by having PayPal make two small deposits into it (which you get to keep).

Send only tangible products. Digital products, such as downloadable software or registration codes, and lunch with your favorite celebrity, aren't covered.

Use tracking numbers. Always ship with a tracking number [Hack #86], and do so promptly. Make sure to keep records of tracking numbers for a minimum of six months. And if the value of the item is more than US$250, require that the recipient sign for the package.

Ship to the right address. When you receive a PayPal payment, PayPal includes the customer's shipping address in the "Notification of an Instant Payment Received" email and on the transaction details page (My Account → History). Make sure you ship only to this address, even if the buyer asks you to ship elsewhere. If a problem arises, you'll need to be able to prove that you shipped to that address, which, of course, is where the tracking number comes into play.

Ship only to confirmed addresses. If your customer is in the United States, the payment is protected only if the customer provides a confirmed address [Hack #33], and then only if you ship to that address.

This is a common sticking point, since most PayPal users have no idea what a confirmed address is. To deal with this, you have two choices: you can either try to educate your customers and then find yourself repeatedly refunding [Hack #90] ineligible payments until they get it right, or you can simply block payments lacking confirmed addresses.

Go to My Account → Profile, and in the Selling Preferences section, click Payment Receiving Preferences. Next, under "Block payments from U.S. users who do not provide a Confirmed Address," choose Yes.

While you're here, take a moment to type something in the Credit Card Statement Name box. The name you provide is what your customers will see on their statements when they send you payments funded by a credit card. If you use your eBay Member ID (as opposed to your real name or business name), it'll be easier for your customers to recognize the charges, and they'll be less likely to open any disputes.

See the next topic for information on the "Block payments funded by... Non-U.S. PayPal accounts" setting on this page.

Accept only eligible payments. For buyers *outside* the USA, there is no "confirmed address" requirement. But there is also no way of knowing whether or not a particular international transaction is eligible for the Seller Protection Policy until you receive it and inspect the corresponding Transaction Details page. (All payments coming from U.S. customers with confirmed addresses should be automatically eligible, so there's no guesswork there.)

The catch is that there's no way to systematically block all payments based on their "Seller Protection" eligibility. So, if you want to sell to customers outside the United States, you can either *accept all* non-U.S. payments and then simply refund [Hack #90] those you find unacceptable, or *block all* non-U.S. payments with the aforementioned "Block payments funded by...Non-U.S. PayPal accounts" option.

If you're diligent about these rules, and you respond quickly if one of your charges is disputed, you'll never be held responsible for buyer fraud, and you'll never lose a dime selling with PayPal.

For more PayPal tips, check out *PayPal Hacks*, by Shannon Sofield, Dave Nielsen, and Dave Burchell. Among other things, you'll learn how to lower your seller fees, protect yourself from chargebacks, and even integrate PayPal with your online business.

Personal and Business Checks

If you're smart, you'll never accept a check as payment for an auction. Checks can bounce, buyers can stop payment, and most eBay sellers have no way of determining if a check is even valid.

If you *must* accept checks, ship only after the check has cleared, and the money has been deposited into your account, a process that can take up to two weeks. If you want to accept payments only via postal mail, you're better off restricting such payments to money orders and cashier's checks, if for no other reason than to avoid having to remember when to check the status of a deposited check.

Money Orders and Cashier's Checks

Money orders and cashier's checks aren't like personal checks; they don't bounce and payment can't be stopped as easily, so in that regard they're more like cash. You don't have to wait for them to clear, but there's still the possibility of fraud, so always have a bank teller inspect the money order or cashier's check.

If you're in the U.S., postal money orders have a better track record and, while they're possible to counterfeit, they can be easily verifed at any post office branch. Probably the safest type of postal-mail payments is BidPay money orders, next.

Western Union Money Order

There are two kinds of Western Union money orders:

The old-fashioned kind. Never, ever, ever, ever, accept a Western Union payment for an eBay transaction. Ever. Such payments turn out to be fraudulent [Hack #69] about 99.9% of the time.

BidPay. The exception to this rule is BidPay [Hack #33], a service that sends Western Union money orders specifically for eBay transactions. BidPay payments are safe because you can verify them in about a minute by going to *www.bidpay.com*. Plus, buyers pay the BidPay fees, so the payments cost sellers nothing. BidPay payments are a particularly handy way for non-U.S. customers to pay U.S. sellers.

Credit Cards

If you directly accept credit cards through a merchant account [Hack #96], you'll always run the risk of chargebacks. Most credit card companies regard this as the cost of doing business and gladly pass that cost on to you.

If someone pays you with a stolen credit card, or if an otherwise legitimate customer simply forgets that they've bought something from you, the charge can be disputed [Hack #40] through the cardholder's credit card company. The company that issues your merchant account then notifies you of any chargeback, and assesses a nonrefundable chargeback fee to your account *in addition* to the amount of the original charge. You can reduce the likelihood of chargebacks by setting the following policies:

Ship only to the cardholder's billing address. When processing the charge, verify that the address the bidder provided matches the one on file with his or her credit card company.

Always ship with a tracking number. When choosing a courier, use a tracking number [Hack #86], insure any packages valued over $100, and ship promptly. Keep records of all tracking numbers for a minimum of six months.

Ask for the CVV code. Require that your customers provide the CVV code, the three-digit number (four digits for American Express) that appears after the card number, typically on the back of the card. This extra bit of information will help ensure that the customer actually has the card in his or her possession, especially in the event of a chargeback.

Be wary of international customers. The odds of credit card fraud increase tenfold when selling internationally [Hack #87].

Don't accept credit cards from newbies. Consider accepting credit card payments only from bidders with a certain minimum feedback rating, say 20 or 50. Make that requirement higher for international credit card payments. Keep in mind, however, that an account takeover [Hack #25] can allow someone to defraud you under the guise of an experienced eBayer, so be cautious if you see any red flags [Hack #69].

See Also

- See "Sell and Ship Internationally" [Hack #87] for ways to protect yourself when receiving payments from other countries.

Ship Cheaply Without Waiting in Line

Generate prepaid shipping labels online to save money and time.

Three things in life are certain: death, taxes, and long lines at the post office.

You know the drill. Take your package down to the post office. Stand in line. Stand in line some more. Then, watch while your package is weighed, listen to your shipping options, and pick whichever one is cheapest. Go home, and do it all again next week. But the worst part is that it's completely unnecessary.

Most major couriers—and nearly all couriers in the United States—offer online shipping services. Here's how it typically works:

1. Go to your courier's web site and sign up for an account; at this time, you'll enter your mailing address and, optionally, payment information. You'll need to do this only once. (See the next section for courier-specific tips.)

Before you're ready to ship, you can get a shipping cost quote from any courier web site. Do this before sending a total to the high bidder [Hack #84], and you'll never underestimate shipping costs again.

2. Enter your recipient's address, as well as the weight and dimensions of the package, into the Web form. (To avoid typos, make sure to use copy-and-paste rather than hand-typing your customer's address.) Figure 6-4 shows this step using the FedEx Ship Manager; note that the return address, which isn't shown, is filled in automatically.
3. Print out a prepaid shipping label and affix the label to your package. (If you're a buyer trying to save money on shipping [Hack #38], the only difference is that you'll be printing to a PDF file instead of a physical printer.)
4. Drop off your package at a local customer counter or, for an extra charge, schedule a pickup. You can find the closest drop-off location on the courier's web site.
5. Track the package using the tracking number generated with your label. Make sure to keep permanent records of all your tracking numbers; if your customer claims the package never arrived, you'll need to be able to find out what really happend by returning to the courier's web site and tracking the package. (For this reason, you should never use a shipment method that doesn't come with a tracking number.)

The entire process takes about a minute and requires no waiting in line and no guesswork. (See "Sell and Ship Internationally" [Hack #87] for any additional forms you might need when shipping to other countries.)

Courier Notes

Here are some tips and considerations for the "big three" shippers in the United States:

United States Postal Service (USPS). Not only can you print prepaid labels from the U.S. Postal Service web site (*sss-web.usps.com*), you actually get a better deal if you do so. (You can also print USPS labels from your PayPal account, as described in the "Shipping with PayPal" sidebar.)

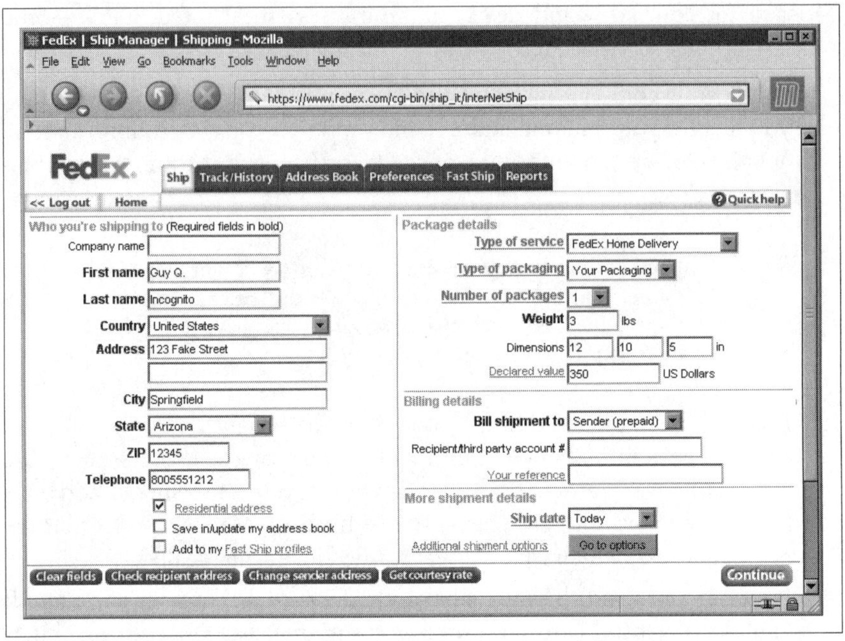

Figure 6-4. The FedEx Ship Manager lets you print out a prepaid shipping label in about a minute

If you need a shipping cost estimate so you can tell your customer how much to pay, go to *ircalc.usps.gov*, and enter the destination, size, and weight of the package. Among other things, you'll get a rundown of the required forms you'll need to affix to your package.

The Delivery Confirmation option, which adds a tracking number to most types of postal mail for an extra charge, is free if you print your mailing labels online. Another perk of USPS is that you can print a label without postage and use ordinary stamps instead; this is useful for those who can't or don't want to pay with a credit card.

Only packages weighing less than one pound can be dropped in mailboxes. Due to postal regulations, any package weighing one pound or more must be handed to a postal employee inside a branch, usually without having to wait in line. If you're using insurance, you'll have to stand in line, however, regardless of the weight of the package or the method used to prepare the label. For this reason, you may wish to use one of the other couriers to ship expensive items.

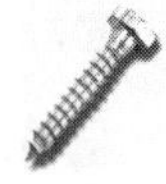

If you have a choice, never use USPS third class (standard) shipping. Although it may be slightly cheaper than Priority Mail, it often takes up to a month to deliver, even within the same state (despite what the USPS web site says). If you're shipping something heavy, use FedEx Ground or UPS Ground instead. The only time when third-class postal mail should be used is when you have no other choice, such as when shipping certain types of chemicals.

Probably the biggest drawback to USPS Click-N-Ship is that, at least at the time of this writing, ordinary international airmail shipments are not supported (unless you want to pay extra for Global Express Mail). This means that if you're shipping to another country [Hack #87], you'll have to use FedEx or UPS if you don't want to wait in line at the post office.

Federal Express (FedEx). Shipping with a FedEx account number is a smooth and easy process. Even when you're not using FedEx Ship Manager (*www.fedex.com*), you can simply handwrite your account number on a FedEx Express airbill or FedEx Ground form, and then drop off your package.

The FedEx Ship Manager, shown back in Figure 6-4, allows you to send any package to just about any destination around the world. Once you've filled out the required fields, but before you print the label, click Get Courtesy Rate to see the estimated shipping cost on the fly.

United Parcel Service (UPS). UPS has gone to great lengths to integrate its services with eBay and PayPal. For instance, eBay's calculated shipping feature [Hack #59] is provided by a UPS subsidiary.

Although you can ship from the UPS web site (*www.ups.com*), it is probably more convenient (and no more expensive) to ship directly from PayPal, as described in the "Shipping with PayPal" sidebar.

Note that these couriers are only a few players in a large field. There are plenty of other companies that you can use to ship eBay purchases, such as DHL (*www.dhl.com*) or FreightQuote (*www.freightquote.com*) for heavy freight.

Shipping on the Cheap

If buyers pay for shipping (and they usually do), then why should sellers care how much it costs to ship a package? If you charge a fixed shipping amount, then every penny saved is a penny earned. And if you charge your customers no more than it costs to ship, then you'll get more bids for being able to ship for less.

Shipping with PayPal

Although you may despise the cross-marketing strategies of large corporations, there are times when such tactics end up removing barriers and making your life easier. In that spirit, PayPal lets you print USPS and UPS shipping labels and pay for them with your PayPal balance.

Say you've just sold a $34 Beanie Baby, and the customer has sent you $40 to cover the item and shipping. Minus the PayPal fees, that leaves you about $4.50 to ship the item. Rather than buying postage separately and doing the bookkeeping later, you can use that $4.50 right on the PayPal site to create a USPS Priority Mail label, prefilled with the customer's comfirmed address [Hack #85]. (Note that this is available only for buyers in the United States.)

Start by logging in to PayPal and going to My Account → Profile → Shipping Preferences to choose the types of transactions for which the Ship button will appear in your transaction list. Then, click the History tab and you'll see the Ship button next to applicable transactions; click Ship to generate a prepaid label for that customer.

Figure 6-5 shows the PayPal shipping form; all you need to specify is the weight of the package (plus the dimensions if you're shipping with UPS). Once you've confirmed the details, the next page displays your invoice and prints your label.

(If your browser has a pop-up blocking feature, the pop-up window with your label might not appear. Just click the Reprint Label link on the confirmation page, another the window will open, and it should print automatically.)

When you're done, just affix the label to the package and drop it off. PayPal records the tracking number in your account history as well as your customer's, and even emails a notification to the customer.

The other major shipping expense comes from packing materials, both in the cost of the materials themselves and the impact they have on the total shipping cost. Here are some ways to save money and time when packing your items:

Save the planet. The number one rule is to never throw out packaging materials; recycle and reuse them as much as possible. Not only will you save money, but you'll help reduce the increased strain on landfills caused by the growing popularity of eBay and mail-order shipping in general.

For instance, don't throw out form-fitted styrofoam, commonly used by manufacturers to pack commercial electronics and other fragile items. Instead, break it apart and use the fragments to fill space in your own packages.

PayPal®

Log Out | Help

My Account | Send Money | Request Money | Merchant Tools | Auction Tools

U.S. Postal Service - Print Your Label See Demo

Create, purchase and print U.S. Postal Service® shipping labels from your PayPal account. Enjoy the affordable Postal Service rates without having to leave your desk.

Shipping tools with U.S. Postal Service are currently only available for transactions where both the sender's and recipient's addresses are in the United States.

Address Information

Ship From: eBay Hacks
Edit this Address 123 Fake Street
San Luis Obispo, CA 93402
United States

Ship To: Jane Buyer
Edit this Address 951 My Street
Helena, MT 61125
United States
Status: Confirmed address

Shipment Options

Shipment Options FAQ

Service Type: Select Service Choose a different shipper
Package Size: Package/Thick Envelope Learn More About Package Sizes
Mailing Date: 3/15/2005
Weight: lbs. oz.
Label Printer: Laser/Ink Jet Printer Edit Printer Settings
Delivery Confirmation: FREE
Label Processing Fee: FREE
Signature Confirmation: Yes ($1.30 USD) No
Note: Signature of receipt is available upon request for Express Mail®.
Display Postage Value on Label:
Email message to Buyer: (optional)

USPS® Insurance

USPS® Insurance FAQ

Purchase Insurance: Yes No
Insured value: 20.00 USD
Provides coverage up to $200.00 USD

Figure 6-5. PayPal Shipping lets you create a prepaid UPS or USPS shipping label without having to type the customer's address, and pay for the shipping charges with your PayPal balance

Hot air. Air is the best packing material on earth—it's lightweight, an excellent heat insulator, and extremely cheap. Bubble wrap and foam peanuts are terrific examples, and can be reused again and again. Tip: use clear trash bags to collect foam peanuts from packages you receive.

Don't use newspaper or shredded paper to wrap or cushion your items. It's heavier than foam peanuts, the ink can rub off, and it won't protect your items as well as bubble wrap.

Free boxes. Never pay for a box again. If you've run out of boxes to recycle, go to *ebaysupplies.usps.com* to order free Priority Mail boxes, co-branded with the eBay logo. Or just go down to your local post office; although they have nondescript boxes for sale, you can get Priority Mail boxes for free. Likewise, most other couriers (UPS, FedEx, etc.) not only provide free cardboard boxes of all sizes, but they will even ship them to you free of charge. All you need to do is ask.

Lots of tape. Buy packing tape in bulk from your local office-supply store. (Avoid independent packing/shipping stores, which usually grossly overcharge for packing materials.) Better yet, use a courier that provides free tape; if you're shipping with USPS Priority Mail, for example, you can use all the Priority Mail tape you want for free.

To label or not to label. You can get labels designed especially for USPS Click-N-Ship at *www.labeluniverse.com* (get part # LUCLICKSLW10). But if you want to save money, you can simply use ordinary paper and a lot of tape (just make sure not to tape over the barcode).

A better choice, and one that works with all kinds of prepaid shipping labels, is to place them in clear, self-adhesive airbill sleeves, freely available from couriers like FedEx and UPS, thus saving the time and expense otherwise spent on wads of packing tape or costly self-adhesive labels.

Sell and Ship Internationally

Make shipping to customers in other countries go more smoothly with these tools and tips.

Nothing so liberalizes a man and expands the kindly instincts that nature put in him as travel and contact with many kinds of people.
–Mark Twain, 1867

With some practice, your international shipments will be nearly as easy as domestic ones **[Hack #86]**. But it takes a little experience to know how to accept payments from customers in other countries, how to ship to other countries, and how to avoid fraud from deadbeats in other countries. Fortunately, the payoff is substantial: expanding your business to include bidders all around the world, while not without its risks, will make trading on eBay more interesting, more challenging, and more profitable.

Accepting International Payments

When you send payment instructions **[Hack #84]** to your customers in other countries, there are a few considerations you'll need to make in addition to anything you already do for your local customers.

First, always keep the language barrier in mind. If your bidder's native language is different from yours, keep your sentences short and avoid slang. Bidders in other countries expect you to write in your own language, but they will usually not have perfect command of it. If you find that the bidder is having a hard time understanding you, you can always try including a translation of your instructions [Hack #37]. Just make sure it's placed alongside your original text in the email, so the bidder gets the complete picture.

Second, be patient. International transactions take longer, partly because of the delays caused by time zone differences and language barriers, and partly because sending payments internationally can be difficult and time-consuming.

Finally, be extremely clear about the types of payments you can accept and the types you cannot. Here are some considerations when accepting payments from other countries:

PayPal. Buyers in nearly 50 countries around the world have access to PayPal, but payments from those members aren't necessarily covered by PayPal's Seller Protection policy [Hack #85].

Credit cards. The incidence of fraud [Hack #69] among credit card payments made by non-U.S. bidders is unfortunately much higher than payments originating in the United States. For this reason, you may wish to impose a limit, either on the amount you'll accept [Hack #85] or on the minimum feedback rating of customers from whom you'll take a credit card. If you contact your merchant account [Hack #96] provider, they'll probably tell you the same thing.

Electronic transfers. Depending on where you live, electronic bank account transfers may be common or unheard of. Sellers in the United States, for instance, largely use PayPal for this purpose, while sellers in Germany frequently initiate electronic transfers directly from their banks. The problem is that international electronic transfers, while safe, are quite expensive, particularly for the buyer. But an electronic transfer may be your best bet if you don't want to accept payments via postal mail, next, and PayPal or credit cards are unavailable. One of the biggest advantages is that your customers can specify the amount to send in your native currency, so you won't have to worry about getting shortchanged as a result of fluctuating exchange rates. Contact your bank for details.

Payments by mail. Any payment received by postal mail is subject to the terms imposed by your bank. Before you instruct an international bidder to mail you a money order [Hack #85], for instance, make sure your bank will accept payment, and try to determine if any additional fees will be incurred. In most cases, however, you can cash an international *postal* money order at your local post office branch. Alternatively, you can use BidPay [Hack #33], and let the buyer handle all the fees.

Although eBay does a fair job in converting currencies right on the auction page, the conversion rates they use are not necessarily the same as those used by your or your customer's bank. To give your customers a more accurate estimate of how much they'll need to send you in their own native currency, contact your bank to get the latest exchange rates, or use the Oanda Currency Converter at *www.oanda.com/converter/classic* for a quick estimate.

Shipping to Other Countries

In many ways, shipping internationally is no different from shipping domestically. It just usually costs a lot more, takes a lot longer, and requires a bunch of cumbersome forms.

Most couriers offer a different assortment of shipping options for international shipments, all of which are explained on your courier's web site. Regardless of the courier or shipping option you choose, though, you'll need to include the appropriate customs forms.

Here's what sellers in the U.S. must do to send packages to other countries:

United States Postal Service (USPS). Include customs form 2976 with all uninsured international packages, or form 2976-A (inside a 2976-E envelope) if you're insuring your package. You can get these forms at your local post office branch. Go to *ircalc.usps.gov* for exclusions and restrictions.

FedEx and UPS. International shipments with these couriers require a commercial invoice, a generic form in which you'll describe the individual contents of the package and specify the value and country of origin. Then, depending on the destination country, you'll need to include three to five copies along with the original. Place all forms in a single clear pouch, the same kind as is used for shipping airbills. You can download a blank commercial invoice form in Adobe Acrobat format from *ups.com* or *fedex.com* in their respective international documents sections.

It's important to understand that somewhat different forms and procedures may be required for different countries. If you've never shipped to a particular country before, make sure to contact the courier and ascertain any restrictions or additional requirements that may apply your package. For example, according to UPS, packages shipped to Mexico may not contain any products made in China. And according to FedEx, packages to Canada require one original and five copies of the commercial invoice, packages to Puerto Rico require only three copies, and some other countries require only originals (no copies). In other words, there's no hard and fast formula that applies in all situations.

Different countries also have restrictions as to the types of items you're permitted to ship into their borders. For instance, according to the United States Postal Service web site, shipments to Italy cannot contain artificial flowers and fruits (or accessories for them), bonnets, caps, or hats of any kind, clocks or supplies for clocks, coral mounted in any way, footwear of any kind, handkerchiefs, human remains, live bees, playing cards of any kind, radioactive materials, ribbons for typewriters, scarves, shawls, or toys not made wholly of wood.

Denied Parties

If you really want to be on the safe side, you might also consider researching so-called "denied parties." For example, FedEx offers the Denied Party Screening tool, which searches for your customer's name among governmental lists of countries, individuals, companies, and other organizations that have had economic and trade sanctions imposed against them. You can try this out by going to *https://gtm.fedex.com/cgi-bin/gtm_dps.cgi*.

Expectation Management

When shipping internationally, take a moment to prepare your customers for any delays (expected or otherwise) that the package might encounter before it arrives. For example, the United States Postal Service web site (*www.usps.com*) estimates that a one-pound package sent from the U.S. to the United Kingdom via airmail parcel post will take anywhere from 4 to 10 days. In practice, however, it may take two or three times as long, given the delays imposed by customs and other unforeseen circumstances.

For this reason, a delivery that takes two weeks might be seen in two different lights, depending on what you've told the customer. If the customer expects the package in 10 days, then she'll be disappointed, and you may be thanked with negative feedback for shipping too slowly. But if you say it will take a month, the recipient will be pleasantly surprised when it gets there in half the time. See "Master Expectation Management" [Hack #50] for other ways to engineer your customers' satisfaction while you're building your listings.

Damage Control Before and After You Ship

Handle problems discovered by either you or the customer.

A diplomat is a person who can tell you to go to hell in such a way that you actually look forward to the trip.
– Caskie Stinnett, 1960

So you're packing up an item to ship to a customer, and you suddenly discover a scratch, scrape, hole, discoloration, or missing part that you hadn't noticed and hadn't mentioned in the auction description. Sure, you can pack it up, ship it, and hope the bidder never notices. But he will, and you know it.

The best approach involves a quick preemptive email to the bidder, like one of the following:

The proactive approach. "I just noticed a nick on the back of the item while I was packing it. Let me know if you no longer want it, and I'll refund your money. Otherwise, I'll ship right away."

Give your customer a way out. In most cases, if the problem is minor, the customer will still want the item. Not only will this note make you appear honest, but your customer will have a more realistic expectation about the condition of the item, and less reason to return it when it finally arrives.

The compulsive approach. "While packing up your item, I discovered a flaw I hadn't noticed when writing up the auction description. I've attached a photo. If you still want it, I'd be happy to send it to you along with a partial refund. Or, if you're no longer interested, I'll refund your payment in full."

The photo gives the customer additional information with which he can make an informed decision and, again, helps set a more reasonable expectation. The partial refund is an excellent compromise that will both sweeten the deal for the customer and save you the trouble and expense of having to relist the item.

The "I'll make it up to you" approach. "I was called out of town for a few days, and I had to leave before I got a chance to ship your package. I shipped your package this morning and upgraded it to second-day air for no extra charge. I'm sorry for the delay; please let me know when the package arrives."

Damage control isn't just for physical damage; it's for dealing with snags in any part of the transaction. Not only should you contact customers before they receive a late package, you should make some concession to help compensate for the delay. For instance, a free shipping upgrade will cost you very little, but will go a long way toward making your customer happy with the product when it finally does arrive.

The "nevermind" approach. "I was getting ready to pack your item, but I couldn't find some of the parts that were listed in the auction description. I apologize for the inconvenience and have refunded your payment."

This is the best approach if you're reasonably certain the customer will no longer want the item, as it doesn't even suggest the possibility.

Assuming you're sufficiently apologetic and your tone is sincere, the customer will be understanding, and will quickly release you of your obligation without further inquiry or negative feedback.

The goal in each case is not only to set reasonable expectations [Hack #50] with the customer, but to save you money, time, and aggravation. The last thing you want is to go to the trouble and expense of shipping an item, only to have the customer complain and ultimately return it to you. Not only would you be obligated to refund the shipping fees (assuming you're at fault), but you'd be stuck with negative feedback and an item you subsequently have to resell.

If you instead refund the customer's money *before* shipping, you'll still be stuck with the item, but you won't get negative feedback, you won't lose money in shipping costs, and you won't have to go through the hassle of dealing with an unsatisfied customer.

Don't forget the partial refund, either. By refunding [Hack #90] some of your customer's money, either by a token amount or perhaps by shipping for free, you'll still be able to complete the sale and the buyer will be happy to get his product for a little less. (If you end up refunding some or all of the customer's payment, make sure to apply for a credit for the appropriate final-value fees [Hack #89].)

After the Fact

If the customer has already received the package, any hopes of setting a reasonable expectation will be dashed. But you can still try to ensure that your customer will be happy with her purchase.

The typical scenario involves a customer who isn't happy with an item for whatever reason. Some customers will be more understanding and reasonable than others, but it's up to you to set the tone for the rest of the transaction and deal with the problem appropriately.

When you receive a complaint, take the following steps:

1. *Watch out for red flags.* Keep your eye open for signs of buyer fraud [Hack #69]; don't let your fear of negative feedback or a buyer's idle threats cloud your judgement.
2. *Analyze feedback.* Check out the customer's history and feedback rating and look for signs that he has harassed other sellers. A customer who has received glowing feedback (and left glowing feedback for others) can be much more readily trusted than one whom other sellers have found to be unreasonable or uncooperative.

   See if the customer has left feedback for you yet. If not, you'll still have a chance at coming out of this unscathed [Hack #6]. Otherwise, you might understandably be less willing to compromise, given that there's seemingly nothing in it for you. But don't forget that feedback can be retracted [Hack #7], meaning that it's never too late for diplomacy.

3. *Check your listing.* Double-check your listing description for evidence of the problem. If the customer's complaint is addressed in your description, then all you need to do is—kindly—inform the bidder that the problem was explained in the auction. A seller should never be held responsible for a complaint based solely on the buyer's hastiness or laziness in not having bothered to read the description.
4. *Check your photos.* Examine your photos of the item to see if you can corroborate (or refute) the seller's story. It will be up to your judgment as to how clearly the problem was illustrated by your photos, and how you wish to proceed.
5. *Start with a partial refund.* Offer a partial refund commensurate with the severity of the problem. If the customer is happy to accept, you won't have to take the item back and refund all the customer's money.

So how do you calculate the amount of a partial refund? One way is to take the difference between the amount the customer paid and the estimated amount the customer would've paid had he known about the specific problem. Barring that, a token refund of the shipping cost, for example, may be all it takes to make the bidder happy.

6. *Consider a full refund.* If the customer rejects the partial refund, then it's up to you whether to give the customer a full refund and whether you include the cost of shipping. For instance, if it looks as though the damage was caused in shipping, and you remembered to insure the package, you can file an insurance claim with your shipper.

Fine Print

Depending on the circumstances, your customer may ask you to refund the shipping charges as well. It's generally accepted that the seller refunds original shipping charges if the seller is at fault; otherwise, the customer is entitled to nothing more than a refund of the final bid price. The shipping cost to return the item to you can be your burden or the buyer's, again depending on who's at fault.

You never need to ask your customer to cover eBay's fees if she returns an item, mostly because eBay will refund any applicable final-value fees [Hack #89]. You can even apply for a partial fee credit should you offer the bidder a partial refund.

HACK #89 Deal with Stragglers, Deadbeats, and Returns

File nonpaying bidder alerts and credit requests in the event of a failed transaction.

Although sellers are responsible for paying all fees associated with an auction, eBay is not unreasonable about refunding those fees when it comes to returns, deadbeat bidders, and other extenuating circumstances.

Regardless of the terms of a failed transaction, every seller can complete the following two-step process to recover any final-value fees associated with an listing. Unfortunately, insertion fees [Hack #43] are nonrefundable, but they are rarely substantial.

Report an Unpaid Item

If a bidder never pays, if a buyer returns an item, or if you and the customer settle a transaction for less than the final bid price, the first (and sometimes only) step is to report an "Unpaid Item." You can initiate this process no sooner than 7 days after the listing has closed, and no later than 45 days after.

Start by going to My eBay → Dispute Console, and choose Unpaid Items from the Choose a Dispute Type box at the top of the page. (Alternatively, you can go to *feedback.ebay.com/ws/eBayISAPI.dll?ViewDisputeConsole*.) Here, you'll see any previous unpaid item disputes you've filed (or other sellers have filed against you).

Click Report an Unpaid Item to start a new claim. When prompted, enter the eBay item number of the disputed transaction, and click Continue.

On the next page, you'll be presented with two questions. The choice you make here will affect the way eBay handles the rest of the process, so make sure to proceed carefully. If you're confused as to how to proceed, forget all the different scenarios listed on the page, and just decide how you feel:

- The buyer is a deadbeat, and I want revenge!
- The buyer is okay; we've resolved things amicably.

Once you've decided, choose the appropriate option:

1. *The buyer has not paid for the item.* Choose this if the buyer hasn't responded, if the buyer hasn't sent payment, or if the buyer is no longer a registered user (possibly as a result of other unpaid items). eBay then sends an email to the bidder reminding him of his obligation to pay.

   This selection also puts the wheels in motion should you need to return to this page and apply for a refund of your final-value fees, discussed in the next section. But you won't be able to do this right away; eBay requires that you wait seven days before escalating the dispute and giving the bidder an unpaid item strike. (The exception is if the buyer is no longer registered, in which case you'll get your refund immediately.)

The result, should the buyer not complete the transaction, is that his or her account will receive an unpaid item strike (thus eBay insists on some time for the buyer to respond). Once a buyer receives two such strikes, sellers can block his or her bids [Hack #64]; after three strikes, the bidder is kicked off eBay.

2. *We have mutually agreed not to complete the transaction.* If you choose this selection, the buyer won't be penalized for not paying. This may be the appropriate choice if:
   - The buyer returned the item, and you issued a refund.
   - You gave the buyer a partial refund, and the buyer kept the item.
   - The buyer never paid, but you want to let him off the hook.
   - The buyer never paid, and has no intention of doing so.
   - The buyer can't abide by your shipping or payment terms [Hack #54].

   The advantage with this second option is that you'll get your final value refund right away.

Regardless of the choice you make here, however, eBay will notify the bidder, and your report will appear in the bidder's Dispute Console (even if the dispute was amicable). This affords some degree of self-policing, so that buyers can notify eBay if a seller abuses the Dispute Console using the Unpaid Item Bidder Appeal form.

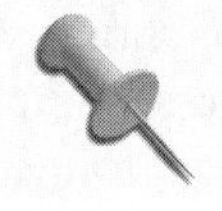

If you file a dispute and then later discover, for instance, that the buyer was in the hospital or simply never got your emails [Hack #9], you can withdraw the unpaid item strike for the buyer. Return to the Dispute Console, click the View Dispute link next to the transaction in question, and then click "remove the Unpaid Item strike for this dispute."

Concerning Feedback

The Dispute Console can also be used to report nonshipping sellers [Hack #41] or dispute items received that were significantly different than advertised.

Whether you use it as a buyer or a seller, a dispute will never directly affect your feedback score, nor will it affect your ability (or the other party's ability) to leave feedback.

For this reason, always check to see whether or not the bidder has left feedback for you (search your profile [Hack #1] look for the bubble icon [Hack #83] in My eBay) before you file a dispute or escalate a case. Although you should never let someone off the hook for fear of feedback retaliation, you may want to think twice before penalizing someone for what may be a marginal violation.

Final Value Fee Credits

If you chose option #2 when filing your dispute, indicating that you and the buyer resolved things peacefully, eBay will refund your final-value fees immediately in most cases.

But if you chose option #1, indicating that the buyer is essentially a deadbeat, you'll have to return to the Dispute Console at least a week after filing your original report. Click the View Dispute link next to the transaction in question, and then choose one of these three options at the top of the page:

We've completed the transaction and we're both satisfied. Select this option if you want to close the dispute, but you don't want your final value fees refunded, and you don't want to give the buyer an unpaid item strike.

We've agreed not to complete the transaction. Select this option if you want to close the dispute and get your final value fees refunded. The bidder won't get an Unpaid Item Strike, and you'll be eligible for a relist credit [Hack #90].

I no longer wish to communicate with or wait for the buyer. Select this option to get your final value fees refunded and give the bidder an unpaid item strike. You'll also be eligible for a relist credit.

Click Continue when you've made your choice.

There's a time limit on all open disputes; if, after 60 days from the close of the listing (*not* the filing of the dispute), the dispute is still open, eBay unceremoniously closes the dispute. (Disputes for items not received have more generous expiration dates.) If this happens, you won't be eligible for a refund of your final value fees, you won't get a relist credit, and you'll have missed your chance to give the bidder an unpaid item strike. To help you keep track of the timing of your open disputes, you may wish to add a note [Hack #83] to the listing in My eBay.

Your credit will take effect immediately. To see how much money has been credited, go to My eBay → My Account → View invoice.

HACK #90 Issue a Refund

Give your customer her money back without incurring additional fees or risking negative feedback, and then relist your item for free.

After you've sold something on eBay, usually the last thing in the world you want is to see it again, let alone part with the money you got for it. But refunds are a fact of life in a trading community where your reputation means everything.

PayPal. If the customer paid for your item with PayPal, use PayPal's Refund feature instead of trying to send the buyer a new payment. Just log into PayPal and go to My Account → History. Find the transaction in the list, click Details, and then click Refund Payment at the bottom of the page.

Next, you'll see the Refund Offer page, shown in Figure 6-6. Fill in Gross Refund Amount with either the total amount of the original payment or the amount of your partial refund **[Hack #88]**, and click Submit.

PayPal gives you 60 days to refund your payments, after which time the feature will no longer be available. If you need to refund a payment after 60 days, you'll need to use the Send Money tab to send an ordinary PayPal payment. This means, among other things, that your seller fees won't be refunded, which should be good incentive to handle returns promptly.

Since your customer may be upset at the prospect of having to pay a percentage of his refund to PayPal, you may wish to spend an extra few bucks and use PayPal's Mass Pay feature to pay the seller fees **[Hack #34]**.

Credit cards. If a customer paid you directly with a credit card, you should be able to process a refund and get your discount fees refunded. Contact your merchant account provider **[Hack #96]** for details.

Payments by postal mail. If a customer sent you a cashier's check, money order, or other payment via postal mail, you can refund the payment by returning the check (if it hasn't been cashed) or by sending a new check for the purchase amount (if it has).

Make sure you send the refund with some form of tracking **[Hack #86]** so that you know when and if the customer has received it. Before you go to the hassle of mailing a refund, though, see if the customer will accept a refund in the form of a PayPal payment.

Note that BidPay payments **[Hack #85]** can't be refunded per se, so you'll need to send a whole new payment to return the customer's money.

Electronic transfers. Contact your bank for the refund procedure for electronic bank account transfers, if available.

PayPal

Log Out | Help

My Account | Send Money | Request Money | Merchant Tools | Auction Tools

Overview | Add Funds | Withdraw | History | Resolution Center | Profile

Refund Offer

You may offer your buyer a refund within 60 days of payment. All refunds will be processed immediately.

Enter the amount you would like the buyer to receive and click **Calculate**. Based on the amount that you enter, PayPal will calculate the fees eligible for refund. Click **Submit** to initiate the refund.

Transaction ID: 4G9473195Y606740H
Name: Ivana Tinkel
Email: ivana@moestavern.com
Original Amount: $20.00 USD

Note: You may offer the buyer a full refund or a partial refund (for example, the transaction amount less shipping and handling).

Gross Refund Amount: 20.00 Calculate ?
Net Refund Amount: $19.12 USD ?
Fee Refunded: $0.88 USD ?
Source of Funds: PayPal balance
Note: If you choose to refund by eCheck and the eCheck doesn't clear, PayPal will process the refund with funds from your PayPal account.

Optional Note to Buyer: (This note will be included with your refund offer) Sorry for the mixup. Here's your money back.

211 characters left

Submit Cancel

Figure 6-6. Use PayPal's Refund feature to return a customer's payment and get your PayPal seller fees back

Relisting and Other Options

When all is said and done, you'll most likely still have the item, which means you'll probably want to relist it and try to sell it again.

Before you relist, make sure to add the deadbeat bidder from the first round to your blocked bidder list [Hack #68] if for no other reason than to prevent the bidder from retaliating by disrupting your new listing. Before you relist, you can also see if any of the other bidders on the auction are still interested by using the Second Chance Offer on your My eBay Selling page.

You can relist any item on eBay by going to the completed auction page and clicking Relist Your Item. You can relist multiple items quickly in the Unsold Items section of your My eBay Selling tab.

Relisting in this way has three advantages over creating a new listing:

It's already done. You don't have to enter all the auction details again; eBay will do it for you. All you need to do is click Go to Review to jump to the last page of the form, and then click Submit Listing to start the new auction.

It's advertised. If you turn on the Relisted Item Link option in the Sell Your Item form [Hack #43], a prominent link will be placed at the top of the old listing page, directing any customers who happen to see it to the new listing. It's a great way to get a little extra free advertising for your item.

It's free. If the first auction failed because it didn't receive any bids or the reserve wasn't met, eBay will waive the listing fees for the relisted auction (provided it ends successfully). Or, if you're relisting because of a deadbeat bidder, and you were successful in filing an unpaid item dispute [Hack #89], eBay will credit the insertion fees for the original listing when you relist the item.

Silver Lining Clause

More often than not, an auction that is relisted after a deadbeat bidder backs out usually closes at a higher price the second time. Why is this?

First, two back-to-back 7-day auctions have twice the exposure (14 days) of a single 7-day auction; if you do it right, anyone who visits the first auction will see a link to the relisted auction. Second, any unsuccessful bidders on the first auction are likely to return and bid more aggressively on the second auction, especially if you're selling something rare. Third, a diligent seller is likely to improve the auction description the second time around, which can result in a higher price.

## CHAPTER SEVEN

Running a Business on eBay

Hacks 91–101

No two people or companies do business in exactly the same way, but there is always common ground when it comes to saving money and time. This chapter illustrates some of the tools—some available for free and some at extra cost—that sellers have at their disposal for increasing automation in their businesses, and shows how some of these tools can be hacked to better suit your needs.

PowerSellers and the Role of Numbers on eBay

eBay recognizes sellers who meet certain sales quotas as *PowerSellers* and awards them a few extra perks:

Better customer support. Depending on your PowerSeller tier, you may have access to priority web-based support, or even toll-free telephone support.

More education. As a PowerSeller, you'll have access to advanced selling educational tools, seminars, and information.

Free stuff. Qualify for promotional offers and get a bunch of eBay promotional merchandise for yourself (or your customers).

Finally, the recognition you deserve. When you join, you'll receive a welcome letter and a PowerSeller certificate of achievement from Meg Whitman. More importantly, it'll become evident who Meg Whitman is. (She's the esteemed President and CEO of eBay, and the person who's followed around at eBay Live! conferences as though she were handing out $5 bills to anyone who asked.)

In order to qualify for the PowerSeller program, you'll need—among other things—to maintain at least $1,000 of average gross monthly sales for three months and a meager 98% positive rating. These bare minimums aren't particularly difficult to achieve, but you'll have to maintain them to keep your PowerSeller status.

To qualify for the higher tiers, you'll need to achieve higher gross monthly sales:

Bronze	Silver	Gold	Platinum	Titanium
$1,000	$3,000	$10,000	$25,000	$150,000

You don't need to sign up for the PowerSeller program; eBay notifies you automatically when you reach any of these levels, and places a PowerSeller icon next to your member ID in your listings.

You'll also have access to the full-size PowerSeller logo to place in your listings. Give it some thought before actually doing so, however. Although the program as a whole can be valuable to sellers, the logo itself can send a message to your customers that you're a big, faceless organization, and they'll be lucky if they receive any personal attention from you at all. The personal touch, after all, is what attracts many bidders to eBay.

It's worth noting that the hacks in this chapter are designed to help all sellers streamline their operations, whether they're Titanium-level PowerSellers moving a quarter-million dollars worth of merchandise every month, or hobbyists trading a few low-cost items every couple of weeks.

Staying Connected to the eBay Community

eBay is constantly revising their web site, policies, features, and associated fees; as a seller on eBay, you have a vested interest in how these changes shape your business. Since even the most minor changes can have an impact (positive or negative), stay connected to the eBay community to ensure that you're aware of potential problems and prepared for upcoming changes; the following resources will help:

General Announcements board. *www2.ebay.com/aw/marketing.shtml*

Go to Site Map → News & Announcements for previews of new features, new category announcements, policy changes, and updates to eBay's various tools and services.

System Announcements board. *http://www2.ebay.com/aw/announce.shtml*

Go to Site Map → News & Announcements → System when something on eBay stops working, to see if there's an explanation here. Scheduled maintenance and unscheduled outages are also documented on this page.

My eBay My Messages. *My eBay → My Messages*

The most important announcements from the General Announcements board, plus occasional tips and promotions appear here from time to time. The number in parentheses next to the My Messages link shows when new messages have been added. This is a good place to look for listing upgrade [Hack #46] sales and discounts.

eBay Community Newsletter. *http://ebay.com/community/chatter*

Go to Site Map → News & Announcements → Newsletter to read *The Chatter*, a monthly e-zine produced by eBay staff members, complete with articles, announcements, and even a *Member Spotlight*.

PowerUp Seller Newsletter. *http://ebay.com/sellercentral/newsflash.html*

Get advance notice of upcoming promotions, such as sweepstakes, free listing days, and listing upgrade sales and discounts, delivered to your email box.

Calendar. *http://ebay.com/community/events*

Go to Site Map → Calendar for a listing of this month's workshops, tradeshows, Share your Wares events, Street Faires, eBay Live! conferences, and eBay University seminars.

Discussion Forums. *http://ebay.com/community/boards*

Go to Site Map → Discussion, Help and Chat → Discussion Boards to discuss nearly all aspects of eBay with other members. Among the roughly 70+ specialized forums are *Checkout*, *Search*, *International Trading*, and my favorite, *Soapbox*.

Use the boards to ask questions, offer help to other eBay users, and voice your opinions (and objections) regarding eBay policies, changes, and trends. For instance, when eBay's Checkout feature [Hack #64] was first introduced, eBay's then-new Checkout forum was crammed with thousands of complaints from members (including several makeshift petitions started by particularly outraged sellers).

Forums are comprised of *threads*, each of which starts as a single message. Any member can start a new thread or add to an existing thread. New threads—as well as old threads that have been updated—are automatically promoted to the top of the list.

Some people post to their own threads to move them to the top in the hopes of invigorating them, which is why you may occasionally see a post with nothing more than "Bump" in the message body.

When eBay staff members post to forums (and they do), their names are shown in a pink-colored stripe, which is why you may occasionally see references to "Pinks" by some of the forum regulars.

API forums. *http://developer.ebay.com/DevProgram/community/forums.asp*

This is a special section of the forums for developers working with the eBay API, discussed in Chapter 8.

eBay Live! *http://www.ebay.com/ebaylive*

The annual eBay Live! conference is a good place to connect with other eBay fanatics in person, attend classes, learn about the latest eBay-related products, and possibly get your favorite eBay book signed by its author.

HACK #91 Open an eBay Store

Open an eBay Store to build a more aggressive presence on eBay and on the Web.

For sellers who want their presence on eBay to be more than just a collection of running auctions, eBay allows you to open a *Storefront*. eBay Stores are permanent, dedicated web sites on which you can list more inventory for less money than ordinary eBay listings.

An eBay Store offers a bunch of perks, including the following:

Longer-lasting listings. You'll be able to create fixed-price listings that last 30, 60, 90, or even 120 days. These listings don't show up in standard eBay search results (except under specific circumstances), but are shown to buyers who enter your store through any of your ordinary eBay listings.

Your standard eBay listings appear alongside your store listings in your eBay Store as long as the listing started after you opened your storefront. Having a few normal eBay listings running concurrently to your store inventory listings is a great way to promote your eBay Store.

Lower insertion fees. eBay Stores items cost only 5 cents for each 30 days they appear in your store.

Private search for your store. A search box appears at the top of your personal category listings, allowing customers to search through only your listings. Of course, you can always add a similar box to your non-Store listings [Hack #61].

Create your own categories. File your store inventory into a handful of custom categories in your store. Although these categories won't get mixed in with eBay's standard categories, they allow you to easily organize the listings in your own store. For instance, if you're selling photographic equipment, you can have a Lenses category and a Film category, making it easy for a customer who has just purchased a camera from you to pick up a few accessories to go along with it.

Cross-promotion. With an eBay store, you can use eBay's cross-promotion feature [Hack #60] to advertise your store items in each of your active listings.

Advertising credits. Depending on the store subscription you choose, you can get discounts on various programs to advertise your store [Hack #99].

Vacation hold. Given the extended period items can be active in your store, it can helpful to put your listings on hold while you're away.

Build a stable presence on eBay. An official storefront will help make your business look more reputable [Hack #8] to customers.

Aside from the expected listing and final-value fees, eBay Stores require an extra-cost monthly subscription. As with most of eBay's advanced programs, you can choose one of several tiers, depending on your needs. Higher tiers cost more money per month—about $16 for a *Basic* store, going up to $500 for an *Anchor* store—but also offer more perks. You can get the details and sign up at *stores.ebay.com*.

Once you open your store, a new option will appear on the first page of the Sell Your Item form, allowing you to create a new store inventory listing [Hack #43].

How Customers Will Find You

Once you've opened an eBay Store, a red open-door icon will appear next to your member ID anywhere it appears on eBay. A bidder looking at one of your eBay listings can click the icon to enter your store and shop among your items.

You'll also receive a tidy URL in this format:

```
www.ebaystores.com/storename
```

This allows you to easily link to your store in your listing descriptions, your About Me page [Hack #62], and any email messages you send to customers. Also, any customers who go to *www.ebaystores.com* will be able to browse or search through all eBay stores, and thus find your store through one of your listings.

But probably the biggest advantage of eBay stores over ordinary eBay listings is that since an individual listing can last for several months, it will stick around long enough to show up in search engines like Google. This means that anyone who goes to *www.google.com* and searches for antique backscratchers may see the seven varieties you're currently selling.

Alternatives

The eBay Store is essentially a *turnkey* solution, allowing any seller to open a prefabricated, fully functional store in just a few minutes, but it's not the only site offering such an option. Other sites offering similar services include Yahoo! Stores (*www.stores.yahoo.com*) and Vendio Stores (*www.shop.vendio.com*).

HACK #92 Find a Market

Research sales trends and find out what to sell and when to sell it.

Most sellers come to eBay when they've got some stuff to sell, but if you're running a business on eBay, you've likely cleaned out your own attic by now. The next step, of course, is to find something new to sell.

There are two basic approaches: buy products inexpensively for the purpose of reselling on eBay for a profit, or sell other people's stuff for a percentage of the profits. To pursue either course, you'll need to know what's currently selling well on eBay.

Find Out What's Hot

While you may be intimately acquainted with a particular market on eBay, such as hand-painted clogs or wind-up walking sushi, there's no reason you couldn't branch out and start selling other kinds of things.

eBay updates its Hot Categories Report every month with the latest list of categories in which, as they put it, "demand is growing faster than supply *and* bid-to-item ratios are relatively high." In other words, these are markets that eBay believes to be untapped of their full potential.

You can download the entire report in Adobe Acrobat PDF format by going to *ebay.com/sellercentral/whatshot.html*. (If you can't open PDF files, you can get the free Acrobat reader at *www.adobe.com*.)

Categories are listed by *level* (e.g., L2, L3, L4), which is another way of saying the "number of layers deep." For instance, in the Antiques top-level (a.k.a. Level 1 and L1) category, you might see a table in the report that looks something like this:

Hot:

Level 2 (L2)	Level 3 (L3)	Level 4 (L4)
Textiles, Linens	Quilts, Bedspreads	Quilts
Silver	Sterling	Cups, Goblets
Silver	Sterling	Candlesticks, Candelabra
Silver	Sterling	Salt Cellars, S&P Shakers
Decorative Arts	Picture Frames	Metal

So, the first entry in the table indicates that the Antiques → Textiles, Linens → Quilts, Bedspreads → Quilts category was "Hot" last month. Check out the first page of the report for an explanation of the technical differences between the Super Hot, Very Hot, and merely Hot classifications.

Now, since there are a number of factors that can lead to a particular category being hot during any given month, you may want to look a little deeper before you go buy a cargo container full of salt and pepper shakers. For example, imagine that a national television network broadcast the classic 1974 movie *Young Frankenstein*, and immediately thereafter, the market for antique sterling silver candelabras skyrocketed for a week or two. Does this mean that candelabras are making a come-back? Of course not.

What's important are the *trends* indicated by the spikes in certain categories, which is something you'll only be able to discern by reviewing historical data. For example, if you could look back at eBay sales over the last few years, you'd probably see spikes in the market for handheld calculators every September, presumably due to the annual back-to-school spending spree. But if you waited for eBay's Hot Categories Report, you wouldn't know that calculators were hot until October, at which point you would've missed your window.

This is where an off-eBay sales analysis tool like Terapeak (*www.terapeak.com*) becomes immeasurably useful. Terapeak's Hot List uses terms similarly to eBay's, such as Hot and Super Hot, but their presentation, shown in Figure 7-1, is infinitely superior to eBay's Hot Categories Report.

terapeak marketplace research | Search Listings | Search | All Categories | Current Category | eBay Stores Only | eBay market data

HOME | BROWSE CATEGORIES | SEARCH LISTINGS | HOT LIST | COMMUNITY | HELP | CATEGORY JUMP: 0

February, 2005
You are in Month mode, Switch to DAY or WEEK
Prev • Next Day | Week | Month | 7Days | 30Days

Categories Which Are Doing Well on eBay.com
PREV • 1 2 3 100 101 102 • NEXT

Category Name	Success	Status	Sales Rank out of 2031 Hot Categories
Home & Garden > Housekeeping & Vacuuming > Vacuum Cleaners > Canister > Kenmore	54.55%	Hot	#2021
Jewelry & Watches > Watches > Pocket Watches > Modern (1970-Now)	26.32%	Hot	#2022
Home & Garden > Home Decor > Baskets > Wood	45.45%	Hot	#2023
Entertainment Memorabilia > Music Memorabilia > Pop > Michael Jackson	34.15%	Hot	#2024
Home & Garden > Home Decor > Afghans, Throws > Patterns	32.88%	Hot	#2025
Collectibles > Comics > Golden Age (1938-55) > Cartoon Character	43.94%	Hot	#2026
Sports Mem, Cards & Fan Shop > Cards > Football-NFL > Singles (1970-79) > Graded > PSA	67.86%	Very Hot	#2027
Cameras & Photo > Binoculars & Telescopes > Telescopes > Refractor	37.50%	Hot	#2028
Sports Mem, Cards & Fan Shop > Cards > Hockey-NHL > Boxes, Cases > Pre-2000	38.46%	Super Hot	#2029
Collectibles > Comics > Silver Age (1956-69) > Superhero > Justice League of America	50.00%	Very Hot	#2030
Sporting Goods > Snowmobiling > Parts & Accessories > Yamaha	17.39%	Hot	#2031

PREV • 1 2 3 100 101 102 • NEXT

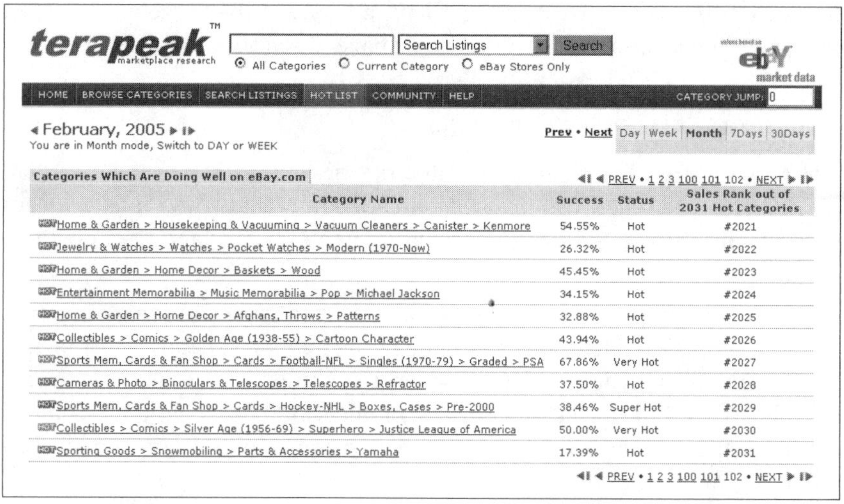

Figure 7-1. Use Terapeak's Hot List to determine the hottest categories for any given month

For one, you can click the column headers to sort by Success rate (the percentage of listings that completed successfully), Status (e.g., Hot, Very Hot, or Super Hot), or Sales Rank.

But the real value is in Terapeak's integration of historical data, which is also useful for determining the effectiveness of extra-cost listing upgrades [Hack #46]. For example, Figure 7-1 shows the Month view of the Hot List, but you can use the Prev and Next links to navigate to any other month (or Day or Week, for that matter). This means you can compare what was hot last month with what was hot six months ago or, more interestingly, what was hot this time last year.

But here's the best part: Terapeak does this for you, too! Just click any category link on the Hot List to see a history of total sales like the one in Figure 7-2. And you can click any of the parent categories (shown at the top of the report) to view larger-scale sales trends. For instance, Figure 7-2 shows the sales for a Level-5 (L5) category, Home & Garden → Housekeeping & Vacuuming → Vacuum Cleaners → Canister → Kenmore. You can click the "Canister" or "Vacuum Cleaners" links to view those L4 or L3 categories, respectively, or view other L5 sibling categories by using the links in the Sub-Categories box to your left.

With these reports (and a little common sense), you can distinguish markets that are truly hot from those that are merely temporary blips on eBay's radar.

Now What?

So you've discovered that you might have a future in the burgeoning field of vacuum cleaner sales. (At least you don't have to sell them door-to-door.)

The next step is to find some products you can buy and then resell, and there are several ways to go about this:

Arbitrage. Most sellers on eBay have no idea what they're doing. As an experienced seller, you probably already know that you can take advantage of this by purchasing poorly listed items cheaply and reselling them for a profit.

Many sellers practice this form of arbitrage to an extent that it becomes a full-time job. Naturally, the value of the items you handle must be sufficient to make it worthwhile given the shipping costs and associated eBay fees, but if you do enough volume, you can make quite a bit of money by doing nothing more than being a particularly good eBay buyer and seller.

Wholesale lots. One of the things you'll find on eBay is wholesale lots, large collections of items offered with the expectation that the items will

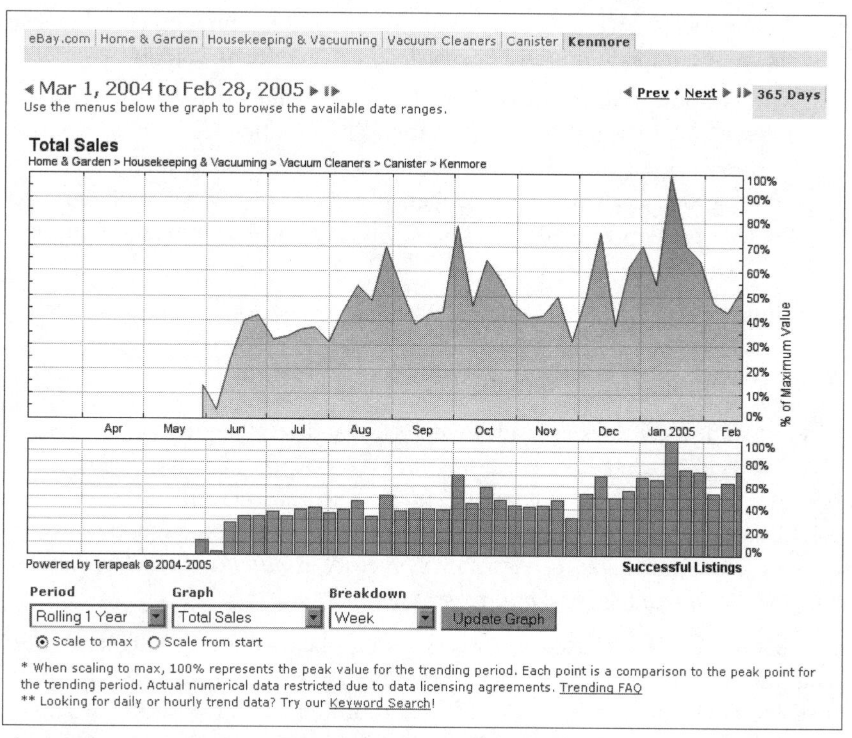

Figure 7-2. View the history of any hot category at Terapeak, and find out if recent activity indicates an up-and-coming market or just a temporary spike

be resold individually. To find the Wholesale Lots section of any eBay category, just go to *listings.ebay.com/aw/plistings/list/categories.html* and use your browser's Find feature (Ctrl-F) to search the page for the word "lots."

Next, do the math. Say a particular lot of 300+ leather watchbands is selling for about $400. To make any kind of profit, all you need to do is resell the bands for a little more than $1 apiece, right? Well, not exactly.

First, add eBay's insertion and final-value fees, which will probably come to at least 65 cents per listing. Then, consider your time creating the listings, communicating with customers, and packing and shipping the items: if you sell enough watchbands, you may be able to get this down to a couple of minutes per band. But the biggest question still remains: how are you going to sell 300 watchbands?

To make it worth your while, you're going to have to make at least a couple dollars on each watchband you sell, which gives you a minimum per-piece price of, say, $4. This, of course, assumes you can sell all 300 bands. Say you end up unloading only 50 of them, for instance; in this case, the per-piece price would have to be at least $10 to eke out a small profit from the lot. Now, do a search on eBay [Hack #42] and see how much other sellers (your competition) have been asking for individual watchbands.

At this point, you may decide to become a *value-added reseller*. In the eBay world, this simply means that you'll probably need to find *another* wholesale lot, this time for 300 wristwatches without watchbands. Then, attach each of the watchbands to each of the wristwatches (get the kids to help you out here), and sell these new unique and complete wristwatches for $25 apiece.

And thus the circle of life on eBay is complete.

Become a Trading Assistant

In some respects, it doesn't matter what's hot and what's not on eBay. A good seller can sell anything [Hack #51] at any time [Hack #48]. To that end, many sellers become proxy sellers, or *trading assistants*, who earn percentages of the successful sales of other people's stuff. This practice is common enough to inspire eBay to publish the Trading Assistant Directory at *http://contact.ebay.com/ws/eBayISAPI.dll?TradingAssistant&page=main*.

If you want to be included in the directory, click Create/Edit Your Profile. You'll need a feedback score of 50 or higher, of which at least 97% is positive, and you'll need to have sold at least four items in the past 30 days.

Once you're in, customers can find you by searching the directory. Since they'll need to deliver the items to you, the search is performed by Zip Code, allowing customers to find trading assistants closest to them. However, you should try a quick search of your own Zip Code before resting your hopes on this program; if you find 300+ other trading assistants in your area, then you're probably not going to get a lot of business as a proxy seller.

Now, consider that the kind of people who are likely to need this service are probably not going to be proficient enough to find their way to eBay's Trading Assistant Directory. In fact, it's probably not going to occur to these people that there are those who will do their selling for them.

This is why the more serious proxy sellers open brick-and-mortar stores. With signs such as "We'll Sell Your Stuff on eBay" in their front windows, and locations in shopping malls and on high-traffic streets, they're much more likely to target the kind of customer that will bring them real business.

Here's how it works. A customer brings you an item and says "sell this for me." You take the item, photograph it, and list it on eBay (under your own, well-established account). To avoid doing extensive market research for a single item, most proxy sellers start their listings at a single dollar.

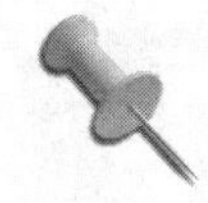

If you want to research a particular item, you can always try a standard completed-items search [Hack #42]. But if you suspect a customer has brought you something of value, you may want to take it a bit further and have it appraised at a site such as CollectingChannel's "Ask the Appraiser" (*www.collectingchannel.com/ata*).

Bidding proceeds normally until the item is successfully sold, at which point you collect payment and ship the item to the new owner. You then keep a healthy cut (15%–25% is customary) and write a check to the original customer for the difference.

If you do enough business, you can make yourself quite a bit of money. But the best part is that you don't have to find a market at all; the markets find you!

HACK #93 Streamline Listings with Turbo Lister

Use eBay Turbo Lister to upload more listings in less time.

The Sell Your Item form [Hack #43] is a simple but limited auction listing tool, adequate only for creating a handful of new listings at a time. It's hopelessly cumbersome for anyone needing to upload a large number of listings or otherwise automate the listing process.

eBay's own Turbo Lister application is what they call a *bulk listing tool*, but in many ways it is simply a more convenient way to create eBay auctions. Turbo Lister, available at *pages.ebay.com/turbo_lister*, is completely free to download and use, and operates on any Windows machine (Mac and Unix are not supported).

Although Turbo Lister provides the same listing options available at *eBay.com*, it sometimes takes a little while (often a few days or even weeks) for eBay to update the software with new features and categories. To make sure Turbo Lister is always up-to-date, go to Tools → Options → Advanced Options, and turn on the "Automatically download updates when I start the program" option. You can also participate in the Beta program and see the latest features and changes sooner than most by going to Tools → Options → Join Beta Program.

Setting Up Turbo Lister

One of Turbo Lister's biggest strengths is that it effectively eliminates the need to enter the same information again and again. Before you use Turbo Lister, take a moment to specify default values by going to Tools → Options, as shown in Figure 7-3.

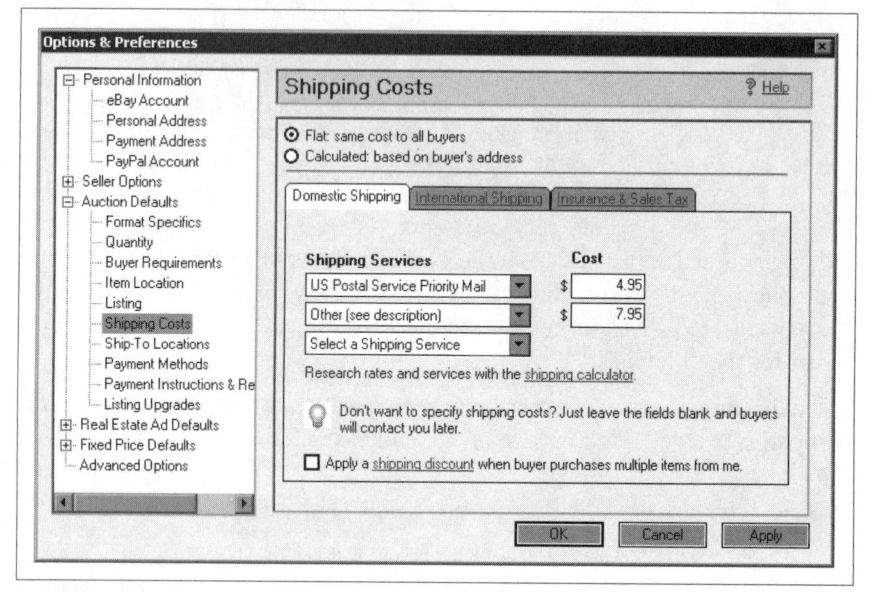

Figure 7-3. Use Turbo Lister's Options & Preferences box to set the defaults for your auctions

The more auction details you specify here, the less work you'll have to do for each listing. For instance, select Auction Defaults → Listing to create an auction description template to be used for all newly created items.

Creating Listings

Ironically, Turbo Lister's listing creation tool starts with a multipage wizard, not unlike eBay's Sell Your Item form. The good news, however, is that you have to use it only once.

Turbo Lister uses the eBay API (Chapter 8) to upload new listings. If you don't like Turbo Lister, you can build your own simple listing upload tool **[Hack #113]**.

Start by clicking the Create New button on the toolbar (or go to File → New → Item) and follow the prompts. If you like, you can fill in all the fields as though you were selling a single item, or just click Next repeatedly to get through the wizard and click Save when you're done. Your new listing will then appear under the Item Inventory tab, awaiting upload.

The best part is where you can go from here. Instead of going through the wizard each time you want to create a new listing, you can simply duplicate an existing item and modify it as needed. Click the Duplicate button on the toolbar (or go to Edit → Duplicate), specify the number of duplicates to create, and click OK. This makes it remarkably easy to create dozens or even hundreds of similar listings in a fraction of the time it would take without Turbo Lister. Then, double-click any entry to show the Edit Item–Auction Details window, shown in Figure 7-4.

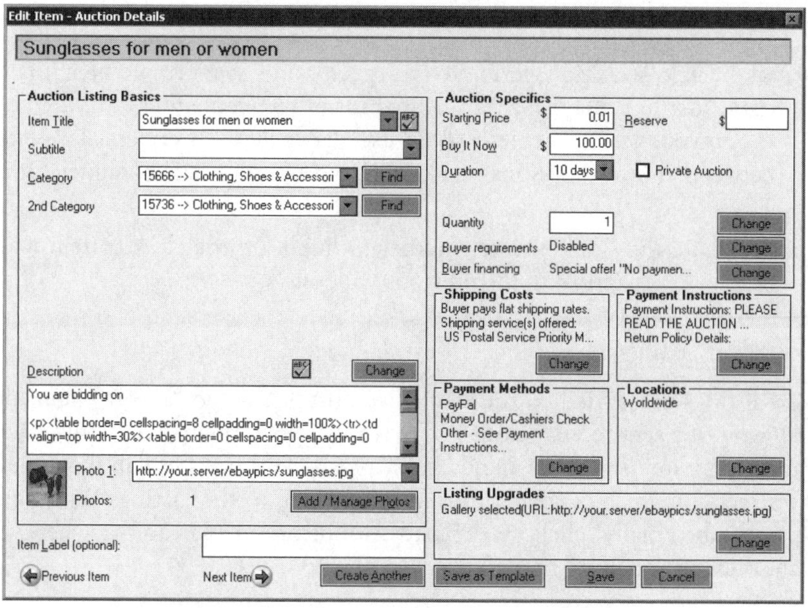

Figure 7-4. The Edit Item – Auction Details window, available only after you've created a listing, allows you to modify all aspects of a listing on one page

Here are a few things to note about this window:

Categories. You can specify the category (or categories) in any of three ways. Click Find to browse the entire category tree. Or, type a category number right in the Category and 2nd Category boxes, and press the Tab key to validate it. Finally, choose from among your most recently used categories in the drop-down listbox.

HTML preview. Click Design View in the Edit Item–Auction Details window to modify the auction description with the WYSIWYG editor. Flip to the HTML View and Preview tabs to edit the HTML directly and see what your auction will look like, respectively.

Although you can put HTML code in any eBay listing with the Sell Your Item form, Turbo Lister really shines in its ability to allow you to put the same HTML code in all your listings without having to cut and paste and fine-tune each one. Thus, you could put a Search by Seller box [Hack #61] in a single listing, customize it the way you want it, and then duplicate it hundreds of times.

Photos. Click Add/Manage Photos to specify one or more pictures for the item. Just like eBay's Sell Your Item form, you can either host the photos on your own server [Hack #76] or use eBay's Picture Services. To switch between the two options, click "Change photo hosting" under Other Tasks.

Quick duplicate. Click Create Another to duplicate the current item without having to return to the previous window.

Uploading Listings

New listings are added to the Item Inventory list as you create them, but they won't be sent to eBay until you're ready upload them. To do this, select one or more items in the list and click Upload. Turbo Lister will then queue the selected items by copying (not moving) them to the Listings Waiting to Upload tab. Finally, click the Upload All button on the toolbar when you want them to "go live."

Since auctions end at the same time of day they start, give some thought to when you upload them. After all, if an auction ends in the middle of the night, you will have far fewer last-minute bidders, so even if you construct your auctions at 2 a.m., you may want to upload them during your lunch break the next day. For an extra fee, you can also upload your listings now and schedule them to start up to two weeks from now.

You can also select individual items and click Upload to send them to eBay in batches, each separated by only a few minutes. By staggering your listings in this way, you'll facilitate further bidding by last-minute bidders who may want to purchase more than one item from you.

Another strength of Turbo Lister is that it maintains a nonexpiring archive of every auction you've ever created with it. This allows you to upload the same item several or even hundreds of times. It can also be very helpful to have access to old listings so that you can reuse descriptions or code for similar items you've sold in the past.

Using Folders

Use folders to organize your items. (If you don't see the folder list pane on the left, click the Show Folders button on the toolbar.) Go to File → New → Folder, and then drag and drop one or more items into the new folder.

Since Turbo Lister doesn't differentiate between items that have been uploaded and those that haven't, you might want to create an Uploaded folder and a Pending folder for precisely that purpose. Or, to make bookkeeping easier, create monthly folders and divide your listings into folders named June, July, August, etc.

Seller's Assistant Pro

Once an item has been uploaded to eBay, Turbo Lister's role in that auction ends. There are plenty of tools you can use to conduct any post-auction tasks, but you may instead wish to use an integrated tool that follows the progress of an auction from conception to completion.

One alternative is eBay Seller's Assistant Pro (*pages.ebay.com/sellers_assistant/pro.html*), shown in Figure 7-5, which is available for a monthly fee (or is free with some eBay Stores subscriptions **[Hack #91]**). Although its interface is somewhat more crude than Turbo Lister, it provides much more complete auction management.

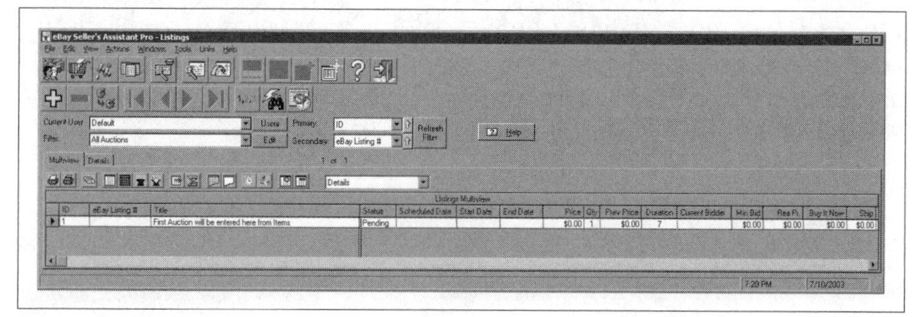

Figure 7-5. eBay Seller's Assistant Pro combines auction creation with post-auction management tools

Essentially, Seller's Assistant Pro combines Turbo Lister with a simple completed-listing tracking system **[Hack #83]** and adds some post-listing automation features **[Hack #96]** and tools to streamline communications **[Hack #95]** with customers.

HACK #94 Boost Sales with Rebates, Incentives, and Discounts

When low prices and slick photos aren't enough, take advantage of these promotions to increase your success rate.

As you've probably figured out by now, you aren't the only seller on eBay. There are millions of other people on eBay, some of whom are likely selling the same thing you are. When it comes to sniffing out deals, your customers can be ruthless, which means they may buy from one of your competitors instead of you just to save a buck or two.

The following are some ways to tip the scales in your favor.

Offer Anything Points

eBay *Anything Points* are like the prize tickets you can win at some video game parlors; get 1,000 tickets, for instance, and you can exchange them at the front desk for an oversized plastic novelty comb. The difference, of course, is that you can use Anything Points to buy stuff on eBay.

As an incentive to your buyers, you can offer Anything Points with your purchases. The catch is that you have to pay for them. Log in to the Anything Points Offer Manager (*anythingpoints.ebay.com/offer.html*) and activate the program for any or all of your currently running listings. Points cost one cent each, and are purchased on a per-dollar basis, relative to the closing costs of your listings. For instance, if you're offering 2 points per dollar, and an listing closes at a final price of $25.00, your bidder will be awarded 50 Anything Points at a cost of 50 cents to you.

The point of programs like this is that you offer incentives to your customers without lowering your prices. Of course, lower prices are another great incentive for buyers, so the choice is up to you. And if you like the idea of offering Anything Points with your purchases, you can always offset the cost by *raising* your prices (in this case, by at least 2%).

Buyers can also purchase Anything Points themselves by exchanging points from other "awards" programs. Got a bunch of airline frequent flyer miles you're not planning on using? Go to *anythingpoints.ebay.com* and exchange them for money you can spend on more junk on eBay.

Here's the best part: as a seller, you can indirectly purchase these points using your own balance of Anything Points. Although eBay won't let you pass points directly to your customers from your Anything Points balance, you can use your points to pay your eBay fees—which, in turn, are used to purchase points for your customers—by going to My eBay → My Account → Make a one-time payment (*cgi3.ebay.com/ws/eBayISAPI.dll?OneTimePayPalPayment*).

Offer Shipping Discounts

Here's a way to increase sales—and it won't cost you anything up front.

Say you charge $6.99 to ship a single item. In reality, this shipment actually costs you about $2 in materials and postage. Obviously, this allows you to turn a tidy profit of about $5 for each sale. But if you look beyond the individual sale, you'll see that there's a way to make more money while simultaneously giving your customers a better bargain.

The key is to give your customers an incentive to buy more than one item from you. For example, offer your customers discounted shipping on additional purchases, say $6.99 for the first item and $2.49 for each additional item. This means that a customer who buys three items from you will be paying you $11.97 to ship a package that probably *still* costs you no more than about $2.00 to ship. All of a sudden, you've made $10.00 in profit from a customer that otherwise would've stopped at one item.

To implement this in your listings, go to My eBay → eBay Preferences, scroll down to the Seller Preferences section, and click the Change link next to "Shipping preferences: Offer combined payment discounts."

Here, you can choose the window of time during which customers can purchase several items from you and receive the discount. If you choose a shorter window, like three days, it'll decrease the odds that your customers will use it, but it will also decrease the amount of time you'll have to wait to receive payment for any given item. In most cases, seven days is a good compromise.

PayPal Buyer Credit

PayPal offers its U.S. customers a personal line of credit, with which they can make purchases on any site (including eBay) that accepts PayPal. This allows them to more easily make purchases—especially large ones—and then pay them down over a period of time (with interest, of course).

The good news is that you'll still get your money right away if a customer pays you with Buyer Credit, and in most cases it won't cost you anything.

If you choose to offer promotional financing (e.g., no payments for six months), PayPal charges you, the seller, a percentage of the financed amount. The percentage you pay varies from 0.5% to 3.75%, depending on the type of financing you offer in your listings. The benefit to you is that you could be more likely to sell your high-priced items.

PayPal also occasionally runs Buyer Credit promotions that offer discounts to your customers who sign up for Buyer Credit (this time at no cost to you). For instance, if you were advertising Buyer Credit on a listing for a $70 fixed-price item, your customers would see an ad right on your listing page offering them $10 off the purchase price if they sign up for PayPal Buyer Credit and use it to purchase your item. You still get the full purchase price of $70—minus the 0.5% fee for offering Buyer Credit, if the purchase is financed—yet your customers pay only $60. These promotions vary, so be sure to check *pages.ebay.com/paypal/buyercredit* for the latest scoop.

Otherwise, PayPal Buyer Credit is free for sellers, and is automatically offered in all eBay listings priced at $199 and higher; you can turn this off by going to My eBay → eBay Preferences → Payment preferences. If you want to offer promotional financing, visit *www.ebay.com/offercredit*.

HACK #95 Streamline Payment Instructions

Use templates to send prewritten emails to your bidders.

As a seller, it is your responsibility to guide your bidders, helping them send payments and complete your transactions. You are the teacher as well as the seller, and—unfortunately—you'll get blamed when something goes wrong.

The email you send to your winning bidders [Hack #84] after a listing closes must communicate several different pieces of information, including the total amount to pay, the methods of payment you accept, and how to actually send payment. As a busy seller, you'll want to do everything you can to simplify this task so that notifying dozens or even hundreds of bidders takes no more time than notifying a single one. Here are three different approaches that offer three different levels of automation.

The Simple Approach

As stated at the beginning of this chapter, sellers have different needs and different capabilities. The simplest way to streamline repetitive emails is to use the Stationery feature of your email program (discussed in the Preface).

Eudora (eudora.com). To start, go to Tools → Stationery. Right-click an empty area of the Stationery window, and select New. Type the subject line and body text that you'd like to send to an average bidder, and close the Untitled window when you're done. Eudora will prompt you for a filename in which to save the stationery; thereafter, your stationery will appear in the Stationery window. Simply double-click your stationery to send it to a new customer.

Your email should be readable by as many bidders as possible. For this reason, avoid using special fonts, colors, and especially pictures in your stationery.

Outlook or Outlook Express (microsoft.com). Go to Message → New Message. Type the subject line and body text that you'd like to send to an average bidder, and then go to File → Save as Stationery when you're done. To send a message with your stationery, go to Message → New Message Using → Select Stationery, find your newly created stationery in the folder, and then click OK.

eBay/PayPal automatic notifications. If you accept PayPal payments, you can customize the automatic email [Hack #84] eBay and PayPal sends to your winning bidders.

The Hacker's Approach

This next approach involves a template, an HTML form, and a Perl script, all of which must be installed on a web server (see "Using CGI Scripts" in the Preface), even if it's a local server on your own machine. A seller enters a few specifics into the form, and the Perl script places them into the template and mails it to the bidder.

Start with this simple HTML form (replace the URL in the first line with the address of your script), saved into a file named something like *contactform.html*:

```
<form method="post" action="http://www.ebayhacks.com/cgi-bin/mail.pl">
Item Number: <input name="item" size=15>
<br>
Title: <input name="title" size=30>
<p>
Customer's name: <input name="name" size=30>
<br>
Customer's email address: <input name="email" size=30>
<p>
High bid: <input name="highbid" size=8>
<br>
Shipping: <input name="shipping" size=8>
<p>
<input type="submit" value="Send">
</form>
```

Next, grab the template from "Send Payment Instructions" [Hack #84] and save it into a plain text file called something like *template.txt*. You can customize the template to your heart's content, but for the sake of simplicity, use the same variables described in "Send Payment Instructions" [Hack #84].

Last, use the following Perl script, *mail.pl*, to tie it all together:

```
#!/usr/bin/perl

require("cgi-lib.pl");
&ReadParse;

$myemail = "paybot\@ebayhacks.com";
$template = "/usr/local/home/template.txt";
$returnurl = "http://www.ebayhacks.com/contactform.html";

if (($in{'item'} eq "") || ($in{'title'} eq "") || ($in{'email'} eq "")
          || ($in{'highbid'} eq "") || ($in{'shipping'} eq "")) {
  print "Content-type: text/html\n\n";
  print "Please fill out all the fields.\n";
  exit;
}

$total = $in{'highbid'} + $in{'shipping'};

open(MAIL,"|/usr/sbin/sendmail -t");
print MAIL "To: $in{'email'}\n";
print MAIL "From: $myemail\n";
print MAIL "Reply-To: $myemail\n";
print MAIL "Subject: $in{'title'}\n\n";

open (COVER, "$template");
  while ( $line = <COVER> ) {
   $line =~ s/{BUYERUSERNAME}/$in{'name'}/g;
   $line =~ s/{ITEM#}/$in{'item'}/g;
   $line =~ s/{TITLE}/$in{'title'}/g;
   $line =~ s/{TOTAL}/$total/g;

   if ($line eq "\n") { $line = "$line\n"; } else { chomp $line; }
   print MAIL $line;
 }
close(COVER);

close(MAIL);
print "Location: $returnurl\n\n";
```

This script requires the *cgi-lib.pl* Perl library (*http://cgi-lib.berkeley.edu/*), used to parse the arguments passed from the HTML form. This simple library works quite well and is particularly nice, because it doesn't require the installation of any Perl modules.

This script is fairly crude, but it does the job. Make sure to change the `$myemail`, `$template`, and `$returnurl` variables at the beginning so that they reflect your email address, the location of your template file, and the URL of your HTML form, respectively.

To make this even more automated, tie the script in with the eBay API (Chapter 8), which, when given an item number, will be able to retrieve the title, the name and email address of the high bidder, and the amounts of the high bid and applicable shipping charges. See "Create a Search Robot" [Hack #21] for more information on the email functionality in this script.

The Business Approach

Sellers who need to send payment instructions to hundreds or thousands of bidders will not have the time to process them individually. This situation requires auction management software [Hack #96], typically available for an additional monthly fee.

A few examples include eBay's own Selling Manager [Hack #97] or Seller's Assistant Pro [Hack #93], Auctiva eBud (*www.auctiva.com*), Andale Checkout (*www.andale.com*), and Vendio Checkout (*www.vendio.com*).

HACK #96 Use an Off-eBay Checkout System

Use this system to integrate payments with shipping and accounting.

In the old days, any seller who wanted to accept credit cards had to get a credit card merchant account. Now, payment services like PayPal [Hack #85] have made merchant accounts largely unnecessary for everyone but the largest sellers, but there are still reasons to get a merchant account. For instance, sellers who do a lot of business may be able to get a better discount rate as a credit card merchant than they could through PayPal, which essentially means they keep a larger percentage of the payments they receive. And anyone who sells merchandise outside of eBay will not want to limit their transactions only to PayPal.

If you use an off-eBay checkout system, you may wish to disable eBay's own checkout [Hack #64] to keep bidders on-track. Better yet, use a payment-collection system that integrates with eBay, such as Marketworks (*www.marketworks.com*).

But if there's any single truth when it comes to accepting payments on eBay, it's this: the more types of payment you accept, the more bids you'll get.

Getting a Merchant Account

This is one thing eBay won't do for you, and one thing that requires more than spending five minutes filling out a form on a web site. The best way to start is by contacting your bank and asking them to recommend a merchant account provider with which they're affiliated.

A representative will then talk to you and request lots of information about you and your business to help them establish your identity. You'll discuss payment plans and discount rates; don't be afraid to ask questions. When all is said and done, you'll be given a terminal or other means of entering credit card information, and you'll be ready to accept credit card payments.

Be warned: setting up a merchant account is not cheap, and is not for the faint of heart. Also, be extremely wary of Internet and email advertisements for merchant accounts.

See "Protect Yourself While Accepting Payments" [Hack #85] for some of the steps you should take to prevent chargebacks and unnecessary fees.

Accepting Credit Card Payments

Once you get your merchant account, the next step is to provide the means for your customers to transmit their credit card numbers and related information to you. This involves an HTML form and a backend script on a public web server (see the Preface). Let's start with a simple order form:

```
<form action="http://www.ebayhacks.com/cgi-bin/checkout.pl"
          method=post name="ccform" onSubmit="return confirmation( );">
<table border><tr><td width=50% valign=top>
  <table border=0 width=100%>
  <tr><td align=right valign=top>eBay auction number(s):</td>
  <td align=left valign=top><input size=12 name="invoice"></td></tr>
  <tr><td align=right valign=top>Total amount of payment:</td>
  <td align=left valign=top><input size=12 name="total"></td></tr>
  <tr><td align=right valign=top>Method of Payment:</td>

  <td align=left valign=top>
  <select name="paytype"><option selected>(please make a selection)
    <option>Visa<option>MasterCard<option>American Express</select>
  </td></tr>
  <tr><td align=right valign=top>Credit card number:</td>
  <td align=left valign=top><input size=25 name="ccnumber"></td></tr>
  <tr><td align=right valign=top>CVV code:<br>(3-4 digits after
                  your CC number, on the back of the card)</td>
  <td align=left valign=top><input size=4 maxlength=4 name="cvv"></td></tr>
  <tr><td align=right valign=top>Expiration Date:</td>
  <td align=left valign=top>
```

```
    <select name="expiremonth"><option selected value="??">(Month)
    <option value="01">1<option value="02">2<option value="03">3
    <option value="04">4<option value="05">5<option value="06">6
    <option value="07">7<option value="08">8<option value="09">9
    <option value="10">10<option value="11">11<option value="12">12
    </select>
    <select name="expireyear"><option selected value="????">(Year)
    <option>2003<option>2004<option>2005<option>2006<option>2007
    <option>2008<option>2009<option>2010<option>2011<option>2012
    <option>2013<option>2014<option>2015<option>2016<option>2017
    </select>
  </td></tr></table>
</td><td width=50% valign=top>
  <table width=100%>
  <tr><td align=right valign=top>First Name:</td>
  <td align=left valign=top><input name="firstname" size=15></td></tr>
  <tr><td align=right valign=top>Last Name:</td>
  <td align=left valign=top><input name="lastname" size=15></td></tr>
  <tr><td align=right valign=top>E-mail Address:</td>
  <td align=left valign=top><input name="email" size=30></td></tr>
  <tr><td align=right valign=top>Mailing Address:</td>
  <td align=left valign=top><input name="address1" size=30>
    <input name="address2" maxlength=50 size=30></td></tr>
  <tr><td align=right valign=top>City:</td>
  <td align=left valign=top><input name="city" size=25></td></tr>
  <tr><td align=right valign=top>State/Province:</td>
  <td align=left valign=top><input name="state" size=4></td></tr>
  <tr><td align=right valign=top>Zip:</td>
  <td align=left valign=top><input name="zip" size=10></td></tr>
  <tr><td align=right valign=top>Country:</td>
  <td align=left valign=top><input name="country" size=25></td></tr>

  <tr><td></td><td align=left valign=top>
    <input type="submit" value="Complete Your Order">
  </td></tr></table>
</td></tr></table>
```

Place this HTML form on your public web server. You'll need to make sure your server supports *Secure Sockets Layer* (SSL), so the information your customers enter can be safely submitted to your server **[Hack #33]**.

Next, install the following backend Perl script, *checkout.pl*, to process the incoming data and store it in a file:

```
   #!/usr/bin/perl

   require("cgi-lib.pl");
❶  &ReadParse;

❷  $checkoutdir = "/usr/local/home";
   $myemail = "checkout\@ebayhacks.com";
   $ordernum = time;

   # *** empty fields ***
```

```
❸ if ((!keys(%in)) || ($in{'firstname'} eq "") || ($in{'lastname'} eq "")
      || ($in{'address1'} eq "") || ($in{'city'} eq "") || ($in{'zip'} eq "")
      || (($in{'state'} eq "") && ($in{'country'} eq "")) ||
      ($in{'paytype'} eq "(please make a selection)")
      || ($in{'ccnumber'} eq "") || ($in{'cvv'} eq "") ||
      ($in{'expiremonth'} eq "??") || ($in{'expireyear'} eq "????")) {
    print &PrintHeader;
    print "<b>Error:</b> Please fill out all the fields and try again.\n";
    exit;
  }

  # *** write data file ***
❹ open(OUTFILE,">$checkoutdir/$ordernum.txt");

    print OUTFILE "[checkout]\r\n";
    print OUTFILE "email=$in{'email'}\r\n";
    print OUTFILE "firstname=$in{'firstname'}\r\n";
    print OUTFILE "lastname=$in{'lastname'}\r\n";
    print OUTFILE "address1=$in{'address1'}\r\n";
    print OUTFILE "address2=$in{'address2'}\r\n";
    print OUTFILE "city=$in{'city'}\r\n";
    print OUTFILE "state=$in{'state'}\r\n";
    print OUTFILE "zip=$in{'zip'}\r\n";
    print OUTFILE "country=$in{'country'}\r\n";
    print OUTFILE "invoice=$in{'invoice'}\r\n";
    print OUTFILE "total=$in{'total'}\r\n";
    print OUTFILE "paytype=$in{'paytype'}\r\n";
❺   print OUTFILE "cc=" . &formatccnumber($in{'ccnumber'}) . "\r\n";
    print OUTFILE "cvv=$in{'cvv'}\r\n";
    print OUTFILE "expiremonth=$in{'expiremonth'}\r\n";
    print OUTFILE "expireyear=$in{'expireyear'}\r\n";
  close(OUTFILE);

❻ open(MAIL,"|/usr/sbin/sendmail -t");
    print MAIL "To: $in{'email'}\n";
    print MAIL "From: $myemail\n";
    print MAIL "Reply-To: $myemail\n";
    print MAIL "Subject: Order Confirmation\n\n";
    print MAIL "Your payment information has been received.\n";
    print MAIL "Here are the details of your order:\n\n";
    print MAIL "   Name: $in{'firstname'} $in{'lastname'}\n";
    print MAIL "Address: $in{'address1'}\n";
    if ($in{'address2'} ne "") { print MAIL "         $in{'address2'}\n"; }
    print MAIL "         $in{'city'}, $in{'state'}  $in{'zip'}\n";
    print MAIL "         \U$in{'country'}\n\n";
    if (substr($in{'total'},0,1) ne "\$") { $in{'total'} = "\$$in{'total'}"; }
    print MAIL "US$in{'total'} will be charged to your $in{'paytype'}.\n\n";
    print MAIL "Your item(s) will be shipped as soon as possible.  If you\n";
    print MAIL "have any questions, please send them to $myemail\n";
  close(MAIL);
```

```
❼  open(MAIL,"|/usr/sbin/sendmail -t");
     print MAIL "To: $myemail\n";
     print MAIL "From: $in{'email'}\n";
     print MAIL "Reply-To: $in{'email'}\n";
     print MAIL "Subject: $in{'product'} Registration\n";
     print MAIL "A customer, $in{'firstname'} $in{'lastname'}, has\n";
     print MAIL "submitted a payment: order number #$ordernum.\n";
   close(MAIL);

❽  print &PrintHeader;
   print "Thank you for your order.\n";
   print "You will receive a confirmation email shortly.\n";
   exit;

❾  sub formatccnumber{

     $cc = "";
     $pos = 0;
     for ($i = 0; $i < length($_[0]); $i++) {
       if ("0123456789" =~ substr($_[0], $i, 1)) {
         $cc = $cc . substr($_[0], $i, 1);
         $pos++;
         if ($pos / 4 == int($pos / 4)) { $cc = $cc . " "; }
       }
     }
     return $cc;
   }
```

This script requires the *cgi-lib.pl* Perl library, which can be found at *http://cgi-lib.berkeley.edu/*, to parse the arguments passed from the HTML form.

The script is pretty straightforward. Using the *cgi-lib.pl* module, the script parses ❶ the incoming data into variables. Next, some custom variables are declared ❷, which you'll want to modify to reflect your system.

A single `if` statement ❸ checks for empty fields and spits out a generic error message if any problems are found; you'll probably want to expand this to provide more specific and appropriate error messages to your customers. The next section ❹ stores the data in a text file, but you can customize this to suit your needs.

Note that on line ❺, the credit card number is modified by the `formatccnumber` function ❾, which does nothing more than insert spaces between every four digits and throw out anything else. You'll most likely want to supplement this with code that encodes the number, so you're never storing a raw credit card number on a server that can be compromised by an intruder.

After the information is stored, three more tasks are performed: a confirmation email is sent to the customer ❻, a notification email is sent to the seller ❼, and a brief confirmation page is shown in the browser window ❽.

How to Use It

With these two elements in place, all that's left is to publicize the URL of your checkout form. You'll notice that in both "Send Payment Instructions" [Hack #84] and "Streamline Payment Instructions" [Hack #95], the example payment instructions email contains a link to a custom order form, complete with the `https://` prefix, signifying a secure SSL connection.

When a customer places an order with your checkout form, you'll automatically be sent an automatic email, and a new order record file will appear in the directory you specified on line ❶. You can further automate this hack by linking the script with your inventory system or setting it up to automatically print a prepaid shipping label [Hack #86].

Checkout Providers

Those who don't want to create their own checkout systems may prefer an extra-cost, all-in-one turnkey solution, such as any of the following.

Andale Checkout. The goal of Andale Checkout (*www.andale.com*) is to effectively eliminate the back-and-forth emails between buyers and sellers, a necessity if you sell more than 100 items a week. Figure 7-6 shows what your customers see when they use Andale Checkout to pay.

Vendio Checkout. Similar to Andale Checkout, Vendio Checkout is available with several of Vendio's subscription-based services, such as Sales Manager (*www.vendio.com*).

Marketworks. Yet another off-eBay payment-collection system, Marketworks (*www.marketworks.com*) has the distinct advantage of being properly-integrated with eBay, such that you don't have to disable checkout [Hack #64] in order to use it.

Selling Manager. eBay's Selling Manager (*pages.ebay.com/selling_manager*) [Hack #97], and Seller's Assistant Pro (*pages.ebay.com/sellers_assistant/pro.html*) [Hack #93] both rely on eBay's checkout system, but provide additional post-auction tools and automation not otherwise available.

eBay Hacks enterprises

Shopping Cart

Status: YOUR INFO — FINAL PRICE — PAYMENT RECEIVED — ITEM SHIPPED

Where would you like your item(s) to be shipped? Use Secure checkout | ▶ = required

▶ Name:
▶ Address:
Address:
▶ City: U.S. Military: APO/FPO
▶ State: Select U.S. Military: AA, AE or AP
▶ Zip/Postal Code:
▶ Country: United States
Region: International customers only
Phone:
Fax:

How would you like to pay and ship your item?

▶ Payment Options: PayPal / Personal Checks / Money Order, Cashiers Check

Do you have any special instructions?

Special Instructions:

Back Continue

Figure 7-6. Your customers will see this page when they pay via Andale Checkout

Obtain Sales Records

Extract detailed accounting data from My eBay, or do it automatically with eBay's Selling Manager.

Sellers pay the bills at eBay. Fees are assessed for the creation of listings [Hack #43] and any upgrades you choose [Hack #46], and eBay gets a percentage of the final value of each successfully completed auction.

You can check your account by going to My eBay → My Account → View Invoice → View Selected Invoice. The fees here are broken down individually and cross-referenced by item number. To see exactly how much a particular auction cost you, just search for the item number, add up the corresponding amounts shown in the Debit column, and subtract any corresponding entries in the Credit column.

Quick and Dirty Spreadsheet Import

Unfortunately, eBay's invoice isn't too flexible. To make the data more useful, you can import it into a spreadsheet to organize the data. (This will also afford you the ability to keep old invoices permanently; eBay stores them for only 18 months.) Since eBay doesn't have a formal Export feature, you'll have to do the conversion manually. In your browser, go to File → Save As in your browser, and save as an HTML file.

If you want to remove the images and search box from the page, open the HTML file in a text editor and do a few search-and-replace operations before importing it into Excel. Replace every occurrence of `<img` with `<ximg`, and every occurrence of `<input` with `<xinput`. Save the file when you're done.

Open the page in a web-capable spreadsheet application like Microsoft Excel. Highlight all the rows above the data table (about 30 rows), and remove them (Edit → Delete). Do the same for all cells below the table. Finally, sort the listing by item number. Select the entire sheet (Ctrl-A), go to Data → Sort, choose "Item" in the first box, and then click OK. It's not pretty, but it does the job in less than two minutes, and it's free.

Sales Reports & Sales Reports Plus

eBay calls them *performance metrics*, which is a fancy way of saying "all your sales figures condensed into a few oversimplified charts and graphs." eBay's Sales Reports tools allow you to view charts and graphs based on your own sales data.

There are two versions of the Sales Reports tool:

Sales Reports. Shows a summary of your sales, completed listings, success rates (percentage of listings that were successful), average sale price, and your eBay and PayPal fees. This subscription is free.

Sales Reports Plus. Includes all of the above, plus "metrics" filtered by category, listing format, or ending date or time, and the ability to download reports. This subscription costs $4.99 per month.

To add either version of the Sales Reports tool to your account, go to *pages.ebay.com/salesreports*, and click Sign Up Now. When you're done, a link to Sales Reports will appear in the Subscriptions box in My eBay.

Step Up to Selling Manager

For a monthly fee, you can have access to eBay's Selling Manager tool. Among other things, Selling Manager keeps an archive of past sales for up to four months, allowing you to download a sales history in a more convenient CSV (comma-separated value) format than the spreadsheet hack discussed earlier. CSV files can be easily imported into any spreadsheet, database, or accounting program.

Selling Manager, shown in Figure 7-7, simply appears as a tab in My eBay, replacing the standard Selling page [Hack #83].

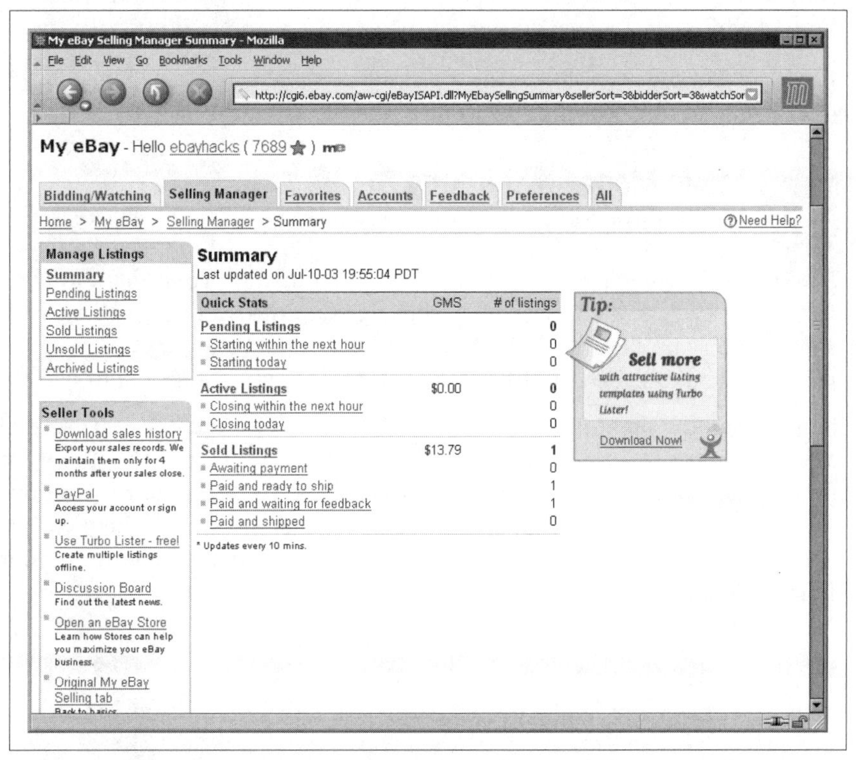

Figure 7-7. Selling Manager provides more robust sales records for an extra fee

You can subscribe to Selling Manager at *pages.ebay.com/selling_manager*. eBay offers a free 30-day trial, and even reminds you a few days before the trial period ends. Selling Manager can also be used for more general-purpose auction management tasks [Hack #95].

One of the drawbacks of Selling Manager is that it won't migrate your past completed listings to the new format; only currently running listings and auctions that end *after* you upgrade will appear in Selling Manager. However, you can always click "Original My eBay Selling tab" to temporarily revert to the old interface and view older completed listings.

Alternatives

If you prefer to do your accounting and reporting off-eBay, you can use Andale Reports (*www.andale.com*) or Auctiva eBud (*www.auctiva.com*), both of which offer some additional functionality at some additional cost.

If you only want to import your sales and fee data into QuickBooks, use eBay's Accounting Assistant (*pages.ebay.com/accountingassistant*).

HACK #98 Make Money by Linking to eBay

Earn affiliate kickbacks without selling anything on eBay.

Like many e-commerce sites, eBay offers an affiliate program that pays *you* money for each new eBay member who signs up through the links on your site. If you're promoting your own eBay auctions off-site [Hack #99], you can make it even more lucrative by turning all the links into affiliate links.

Start by signing up at *affiliates.ebay.com*. At any point there may be several affiliate programs, but the Commission Junction link is probably the most applicable. Commission Junction offers kickbacks for new user registrations (up to $45 for each new user who signs up with eBay) as well as a percentage of individual bids (up to 25 cents for each bid that results from your links). There's no fee to apply.

Creating Links with Commission Junction

eBay is one of many affiliate sites partnered with Commission Junction, a fact that will become all too clear when you first try to create links.

You'll have to dig a bit just to find eBay on the site. The quickest way is to go to Get Links → By Relationship → My Advertisers, and you'll see a list of sites with whom you've signed up. (If you join Commission Junction through eBay, you'll be automatically signed up as an eBay affiliate.)

You may see references to cryptic terms like "EPC," followed by dollar amounts that look like fees. EPC is marketing lingo for "Average Earnings Per One Hundred Clicks" and translates to the money they expect you to earn through your affiliate links.

Next, click View Links to show the assortment of links and banners you can use (there were 144 at the time of this writing). The listing can be sorted by clicking the column headers; click 7-Day EPC, for instance, to show the links that, statistically, are supposed to earn the most money.

Hacking the Links

But as we learned in *How to Lie with Statistics* by Darrell Huff, "There is terror in numbers." Instead of using the links that Commission Junction says are most profitable, you might want to use the links that will further your specific interests and have the least impact on your site.

One of the most useful is Link ID 5463217, *Flexible Destination Tool*, which lets you link to any specific page at eBay. Since this tool may have expired by the time you read this, you may have to wade through all the obnoxious banner ads to find the most recent equivalent, but try typing the word "flexible" into CJ's search box.

The details box for Link 5463217 will eventually lead you back to eBay's Flexible Destination Tool (*affiliates.ebay.com/tools/linking/*), shown in Figure 7-8.

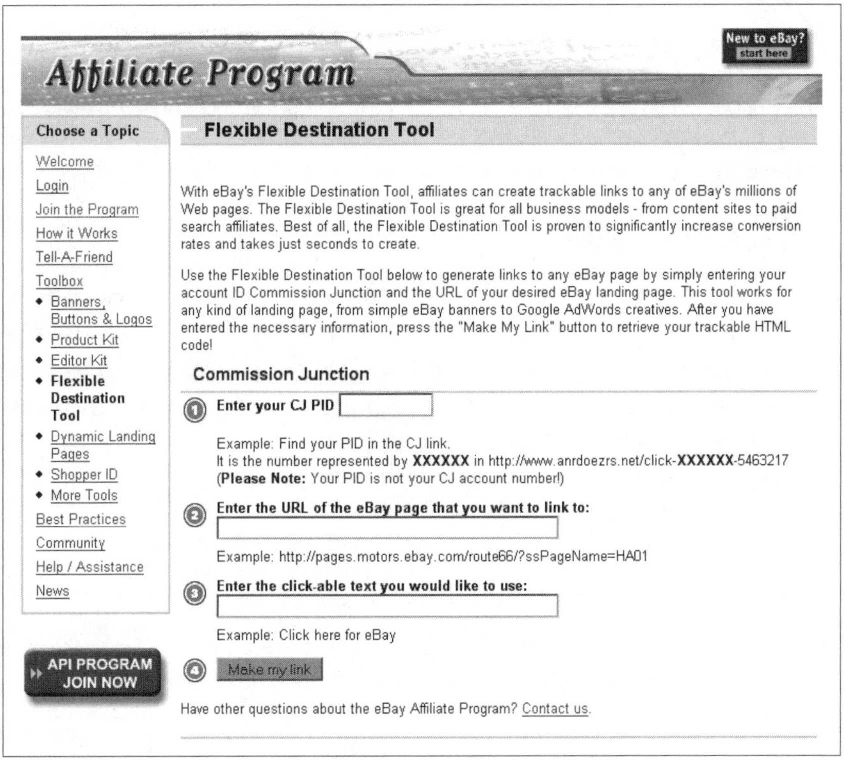

Affiliate Program
New to eBay? start here
Choose a Topic
Welcome
Login
Join the Program
How it Works
Tell-A-Friend
Toolbox
• Banners, Buttons & Logos
• Product Kit
• Editor Kit
• Flexible Destination Tool
• Dynamic Landing Pages
• Shopper ID
• More Tools
Best Practices
Community
Help / Assistance
News
API PROGRAM JOIN NOW
Flexible Destination Tool
With eBay's Flexible Destination Tool, affiliates can create trackable links to any of eBay's millions of Web pages. The Flexible Destination Tool is great for all business models - from content sites to paid search affiliates. Best of all, the Flexible Destination Tool is proven to significantly increase conversion rates and takes just seconds to create.
Use the Flexible Destination Tool below to generate links to any eBay page by simply entering your account ID Commission Junction and the URL of your desired eBay landing page. This tool works for any kind of landing page, from simple eBay banners to Google AdWords creatives. After you have entered the necessary information, press the "Make My Link" button to retrieve your trackable HTML code!
Commission Junction
1 Enter your CJ PID
Example: Find your PID in the CJ link.
It is the number represented by XXXXXX in http://www.anrdoezrs.net/click-XXXXXX-5463217
(Please Note: Your PID is not your CJ account number!)
2 Enter the URL of the eBay page that you want to link to:
Example: http://pages.motors.ebay.com/route66/?ssPageName=HA01
3 Enter the click-able text you would like to use:
Example: Click here for eBay
4 Make my link
Have other questions about the eBay Affiliate Program? Contact us.

Figure 7-8. Create links to specific pages with the Flexible Destination Tool

Here, you enter your CJ PID, a seven-digit number representing your Commission Junction account (but not the same as your account number, paradoxically), the URL [Hack #13] of the destination page, and the caption for the text link. After a bit of fussing with this page, you'll get a URL that looks something like this:

```
http://www.anrdoezrs.net/click-xxxxxxx-5463217?loc=http%3A//listings.ebay.com/
aw/plistings/list/all/category19116/index.html
```

where *xxxxxxx* is your CJ PID, and the URL following the `loc` parameter is merely the URL you typed on the last page. Likewise, a link to eBay's Advanced Search page will look something like this:

```
http://www.anrdoezrs.net/click-xxxxxxx-5463217?loc=http%3A//search.ebay.com/
```

You may notice that some of the characters present in the original URL have been converted to hex codes to keep them from interfering with the link. For instance, the colon (:) becomes `%3A`, the ampersand (&) becomes `%26`, the question mark (?) becomes `%3F`, and the equals sign (=) becomes `%3D`.

If you feel like doing this simple conversion manually, you can create all your links without having to repeatedly return to the Flexible Destination Tool. For instance, a link to a specific listing will look like this:

```
http://www.anrdoezrs.net/click-xxxxxxx-5463217?loc=http%3A//cgi.ebay.com/ws/
eBayISAPI.dll%3FViewItem%26item%3Ditemnumber
```

where *`itemnumber`* is the item number of your auction. You can even use these links right in your listing descriptions [Hack #60] or when advertising your listings on another site [Hack #99].

A Simplified Search Box

Among the 140+ link types at Commission Junction are several search boxes you can put on your site. Unfortunately, they all come with banner advertisements, and most of them don't work properly.

Instead, use this simple form. The JavaScript simply assembles a URL from the CJ URL found earlier in this hack, the standard eBay Search URL [Hack #13], and the words your visitors type into the box:

```
<script language="JavaScript1.1">
<!--
var baseurl = "http://www.anrdoezrs.net/click-xxxxxxx-5463217?loc=";
var ebaysearch = "http://search.ebay.com/"

function buildurl(form,url){
  document.location = baseurl + ebaysearch + form.satitle.value;
}
```

```
// -->
</script>

<form action="http://search.ebay.com/" onsubmit="buildurl(this); return
false;" method="get">
  <nobr>
  <input name="satitle" maxlength=300 size=20 value="">
  <input type="submit" value="Search">
  </nobr>
</form>
```

The only thing you have to do to get this to work is replace *xxxxxxx* with your Commission Junction ID.

See Also

- See "Allow Visitors to Search Through Your Listings" **[Hack #61]** for details on making this box look like the standard eBay search box.

HACK #99 Advertise Your eBay Listings

Use the eBay Editor Kit and Merchant Kit to promote your listings off-eBay, or promote your eBay Store right in eBay search results.

The age-old practice of advertising is alive and well on the Net, so why be left out? There are several ways to advertise your eBay listings to help turn your small business into a big one, and what's better is that most of them are free.

Once you've signed up with one of eBay's affiliate programs **[Hack #98]**, you can use either of eBay's two tools for creating lists of auctions on your own site. Not only will this help promote your auctions and increase traffic to specific items, but you'll make money for each new user who signs up and for each bid that is placed as a result of your links.

Alternatively, you can promote your listings to other eBay members by paying (as little as US$20) for banner ads to appear in eBay search results, as described later in this hack.

The Editor Kit

The Editor Kit couldn't be slicker. Just go to *cgi3.ebay.com/ws/eBayISAPI.dll?EKCreate* and fill out the fields, as shown in Figure 7-9.

Select Commission Junction in the Provider box and enter your CJ ID in the Tracking ID field (paradoxically, you leave the Commission Junction SID field blank). The rest of the fields should be self-explanatory, and the only one that is required is the Search Term. Since you probably want to limit the search to your own listings, type your eBay Member ID in the eBay Seller IDs box.

Create Your Editor Kit
Download User's Guide

Tracking Services

Provider *
Commission Junction
Not an affiliate? Join now

Tracking ID
394578349
Help for Tracking and Payment
If you choose Mediaplex as your Provider, please contact your eBay account manager for your Tracking ID

Commission Junction SID
What is SID?
Enter up to 30 alpha-numeric characters as your tracking code for this Editor Kit (e.g., U2 DVD 1, Harry Potter).

Search Criteria

At least one of the first three search criteria are required.*

Search term
test
Tips
Search title **and** description to find more items

eBay Seller IDs
your_ebay_id
See items only from these sellers.
Enter up to 10 User IDs separated by commas (example: userid1,userid2)

Category numbers
Enter up to 10 category numbers separated by commas. See all Category numbers

Figure 7-9. Use the Editor Kit to create a custom search results listing on your own site

When you're done, click Preview to create the JavaScript code and show the resulting search box, shown in Figure 7-10.

Hacking the Editor Kit

The big drawback to the Editor Kit is that it shows only results of a keyword search; you can't leave the Search Term field blank in order to show all your auctions. But with a little hacking, you can make the Editor Kit do anything you want.

The code produced by the Editor Kit is just a long URL—encased in a `<script></script>` structure—with all the details you specified on the Create Your Editor Kit page in plain sight.

If you've specified a seller ID (such as your own), you can hack the code to show all your current listings. Just find the query parameter in your code:

```
...&amp;query=my_search_keywords&amp;...
```

an ebaY marketplace

Product	Price	Bids	Time Left
USB CABLE for OLYMPUS CAMEDIA digital camera	$8.95	-	2h 06m
Kodak Leather Like Digital Camera Bag	$2.95	-	2h 07m
~NEW~ EN-EL3 Li-Ion Camera Battery Nikon D100	$9.99	-	2h 07m
USB Cable for Toshiba PDR-2300 Camera	$6.90	-	2h 07m
Polaroid PhotoMax Digital 320 Camera	$5.00	1	2h 08m
NEW CASIO EXILIM EX-Z3 DIGITAL CAMERA W/ DOCK	$300.00	8	2h 08m
USB Cable for Canon PowerShot Pro90 IS Camera	$12.90	Buy It Now	2h 08m
Olympus IS-1 Quartzdate Auto 35mm camera ED	$31.00	4	2h 09m
DIGITAL CAMERA 3 CAMERAS IN ONE w/video NEW !	$34.99	-	2h 09m
FED-2 Russian Camera LEICA copy 35mm NR	$10.50	2	2h 09m
ZORKI-4 Russian Camera Leica copy /industar50	$24.99	-	2h 09m

View all 37698 items on eBay — disclaimer

Figure 7-10. The code produced by the Editor Kit will create this dynamic listing on your site

Remove the search term you typed on the last page. When you're done, it'll look like this:

```
...&amp;query=&amp;...
```

Save the code in an *.html* file and open it in your browser to view the results.

If you want to take this a bit further, you can use the Editor Kit in conjunction with a simple search box **[Hack #62]**. Start by editing your Editor Kit code; find the query parameter again, and replace it with the following:

```
...&amp;query=@query@&amp;...
```

Save the Editor Kit code into a file named *ek.txt* when you're done, and then place this simple HTML form elsewhere in the file:

```
<form action="http://my.server/cgi-bin/ek.pl">
  <nobr>
  <input name="satitle" maxlength=300 size=20 value="">
  <input type="submit" value="Search">
  </nobr>
</form>
```

Just replace *`http://my.server/cgi-bin/`* with the full URL of the CGI directory on your own web server (see the Preface). Save *ek.txt* when you're done.

And here's the Perl script that does all the work:

```
#!/usr/bin/perl

require("cgi-lib.pl");
&ReadParse;
$content = "";
open (COVER, "ek.txt");
```

```
    while ( $line = <COVER> ) {
     $line =~ s/\@query\@/$in{'satitle'}/g;
     $content = $content . $line;
    }
  close (COVER);
  print $content;
  exit;
```

Save this script into a plain text file, name the file *ek.pl*, and place it in the cgi folder on your server. You'll also need to include the *cgi-lib.pl* Perl library [Hack #95] in the same folder.

To run the hack, open up the web form, type a search query, and click Search. Your browser sends the query to the Perl script, which will insert it into your Editor Kit code, and output it to the browser. If you want the output to appear in another page, you can use the `<iframe>` HTML tag (just not in eBay listings).

Another way to get custom search results on your own site is to use the Merchant Kit, next.

The Merchant Kit

Like the Editor Kit, the Merchant Kit creates simple JavaScript snippets, but it focuses on category listings rather than search results.

Start by going to *pages.ebay.com/api/merchantkit.html* and using the Merchant Kit, shown in Figure 7-11, to create your code.

The code is little more than a URL that can be easily tweaked without having to return to the Merchant Kit. The resulting box, shown in Figure 7-12, lists all your auctions, optionally filtered by category.

Advertise Your eBay Store

If you have an eBay Store [Hack #91], you have the option of buying banner ads that appear at the top eBay pages whenever you perform a search. Although the banners cost money, this form of advertising (called eBay Keywords) targets an essential market for your business: existing eBay users.

Here's how to put your own ads on eBay search results. First, create some listings [Hack #43] for your eBay Store, if you haven't done so already. Next, go to *ebay.admarketplace.net*, and click Get Started Now.

Once you've created an account, you start your ad campaign using the Campaign Creation page shown in Figure 7-13.

On this page, type a name for your advertising campaign and specify a budget by typing a dollar amount into the Campaign Funds field (the minimum is US$20). Ads are delivered to other eBay customers as they search, and you're charged a fixed amount for each ad displayed (whether or not someone clicks it).

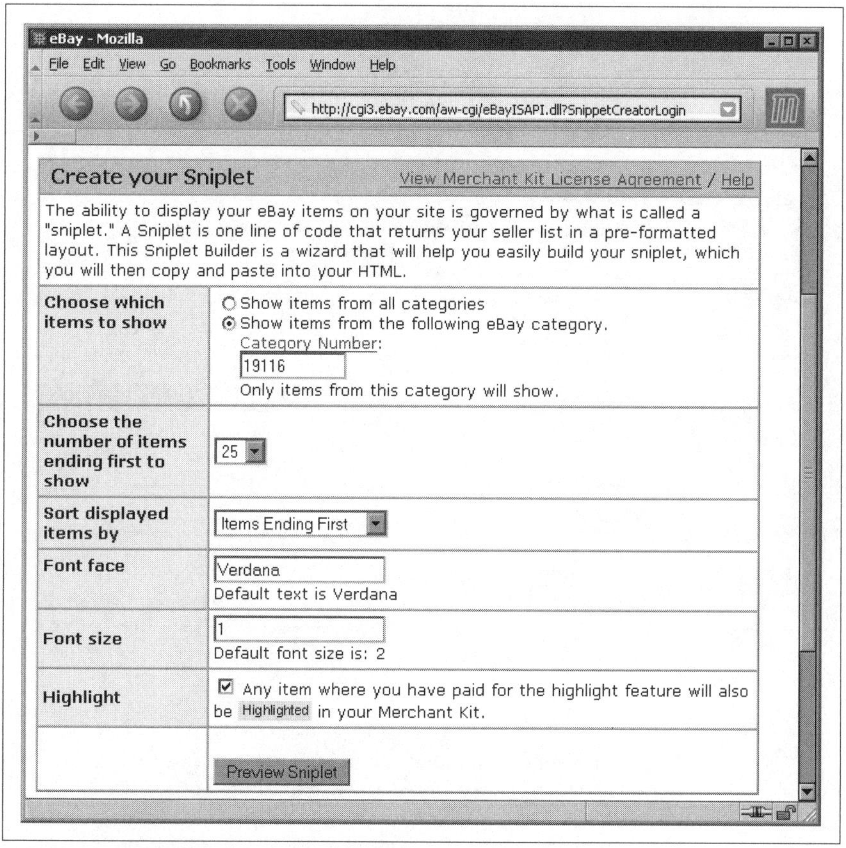

Figure 7-11. The Merchant Kit has only a few options, but the code it creates is not limited by search terms

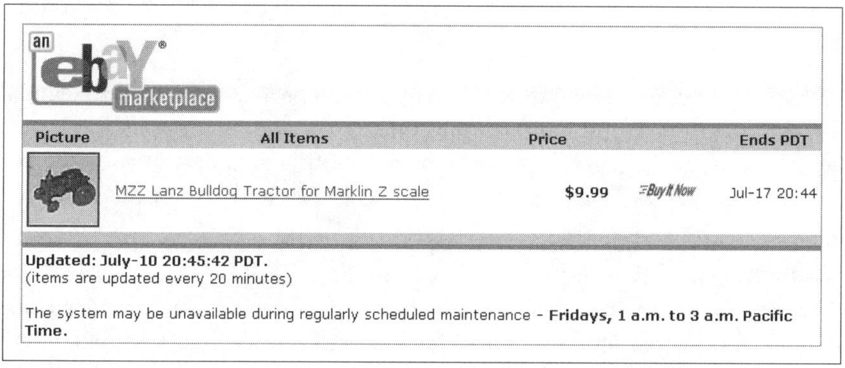

Figure 7-12. Use the Merchant Kit to produce dynamic listings of all your auctions on any site

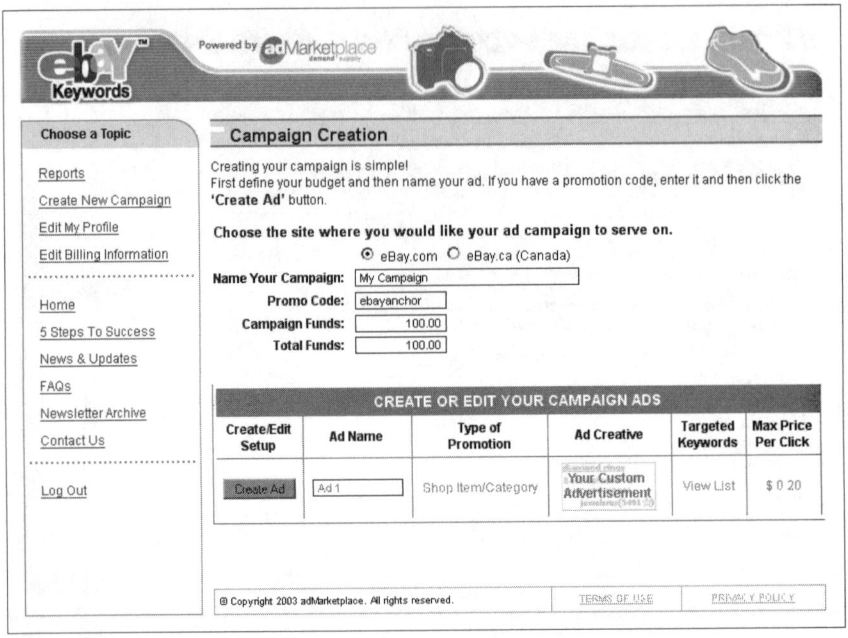

Figure 7-13. *Use the Campaign Creation page to build banner ads that appear in eBay search results*

> You can also enter a Promo Code here. If you've opted for one of the higher-level eBay Stores tiers (e.g., Featured or Anchor), eBay gives you an allowance of sorts (up to $300 per month at the time of this writing), which you can spend on ad space. For instance, if you have a Featured Store, you get $90 worth of advertising for free. Check eBay's Promoting Your Store page at *pages.ebay.com/storefronts/Promoting.html* for the latest promotions.

When you're done, click Create Ad. Next, you'll be able to customize your ad by choosing a link destination—presumably the address of your eBay Store—from the Ad Targeting box, and typing a subtitle to appear in your ad. The "5 Steps To Success" page has some good examples and tips for this step.

The next step is the most important, as it's where you select the keywords **[Hack #47]** that will bring up your ad. If you specify "plastic sushi," for instance, your ad will appear whenever someone searches for "plastic sushi." If you choose particularly arcane and specific keywords, your ad won't appear as often, but your campaign funds will last longer and your ad will better target those who are likely to make a purchase.

When you're done, your ads will begin to appear in eBay search results whenever someone searches for your keywords. The ads will continue to appear until you've exhausted your campaign funds, so be careful not to accelerate the process by needlessly "testing" your keywords.

HACK #100 Accept PayPal Payments from Your Own Site

Integrate PayPal into your web site with a simple HTML form.

PayPal is more than a standalone auction payment service: it's an engine that you can use to power transactions on or off eBay. Any site that sells products can accept PayPal payments, and can do so without forcing customers to manually type the seller's email address and a dollar amount into their browsers.

Somewhat like an API, PayPal provides a simple HTTP interface to their payment system that works just like the Pay Now button at the top of completed eBay auctions. This allows you, as the seller, to streamline the payment process by specifying an amount, a product name, and any other bits of information you'd like to associate with the payment.

There are three ways to integrate PayPal into your site: URLs, Pay Now buttons, and Shopping Cart forms. Anyone with a PayPal account can use these links; you don't need to sign up for any special programs or install any special software. All you need is a basic working knowledge of URLs **[Hack #13]** and HTML **[Hack #52]**.

> Once you've set up a PayPal payment link, you can use Instant Payment Notification **[Hack #101]** to have your server handle the payment automatically. For more tips relating to payment buttons and Instant Payment Notifications, check out *PayPal Hacks* by Shannon Sofield, Dave Nielsen, and Dave Burchell.

Just a Link

The simpler of the three methods involves nothing more than a link placed on your site. For instance, this URL:

```
https://www.paypal.com/xclick/business=paybot@ebayhacks.com&item_
name=wicket&amount=58.00&no_note=1
```

specifies the email address (`paybot@ebayhacks.com`), the product name (`wicket`), and the amount (`$58.00`).

If you want to link the URL to an image (like the PayPal logo), use this code:

```
<a href="https://www.paypal.com/xclick/business=paybot@ebayhacks.com&item_
name=wicket&amount=58.00&no_note=1"><img src="https://www.paypal.com/images/
x-click-but01.gif" border=0></a>
```

Other Pay Now button images are available at PayPal. When your customers click the link, they will see a window like the one in Figure 7-14. When they click Continue, the only things they'll be able to change on the next page are the funding source and the shipping address. If you want your customers to be able to enter a note or special instructions, remove the `&no_note=1` parameter from the URL.

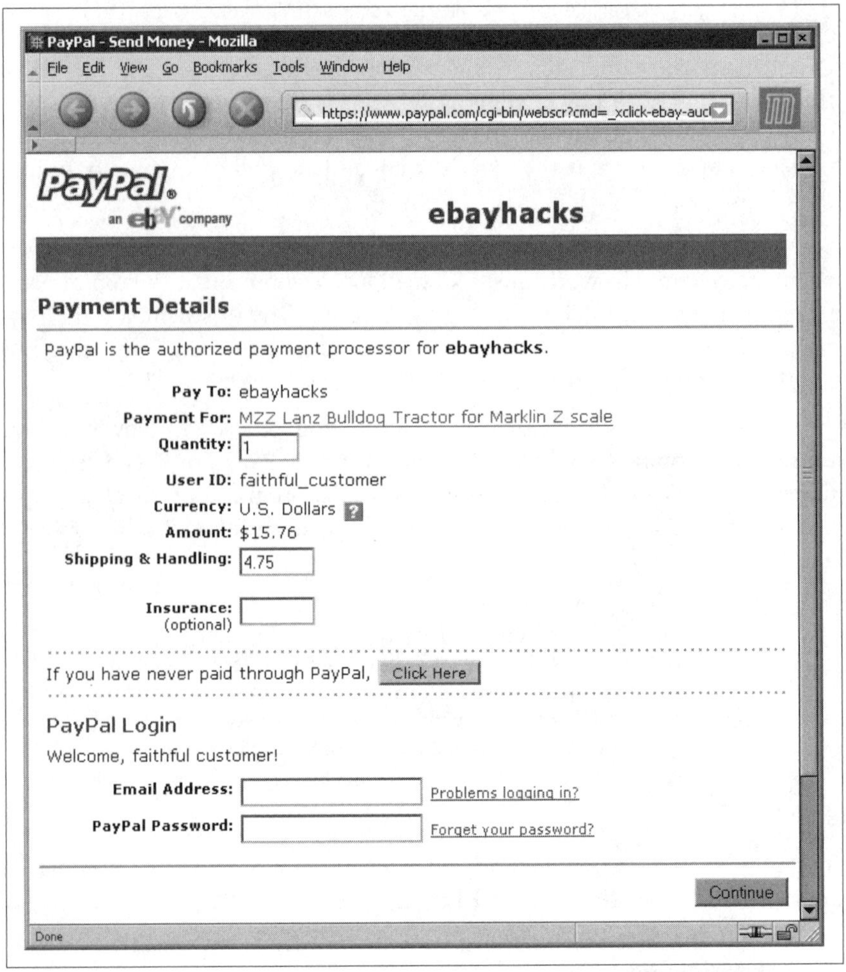

Figure 7-14. The PayPal checkout counter shows your product and the price

Look out for devious customers who might try to short-change you by altering the amount in the URL. Make sure to verify the amount before shipping your product. Use a form (described next) for a slightly more tamper-proof solution.

You can further customize your customers' experience by including additional fields in the URL, many of which are discussed in the next section.

The Form

The more robust approach requires a little more code:

```
<form action="https://www.paypal.com/cgi-bin/webscr" method="post">
<input type="hidden" name="cmd" value="_xclick">
<input type="hidden" name="business" value="paybot@ebayhacks.com">
<input type="hidden" name="return"
                 value="http://www.ebayhacks.com/thankyou.html">
<input type="hidden" name="cancel_return"
                 value="http://www.ebayhacks.com/cancelled.html">
<input type="hidden" name="no_note" value="1">
<input type="hidden" name="item_name" value="Extra-Strenth Wicket">
<input type="hidden" name="item_number" value="63123">
<input type="hidden" name="amount" value="$77.00">
<input type="hidden" name="on0" value="Name">
<input type="hidden" name="on1" value="Color">

Please type your name:
<input name="os0" value="" maxlength=60 size=22>
<p>
Please choose a color
<select name="os1">
  <option>Mustard Yellow
  <option>Metallic Puce
  <option>Chartreuse
  <option>Clear
  <option>Candy Apple Gray
</select>
<p>

<input type="submit" name="submit" value="Continue...">
</form>
```

The advantages of the form interface are clear: in addition to the standard fields (listed at the beginning in the hidden `<input>` tags), you can include up to two custom fields to be filled out by your customers. The names of the custom fields are specified in the hidden `on0` and `on1` fields, and their contents are specified in the `os0` and `os1` fields. In the example, the custom fields, `name` and `color`, are comprised of a standard text box and a drop-down listbox, respectively.

Also new in this form are the `return` and `cancel_return` fields, which contain the URLs to which your customers will be sent when they complete (or cancel) the payment process, and the `item_number` field, which can be your stock number (SKU) or part number.

If you don't want to build the form yourself, PayPal will do it for you. Go to Merchant Tools → Web Site Payments → Buy Now Buttons to choose the options you want and review the resulting HTML code.

Shopping Cart

PayPal also supports a shopping cart interface in which customers can specify—and pay for—multiple items from your store. The code is nearly identical to the form in the previous section, except for two fields. First, change the contents of the `cmd` field to `_cart` (with the underscore), like this:

```
<input type="hidden" name="cmd" value="_cart">
```

Next, add the following new field:

```
<input type="hidden" name="add" value="1">
```

Finally, change the caption of the submit button like this:

```
<input type="submit" name="submit" value="Add to Cart...">
```

When your customers add items to their shopping carts, they'll see a page like the one in Figure 7-15.

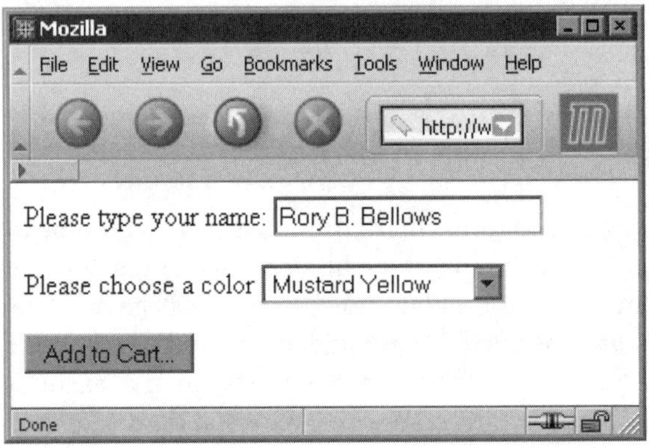

Figure 7-15. Integrate a PayPal shopping cart interface with a simple HTML form

See Also

- You'll be notified of any completed sales with a payment notification email to your registered PayPal email address. To eliminate the human interaction required to process the emails and further integrate your business with PayPal, you can use Instant Payment Notification [Hack #101].
- You can fine-tune the way PayPal is integrated with your completed eBay listings by customizing the checkout process [Hack #64].

Process PayPal Payments Automatically

Use Instant Payment Notification to fulfill orders without human intervention.

When a bidder pays for an auction with PayPal or sends a PayPal payment from your online store [Hack #100], PayPal notifies you with a single email. Since the last thing any busy seller wants to do is deal with a bunch of emails, PayPal offers the free Instant Payment Notification (IPN) feature.

Setting Up IPN

The premise is pretty simple: as soon as a payment is received, PayPal contacts your server and submits all the details of the transaction to your script. Your script then processes and stores the data in whatever way you see fit.

To start using IPN, all you need to do is enable the feature and specify the URL of your script. Log into PayPal and go to My Account → Profile → Instant Payment Notification Preferences. Click Edit to change the current settings.

The Code

The following Perl script* does everything required to accept IPN notifications; all you need to do is modify the $workdir variable to reflect a valid path on your server:

```
#!/usr/bin/perl
$workdir = "/usr/local/home";

❶ read (STDIN, $query, $ENV{'CONTENT_LENGTH'});
❷ $query .= '&cmd=_notify-validate';

use LWP::UserAgent;
$ua = new LWP::UserAgent;
$req = new HTTP::Request 'POST','http://www.paypal.com/cgi-bin/webscr';
$req->content_type('application/x-www-form-urlencoded');
$req->content($query);
❸ $res = $ua->request($req);

❹ @pairs = split(/&/, $query);
$count = 0;
foreach $pair (@pairs) {
  ($name, $value) = split(/=/, $pair);
  $value =~ tr/+/ /;
  $value =~ s/%([a-fA-F0-9][a-fA-F0-9])/pack("C", hex($1))/eg;
```

* Portions based on sample code by PayPal and David W. Van Abel (*Perlsources.com*).

```
    $variable{$name} = $value;
    $count++;
  }

❺ if ($variable{'payment_status'} ne "Completed") { &SendOK( ); }
❻ if (-e "$workdir/$variable{'txn_id'}.txt") { &SendOK( ); }

❼ open(OUTFILE,">$workdir/$variable{'txn_id'}.txt");
    print OUTFILE "[ipn_data]\r\n";
    print OUTFILE "email=$variable{'payer_email'}\r\n";
    print OUTFILE "firstname=$variable{'first_name'}\r\n";
    print OUTFILE "lastname=$variable{'last_name'}\r\n";
    print OUTFILE "address1=$variable{'address_street'}\r\n";
    print OUTFILE "address2=$variable{'address_status'}\r\n";
    print OUTFILE "city=$variable{'address_city'}\r\n";
    print OUTFILE "state=$variable{'address_state'}\r\n";
    print OUTFILE "zip=$variable{'address_zip'}\r\n";
    print OUTFILE "country=$variable{'address_country'}\r\n";
    print OUTFILE "product=$variable{'item_name'}\r\n";
    print OUTFILE "quantity=$variable{'quantity'}\r\n";
    print OUTFILE "total=$variable{'payment_gross'}\r\n";
    print OUTFILE "custom1=$variable{'option_selection1'}\r\n";
    print OUTFILE "custom2=$variable{'option_selection2'}\r\n";
  close(OUTFILE);
❽ &SendOK( );


  sub SendOK( ) {
❾   print "content-type: text/plain\n\nOK\n";
    exit;
  }
```

This script requires the `LWP::UserAgent` Perl module by Alan E. Derhaag, available at *search.cpan.org/perldoc?LWP::UserAgent*, necessary to facilitate communication with the PayPal server. See the Preface for installation instructions.

Here's how it works. First, the data received from PayPal ❶ is appended with an additional variable ❷, and then sent back to PayPal for validation ❸. This will prevent an unscrupulous user from attempting to trick your server into thinking an order has been received. Immediately thereafter, PayPal returns the data, and the script parses it into separate variables ❹.

Next, the script checks to see if the transaction status is "Completed" ❺ and if the transaction ID (txn_id) has been processed ❻. If either test fails, the script quits by way of the `SendOK` function.

Finally, the script writes the pertinent information to a file ❼, the name of which is simply the transaction ID. You'll undoubtedly want to change the fields that are recorded, the format of the file, and the path (`$workdir`) in which the files are stored.

To ensure that your server is properly notified of the transaction, PayPal sends the data repeatedly until it receives an OK signal ❾ from your script. Furthermore, a single transaction can trigger a bunch of notifications, which is why you'll need to filter out incomplete or duplicate entries (lines ❺ and ❻).

Hacking the Hack

Ultimately, the only thing this script does is read the data received from IPN, validate it, and store it in a text file. The format of the file in this example is that of a Windows INI Configuration File, making it easy for a Windows application to read the data using the `GetPrivateProfileString` API call.

Naturally, you can store the data in whatever format you choose, including a database or even a specially formatted email. IPN is commonly used for automatic order fulfillment, wherein the server sends the customer a software registration key, subscription password, or other electronically transmitted product. But you can also use IPN to integrate incoming payments with your shipping system to produce prepaid shipping labels [Hack #86] automatically.

PayPal email notifications can sometimes be unreliable, either taking a while to show up or not showing up at all. You can remedy this by supplementing with your own email notification by placing the following immediately before line ❽:

```
open(MAIL,"|/usr/sbin/sendmail -t");
  print MAIL "To: $variable{'receiver_email'}\n";
  print MAIL "From: $variable{'payer_email'}\n";
  print MAIL "Reply-To: $variable{'payer_email'}\n";
  print MAIL "Subject: New IPN Order Received\n\n";
  print MAIL "Order $variable{'txn_id'} has been received via IPN\n";
  print MAIL "and stored in file $workdir/$variable{'txn_id'}.txt\n";
close(MAIL);
```

See Also

- Full documentation, including a list of all supported fields, is available in the PayPal Instant Payment Notification Manual, available at *www.paypal.com*. Further examples and commercial versions of the script are available from a variety of sources, including *www.ipnhosting.com*, *www.paypalipn.com*, and *www.perlsources.com*.
- The best single resource for PayPal code, tips, and strategies is *PayPal Hacks* by Shannon Sofield, Dave Nielsen, and Dave Burchell.

CHAPTER EIGHT

The eBay API

Hacks 102–125

eBay is more than just a web site. It's a platform upon which you can build your own applications and with which you can extend your business.

The eBay *Application Programming Interface* (API) is a set of functions you can integrate with your applications to communicate directly with eBay. Use the API to retrieve details about an auction, perform searches, list a seller's current items, and even create new auction listings. Think of the API as a back door of sorts, a way for developers to interact with the eBay engine and auction database without using the standard web interface.

The possibilities of such a system are limitless. Businesses can use the eBay API to link their inventory and sales databases with listings, cutting out most of the labor that would otherwise be involved in selling large numbers of items. Developers can use the API to construct auction management applications for themselves, their companies, or even for commercial sale. And, of course, individual buyers and sellers on eBay can use the API to do a little friendly hacking, as described throughout the rest of this chapter.

How the eBay API Works

The underlying process of placing a call to the API is conceptually quite simple. First, your program sends an XML string to eBay with the name of the API call and any additional required fields. Here's an example XML request for the `GetSearchResults` function:

```
<?xml version='1.0' encoding='iso-8859-1'?>
<request>
  <RequestUserId>my_user_id</RequestUserId>
  <RequestPassword>my_password</RequestPassword>
  <ErrorLevel>1</ErrorLevel>
  <DetailLevel>0</DetailLevel>
  <Verb>GetSearchResults</Verb>
  <SiteId>0</SiteId>
```

```
    <Query>![CDATA[*abbey road*]]</Query>
</request>
```

eBay then responds with more XML, from which your application extracts the desired data. The components of the input and output XML will vary with the particular function and the needs of the application, but the overall methodology is the same regardless of the API call being used.

Every single XML request sent to eBay must contain three developer-specific keys, `DevID`, `AppID`, and `CertID`, all of which are provided to you when you join eBay's Developers Program.

At some point in 2006, eBay will be deprecating this XML-based API schema in favor of a new Web Services SOAP API. At that point, you'll likely need to replace the *ebay.pl* and *config.pl* scripts in the next section with new SOAP-compatible versions. By the time you read this, this migration may have already taken place. Please visit *www.ebayhacks.com* for any applicable updates and code.

Getting Started

Before using the eBay API, you will need to sign up at *developer.ebay.com*. There are four different license types (or *tiers*):

Individual. This is the free license designed for individual developers. It includes full access to all API calls, but limits usage to only 50 calls per day. The only tangible cost is Certification [Hack #102], required for all users.

Developers using the Individual license have no access to developer technical support (though they can access developer forums), and cannot use Platform Notifications [Hack #118] or sell their programs commercially.

Basic. The lowest commercial tier, Basic includes 30,000 calls per month (significantly more than the 50 allotted to Individual developers), with a nominal charge for additional calls. But it also has an annual fee and a higher certification cost, all offset by the ability to create commercial applications (like auction management tools).

Professional. The Professional tier is similar to the Basic tier, but with more expensive annual membership fees, less expensive API usage fees, and more free technical support incidents.

Enterprise. The highest commercial tier, Enterprise differs from the Basic and Professional tiers only in the fees and number of free technical support incidents.

Once you've signed up, you can log in and download the eBay API Software Development Kit (SDK).

Although the SDK comes with documentation, the online API Technical Documentation at *developer.ebay.com/DevZone/docs/API_Doc/* is the best source for technical information about the API.

Using the Scripts in This Chapter

All of the example scripts in this chapter are written in Perl. Not only is Perl code concise and extremely easy to read, but Perl interpreters are freely available for nearly every computing platform on earth.

Every script in this chapter relies on the following two scripts. Make sure all your scripts are stored in the same directory. As with all the scripts in this book, you can download them from *www.ebayhacks.com*.

ebay.pl

This script contains the common code used in all scripts in this chapter, including the aptly named call_api function:

```
#!/usr/bin/perl
use LWP::UserAgent;
use HTTP::Request;
use HTTP::Headers;
use XML::Simple;
require 'config.pl';

sub call_api {
  my ($arg) = @_;
  return undef unless $arg->{Verb};
  $arg->{RequestToken} = $authtoken unless defined $arg->{RequestToken};
  $arg->{DetailLevel} = "0" unless defined $arg->{DetailLevel};
  $arg->{ErrorLevel} = "1" unless defined $arg->{ErrorLevel};

  my $ua   = LWP::UserAgent->new;
  my $head = HTTP::Headers->new
       ('X-EBAY-API-COMPATIBILITY-LEVEL' => $compat_level,
        'X-EBAY-API-SESSION-CERTIFICATE' => "$dev_id;$app_id;$cert_id",
                   'X-EBAY-API-DEV-NAME' => $dev_id,
                   'X-EBAY-API-APP-NAME' => $app_id,
                  'X-EBAY-API-CERT-NAME' => $cert_id,
                  'X-EBAY-API-CALL-NAME' => $arg->{Verb},
                     'X-EBAY-API-SITEID' => $site_id,
               'X-EBAY-API-DETAIL-LEVEL' => $arg->{DetailLevel}
  );

  my $body = XMLout($arg,
                keeproot => 1,
                 keyattr => undef,
                  noattr => 1,
```

```
                rootname => 'request',
                 xmldecl => 1);
  print STDERR "calling: $body" if $DEBUG;
  my $req = HTTP::Request->new("POST", $api_url, $head, $body);
  my $rsp = $ua->request($req);
  print STDERR "response: $rsp->content" if $DEBUG;
  return undef if !$rsp->is_success;
  return XMLin($rsp->content,
                 forcearray => [qw/Error Item FeedbackDetailItem/],
                    keyattr => undef);
}

sub print_error {
  my ($xml) = @_;
  foreach (@{$xml->{Errors}{Error}}) {
    print "$_->{Severity}: $_->{LongMessage}\n";
  }
}

sub formatdate {
  ($sec,$min,$hour,$mday,$mon,$year,$wday,$yday,$isdst) = gmtime($_[0]);
  $year = $year + 1900;
  $mon = $mon + 1;
  return sprintf("%0.4d-%0.2d-%0.2d %0.2d:%0.2d:%0.2d",
                               $year,$mon,$mday,$hour,$min,$sec);
}

return true;
```

config.pl

Next, the *config.pl* script is used to store personal information such as the developer keys eBay sends you, your username and password, and other variables used throughout this chapter.

```
#!/usr/bin/perl
$api_url      = 'https://temp-sandbox.ebay.com/ws/api.dll';

$loc          = ".com";
$itemurl      = "http://cgi.ebay$loc/ws/eBayISAPI.dll?ViewItem&item=";
$compat_level = 399;
$site_id      = 0; # US
$DEBUG        = 0;

$dev_id       = 'your_DevID';
$app_id       = 'your_AppID';
$cert_id      = 'your_CertID';
$authtoken    = 'your_auth_token';
$selleremail  = "your_email_address";
$localdir     = "c:\my folder\";

return true;
```

Make sure to fill in all the "your" fields in *config.pl* with your information. eBay provides the `DevID`, `AppID`, and `CertID` keys when you join the eBay Developers Program. Use the Authentication Token Tool [Hack #103] to generate `$authtoken`.

Next, for `$localdir`, specify the full path to a working folder on your hard disk, such as `c:\stuff` (in Windows) or `/usr/local/etc/stuff` (in Unix). This folder is used by several hacks in this chapter to store data files.

If you're outside the U.S., change `$site_id` accordingly, and change `$loc` to match the URL extension for your localization [Hack #19]. See "Climb Out of the Sandbox" [Hack #102] for more information on the Compatibility Level (`$compat_level`). Finally, the two URL variables shouldn't have to be changed.

Nearly everything in Perl (and the eBay API, for that matter) is case sensitive. Always mind your upper- and lowercase when working with the scripts in this chapter.

Why Perl?

With the exceptions of "Receive Search Results via RSS" [Hack #106], "Create Custom-Formatted eBay Search Results with the REST API" [Hack #107], and "Search with PHP 5 and a Web Services Interface to the XML API" [Hack #108], each of the hacks in this chapter uses Perl to access the API. You can copy any script from this chapter and run it from a terminal window, and it should work with minimal modification.

Perl was chosen for several reasons. First, it's free; you can compose Perl programs with a simple text editor and run them with the free Perl interpreter, which is probably already installed on your server. Second, Perl is concise, a fact that allows most of the scripts in this chapter to consume no more than a few lines, or a page at the most. And third, Perl is widely used and relatively easy to understand; even if you're new to programming, you should be able to follow most of the logic of a Perl script by simply reading the code.

Now, the beauty of the eBay API (and, in theory, any API), is that you can interface with eBay using any development environment on any platform. If you prefer PHP, ASP.NET, C++, C#, Visual Basic, or almost anything else, you can use the Perl scripts contained herein merely for inspiration, and then build your own hacks with your favorite platform.

See the Preface for more information about using the code in this book.

Special thanks to Todd Larason, whose help with this chapter helped make the first edition possible. Thanks also to Adam Trachtenberg, manager of technical evangelism for eBay, who provided the PHP hacks and help with some other details for the second edition.

HACK #102 Climb Out of the Sandbox

Deal with certification and go "live."

eBay is understandably protective about any access it permits through its API. To that end, they provide the Sandbox, a "dummy" eBay site with which you can test your programs to your heart's content.

The Sandbox is located at *sandbox.ebay.com*, and looks (and acts) just like *eBay.com*. Although it's nearly fully functional (some features don't work at all), its auction and user databases are completely separate from the main eBay site.

The idea is that you can create user accounts, list items, bid, and even check out, all without incurring the fees and API call limits that would otherwise prevent you from freely testing your application or scripts on the main site.

Although the Sandbox is not bug-free and is often a few months behind *eBay.com* when it comes to new features and interface changes, it's stable where it counts. It's accepted as fact that any code that works in the Sandbox will work on the live *eBay.com* site.

Certification

Before your application goes live, meaning that it can be used on what eBay calls the "production servers" (not just the Sandbox), you must complete certification.

Now, the fact that certification is a required step and costs money ($100 for Individual-tier developers) may make it seem more like a barrier than a service. However, eBay's reasoning is that it ultimately benefits developers as much as it benefits eBay.

For developers working under the Individual license, the certification fee is the only tangible cost of entry to going live.

First and foremost, certification involves using your script or application against eBay's test server to ensure that it operates efficiently and causes minimal impact on the performance of the production site. Certification also permits developers to display the eBay Certified Developer Logo in their applications; while this may not mean so much to individual developers (it is not even available under the Individual license), it is absolutely vital for those creating commercial applications to gain the confidence of their customers.

Here's how certification works:

1. Review the certification requirements (see the next section).
2. Submit the API Usage Document (available at *developer.ebay.com*), which helps provide the certification test team with enough information to understand how your product will be accessing the eBay API and eBay content.
3. Submit a Certification Request.
4. eBay works with you to test your application, which essentially involves hooking it up to a special debug server and analyzing the traffic it generates.
5. Provided that you've met the certification requirements, eBay estimates that your program should be certified within a week.
6. Recertification is necessary only if your application substantially changes the way it uses the API.

Certification Requirements

The following requirements must be met by your application in order for it to pass certification:

Error handling. Make sure you look for and handle any errors received from API calls. For instance, if you're using a single API call repeatedly, make sure the loop halts if it encounters an error. All of the scripts in this chapter incorporate some degree of error checking.

Efficiency. One of the primary reasons for certification is to ensure that your application or script handles communication with eBay responsibly and efficiently [Hack #125].

Compatibility levels. The eBay API is constantly changing and evolving to keep up with the production site. It's important to keep track of these changes, especially if you're using some of the more obscure fields or API calls listed in the documentation. The compatibility level (`$compat_level`) specified in *config.pl* ensures that these changes won't affect your program, at least until eBay removes support for your compatibility level (which they do periodically).

For instance, the `Seller.User.Sunglasses` field was replaced with the `Seller.User.NewUser` and `Seller.User.UserIdChanged` fields as of API version 305, to correspond with changes to the main eBay site. If your program were to submit an API call with compatibility level 309 or later, you wouldn't have access to the `Seller.User.Sunglasses` field.

All the scripts in this book have been tested with compatibility level 399. If you encounter a script or function that doesn't work for you, refer to the API documentation for possible changes associated with later compatibility levels. Eventually, any given compatibility level will be deprecated and ultimately retired, meaning that you'll have to maintain your application to keep it functional with the live site.

Specific call requirements. In addition to the previous, rather general requirements, certification also requires certain procedures to be followed with regard to many of the individual API calls. Here are a few examples:

`GetFeedback`
: Every time your application retrieves comments from a feedback profile [Hack #121], it should cache or record the data so that it retrieves only newly added feedback records each time.

`GetItem`
: You should use the `GetItem` [Hack #109] call only if the information you need cannot be retrieved through more efficient means such as `GetSellerList` [Hack #112].

`GetSellerList`
: Use the `GetSellerList` call only to retrieve listing data for the first time; use `GetSellerEvents` to subsequently retrieve price changes, bids, item revisions, or other changes that might have occurred since the auction data was last retrieved.

License requirements. Finally, your application must fall within the limits of your license agreement. For instance, if you're working under the free Individual license, you can't redistribute your applications (nor would you want to, given the number of daily API calls that would be required by hundreds of users).

As the API gains popularity, it remains to be seen how strict the certification requirements will remain, and how rigorously eBay will enforce recertification for large changes to your code.

Validating Users

In order to use some of the hacks in this chapter, you'll need to create some test users in the Sandbox. Before you can use a sandbox user with the API, you'll need to "validate" the user account with this simple script:

```
#!/usr/bin/perl
require 'ebay.pl';

my $rsp = call_api({Verb => 'ValidateTestUserRegistration',
           RequestUserId => $ARGV[0],
         RequestPassword => $password,
             DetailLevel => 0
});

if ($rsp->{Errors}) {
  print_error($rsp);
} else {
  print "Status:
$rsp->{ValidateTestUserRegistration}{ValidateTestUserRegistrationStatus}\n";
}
```

Save the script as *validate.pl*. To validate a user, type:

```
validate.pl username
```

where *username* is the eBay member ID of the account to validate.

HACK 103 Authenticate Users

Use Authentication & Authorization to allow your users to pass eBay login information to your applications.

Whether you're playing around with the eBay API for your own amusement or building an enterprise application for thousands of users, you'll have to implement a schema eBay calls "Auth & Auth" to pass login information to eBay along with your calls.

If you only need to access the API for your own eBay account (so you can, for instance, do simple searches [Hack #104] or create listings [Hack #113]), this process is simple.

Open the Authentication Token Tool at *developer.ebay.com/tokentool*, show in Figure 8-1. Select the environment you're using, either Production or Sandbox [Hack #102], and then paste the security keys you got when you signed up (described at the beginning of this chapter).

Click "Continue to generate token" when you're done. On the next page, you'll be asked to sign into eBay. Fill in your eBay User ID and password and submit the form. After clicking "Agree and Continue," you'll be presented with your Auth token, along with lots of other information. Copy the token (Ctrl-C) and paste it (Ctrl-V) into the *config.pl* script shown at the ebay® Developers Program Developer Zone Dz

Authentication Token Tool

Use this tool to create authentication tokens for applications that make calls on behalf of a single eBay user. For applications that make calls on behalf of multiple users, you should generate a token for each user within the flow of your application. For a description of how this works, click here.

To generate a single-user token, fill out the information in the form below, then click on the "Generate Token" link. The tool will redirect you to eBay's sign-in page to validate your eBay user ID and password, then return you to this page, where your authentication token will be displayed.

The token generated by this tool should be used for API calls (including those made through SDKs and the REST API) made on behalf of the application and eBay user you authorize.

For complete documentation on this tool, click here. For more information on authentication and authorization, please refer to the API Documentation.

Select the environment: Please choose

Include the **REST** token: ☐

Enter your security keys:

Developer ID:

Application ID:

Certificate:

Continue to generate token

Figure 8-1. Use the Authentication Token Tool to generate the security keys you'll need to access the API under your own eBay account

beginning of this chapter (or into any application you're writing that uses the eBay API).

Auth & Auth gets much more complicated when you need to provide access to other users. For instance, if you've written a web-based listing creation tool, you'll need to integrate Auth & Auth with your service so that users can sign into eBay to authenticate themselves. For details, see eBay's documentation on Authentication & Authorization. (For the XML API, this is located at *http://developer.ebay.com/DevZone/docs/API_Doc/Developing/AuthAndAuth.htm*.)

HACK #104 Search eBay Listings

Perform reliable searches with GetSearchResults.

In "Create a Search Robot" [Hack #21], a Perl script is used to perform an automated eBay search and then email new listings as they're discovered. Although the script serves a valuable function, it has the notable handicap of relying entirely on "scraping" (using a series of Perl modules) to retrieve its search results.

Scraping involves parsing standard web pages in order to retrieve the desired data. As you might expect, any changes to eBay's search pages, even minor ones, may break the script until the script or modules on which it relies are updated to work with the new version.

The API, on the other hand, provides an officially supported interface to eBay's search engine, which means that scripts based on the API will be much more robust and nearly invulnerable to changes in eBay's search pages.

A Simple Search

Here's a simple Perl script, *search.pl*, that performs a search and displays the results:

```
#!/usr/bin/perl
require 'ebay.pl';

use Getopt::Std;
getopts('d');
$keywords = shift @ARGV or die "Usage: $0 [-d] keywords";

❶ PAGE:
while (1) {
❷ my $rsp =  call_api({ Verb => 'GetSearchResults',
                    DetailLevel => 0,
                          Query => $keywords,
            SearchInDescription => $opt_d ? 1 : 0,
                           Skip => $page_number * 100,
  });
  if ($rsp->{Errors}) {
    print_error($rsp);
    last PAGE;
  }
❸ foreach (@{$rsp->{Search}{Items}{Item}}) {
    my %i = %$_;
❹ ($price, $time, $title, $id) = @i{qw/CurrentPrice EndTime Title Id/};
    print "($id) $title [\$$price, ends $time]\n";
  }
❺ last PAGE unless $rsp->{Search}{HasMoreItems};
  $page_number++;
}
```

Given that searches can return hundreds or even thousands of results, the `GetSearchResults` API call ❷ divides the results into pages, not unlike the search pages at *eBay.com*. The loop, which begins on line ❶, repeatedly resubmits the call, downloading a maximum of 100 results each time, until `$rsp->{Search}{HasMoreItems}` is `false` ❸. That means that if there are 768 matching listings, you'll need to retrieve eight pages, or make eight API calls.

Your script might not need to retrieve all matching search results, as this one does. Instead, you may be content to search until a single auction is found, or perhaps to search only the auctions that have started in the last 24 hours. See the API documentation for more ways to limit the result set.

For each page that is found, a secondary loop ❺, iterates through the result set for the current page, extracts relevant data ❹, and prints it out.

Performing a Search

Run the script to perform a title search, like this:

```
search.pl keyword
```

where *keyword* is the word you're looking for. To search for multiple keywords, enclose them in single quotes, like this:

```
search.pl 'wool mittens'
```

Or to search titles and descriptions, type:

```
search.pl -d 'wool mittens'
```

But the real beauty of API searches is how they can be used in an automated fashion.

Revising the Robot

Now, if you tie the API search into the script from "Create a Search Robot" [Hack #21], you get the following new, more robust search robot script:

```
#!/usr/bin/perl
require 'ebay.pl';

my $searchstring = "steam";
my $email = "dave\@ebayhacks.com";
my $mailserver = "my.smtpserver.com";
my $localfile = "searchresults.txt";
my $searchdesc = 0;

my (%searchresults, %olditems, $title, $itemnumber);

# *** perform search ***
PAGE:
while (1) {
  my $rsp =  call_api({ Verb => 'GetSearchResults',
                 DetailLevel => 0,
                       Query => $keywords,
         SearchInDescription => $opt_d ? 1 : 0,
         Skip                => $page_number * 100,
```

```
    });
    if ($rsp->{Errors}) {
      print_error($rsp);
      last PAGE;
    }
    $current_time = $rsp->{eBayTime};

    foreach (@{$rsp->{Search}{Items}{Item}}) {
      my %i = %$_;
      ($title, $itemnumber) = @i{qw/Title Id/};
      $searchresults{$itemnumber} = $title;
      write;
    }
    last PAGE unless $rsp->{Search}{HasMoreItems};
    $page_number++;
  }

  # *** eliminate entries already in file ***
  if (-s $localfile) {
    open (INFILE, "$localfile");
      my %olditems = map { split(/=/, $_) } <INFILE>;
    close (INFILE);
    chomp %olditems;

    foreach $itemnumber (keys %olditems) {
      if (exists($searchresults{$itemnumber})) {
        delete $searchresults{$itemnumber};
      }
    }
  }

  # *** save any remaining new entries to file ***
  open (OUTFILE, ">>$localfile");
    foreach $itemnumber (keys %searchresults) {
      print OUTFILE $itemnumber . "=1\n";
    }
  close (OUTFILE);

  my $mailbody = "The following new items have been listed on eBay:\n";
  foreach $itemnumber (keys %searchresults) {
    $mailbody = $mailbody . &get_title($searchresults{$itemnumber}) . "\n";
    $mailbody = $mailbody . $itemurl . $itemnumber . "\n\n";
  }

  if ($mailbody ne "") { &sendemail($email, $email,
                           "New $searchstring items found", $mailbody); }
  exit;
```

Note that the only difference between the search portion of this script and the one at the beginning of this hack is that the title and item number are stored in the `%searchresults` hash instead of being sent to `stdout`.

To get the email portion of the script to work, you'll need to include one of the two sendemail routines from "Create a Search Robot" [Hack #21], depending on your platform.

If you end up scheduling this script [Hack #21], you may not need to retrieve all matching search results each time. Probably the best way is to set the Order input value to MetaStartSort, which will retrieve newly listed items first. Then, assuming you've scheduled your search robot to run every 24 hours, you could then stop retrieving results as soon as an auction older than 24 hours is encountered. Use the $yesterday variable from [Hack #110] to do your date calculations.

Finally, as described in the Hacking the Hack section of [Hack #21], you can include gallery images in your search email. Rather than assuming the URL remains constant, you can retrieve each Gallery URL with the API. To do this, start by replacing this line:

```
($title, $itemnumber) = @i{qw/Title Id/};
```

with:

```
($title, $itemnumber, $galtemp) = @i{qw/Title Id GalleryURL/};
```

Then, place this code immediately thereafter to place the retrieved Gallery URL into the %gallery hash:

```
$gallery{$itemnumber} = $galtemp if ref $gallery;
```

Finally, replace line ❽ in "Create a Search Robot" [Hack #21] with this code:

```
$mailbody = $mailbody . "<p><a href=\"" . $itemurl . $itemnumber . "\">";
$mailbody = $mailbody . "<img src=\"" . $gallery{$itemnumber} . "\"><br>"
$mailbody = $mailbody . &get_title($searchresults{$itemnumber}) . "</a>\n";
```

And you're done!

HACK #105 Create a Split-Pane Search Tool

Replace eBay's search page with a framed version that makes it easier to go through a large number of search results in a short time.

The JavaScript solution in "Open Search Results in a New Window" [Hack #16] works, but it does so by hacking into existing search results pages. A better solution is to use the API to create a custom search tool.

This hack uses frames to list search results and individual listings side-by-side. First, set up your frames:

```
<frameset cols="20%,80%" frameborder=no>
    <frame src="http://your.server/cgi-bin/search.pl" name="search">
    <frame src="http://my.ebay.com/ws/ebayISAPI.dll?MyeBay" name="listing">
</frameset>
```

Save this into a file called *framesearch.html*.

The Code

Next, modify the *search.pl* script from "Search eBay Listings" [Hack #104] so that it spits out HTML instead of plain text, including a simple HTML search form:

```
#!/usr/bin/perl
require 'ebay.pl';
require 'cgi-lib.pl';

&ReadParse;
$keywords = $in{'keywords'};

print "<html><body>";
print "<form action=\"http://your.server/cgi-bin/search.pl\">";
print "<input name=\"keywords\" value=\"$keywords\">\n";
print "<input type=\"submit\" value=\"Search\">\n";
print "</form>\n";

if ($keywords eq "") { exit; }

print "<p><hr><p>\n";
print "<nobr>\n";

PAGE:
while (1) {

my $rsp =  call_api({ Verb => 'GetSearchResults',
                DetailLevel => 0,
                      Query => $keywords,
        SearchInDescription => $opt_d ? 1 : 0,
                       Skip => $page_number * 100,
  });
  if ($rsp->{Errors}) {
    print_error($rsp);
    last PAGE;
  }

foreach (@{$rsp->{Search}{Items}{Item}}) {
  my %i = %$_;
  ($price, $time, $title, $id) = @i{qw/CurrentPrice EndTime Title Id/};
  print "<a href=\"$itemurl$id\" target=\"listing\">$title</a><br>\n";
}

  last PAGE unless $rsp->{Search}{HasMoreItems};
  $page_number++;
}

print "<nobr>\n";
print "</body></html>";
```

Running the Hack

The only thing you'll have to do is replace *http://your.server/cgi-bin/* (found in both the *framesearch.html* and *search.pl* files listed here) with the complete URL of your web server and its *cgi-bin* directory (see the Preface for details).

Next, put the *search.pl* script in the aforementioned *cgi-bin* directory, and make it executable (again, see the Preface).

To run the hack, double-click *framesearch.html*. In the left pane, you should see a simple search box, and in the right you'll see your My eBay page (or possibly the eBay Sign In page). Just type a search in the box in the left pane, and you'll see your search results below. Click any title to view the listing in the right pane. That's it!

Receive Search Results via RSS

Use PHP to distill eBay search results into a format that can be read by an RSS news aggregator.

RSS is a popular way to track changes to news sites and blogs. When a site adds new content, it updates its RSS feed with information on the new item, including the title, URL, and description.

Using a news aggregator program, you can subscribe to RSS feeds for your favorite sites. These programs watch for changes in RSS feeds. When they find something new, they retrieve the listing and display it to you. This allows you to easily keep up-to-date on hundreds of web sites without needing to continually go back to each site looking for new material.

While RSS is most commonly used to track articles and blog posts, you can also use it to track eBay listings. This hack creates a PHP 5 script that searches eBay and converts the results to RSS using XSLT. This hack reuses many of the components from "Create Custom-Formatted eBay Search Results with the REST API" [Hack #107], so you may want to read that one before continuing with this one.

The Code

RSS readers, however, can't understand eBay's XML results, so you need to convert the output into RSS. Conveniently, RSS is also an XML-based format, so it's easy to use XSLT to turn eBay XML into RSS XML.

Here's an XSL stylesheet that does that:

```
<?xml version="1.0"?>
<xsl:stylesheet xmlns:xsl="http://www.w3.org/1999/XSL/Transform"
                xmlns:date="http://exslt.org/dates-and-times"
                xmlns:ebay="http://ebay.com/api/functions"
                xmlns:func="http://exslt.org/functions"
```

```
                extension-element-prefixes="func date"
                version="1.0">
<xsl:output method="xml" version="1.0" encoding="utf-8" indent="yes" />

<!-- Takes EBayTime, formatted as: "2005-03-02 21:30:47" and is in GMT  -->
<!-- Returns RFC822 time, formatted as: "Wed, 02 Mar 2005 21:30:47 GMT" -->
<func:function name="ebay:rfc822-datetime">
  <xsl:param name="ebay-date"/>
  <xsl:variable name="rfc822-date" select="translate($ebay-date,' ','T')" />
  <func:result select="concat(date:day-abbreviation($rfc822-date), ', ',
    format-number(date:day-in-month($rfc822-date), '00'), ' ',
    date:month-abbreviation($rfc822-date),' ',date:year($rfc822-date), ' ',
        format-number(date:hour-in-day($rfc822-date), '00'), ':',
        format-number(date:minute-in-hour($rfc822-date), '00'), ':',
        format-number(date:second-in-minute($rfc822-date), '00'), ' GMT')"/>
  </func:function>

  <xsl:template match="/">
    <xsl:apply-templates select="/eBay"/>
  </xsl:template>

  <xsl:template match="/eBay">
    <rss version="2.0">
      <channel>
      <title>eBay Search for "<xsl:value-of select="$query"/>"</title>
      <link>http://www.ebay.com/</link>
      <description>eBay results for "<xsl:value-of select="$query"/>"
                                  delivered via RSS.</description>
      <language>en-us</language>
      <lastBuildDate><xsl:value-of select="ebay:rfc822-datetime(EBayTime)"/>
                                  </lastBuildDate>
      <xsl:apply-templates/>
      </channel>
    </rss>
  </xsl:template>

  <xsl:template match="/eBay/Search/Items/Item">
    <item>
      <link><xsl:value-of select="Link"/></link>
      <guid><xsl:value-of select="Link"/></guid>
      <title><xsl:value-of select="Title"/></title>
        <description>
        &lt;p&gt;
        <xsl:if test="ItemProperties/Gallery = 1">&lt;img src="<xsl:value-of
           select="normalize-space(ItemProperties/GalleryURL)"/>"
           alt="<xsl:value-of select="Title" />" align="left"/&gt;</xsl:if>
        <xsl:if test="SubtitleText != ''"><xsl:value-of
                               select="SubtitleText"/>&lt;br /&gt;</xsl:if>

        <xsl:if test="ItemProperties/IsFixedPrice = 1">
          Price <xsl:value-of select="LocalizedCurrentPrice" />
          <xsl:if test="LocalizedCurrentPrice != ConvertedPrice">
          (Approximately <xsl:value-of select="ConvertedPrice" />)</xsl:if>
          <xsl:text> BuyItNow!&lt;br /&gt;</xsl:text>
```

```
        </xsl:if>

        <xsl:if test="ItemProperties/IsFixedPrice = 0">
          Price <xsl:value-of select="LocalizedCurrentPrice" />
          <xsl:if test="LocalizedCurrentPrice != ConvertedPrice">
          (Approximately <xsl:value-of select="ConvertedPrice" />)</xsl:if>
          &lt;br /&gt;
        </xsl:if>

        <xsl:if test="ItemProperties/BuyItNow = 1">
          Price <xsl:value-of select="BINPrice" />
          <xsl:text> BuyItNow!</xsl:text>
          &lt;br /&gt;
        </xsl:if>

        <xsl:if test="ItemProperties/IsFixedPrice = 0">
          Bids <xsl:value-of select="BidCount"/>
          &lt;br /&gt;
        </xsl:if>
        &lt;/p&gt;
      </description>
    </item>
  </xsl:template>
</xsl:stylesheet>
```

This stylesheet is a lot more complex than the one in "Create Custom-Formatted eBay Search Results with the REST API" [Hack #107], but its essential nature is the same. It's looping through the individual items in the eBay search results XML file and reformatting them. In the first case, the XML was converted to plain text. In this case, XML is being converted to XML, but many of the elements have been moved around to convert the file from the way eBay returns search results to the way RSS readers view listings.

Save this stylesheet as *rss.xml* on your web server, and then use this script to access it:

```
<?php
// Insert convert_ebay_xml() code below this line

if (empty($_GET['query'])) {
  $me = $_SERVER['PHP_SELF'];
  print "eBay Search Terms <form action=\"$me\" method=\"get\">";
  print "<input type=\"text\" name=\"query\"
                                     /><input type=\"submit\"></form>";
} else {
  header('Content-Type: text/xml');
  print convert_ebay_xml($_GET['query'], 'rss.xsl');
}
?>
```

This script is nearly identical to the one in "Create Custom-Formatted eBay Search Results with the REST API" [Hack #107], with two small changes. First, it references your new XSLT file, *rss.xsl*, instead of *plain.xsl*. Second, it tells the browser that you're serving up XML, by setting a `Content-Type` header of `text/xml`.

Running the Hack

With all this in place, you can go ahead and create RSS feeds to which you can subscribe. If you don't already have an RSS reader, you can use Yahoo!'s My Yahoo area (*my.yahoo.com*), or download a program such as SharpReader (*www.sharpreader.net*) or NetNewsWire (*ranchero.com/netnewswire*) for the Macintosh. Some web browsers, including Firefox and Safari, also support RSS directly.

If your web browser doesn't automatically hand off the results to an RSS reader, copy the URL into the clipboard. Now go ahead and subscribe to a new news feed in your RSS reader. When it asks for a URL, paste in the saved string.

It's important to remember that this RSS feed works only when your web site is available. The results aren't coming directly from eBay to the RSS reader; instead, the script is acting as a middleman that reformats the content. If the script goes away, so does the RSS feed.

—*Adam Trachtenberg*

HACK #107 Create Custom-Formatted eBay Search Results with the REST API

Save your favorite searches in your web browser as bookmarks.

As with "Create a Split-Pane Search Tool" **[Hack #105]** and "Receive Search Results via RSS" **[Hack #106]**, this hack retrieves eBay search results in a way that can be customized for a very specific application.

Instead of using eBay's XML or SOAP APIs, this script uses eBay's little-known REST API. The REST API is simpler to use, but currently only supports a single function: `GetSearchResults`. Fortunately, this is exactly the one call you need.

The first step is to retrieve a special REST Auth & Auth token **[Hack #103]**. The only thing different you'll have to do for this hack is to click the "Include the REST token" checkbox.

Now you're ready to make an eBay REST request. REST requests are simple because they're just HTTP URLs, so you can test them out in your web browser. Here's the format:

```
http://rest.api.ebay.com/restapi?Query=<Insert Your Query>
&RequestToken=<Insert your REST Token>&RequestUserId<Insert Your eBay User
Id>&CallName=GetSearchResults.
```

Replace the placeholders with appropriate values: the Query (what you want to search for), the RequestToken (the value you just generated), and the RequestUserId (your eBay member ID). Make sure to replace any spaces in your query with plus signs.

Here's an example that searches for "eBay Hacks":

```
http://rest.api.ebay.com/restapi?Query=eBay+Hacks&RequestToken=hkK1wDpFw...
```

When you enter this into your browser's address bar, it makes a REST API request to eBay, and eBay returns search result XML. You can easily turn this output into HTML using XSLT. XSLT is an XML-based language for turning XML into other formats, including HTML. For example, this short XSLT file prints out the title and price of every item found:

```
<?xml version="1.0"?>
❶   <xsl:stylesheet xmlns:xsl="http://www.w3.org/1999/XSL/Transform"
                                                version="1.0">
❷   <xsl:output method="text" encoding="utf-8"/>

❸   <xsl:template match="/">
❹   <xsl:apply-templates select="/eBay/Search/Items/Item"/>
    </xsl:template>

❺   <xsl:template match="/eBay/Search/Items/Item">
❻   <xsl:value-of select="Title"/>
❼   <xsl:text> </xsl:text>
❽   <xsl:value-of select="LocalizedCurrentPrice"/>
❾   <xsl:text>&#10;</xsl:text>
    </xsl:template>
</xsl:stylesheet>
```

The beginning line ❶ says that this XML file is an XSLT stylesheet. XSLT has different display rules for HTML, XML, and plain text. Line ❷ tells the XSLT processor that you want to use the text rules.

XSL uses a concept of templates to determine what parts of the XML document it should display. This file has two templates, the `<xsl:template>` elements in ❸ and ❺.

The template's `match` attribute specifies when the processor should invoke that particular template. The first template matches `/`, the root element. Inside that template, line ❹ tells the processor to only process a certain subset of elements, the ones matching `/eBay/Search/Items/Item`, or `Item` elements living under the hierarchy of `eBay`, `Search`, and `Items`.

This pattern is exactly what the second template is set up to handle. Lines ❻ and ❽ pick out different elements from the document for display (in this case the `Title` and the `LocalizedCurrentPrice`), while lines ❼ and ❾ insert a space and a return.

Now that you have both XML and XSLT files, you need to feed them into an XSLT processor. This processor takes the XML file, applies the transformation rules set out in the XSLT file, and prints the results.

Here's a short PHP 5 function to do this:

```
    function convert_ebay_xml($query, $stylesheet) {

        // Your REST token
❶      $token = "<insert token here>"
        // Your eBay User ID
❷      $userid = "<insert user id here>";

        $params = array(
          'Query' => $query,
          'RequestToken' => urldecode($token),
          'RequestUserId' => $userid,
          'CallName' => 'GetSearchResults');

❸      $callParams = http_build_query($params);

        // Set the eBay REST query
❹      $restURL = "http://rest.api.ebay.com/restapi?$callParams";

        // Load XSL template
        $xsl = new DOMDocument;
❺      $xsl->load($stylesheet);

        // Create new XSLTProcessor
        $xslt = new XSLTProcessor( );
        // Load stylesheet
❻      $xslt->importStylesheet($xsl);

        // Pass in the search term
❼      $xslt->setParameter(NULL, 'query', $query);

        // Load REST XML input file
        $xml = new DOMDocument;
❽      $xml->load($restURL);

        // Transform and display
❾      return $xslt->transformToXML($xml);
    }
```

This function, `convert_ebay_xml( )`, combines your search terms and token to create an eBay REST API URL. This is done on lines ❸ and ❹.

The contents of the XSLT stylesheet and REST URL are then retrieved (lines ❺ to ❽) and combined with the XSLT stylesheet to create the newly formatted information. That data is then returned by the function on line ❾.

Before you can use the function, you must replace the value assigned to the `$token` and `$userid` variables with your REST token and eBay User ID. These are on lines ❶ and ❷.

Running the PHP Script

In order to run a PHP script, you need a web server with PHP 5 installed. PHP 5 also need to be configured with the DOM and XSL extensions. If you don't know if your web server supports PHP, ask your ISP. To discover if your ISP provides DOM and XSL support, enter this line into a file:

```
<?php phpinfo( ); ?>
```

Save it on your web site as *phpinfo.php*, and view that page in a web browser. On a web site with PHP support, you will receive a long web page with lots of technical information.

Scroll down looking for sections labeled DOM and XSL. If you see them, you can run this script. If not, you need to talk to your ISP to get them to enable these extensions.

Many web sites still run PHP 4, an older version of PHP. These scripts will not work under PHP 4. They use new PHP 5-only language.

For more on PHP, go to *www.php.net*. Information on DOM and XSL in PHP is located at *www.php.net/dom* and *www.php.net/xsl*.

To put everything together, save the contents of the stylesheet in a file named *plain.xsl*, and place it in a directory on your web site. Then, place the `convert_ebay_xml( )` function in a file, *plain.php*, along with the following PHP code:

```
<?php
// Insert convert_ebay_xml( ) code below this line

if (empty($_GET['query'])) {
  $me = $_SERVER['PHP_SELF'];
  print "eBay Search Terms <form action=\"$me\" method=\"get\">";
  print "<input type=\"text\" name=\"query\" /><input type=\"submit\">
                                                           </form>";
} else {
  header('Content-Type: text/plain');
  print convert_ebay_xml($_GET['query'], 'plain.xsl');
}
?>
```

This code checks to see if you've provided the script with search terms. If you haven't, it displays a short HTML form. If you have, it passes them along to the convert_ebay_xml( ) function, which does the REST query and XSLT transform, and then prints out the results.

Best of all, it's simple to save this search for future use. All the information is stored in the URL, so all you need to do is bookmark the page. That's it.

Updating the results display only requires modifying the XSLT file, so this is a very flexible way to generate custom search results.

—*Adam Trachtenberg*

HACK #108 Search with PHP 5 and a Web Services Interface to the XML API

Connect PHP 5 to the eBay API with the `Services_eBay` PEAR package.

Like many web services, the eBay API comes in multiple flavors. There's the original XML-over-HTTPS POST interface used by most of the hacks in this chapter, a format that's quite similar to REST [Hack #107]. There's also a newer, more fashionable SOAP interface, which uses the Doc/Literal format.

Both have benefits and weaknesses. Pure XML is easy to produce and consume on any platform, something that's vital given the shaky state of PHP's SOAP support. However, SOAP has the advantage of eliminating the trouble of manually parsing XML into usable data structures.

PHP programmers have a third alternative, which combines the best parts of both interfaces: Services_Ebay. Written primarily by Stephan Schmidt, Services_Ebay is a PEAR package that wraps around the XML API to provide an object-oriented interface to eBay. Additionally, it takes advantage of several new PHP 5 features to create powerful code that's simple to use. You can't run this code under PHP 4 because PHP 5 plays such a key role.

This hack uses Services_Ebay to search eBay and display results, similar to what an eBay affiliate might write. In the process, it gives a small taste of what you can begin to do with the package. Additionally, it shows off a real-world implementation of a PHP 5 program, one that showcases many of the reasons to upgrade from PHP 4 to PHP 5.

Installation and Configuration

Before you can use Services_Ebay, you need to install it using the PEAR package manager tool. The easiest way to do this is with the upgrade -a command:

```
$ pear upgrade -a Services_Ebay-alpha
```

The upgrade -a flag causes PEAR not only to install Services_Ebay but also to automatically upgrade all package dependencies. The -alpha portion at the end lets PEAR know that it's OK to install an alpha version of the package, which is necessary because Services_Ebay is not yet tagged as stable.

Now that you've installed Services_Ebay, you need to configure it with your authentication credentials. This is developer-specific information that allows eBay to identify you and your application.

```
require_once 'Services/Ebay.php';

// load authentication data from config file
$config = parse_ini_file('ebay.ini');

// pass authentication data to Services_Ebay
$session = Services_Ebay::getSession($config['devId'],
                                     $config['appId'],
                                     $config['certId']);

$session->setToken($config['authToken']);
$session->setUrl(Services_Ebay_Session::URL_PRODUCTION);
```

After including the Services_Ebay package, the code loads in a configuration file, *ebay.ini*, using parse_ini_file( ). This file contains the credentials you must provide when making an eBay services API call. Specifically, these are your developer an application ID (described in the beginning of this chapter), your Certification ID [Hack #102], and Auth & Auth Token [Hack #103].

Now that you have the data loaded, the next step is to create an eBay web services session. This session is an object that holds your credential data. Create a session by calling Services_Ebay::getSession( ) and passing your keys as arguments. In this case, the keys are in the $config array created by parse_ini_file( ).

The next two steps modify the session to set the Auth & Auth Token and the URL of the web service by using the setToken( ) and setUrl( ) methods. By default, the session points itself at eBay's testing server [Hack #102]. To override this value and direct the server at the live Production site, pass the Services_Ebay_Session::URL_PRODUCTION constant.

Searching

With the session configured, it's time to create the Services_Ebay object used to make eBay web services API calls. Instantiate a new instance, passing $session to the constructor:

```
// create new proxy object
$ebay = new Services_Ebay($session);

// search eBay
$searchTerms = 'new ipod mini';
$items = $ebay->GetSearchResults($searchTerms);
```

```
// print the results
foreach ($items as $item) {
  echo $item;
  echo "<br />";
}
```

Now you can go ahead and search eBay using the `GetSearchResults()` method, or GSR for short. The easiest way to use GSR is to pass a single argument: your search terms (e.g., "new ipod mini").

Calling this method causes `Services_Ebay` to construct an XML web services request, contact eBay's servers, fetch a response, and then return the returned items in $items. In many ways, this process is similar to what occurs when you use a SOAP client; however, it has the benefits of being able to extend beyond the definitions in the WSDL file.

You can't tell from the code, but the `Services_Ebay` class doesn't actually define the GSR method. Instead, `Services_Ebay` uses the magical `__call()` method to trap the method invocation and automagically load in and execute the appropriate code. In PHP 5, you can define a method named `__call()`; then, any time you call an unimplemented method, PHP will invoke `__call()` instead of dying an ugly death.

Normally, once you've retrieved a list of search results, you want to loop through them and print them out. That's why the `$items` object uses a new PHP 5 feature, iterators, to allow to you cycle through the items inside of a `foreach()` loop.

Inside the `foreach()`, you receive an `$item`, which is an object that represents an eBay item. This class uses yet another PHP 5 feature that allows you to specify an object's *stringification*. When you `print` or `echo` an object, PHP calls the object's `__toString()` method and displays what it returns.

Printing out a list of search results is a piece of cake:

```
// print the results
foreach ($items as $item) {
  echo $item;
  echo "<br />";
}
```

There's no need to extract the individual items from the object, nor to retrieve their individual properties to create a string description. It's all encapsulated inside the class, and accessible using regular PHP language constructs.

You've just seen how easy it is to write an eBay web services search application in PHP with the help of `Services_Ebay`. `Services_Ebay` uses much of the power of PHP 5: the whole spectrum of the new object model, the rewritten

XML and XSL extensions, iterators and SPL, reflection, and exceptions. These components combine to create a kick-ass tool that PHP 4 can't replicate without lots of work, if at all.

Furthermore, the eBay API is not restricted to read-only calls, such as searching for and viewing listings. You can do almost everything through the API, including listing items, giving and checking feedback, managing eBay Stores, retrieving data from your My eBay page, and setting preferences. Services_Ebay supports most of these calls today and is quickly adding the rest.

—Adam Trachtenberg

HACK #109 Retrieve Details About a Listing

Use the GetItem API call to get listing details.

The GetItem API call is used to retrieve all the details of a listing, including the title, description, starting price, category, and about 180 other individual bits of information.

The Code

Here's a simple script that, when provided with the item number, returns the title, seller ID, amount of time left, number of bids, and the current price:

```
#!/usr/bin/perl
require 'ebay.pl';

$item_id = shift @ARGV or die "Usage: $0 itemnumber";

❶ my $rsp = call_api({ Verb => 'GetItem',
                DetailLevel => 0,
                         Id => $item_id
  });

  if ($rsp->{Errors}) {
    print_error($rsp)
  } else {
    my %i = %{$rsp->{Item}[0]};
❷   my ($price, $currency, $bids, $time_left, $seller, $title) =
          @i{qw/CurrentPrice CurrencyId BidCount TimeLeft Seller Title/};

❸   $d = $time_left->{Days};
    $h = $time_left->{Hours};
    $m = $time_left->{Minutes};
    $s = $time_left->{Seconds};
    $seller_id = $seller->{User}{UserId};
    $seller_fb = $seller->{User}{Feedback}{Score};

    print "Item #$item_id: $title\n";
```

```
    print "For sale by $seller_id ($seller_fb)\n";
    print "Currently at $currency$price, $bids bids\n";

    if ($d > 0) { print "$d days, $h hours left.\n"; }
    elsif ($h > 0) { print "$h hours, $m minutes left.\n"; }
    elsif ($s > 0) { print "$m minutes, $s seconds left.\n"; }
    else { print "auction ended.\n"; }
}
```

This script is fairly straightforward. The `GetItem` API call is submitted on line ❶, and the desired fields are extracted on line ❷. Naturally, you can specify any of the 180+ field names specified in the API documentation (look up GetItem → Return Values in the index), as long as the variables on the left side of the equals sign on line ❷ match up with the field names on the right.

Note that some variables are hashes (which eBay calls "container nodes"), from which relevant data must be extracted. For instance, in the documentation you'll see entries for `TimeLeft` as well as `TimeLeft.Days`, `TimeLeft.Hours`, `TimeLeft.Minutes`, and `TimeLeft.Seconds`. In Perl, these elements of the hash are accessed with the -> arrow (infix dereference) operator, as shown on line ❸.

Running the Hack

To use the script, simply specify the item number, like this:

```
getitem.pl 3136272129
```

and you'll get output like this:

```
Item #3136272129: Little Red Steam Shovel
For sale by ebayhacker
Currently at $71.00, 9 bids
1 days, 22 hours left.
```

However, you'll find it much more useful when used in conjunction with other scripts, like the ones in "Automatically Keep Track of Auctions You've Won" [Hack #110] and "Automatically Keep Track of Items You've Sold" [Hack #112].

Hacking the Hack

The `DetailLevel` field in the API call on line ❶ determines how much information is retrieved. In most cases, a value of `0` is sufficient. However, if you want to retrieve the description, you'll need to raise this to at least `2`. See "Spellcheck All Your Listings" [Hack #116] for an example.

Provided that you're the seller or the high bidder and the auction is completed, you can retrieve the `HighBidder.User.Email` and `Seller.User.Email` fields by specifying a detail level of at least `8`, as shown in "Automatically Keep Track of Items You've Sold" [Hack #112].

The DetailLevel tag is used for most API calls, but its usage isn't necessarily the same for all of them. In most cases, a higher detail level will result in more data received (and more time taken), but for some API calls, a high detail level (usually 32 and above) is used for special "abbreviated" result sets. Regardless, if you're not getting the results you expect from an API call, make sure you supply the appropriate DetailLevel, as instructed by the API documentation.

HACK #110 Automatically Keep Track of Auctions You've Won

Maintain a permanent record of everything you've ever purchased.

Since eBay keeps auctions on site only for a few months and lists them in My eBay for only 60 days, all bidders should maintain permanent, off-site records of the items they've purchased.

As long as you keep a permanent archive of all email you've received (see the Preface), you'll always have records of the item numbers, titles, seller IDs and email addresses, and closing prices of the items you've won. But this data is stored in a less-than-convenient format, and the descriptions aren't stored at all.

Here's a script that will automatically retrieve and store details for every auction you've won:

```
    #!/usr/bin/perl
    require 'ebay.pl';

❶   $today = &formatdate(time);
❷   $yesterday = &formatdate(time - 86400);

❸   my $rsp = call_api({ Verb => 'GetBidderList',
                  DetailLevel => 32,
                       UserId => $user_id,
                       SiteId => $site_id,
                  EndTimeFrom => $yesterday,
                    EndTimeTo => $today,
    });

    if ($rsp->{Errors}) {
      print_error($rsp);
    } else {
      foreach (@{$rsp->{BidderList}{Item}}) {
        my %i = %$_;
❹       ($highbidder, $title, $id) = @i{qw/HighBidderUserId Title Id/};

❺       if ((! -e "$localdir/$id") && ($highbidder eq $user_id)) {
❻         my $rsp = call_api({ Verb => 'GetItem',
                        DetailLevel => 2,
                                 Id => $id
```

```
            });

            if ($rsp->{Errors}) {
              print_error($rsp)
            } else {
              my %i = %{$rsp->{Item}[0]};
❼             my ($price, $currency, $seller, $title, $description) =
                     @i{qw/CurrentPrice CurrencyId Seller Title Description/};

❽             open (OUTFILE,">$localdir/$id");
                print OUTFILE "[$id]\n";
                print OUTFILE "title=$title\n";
                print OUTFILE "seller=".$seller->{User}{UserId}."\n";
                print OUTFILE "price=$currency$price\n";
                print OUTFILE "description=$description\n";
              close (OUTFILE);
            }
          }
        }
      }
```

The GetBidderList API verb, called on line ❸, returns a maximum of 200 items, but doesn't support paging like GetSearchResults [Hack #104]. This means that you need to be a little creative. So instead of trying to grab as many listings as possible, grab only the auctions that have ended in a certain interval, say, a day. (If you bid infrequently, you can change this to a week or even a month, and help keep down your API calls). So, you set the EndTimeTo and EndTimeFrom fields to today's and yesterday's dates, respectively. The formatdate subroutine is used on lines ❶ and ❷ to convert the Perl dates to something eBay understands.

Next, the script runs through the list of auctions you've bid on and retrieves ❹ the high bidder, title, and item number for each. (You don't actually need the title here, but it's nice to have.)

On line ❺, a check is performed to see if the auction has been recorded previously and if you're indeed the high bidder. Note that since the script uses a DetailLevel of 32 (specified on line ❸), you get back an "abbreviated result set" from which, as the documentation explains, the user ID of the high bidder is retrieved with the HighBidderUserId tag. You could also use a DetailLevel of 0, but you'd have to deal with the HighBidder hash (see "Retrieve Details About a Listing" [Hack #109] for more information on container nodes). Refer to the API documentation for the somewhat confusing circumstances surrounding the DetailLevel tag with regards to GetBidderList.

Finally, the auction details for each item are retrieved with `GetItem` (line ❻ and then line ❼). Note that the `DetailLevel` for this call is set to `2` to retrieve the descriptions as well [Hack #109].

The `$description` variable contains the raw description, including any HTML code. See "Spellcheck All Your Listings" [Hack #116] for details on extracting plain text from HTML code.

Line ❽ then saves the retrieved data into a file, named for the item number of the listing. Naturally, you can retrieve and store as many or as few fields as you like and store them whatever format is convenient (e.g., in a database, comma-delimited (CSV) text file, or the generic format used here).

Since the script retrieves only auctions that have ended in the last 24 hours, this script should be scheduled [Hack #21] to run once a day, every day. If you want to run it less (or more) often, just change the `EndTimeTo` and `EndTimeFrom` fields accordingly.

HACK #111 Track Items in Your Watching List

Link an off-eBay auction tracker with eBay's Items I'm Watching list.

eBay provides the Items I'm Watching list (in My eBay → Bidding/Watching) to help you keep track of auctions on which you haven't yet bid. A corresponding API call, `GetWatchList`, allows you to access the contents of that list.

But the Items I'm Watching list is rather limited and can be replaced with a custom tracking list [Hack #29]. Although the hack works, there are two simple ways to use the eBay API to make the script more robust and efficient:

- Retrieve the title and end date with the `GetItem` API call instead of using the flakier method of extracting them from the auction page title.
- Supplement the tracking list with any auctions in the Items I'm Watching list.

The following is a revised auction-tracking script with both of these improvements.

This script requires all the Perl modules specified in "Keep Track of Auctions Outside of eBay" [Hack #29], as well as `Time::Local`, by Tom Christiansen, Graham Barr, and Dave Rolsky (*search.cpan.org/perldoc?Time::Local*), which is used to convert dates retrieved from the API from GMT to local time.

```
#!/usr/bin/perl
require 'ebay.pl';
use Time::ParseDate;
use Time::Local;
use POSIX qw(strftime);
require 'cgi-lib.pl';

&ReadParse;
$selfurl = "http://www.ebayhacks.com/exec/track.pl";
$localfile = "ebaylist.txt";
$timeoffset = 0;
@formatting=("color=#EE0000 STYLE=font-weight:bold",
                "color=#000000 STYLE=font-weight:bold", "color=#000000");
$i = 0;
$exists = 0;
$numlevels = 2;

# *** read stored list ***
open (INFILE,"$localdir/$localfile");
  while ( $line = <INFILE> ) {
    $line =~ s/\s+$//;
    $i++;
    ($enddate[$i],$priority[$i],$item[$i],$title[$i])=split(",", $line, 4);
    if (($item[$i] ne "") && ($item[$i] eq $in{'item'})) { $exists = $i; }
  }
close (INFILE);

# *** add latest auction if specified ***
if (($in{'auction'} =~ "ebay.com") && ($in{'item'} != "") && ($exists==0)) {
❶ my $rsp = call_api({ Verb => 'GetItem',
                DetailLevel => 0,
                        Id => $in{'item'}
  });

  if (! $rsp->{Errors}) {
    $i++;
    $item[$i] = $in{'item'};
❷   $title[$i] = $rsp->{Item}[0]{Title};
    $priority[$i] = 2;
❸   $enddate[$i] = timegm(localtime(parsedate($rsp->{Item}[0]{EndTime})));
  }
}
elsif (($in{'do'} eq "promote")) {
  $priority[$exists]--;
  if ($priority[$exists] < 0) { $priority[$exists] = 0; }
}
elsif (($in{'do'} eq "demote")) {
  $priority[$exists]++;
  if ($priority[$exists] > 2) { $priority[$exists] = 2; }
}
```

```
elsif (($in{'do'} eq "delete")) {
  splice @enddate, $exists, 1;
  splice @priority, $exists, 1;
  splice @item, $exists, 1;
  splice @title, $exists, 1;
  $i--;
}

# *** scan watch list  ***
my $rsp = call_api({ Verb => 'GetWatchList',
              DetailLevel => 0,
                   UserId => $user_id,
                   SiteId => $site_id,
});
if (! $rsp->{Errors}) {
  $ebaytime = $rsp->{EBayTime};
  foreach (@{$rsp->{WatchList}{Items}{Item}}) {
    my %ii = %$_;
    ($id, $title, $timeleft) = @ii{qw/Id Title TimeLeft/};

    $seconds_left = $timeleft->{Days}*86400 +
                    $timeleft->{Hours}*3600 +
                    $timeleft->{Minutes}*60 +
                    $timeleft->{Seconds};
    $alreadythere = grep /$id/, @item;

    if ($alreadythere == 0) {
      $i++;
      $item[$i] = $id;
      $title[$i] = $title;
      $priority[$i] = 2;
      $enddate[$i] =
                 timegm(localtime(parsedate($ebaytime) + $seconds_left));
      $in{'do'} = "silentadd";
    }
  }
}

# *** update list ***
if (($in{'do'} ne "")) {
  open (OUTFILE,">$localdir/$localfile");
    for ($j = 1; $j <= $i; $j++) {
      print OUTFILE "$enddate[$j],$priority[$j],$item[$j],$title[$j]\n";
    }
  close (OUTFILE);

  if ($in{'do'} ne "silentadd") {
    print "Location: $selfurl\n\n";
    exit( 0);
  }
}
```

```
# *** sort list ***
@idx = sort criteria 0 .. $i;

# *** display list ***
print "Content-type: text/html\n\n";
print "<table border cellspacing=0 cellpadding=6>\n";

for ($j = 1; $j <= $i; $j++) {
  $formatteddate = strftime("%a, %b %d - %l:%M:%S %p",
                             localtime($enddate[$idx[$j]]));
  $formattedtitle = "<a href=\"$itemurl$item[$idx[$j]]\" target=\"_blank\">
       <font $formatting[$priority[$idx[$j]]]>$title[$idx[$j]]</font></a>";

  if (strftime("%v", localtime($enddate[$idx[$j]])) eq
                              strftime("%v", localtime(time))) {
    $formattedtitle = "<li>" . $formattedtitle;

  }
  if ($enddate[$idx[$j]] < time) {
    $formattedtitle = "<strike>" . $formattedtitle . "</strike>";

  }
  else {
    $timeleft = ($enddate[$idx[$j]] - time) / 60 + ($timeoffset * 60);
    if ($timeleft < 24 * 60) {
      $hoursleft = int($timeleft / 60);
      $minleft = int($timeleft - ($hoursleft * 60));
      if ($minleft < 10) { $minleft = "0" . $minleft; }
      $formattedtitle = $formattedtitle .
                " <font size=-1>($hoursleft:$minleft left)</font>";

    }
  }

  print "<tr><td>$formattedtitle</td>";
  print "<td><font size=-1>$formatteddate</font></td>";
  print "<td><a href=\"$selfurl?item=$item[$idx[$j]]&do=promote\">+</a>";

  print " | <a href=\"$selfurl?item=$item[$idx[$j]]&do=demote\">-</a>";
  print " | <a href=\"$selfurl?item=$item[$idx[$j]]&do=delete\">x</a></td>";
  print "</tr>\n";
}

print "</table>\n";

sub criteria {
  # *** sorting criteria subroutine ***
  return ($priority[$a] <=> $priority[$b] or $enddate[$a] <=> $enddate[$b])
}
```

Although much of this script is documented in "Keep Track of Auctions Outside of eBay" **[Hack #29]**, a few minor changes have been made to accommodate the new portions that deal with the API. In other words, it's the same, but different.

First, when a new listing is added through the JavaScript link from **[Hack #29]**, only the item number, `$in{'item'}`, is used. The `GetItem` API call ❶ uses the item number to retrieve the title ❷ and end date ❸. Note that the end date has to be converted from GMT to local time, with the help of the `timegm` function in `Time::Local`. This process is much more robust and reliable (albeit ultimately a little slower) than the original method of parsing the page title.

Next, the `GetWatchList` API call retrieves the contents of your Items I'm Watching list ❹, and checks to see if the item number is already in the list ❻.

Unfortunately, the result set doesn't include `EndTime`, so unless you want to call `GetItem` a bunch of times, you need to be a little creative. All you have to do is retrieve eBay time from the `EBayTime` field ❺ (note the capitalization) and add it to `TimeLeft` ❼ for each auction. (It kind of feels like cheating, but it works.) Once again, this time needs to be converted from GMT to local time.

Every time you "watch" a new auction, just reload *track.pl* to import it into your list. Note that at the time of this writing there was no way to modify the watching list, so the script will simply retrieve the same list over and over. Presumably, you'll want to clear out the Items I'm Watching list (My eBay → Bidding/Watching) as soon as they appear in your tracking list.

See Also

- See the Preface for details on setting up this script in your *cgi-bin* directory.

HACK #112 Automatically Keep Track of Items You've Sold

Retrieve and store completed listing data without typing.

As explained in "Keep Track of Items You've Sold" **[Hack #83]**, it's vital for every seller to keep permanent, off-site records of every single auction he or she has sold.

This script, when run daily **[Hack #21]**, does it all:

```
#!/usr/bin/perl
require 'ebay.pl';

$today = &formatdate(time);
$yesterday = &formatdate(time - 86400);
```

```
my $page_number = 1;
PAGE:
while (1) {
    my $rsp = call_api({ Verb => 'GetSellerList',
                    DetailLevel => 8,
                         UserId => $user_id,
                   EndTimeFrom => $yesterday,
                     EndTimeTo => $today,
                    PageNumber => $page_number
    });

    if ($rsp->{Errors}) {
      print_error($rsp);
      last PAGE;
    }
    foreach (@{$rsp->{SellerList}{Item}}) {
      my %i = %$_;
      ($id, $enddate, $title, $currency, $price, $highbidder) =
             @i{qw/Id EndTime Title CurrencyId CurrentPrice HighBidder/};

      if (! -e "$localdir/$id") {
        open (OUTFILE,">$localdir/$id");
          print OUTFILE "[Details]\n";
          print OUTFILE "enddate=$enddate\n";
          print OUTFILE "itemnumber=$id\n";
          print OUTFILE "title=$title\n";
          print OUTFILE "price=$currency$price\n";
          print OUTFILE "bidder=".$highbidder->{User}{UserId}."\n";
          print OUTFILE "bidderemail=".$highbidder->{User}{Email}."\n";
        close (OUTFILE);
      }
    }
    last PAGE unless $rsp->{SellerList}{HasMoreItems};
    $page_number++;
}
```

This script works similarly to the one in "Automatically Keep Track of Auctions You've Won" [Hack #110], but it retrieves a list of auctions *by seller* that have ended between the specified dates. Here are a few important things to note about this script:

- Unlike the `GetBidderList` API call, which is limited to only 200 results, `GetSellerList` supports paging, and when used properly, will continue to retrieve results until you've got them all.
- Since the `DetailLevel` input field [Hack #109] is set to 8, the `GetSellerList` retrieves all relevant information about an auction so you don't have to issue separate `GetItem` calls. This means you can retrieve the auction details for hundreds of listings with only one or two API calls.

- The fields saved correspond to those listed in "Keep Track of Items You've Sold" [Hack #83], with the exception of the shipping charge (see the following bullet) and any fields you'd normally enter manually (such as whether the bidder has yet paid).
- If you've specified a fixed shipping charge in the listing or are using the Calculated Shipping option, you can retrieve this information with the `GetItemShipping` API call. Also of interest is `GetShippingRates`, a non-item-specific function that helps determine the shipping rates for different combinations of destination Zip Codes, package types, weights, and shipping services.

HACK #113 Submit an Auction Listing

Use AddItem to start new listings and make scheduling easier.

eBay's Turbo Lister [Hack #93] is an API-based tool used to submit new listings to eBay. It provides a complete interface with which you can create and modify listings, as well as a database engine that stores them.

35% of eBay listings are reportedly submitted with the API, including those uploaded with Turbo Lister.

The Code

All the work is done by the `AddItem` API call, illustrated by this extremely simple script:

```
#!/usr/bin/perl
require 'ebay.pl';

$category    = shift @ARGV;
$title        = shift @ARGV;
$description = shift @ARGV;
$minimum_bid = shift @ARGV;
defined($minimum_bid)
              or die "Usage: $0 category title description minimumbid";

$country = 'us';
$location = 'My home town';
$duration = 7;
$quantity = 1;
$currency = 1;

❶ my $rsp = call_api({ Verb => 'AddItem',
               DetailLevel => 0,
                    SiteId => $site_id,
                  Category => $category,
   CheckoutDetailsSpecified => 0,
```

```
                    Country => $country,
                   Currency => $currency,
                Description => $description,
                   Duration => $duration,
                   Location => $location,
                 MinimumBid => $minimum_bid,
               PaymentOther => 1,
                   Quantity => $quantity,
                     Region => 0,
                      Title => $title
    });
    if ($rsp->{Errors}) {
        print_error($rsp)
    } else {
❷       print "New listing created: #$rsp->{Item}[0]{Id}\n";
        print "Ends $rsp->{Item}[0]{EndTime}\n";
    }
```

Save this script as *additem.pl*.

Running the Hack

The simplest way to use this script is to call it from the command line, like this:

```
additem.pl 7276 'Little Red Steam Shovel' 'My description...' 5.00
```

However, it will probably make more sense to call it from another script or program (or integrate it with another script, such as the one in "List Your Entire Inventory on eBay" **[Hack #114]**, especially since you'll likely want more of a description than simply "My description..." and more options than the four required by this sample script.

Although `AddItem` calls do not count against your daily (or monthly) API-call allotment, the listing fees normally associated with starting new auctions still apply. The same goes for the `RelistItem` call **[Hack #117]**.

Hacking the Hack

Of the more than 120 individual input fields supported by the `AddItem` call, only 11 are required: `Category`, `CheckoutDetailsSpecified`, `Country`, `Currency`, `Description`, `Duration`, `Location`, `MinimumBid`, `Quantity`, `Region`, and `Title`. But when submitting a live listing, you'll most likely want to include as many options as possible, everything from the shipping charges to the extra-cost listing upgrades. Refer to the API documentation for a complete listing, and place any additional fields alongside the others on line ❶.

It's important to save as much retrieved information as possible **[Hack #125]** so that you can reduce the number of subsequent API calls needed. If you submit listings only with the `AddItem` API call (never through *eBay.com*), you should record the item numbers it returns (`$rsp->{Item}[0]{Id}`) for further use. This would reduce (or eliminate) your need for the `GetSellerList` API call—used in so many of the hacks in this chapter—at least when it comes to retrieving a listing of your own auctions.

See Also

- The eBay API SDK comes with the eBay Sample Selling Application, a Microsoft Visual Studio .NET–based listing creation tool similar to Turbo Lister. If you're interested in creating a similar tool, you'll want to poke around in the included C source code.

HACK #114 List Your Entire Inventory on eBay

Tie your inventory database into a custom eBay listing-creation tool and create listings for all your products automatically.

As a seller on eBay, one of the most time-consuming tasks is to create new listings. If you already have a product database for your business, you can create a tool to convert individual products into eBay listings.

For this to work, your database will need several fields that look something like the following:

Field name	Type	Description
ID	Number (int)	A unique number for each record (product) in your database
Name	Text (20-char max)	The name of the product, to be used as the first part of the listing title (e.g., "Acme Hy-7713")
Synopsis	Text (30-char max)	A very brief description of the product, to be used as the second part of the listing title (e.g., "7 Quart Mixer")
Long description	Text	What will eventually become the heart of your listing description (e.g., "This is one of the best mixers…")
Sale price	Number	The dollar amount to be used as the Buy It Now price for fixed-price listings
Shipping	Number	The amount to charge for fixed-price shipping
Category	Number (int)	The eBay category number [Hack #13] in which to list the item
Quantity	Number (int)	The number of products you have in stock (or on hand), used to ensure that your program won't list any products you're not able to ship right away
Sell on eBay	Boolean	A checkbox that, when checked, indicates that you want this particular item listed on eBay

Naturally, your database will look different; it should be relatively easy to modify the following code to work with whatever structure your product list is in. Probably the only fields you'll need to add to your database are "Sell on eBay"—unless you want to list your entire inventory each time you run the program—and "Category," discussed later in this hack.

The Code

This hack uses Perl and the DBI Perl Module (*search.cpan.org/perldoc?DBI*) to interface with a MySQL database (*dev.mysql.com*). Of course, the same methodology will work on any platform, although the code will be different. If you're using a Microsoft Access database, for instance, you could create a simple listing tool with Visual Basic and the Microsoft DAO 3.6 Object Library.

Here's the script:

```
#! /usr/bin/perl
use DBI;
require 'ebay.pl';

❶ $db = DBI->connect("DBI:mysql:database=products", "user", "password")
                                    or die "Can't connect to database.";

❷ $sql = "SELECT * FROM productlist WHERE 'Sell on eBay'=TRUE";
$query = $db->prepare($sql);
$query->execute( );

while ($productinfo = $query->fetchrow_hashref( )) {
  $id = $productinfo->{'ID'};
❸ $title = $productinfo->{'Name'} + " " + $productinfo->{'Synopsis'};
  $description = $productinfo->{'Long Description'};
  $price = $productinfo->{'Sale Price'};
  $ship = $productinfo->{'Shipping'};
  $category = $productinfo->{'Category'};
  $quantity = $productinfo->{'Quantity'};

  $bodytext = "";
  open (INFILE,"$localdir/listingtemplate.txt");
  while ( $line = <INFILE> ) {
    if ($line eq "\@description\@\n") {
      $bodytext = $bodytext . $description;
    } else {
      $bodytext = $bodytext . $line;
    }
  }
  $bodytext = "<![CDATA[" . $bodytext . "]]>";

  if ($quantity > 0) {

❹     my $rsp = call_api({ Verb => 'AddItem',
                           DetailLevel => 0,
```

```
                       SiteId => $site_id,
                     Category => $category,
      CheckoutDetailsSpecified => 1,
                      Country => 'us',
                     Currency => 1,
                  Description => $bodytext,
                     Duration => 7,
                     Location => 'My home town',
                   MinimumBid => $price,
                 PaymentOther => 1,
                     Quantity => 1,
                       Region => 0,
                 ShippingType => 1,
ShippingServiceOptions.ShippingServiceOption.ShippingServiceCost => $ship,
                        Title => $title,
                         Type => 9
      });

      if ($rsp->{Errors}) {
        print_error($rsp)
      } else {
        $quantity--;
❺       $sql = "UPDATE productlist SET 'Quantity'=? WHERE ID=$id";

        $query = $db->prepare($sql);
        $query->execute($quantity);
        $query->finish;

        print "Listing created: $title\n";
      }
    }
  }
```

Next, you'll need to create a listing description template file named *listingtemplate.txt*, and place it in the folder specified in the `$localdir` variable (explained at the beginning of this chapter). The template should contain the information you want to appear in each of your listings, as well as this placeholder for the product-specific information taken from the database:

```
@description@
```

The completed template should look something like this:

```
Thank you for visiting Acme Auctions! You are bidding on:

@description@

I accept PayPal, and ship as soon as payment is received.
Please <a href="http://cgi3.ebay.com/aw-cgi/eBayISAPI.dll?
                         ReturnUserEmail&requested=ebayhacks">contact
me</a> with any questions.
```

Naturally, your descriptions can be embellished with as much decor **[Hack #56]** and policy information **[Hack #54]** as you like.

Running the Hack

Save the Perl script into a file named something like *uploadall.pl*, and then run it to begin listing the products in your database.

This script has been designed to be essentially noninteractive. It starts by connecting to your database ❶ and issuing a query ❷ to return a hash containing all the products in your database for which the `Sell on eBay` column is `TRUE`. Then, it plows through the hash and creates a listing ❹ for each product with a quantity greater than zero. And as its last order of business, the script updates the Quantity column ❺ for each product that has been successfully listed, lowering it by one to reflect the new listing.

Hacking the Hack

The `Type` parameter at the end of line ❹ is set to `9` to indicate a fixed-price listing [Hack #43]. Change this to `1` (the default) for a Chinese auction, `2` for a Dutch auction [Hack #44], or `7` for an eBay Store listing [Hack #91]. Refer to the API documentation for the requirements for other listing formats.

One of the things this script illustrates is that the fields in your database don't necessarily need to mirror the options in eBay's Sell Your Item form [Hack #43]. For instance, the database in this example has no `title` field, but rather composes the title of each listing by combining the product name (`Name`) and short description (`Synopsis`) on line ❸. When you implement an automated listing tool to work with your own database, you may have to find other creative ways to fabricate the required listing options on the fly without having to dramatically change the structure of your database.

For instance, the example script in this hack requires that each record have a `Category` field to ensure that each listing is placed in the correct eBay category. If you wanted to be a little more adventurous, you could eliminate the field and instead automate the category selection. First, you'd have to conduct a search [Hack #104] for each listing title. Then, find the single category in which the largest percentage of search results are filed, and use the respective category number when creating the listing.

You could also do some creative things with the pricing, such as including only *your cost* in the database, and then adding, say, a 20% profit margin to calculate the listing price for each item. Then, if you wanted to be somewhat more aggressive, you could write a script to automatically lower the price and then relist each unsuccessful listing [Hack #117].

To make this script more robust, you'll want to implement some error checking. Take eBay listing titles, which can be no longer than 55 characters. As shown in the field summary at the beginning of this hack, the maximum lengths for the Name and Synopsis fields are 20 and 30 characters, respectively. When they're concatenated on line ❸, the combined length of `$title` (including the intermediate space) is never more than 51 characters. Another way to ensure that no field is longer than eBay's allowed maximum is to correct each variable before creating the listing; for instance, you could add the following immediately after line ❸:

```
$title = substr($title, 0, 55);
```

to chop off any text past the 55-character limit. Along the same lines, the description (`$description`) is encased in a CDATA wrapper to accommodate any HTML codes.

Another reason to automate the listing of your inventory with a tool like the one in this hack is to simplify bookkeeping. Among the return values generated by the `AddItem` API call is a collection of `Fees` values (e.g., `Fees.GalleryFee` and `Fees.InsertionFee`). To calculate how much eBay charges you to create each listing, just add them all together, and then (optionally) insert them back into your database to keep a running tally of how much it's costing you to sell on eBay.

HACK #115 Automate Auction Revisions

Simplify the task of revising several auctions at once with the ReviseItem API call.

Once an auction has started, you can normally change most aspects of the listing using the procedure outlined in "Make Changes to Running Auctions" [Hack #65]. But it's also possible to submit a revision using the API.

ReviseItem

Start with a simple script, *reviseitem.pl*, that will let you change any aspect of an active listing:

```
#!/usr/bin/perl
require 'ebay.pl';

my $item_id = shift @ARGV;
my %ARGS    = @ARGV;

my @options = qw/AdditionalShippingCosts AmEx AutoPay BoldTitle
  BuyItNowPrice CashOnPickupAccepted Category Category2 CCAccepted
  CheckoutDetailsSpecified CheckoutInstructions COD Counter Description
  Discover Duration Escrow EscrowBySeller Featured Gallery GalleryFeatured
  GalleryURL GiftExpressShipping GiftWrap Highlight InsuranceOption
  InsuranceFee LayoutId Location MinimumBid MoneyXferAccepted
  MoneyXferAcceptedinCheckout MOCashiers PackageHandlingCosts
  PaymentOther PaymentOtherOnline PaymentSeeDescription PayPalAccepted
```

```
    PayPalEmailAddress PersonalCheck PhotoCount PhotoDisplayType PictureURL
    Private Quantity Region ReservePrice SalesTaxPercent SalesTaxState
    SellerPays ShipFromZipCode ShippingHandlingCosts ShippingInTax
    ShippingIrregular ShippingOption ShippingPackage ShippingService
    ShippingType ShipToAfrica ShipToAsia ShipToCaribbean ShipToEurope
    ShipToLatinAmerica ShipToMiddleEast ShipToNorthAmerica ShipToOceania
    ShipToSouthAmerica SuperFeatured ThemeId Title VisaMaster WeightMajor
    WeightMinor WeightUnit/;

my %args = ( Verb => 'ReviseItem',
       DetailLevel => 0,
            SiteId => $site_id,
            ItemId => $item_id);
    foreach (@options) {
        $args{$_} = $ARGS{$_} if defined $ARGS{$_};
}

my $rsp = call_api(\%args);
if ($rsp->{Errors}) {
    print_error($rsp)
} else {
    print "Revised item #$rsp->{Item}[0]{Id}\n";
}
```

To use the script from the command line, include only the item number and the fields you want to change. For example, to change the title, type:

```
reviseitem.pl 4500205202 Title 'This is My New Title'
```

(Notice the single quotes used around text with spaces.) To change the starting bid to $8.50, type:

```
reviseitem.pl 4500205202 MinimumBid 8.50
```

To add the Bold listing upgrade **[Hack #46]**, type:

```
reviseitem.pl 4500205202 BoldTitle 1
```

where `1` means on (or true) and `0` means off (or false).

Note that the field names (`Title`, `MinimumBid`, and `BoldTitle`) are all case sensitive; make sure to type them exactly as they appear in the script.

Revisions made through the API follow the same rules as those made through *eBay.com*; for instance, you can't change your title if the item has received bids. See "Make Changes to Running Auctions" **[Hack #65]** for details.

AddToItemDescription

If the item has received bids, the changes [Hack #65] you'll be able to make will be diminished greatly. But, just like on *eBay.com*, you can add to the item description with the API using the *addtodescription.pl* script:

```
#!/usr/bin/perl
require 'ebay.pl';

my $item_id = shift @ARGV;
my $addition = shift @ARGV;

my $rsp = call_api({ Verb => 'AddToItemDescription',
              DetailLevel => 0,
                   ItemId => $item_id,
                   SiteId => $site_id,
              Description => $addition
});

if ($rsp->{Errors}) {
  print_error($rsp)
} else {
  print "Successfully added to the description.\n";
}
```

This much simpler script is used somewhat like the first one. For instance:

```
addtodescription.pl 4500205202 'Just a quick note.'
```

will add the following to the end of your auction description:

```
--------------------------------------------------------------------
On Nov-28-54 at 12:11:06 PDT, seller added the following information:
Just a quick note.
```

Note that you probably want to use this only if your item has received bids.

Let's Automate

The power of the API lies in its ability to turn a laborious task into a simple one. Combining these scripts with the ability to retrieve a list of all running auctions, you can create a script, *reviseall.pl*, that will make the same revision to an arbitrary number of listings in a single step:

```
#!/usr/bin/perl
require 'ebay.pl';

$today = &formatdate(time);
$tendays = &formatdate(time + 864000);

my $page_number = 1;
PAGE:
while (1) {
    my $rsp = call_api({ Verb => 'GetSellerList',
```

```
                    DetailLevel => 0,
                         UserId => $user_id,
                    EndTimeFrom => $today,
                      EndTimeTo => $tendays,
                     PageNumber => $page_number
    });

    if ($rsp->{Errors}) {
      print_error($rsp);
      last PAGE;
    }
    foreach (@{$rsp->{SellerList}{Item}}) {
      my %i = %$_;
      $id = @i{qw/Id/};

      if ($ARGV[0] eq "AddToDescription") {
        system './addtodescription.pl', $id, $ARGV[1];
      } else {
        system './reviseitem.pl', $id, @ARGV;
      }
    }
    last PAGE unless $rsp->{SellerList}{HasMoreItems};
    $page_number++;
  }
```

This script requires the *reviseitem.pl* and *addtodescription.pl* scripts listed earlier in this hack. To submit a global change, type:

```
reviseall.pl BoldTitle 1
```

Note that the syntax is the same as *reviseitem.pl* except that the item number is obviously not required, since the changes apply to all running auctions.

There are many things you can do with this tool. For example, you can inform all your potential customers that you'll be out of town:

```
reviseall.pl AddToDescription 'Note to customers: I will be out of town from
    August 3rd to the 6th, and will respond to all questions when I return.'
```

Add the American Express option to all your auctions:

```
reviseall.pl AmEx 1
```

Change the shipping surcharge to $4.50 for all your auctions:

```
reviseall.pl CheckoutDetailsSpecified 1
reviseall.pl ShippingHandlingCosts 4.50
```

It's important to note that all revisions are absolute. That is, if you change the shipping surcharge to $4.50, that change will be made regardless of the original amount entered for each listing. If you want to do more complex revisions, such as lowering the starting bid or reserve price by 15% for items that have not yet received bids, you'll either have to raise the `DetailLevel` value for `GetSellerList` [Hack #112] or use the `GetItem` API call [Hack #116]. Refer to the API documentation for details.

HACK #116 Spellcheck All Your Listings

Implement passive, configurable spellchecking to create correctly-spelled listings in less time.

The success of any auction is largely due to how readily it can be found in eBay searches. As described in Chapter 2, eBay searches show only exact matches (with very few exceptions), which means, among other things, that spelling most definitely counts.

Turbo Lister and eBay's Sell Your Item form have spellcheck features, both of which use the old-school, manual approach that forces you to interrupt your work to review each individual mistake. This hack streamlines the process by summarizing the spelling errors in all your listings in one place.

The Code

The following script requires the following modules and programs:

Module/program name	Available at
`HTML::FormatText` (by Sean M. Burke)	*search.cpan.org/perldoc?HTML::FormatText*
`HTML::TreeBuilder` (by Sean M. Burke)	*search.cpan.org/perldoc?HTML::TreeBuilder*
`HTML::Entities` (by Gisle Aas)	*search.cpan.org/perldoc?HTML::Entities*
`Lingua::Ispell` (by John Porter)	*search.cpan.org/perldoc?Lingua::Ispell*
ispell program (by Geoff Kuenning)	*fmg-www.cs.ucla.edu/geoff/ispell.html*

Here's the script:

```
#!/usr/bin/perl
require 'ebay.pl';

require HTML::TreeBuilder;
require HTML::FormatText;
use Lingua::Ispell qw( spellcheck );
Lingua::Ispell::allow_compounds(1);

$out1 = "";
$outall = "";
$numchecked = 0;
$numfound = 0;

$today = &formatdate(time);
$yesterday = &formatdate(time - 86400);

my $page_number = 1;
PAGE:
while (1) {
❶    my $rsp = call_api({ Verb => 'GetSellerList',
                         DetailLevel => 0,
```

```
                    UserId => $user_id,
             StartTimeFrom => $yesterday,
               StartTimeTo => $today,
                PageNumber => $page_number
    });

    if ($rsp->{Errors}) {
      print_error($rsp);
      last PAGE;
    }
    foreach (@{$rsp->{SellerList}{Item}}) {
      my %i = %$_;
      $id = @i{qw/Id/};

      if (! -e "$localdir/$id") {
        my $rsp = call_api({ Verb => 'GetItem',
                      DetailLevel => 2,
                               Id => $id
        });

        if ($rsp->{Errors}) {
          print_error($rsp)
        } else {
          my %i = %{$rsp->{Item}[0]};
          my ($title, $description) = @i{qw/Title Description/};

❷          $spellthis = $title . " " . $description;
❸          $tree = HTML::TreeBuilder->new_from_content($spellthis);
          $formatter = HTML::FormatText->new();
          $spellthat = $formatter->format($tree);
❹          $tree = $tree->delete;

❺          for my $r ( spellcheck( $spellthat ) ) {
            if ( $r->{'type'} eq 'miss' ) {
              $out1 = $out1."'$r->{'term'}'";
              $out1 = $out1." - near misses: @{$r->{'misses'}}\n";
              $numfound++;
            }
            elsif ( $r->{'type'} eq 'guess' ) {
              $out1 = $out1."'$r->{'term'}'";
              $out1 = $out1." - guesses: @{$r->{'guesses'}}\n";
              $numfound++;
            }
            elsif ( $r->{'type'} eq 'none' ) {
              $out1 = $out1."'$r->{'term'}'";
              $out1 = $out1." - no match.\n";
              $numfound++;
            }
          }

        $numchecked++;
        if ($out1 ne "") {
```

```
            $outall = $outall."Errors in #$id '$title':\n";
            $outall = $outall."$out1\n\n";
            $out1 = "";
          }

          }
        }
      }
      last PAGE unless $rsp->{SellerList}{HasMoreItems};
      $page_number++;
    }

⑥ print "$numfound spelling errors found in $numchecked auctions:\n\n";
   print "$outall\n";
```

This script is based on the one in "Automatically Keep Track of Items You've Sold" [Hack #112], but it has a few important additions and changes.

First, instead of listing recently completed auctions, the `GetSellerList` API call ❶ is used to retrieve auctions that have started in the last 24 hours. This will work perfectly if you want to review your listings daily or schedule [Hack #21] it to run every 24 hours, say, at 3:00 P.M. every day.

Second, since you want the auction descriptions, you need to use the `GetItem` API call for each auction we spellcheck. This means that spellchecking a dozen auctions will require 13 API calls: one call to retrieve the list, and one for each auction.

The code actually responsible for performing spellcheck starts on line ❷, where the title and description are concatenated into a single variable, `$spellthis`, so that only one spellcheck is necessary for each auction. Next, the `HTML::FormatText` module is used (lines ❸ to ❹) to convert any HTML-formatted text to plain text.

Finally, the `Lingua::Ispell` module ❺ uses the external *ispell* program to perform a spellcheck on `$spellthat` (the cleaned-up version of `$spellthis`). As errors are found, suggestions are recorded into the `$out1` variable, which is merged with `$outall` and displayed when the spellcheck is complete.

Hacking the Hack

Here are a few things you might want to do with this script:

- Instead of simply printing out the results of the spellcheck, as the script does on line ❻, you can quite easily have the results emailed to you [Hack #118].
- Currently, the script performs a spellcheck on every running auction started in the last 24 hours. If you run the script every 24 hours, then

this won't pose a problem. But if you choose to run the script manually and therefore specify a broader range of dates, you may wish to include error checking to prevent the script from needlessly checking the same auction twice.

- Most spellcheckers have a means of adding new words to the dictionary, and this one should be no exception. An easy solution is to create a text file with the proper names, technical terms, and other words the spellchecker doesn't recognize. Then, include code to read the list and eliminate any matches that are found immediately after line ❺, so that only newly unrecognized terms are caught.

Automatically Relist Unsuccessful Listings

Save time by automatically relisting items that received no bids or have a reserve that wasn't met.

Most of the time, when an auction ends without receiving any bids or with a reserve that wasn't met, sellers end up relisting the item, but this can be rather laborious, especially if you have more than a few auctions to relist.

The following script will relist for you, and when run on a regular basis—say, every day—you'll never have to manually relist an auction again:

```
#!/usr/bin/perl
require 'ebay.pl';

❶ $localfile = "autorelist.txt";
$today = &formatdate(time);
$yesterday = &formatdate(time - 86400);

my $page_number = 1;
PAGE:
while (1) {
    my $rsp = call_api({ Verb => 'GetSellerList',
                  DetailLevel => 8,
                       UserId => $user_id,
                  EndTimeFrom => $yesterday,
                    EndTimeTo => $today,
                   PageNumber => $page_number
    });

    if ($rsp->{Errors}) {
      print_error($rsp);
      last PAGE;
    }
    LOOP:
    foreach (@{$rsp->{SellerList}{Item}}) {
      my %i = %$_;
      ($id, $bidder) = @i{qw/Id HighBidder/};
```

```
❷       if ($bidder->{User}{Email} !~ "\@") {
          open (INFILE,"$localdir/$localfile");
            while ( $line = <INFILE> ) {
❸             if ($line eq "$id\n") { last LOOP; }
            }
          close (INFILE);

❹         my $rsp = call_api({Verb => 'RelistItem',
                       DetailLevel => 0,
                            SiteId => $site_id,
                            ItemId => $id
          });

          if ($rsp->{Errors}) {
            print_error($rsp)
          } else {
            print "Relisted item $id as #$rsp->{Item}[0]{Id}\n";

            open (OUTFILE,">>$localdir/$localfile");
❺             print OUTFILE "$id\n";
            close (OUTFILE);
          }
        }
      }

      last PAGE unless $rsp->{SellerList}{HasMoreItems};
      $page_number++;
    }
```

This script starts by listing all your auctions that have ended in the last 24 hours, similarly to "Automatically Keep Track of Items You've Sold" **[Hack #112]**. For information on scheduling this script to run at regular intervals, see "Create a Search Robot" **[Hack #21]**. If you decide to have the script run less frequently—say, once a week—make sure to increase the window of dates for which auctions are retrieved accordingly.

The script determines that an auction ended unsuccessfully if the high bidder's email address is not specified, or, more specifically, that the email address field does not contain an `@` sign ❷. For auctions that have received no bids, the `HighBidder.User.Email` field will be empty, or, if the reserve wasn't met, it will be set to "Invalid Request."

Then, the script checks to see if the auction has been previously relisted ❸; if it hasn't, the script proceeds to relist the auction ❹. If the relist operation is successful, a confirmation is shown and the auction number is recorded ❺ into the filename specified on line ❶.

There's no need to use the `VerifyAddItem` API call to confirm a successful relist, since the script already checks for errors.

Hacking the Hack

If you don't want to automatically relist each and every unsuccessful auction, you can set restrictions. For example, you may not wish to relist any item under five dollars or any item that has already been relisted three times.

One thing you can do to improve the success of your relisted auctions is to lower the starting bid and/or reserve price. Now, if you don't explicitly specify the value of a particular option for the relisted auction, the script will simply use the value from the original auction. But, for example, if you specify a new starting bid or reserve price (perhaps 15% lower than the previous values) on line ❹, those values will be used for the new auction. Most of the input arguments available for the AddItem API call [Hack #113] can be used in `RelistItem` as well; see the API documentation for details.

HACK #118 Send Automatic Emails to High Bidders

Send payment instructions to your customers automatically.

Here's a simple script that will scan all your auctions that have ended in the last 24 hours and send a payment-instructions email to each high bidder:

```
#!/usr/bin/perl
require 'ebay.pl';

$template = "template.txt";

$today = &formatdate(time);
$yesterday = &formatdate(time - 864000);

my $page_number = 1;
PAGE:
while (1) {
    my $rsp = call_api({ Verb => 'GetSellerList',
                  DetailLevel => 8,
                       UserId => $user_id,
                  EndTimeFrom => $yesterday,
                    EndTimeTo => $today,
                   PageNumber => $page_number
    });

    if ($rsp->{Errors}) {
      print_error($rsp);
      last PAGE;
    }
    foreach (@{$rsp->{SellerList}{Item}}) {
```

```
        my %i = %$_;
        ($id, $title, $currency, $price, $highbidder, $checkout) =
              @i{qw/Id Title CurrencyId CurrentPrice HighBidder Checkout/};

        $bidderemail = $highbidder->{User}{Email};
        if ($bidderemail =~ "\@") {
          $shipping = $checkout->{Details}{ShippingHandlingCosts};
          $total = $price + $shipping;

          open(MAIL,"|/usr/sbin/sendmail -t");
          print MAIL "To: $bidderemail\n";
          print MAIL "From: $selleremail\n";
          print MAIL "Reply-To: $selleremail\n";
          print MAIL "Subject: $title\n\n";

          open (COVER, "$localdir/$template");
            while ( $line = <COVER> ) {
              if ($line eq "<insert title here>\n") { print MAIL $title; }
              elsif ($line eq "<insert item here>\n") { print MAIL $id; }
              elsif ($line eq "<insert shipping here>\n") {
                       print MAIL $currency . sprintf("%0.2f", $shipping); }
              elsif ($line eq "<insert total here>\n") {
                       print MAIL $currency . sprintf("%0.2f", $total); }
              else {
                if ($line eq "\n") { $line = "$line\n"; }
                       else { chomp $line; }
                print MAIL $line;
              }
            }
          close(COVER);
          close(MAIL);
        }
      }
      last PAGE unless $rsp->{SellerList}{HasMoreItems};
      $page_number++;
}
```

This script requires the email template from "Streamline Payment Instructions" **[Hack #95]**; just place it in the directory specified by `$localdir` in your *config.pl* include file.

The amount charged for shipping is taken from the `Checkout.Details.ShippingHandlingCosts` field, which is suitable if you've specified fixed shipping costs. If you're using eBay's Calculated Shipping feature **[Hack #59]**, then you'll need to use the `GetShippingRates` function. Simply pass it these fields (all children of `Checkout.Details`), and it will give you the same information your winning bidder sees:

```
ShipFromZipCode, ShipToZipCode, ShippingPackage,
WeightUnit, WeightMajor, and WeightMinor
```

Note also that this script will need to be modified in order to accommodate Dutch auctions. Use the GetHighBidders API call to retrieve multiple high bidders and the quantities they purchased for any single Dutch auction. Naturally, you'll need to supplement the shipping cost calculations to account for any per-item shipping expenses.

AuctionEndOfAuction Notifications

The script in this hack retrieves the list of completed auctions for the last 24 hours, just like most of the other scripts in this chapter that use GetSellerList.

Refer to "Automatically Keep Track of Auctions You've Won" [Hack #110] for details on scheduling and running the script at regular intervals.

There is another approach. Sign up to receive notifications such as AuctionEndOfAuction, CheckoutBuyerRequestsTotal, AuctionCheckoutComplete, and FixedPriceEndOfTransaction, and eBay's server will send the appropriate information to you as soon as the event is triggered, and you can then do your post-auction processing on an auction-by-auction basis.

Unfortunately, notifications are not available to developers with the free Individual license (discussed at the beginning of this chapter), but if you're operating under a Basic, Professional, or Enterprise license, you can sign up to receive notifications at *developer.ebay.com*. Look up "Getting Started with eBay Platform Notifications" in the API documentation for details.

HACK #119 Leave Feedback with the API

Use the LeaveFeedback API call to more easily leave feedback.

The eBay API includes extensive support both for leaving feedback for other users and for retrieving comments from your own feedback profile.

The Code

Here's a sample script used to leave feedback for another user with whom you've had a transaction (save it as *leavefeedback.pl*):

```
#!/usr/bin/perl
require 'ebay.pl';

$item_id      = shift @ARGV;
$target_user  = shift @ARGV;
$comment_type = shift @ARGV;
$comment      = shift @ARGV;
```

```
defined($comment) && $comment_type =~ m:^(positive|negative|neutral)$:
        or die "Usage: $0 item user positive/negative/neutral comment";

my $rsp = call_api({ Verb => 'LeaveFeedback',
              DetailLevel => 0,
                   ItemId => $item_id,
               TargetUser => $target_user,
              CommentType => $comment_type,
                  Comment => $comment});
if ($rsp->{Errors}) {
    print_error($rsp)
} else {
    print "Status: $rsp->{LeaveFeedback}{Status}";
}
```

Running the Hack

You can leave feedback with this script by calling it from the command line, like this:

```
leavefeedback.pl item other_user positive 'Smooth transaction'
```

where *item* is the item number of the transaction and *other_user* is the user ID of the user for whom you're leaving feedback.

The LeaveFeedback API call follows the same rules as does *eBay.com*, namely that you can leave feedback only for a user with whom you're involved in a transaction. When testing this feature in the Sandbox **[Hack #102]**, you'll need to set up two users and a handful of auctions. If the seller has a feedback rating of less than 10, however, you won't be able to use Fixed-Price listings or the Buy It Now feature. Instead, you'll have to start an ordinary auction, bid on it with the other user ID, and then wait for it to end.

Note that this script is required by "Automatic Reciprocal Feedback" **[Hack #122]**.

See Also

- See "Negative Feedback Notification" **[Hack #121]** for a script that retrieves feedback comments from your profile.

Negative Feedback Bidder Alert

Have a script automatically notify you if an eBay member with negative feedback has bid on one of your auctions.

One of the best ways to keep away deadbeat bidders [Hack #68] is to monitor your auctions and look for potential troublemakers, namely those with negative feedback ratings.

The Code

This script scans through your currently running auctions and notifies you via email whenever a high bidder has a feedback rating of less than zero:

```
#!/usr/bin/perl
require 'ebay.pl';

$today = &formatdate(time);
$tendays = &formatdate(time + 864000);

my $page_number = 1;
PAGE:
while (1) {
    my $rsp = call_api({ Verb => 'GetSellerList',
                  DetailLevel => 8,
                       UserId => $user_id,
                  EndTimeFrom => $today,
                    EndTimeTo => $tendays,
                   PageNumber => $page_number
    });

    if ($rsp->{Errors}) {
      print_error($rsp);
      last PAGE;
    }
    foreach (@{$rsp->{SellerList}{Item}}) {
      my %i = %$_;
      ($id, $bidder) = @i{qw/Id HighBidder/};

      if ($bidder->{User}{Feedback}{Score} < 0) {
        open(MAIL,"|/usr/sbin/sendmail -t");
        print MAIL "To: $selleremail\n";
        print MAIL "From: $selleremail\n";
        print MAIL "Subject: Negative Feedback Bidder Alert\n\n";
        print MAIL "A bidder with negative feedback has placed a bid on
                                              one of your auctions:\n";
        print MAIL "$itemurl$id\n";
        close(MAIL);
      }
    }
    last PAGE unless $rsp->{SellerList}{HasMoreItems};
```

```
        $page_number++;
    }
```

This script is similar to the one in "Automatically Keep Track of Items You've Sold" [Hack #112], with the notable exception that listings are retrieved for auctions ending any time in the *next* 10 days. This is an easy way to filter out completed auctions, and illustrates how to use the input fields (such as `EndTimeFrom` and `EndTimeTo`) to your advantage.

See the discussion of `GetSellerEvents` in the API documentation for a way to retrieve only those listings that have undergone price changes in the past 48 hours, typically as the result of bids placed.

Running the Hack

To use this script, make sure to modify the `$selleremail` variable to reflect your own email address. Note that if you had issued a separate `GetItem` API call for each auction (or even just one of the auctions), as is necessary in some of the other scripts in this chapter (such as "Spellcheck All Your Listings" [Hack #116]), you could have retrieved the seller's email address automatically.

See Also

- See "Negative Feedback Notification" [Hack #121] for a script that notifies you when a user has left a negative or neutral feedback comment for you.

HACK #121 Negative Feedback Notification

Have a script notify you whenever you've received negative feedback.

Given the importance of feedback, especially to sellers, it's a good idea to routinely check your feedback profile for complaints or comments that should be addressed [Hack #5]. But doing this every day, especially for sellers who receive dozens or even hundreds of feedback comments every week, can be a chore.

The Code

This script routinely scans your feedback profile and notifies you of any new negative or neutral feedback you've received:

```
#!/usr/bin/perl
require 'ebay.pl';

$localfile = "feedbackalert.txt";
%roles = ('S', 'seller', 'B', 'buyer');
```

```
❶ my $rsp = call_api({ Verb => 'GetFeedback',
                DetailLevel => 1,
                     UserId => $user_id,
                     SiteId => $site_id,
               StartingPage => $page_number,
               ItemsPerPage => 1
  });
  $totalcomments = $rsp->{Feedback}{FeedbackDetailItemTotal};

  $oldtotal = 0;
  if (-e "$localdir/$localfile") {
    open (INFILE,"$localdir/$localfile");
❷     $oldtotal = <INFILE>;
    close (INFILE);
  }

❸ $newcomments = $totalcomments - $oldtotal;
  if ($newcomments == 0) { exit; }

  if ($newcomments > 200) {
    $num_pages = int($newcomments / 200) + 1;
    $page_size = 200;
  } else {
    $num_pages = 1;
    $page_size = $newcomments;
  }

  PAGE:
  for (my $page_number = 1; $page_number <= $num_pages; $page_number++) {
❹   my $rsp = call_api({ Verb => 'GetFeedback',
                  DetailLevel => 1,
                       UserId => $user_id,
                       SiteId => $site_id,
                 StartingPage => $page_number,
                 ItemsPerPage => $page_size
    });

    if ($rsp->{Errors}) {
      print_error($rsp);
      last PAGE;
    }

    FEEDBACK:
    foreach (@{$rsp->{Feedback}{FeedbackDetail}{FeedbackDetailItem}}) {
      my %i = %$_;
      ($text, $type, $from, $item, $id, $role) = @i{qw/CommentText CommentType
                     CommentingUser ItemNumber TransactionId FeedbackRole/};

❺     if (($type eq "Complaint") || ($type eq "Neutral")) {
        open (INFILE,"$localdir/$localfile");
          while ( $line = <INFILE> ) {
            if ($line eq "$id\n") { next FEEDBACK; }
          }
```

```
        close (INFILE);

        open(MAIL,"|/usr/sbin/sendmail -t");
        print MAIL "To: $selleremail\n";
        print MAIL "From: $selleremail\n";
        print MAIL "Subject: Negative Feedback Alert\n\n";
        print MAIL "A ".$roles{"$role"}.", $from, has left this feedback:\n";
        print MAIL "$type: '$text'\n";
        print MAIL "regarding this transaction:\n";
        print MAIL "$itemurl$item\n";
❻       close(MAIL);
      }
    }
  }

  open (OUTFILE,">$localdir/$localfile");
❼ print OUTFILE $totalcomments;

  close (OUTFILE);
```

What may seem like an unnecessary extra call at the beginning of the script ❶ is actually quite necessary to achieve compliance with eBay's Production Access Rules. This call retrieves a single comment entirely for the purpose of determining the total number of feedback comments in the profile, `$totalcomments`.

The number of new comments (`$newcomments` ❸) is calculated by subtracting the previous total (`$oldtotal` ❷) from the current total. Then, all new comments are retrieved with the second `GetFeedback` API call ❹.

All this needs to be done because `GetFeedback` doesn't support the `EndTimeFrom` or `EndTimeTo` arguments (possibly signifying the dates that feedback comments were left) that are supported by most of the other API calls discussed in this chapter. Paradoxically, adding an extra call ❶ prevents the script from issuing too many calls later on. Since the script doesn't need to download the entire feedback profile every time, you also don't need to cache feedback, as eBay suggests.

The script then iterates through the profile and sends an email every time a new negative or neutral feedback comment is encountered. Finally, the script records the new total ❼.

Running the Hack

To automate this script, schedule it [Hack #21] to run regularly (every day, every week, etc.). Run it more often to reduce your response time, or use it less frequently to conserve your API calls.

See Also

- See "Negative Feedback Bidder Alert" [Hack #120] for a script to notify you when a user with a negative feedback rating bids on one of your auctions.

Automatic Reciprocal Feedback

Leave automatic feedback for any customer who has left positive feedback for you.

As much as you should respond quickly to any complaints lodged against you in your feedback profile, you'll also want to leave positive reciprocal feedback [Hack #6] for each and every positive comment you receive from buyers. As you might expect, this is also something that can be done with the eBay API.

But let's add a little spice to the mix. Instead of leaving the same feedback comment every time, have the script choose a random comment. Start by creating a plain-text file with a handful of positive comments, one on each line:

```
Lightning-fast payment. Reliable buyer. Thanks for your business!
Quick to pay, friendly emails. This eBayer makes selling a pleasure!
Very fast payment, good communication. All-around excellent customer!
```

Save the file as *prefabpraise.txt* and place it in the directory specified in your *config.pl* file (discussed at the beginning of this chapter).

Next, take the script from "Negative Feedback Notification" [Hack #121] and replace the code between line ❺ and line ❻ with this code:

```
if ($type eq "Praise") {
  open (INFILE,"$localdir/prefabpraise.txt");
    @line = <INFILE>;
  close (INFILE);
  chomp @line;
  $lines = @line;
  $choice = int rand ($lines);

  system './leavefeedback.pl', $item, $from, 'positive', $choice;
}
```

Or, if you want a single script to leave positive reciprocal feedback *and* notify you of negative feedback, instead place this code *before* line ❺.

Note that this script also requires the *leavefeedback.pl* script from "Leave Feedback with the API" [Hack #119].

HACK #123 Make a Feedback Search Tool

Quickly find a specific feedback comment or list a specific type of comment in a person's profile.

eBay provides no searching or sorting tools on the Member Profile page, a fact that makes finding specific feedback [Hack #1] a rather clumsy process.

Fortunately, you can use a few API calls to make searching a member's feedback profile an almost trivial excercise.

The Code

Start with the script from "Negative Feedback Notification" [Hack #121], and just after line ❶, replace this:

```
UserId => $user_id,
```

with this:

```
UserId => $ARGV[0],
```

Next, replace the code between line ❺ and line ❻ with this code:

```
if ((("\L$ARGV[1]" eq "item") && ($item eq $ARGV[2])) || (("\L$ARGV[1]" eq
"type") && ("\$type" eq "\L$ARGV[2]")) {
  print "-- $item-$type from $from\n";
  print "\"$text\"\n";
}
```

When you're done, save this script as *findfb.pl*.

Running the Hack

To find feedback pertaining to a particular item number, type:

```
findfb.pl user item 5958951586
```

Or, to find all feedback of a certain type, say "negative," type:

```
findfb.pl user type negative
```

where, in both cases, *user* is the eBay member ID of the person whose feedback you're searching.

HACK #124 Queue API Calls

Work around eBay's API call limit.

Developers working under the Individual license, explained at the beginning of this chapter, have a strict limit as to the number of eBay API calls they are allowed to make each day.

Provided that your application uses the API efficiently [Hack #125], this shouldn't pose a problem. And as the theory goes, anyone needing more than 50 API calls per day is probably running a business on eBay and can justify the cost of one of the higher developer tiers.

Consider the following scenario. As a seller, you might have 55 separate auctions ending on a single day. If you use the script in "Automatically Keep Track of Items You've Sold" [Hack #112], you can retrieve sufficient data for all your recently closed auctions with only a single `GetSellerList` call. But if you use the script in "Spellcheck All Your Listings" [Hack #116], you'll need a minimum of 56 calls: one to retrieve the list of auctions, and 55 more to retrieve the individual auction descriptions. Run this single script just once, and you'll exceed your API quota for the day.

If you feel that exceeding your quota is a possibility, you can take some extra steps to ensure both that your software understands this limit, and that if your software reaches the limit, it can queue additional API calls and complete its work the next day.

The first step is to begin recording your API call usage. Probably the best way to do this is by adding a counter to the `call_api` subroutine in the *ebay.pl* script listed at the beginning of this chapter. The counter code might look something like this:

```
    open (INFILE,"$localdir/apiquota.txt");
❶     my %count = map { split(/,/, $_) } <INFILE>;
    close (INFILE);
    chomp %count;

    my ($today, $dummy) = split(/ /, &formatdate(time));
❷   $count{$today}++;
    open (OUTFILE,">$localdir/apiquota.txt");
      while (($date,$count) = each %count) {
❸       print OUTFILE "$date,$count\n";
      }
    close (OUTFILE);

❹   if ( $count{$today} > 50 ) {
      ...
      # queue this API call for later processing
      ...
      return undef;
      exit;
    }
```

Here's how it works. The script retrieves the counts ❶ for all recorded days from the *apiquota.txt* file (located in the directory specified by `$localdir` in your *config.pl* script). It then adds `1` to today's count ❷ and writes the updated data back to the file ❸.

Finally, if today's count is above 50 ❹, it runs some code you provide (sorry, I'm not going to do *all* the work for you!) to queue the next API call. You could, for example, set up a temporary cron job [Hack #21], to run another script that resubmits queued API calls.

If nothing else, this nifty snippet of code records accounting data for your API usage. After a few days of using the API, your *apiquota.txt* file will look something like this:

```
2005-07-11,3
2005-07-12,11
2005-07-13,0
2005-07-14,60
2005-07-15,4
```

This shows that on July 14, 2005, 60 calls were made, while only 4 calls were made the next day. (Note that since the data is manipulated as a hash by this script, the records won't necessarily be recorded in order in the file.)

HACK #125 Cache Listing Data to Improve API Efficiency

Reduce the number of API calls your program makes and work within your daily API allotment.

One of the requirements of certification [Hack #102] is that your application or script does not make more calls or retrieve more data than is absolutely necessary. This is typically accomplished in any of three ways:

- Restricting the result set to a specific date range [Hack #110]
- Downloading only new entries by comparing the current total of entries with the total you recorded the last time the call was used [Hack #121]
- Caching retrieved data so that it doesn't have to be retrieved again, as described in this hack

Which data you cache and how you do it depends on the type of data you're working with.

When caching input, probably the most useful place to start is by recording the item numbers of all auctions you're currently selling. Assuming you're using GetItem to upload your listings to eBay [Hack #113], you can simply save the resulting item number in a file, like this:

```
open (OUTFILE,">>$localdir/auctionlist.txt");
  print OUTFILE "$rsp->{Item}[0]{Id},$rsp->,{Item}[0]{EndTime}\n;;
close (OUTFILE);
```

Eventually, the file will look like this:

```
4500207651, 2005-07-15 20:43:32
```

```
4500207783, 2005-07-16 08:14:18
4500208002, 2005-07-18 19:00:31
```

with each line containing one item number and one end date, separated by a comma. Then, instead of using the `GetSellerList` API call found in many hacks in this chapter, you can simply load the list, like this:

```
open (INFILE,">>$localdir/auctionlist.txt");
  my %items = map { split(/,/,$_) } <INFILE>;
close (INFILE);
chomp %items;
```

which will create a hash of item numbers and end times. To fill an array with all the item numbers, use the keys function:

```
@itemnumbers + keys %items;
```

To retrieve the end date for a single auction, reference the hash like this:

```
$endtime = $items{'4500207783'}
```

Naturally, if you want to store more than just item numbers and end times, you'll need a more complex storage system, but the metholology will be the same. Not only will this approach significantly reduce your API usage, it will end up being a lot faster than repeatedly downloading large amounts of data from eBay.

Index

We'd like to hear your suggestions for improving our indexes. Send email to *index@oreilly.com*.

B

C

D

E

F

G

H

I

P

Q

R

S

T

U

V

W

X

Colophon

Our look is the result of reader comments, our own experimentation, and feedback from distribution channels. Distinctive covers complement our distinctive approach to technical topics, breathing personality and life into potentially dry subjects.

The tool on the cover of *eBay Hacks,* Second Edition is a corkscrew. The exact time origin of the corkscrew is not really known, but corkscrews descended from bulletscrews (also called gun worms)—a tool used for cleaning jammed bullets or unspent powder out of musket barrels, which shared a similar spiral tip. By the 17th century, the corkscrew was fairly common, as cork stoppers were now well-established throughout Europe, not only for wine, but for beer, medicine, and cosmetics.

Corkscrews come in a variety of styles, including direct-pull (the simplest), assisted-pull, single-lever, double- (or wing-) lever, and torsional. The corkscrew pictured on the cover is a concertina corkscrew, sometimes called a compound-lever corkscrew. Concertina corkscrews date back to the late 1800s, and many fine examples can be found on eBay

Jamie Peppard was the production editor and copyeditor for *eBay Hacks,* Second Edition. Matt Hutchinson, Lydia Onofrei, Claire Cloutier, and Darren Kelly provided quality control. John Bickelhaupt wrote the index.

Emma Colby designed the cover of this book, based on a series design by Edie Freedman. The cover image is a photograph taken from the Stockbyte Work Tools CD. Karen Montgomery produced the cover layout with QuarkXPress 4.1 using Adobe's Helvetica Neue and ITC Garamond fonts.

David Futato designed the interior layout. This book was converted by Keith Fahlgren to FrameMaker 5.5.6 with a format conversion tool created by Erik Ray, Jason McIntosh, Neil Walls, and Mike Sierra that uses Perl and XML technologies. The text font is Linotype Birka; the heading font is Adobe Helvetica Neue Condensed; and the code font is LucasFont's TheSans Mono Condensed. The illustrations that appear in the book were produced by Robert Romano and Jessamyn Read using Macromedia FreeHand MX and Adobe Photoshop CS. This colophon was written by David Futato.